Publishing Forms and Contracts

VALPARAISO UNIVERSITY LAW LIBRARY

Publishing Forms and Contracts

Roy S. Kaufman

UNIVERSITY PRESS

2008

OXFORD
UNIVERSITY PRESS

Oxford University Press, Inc., publishes works that further Oxford University's objective of excellence in research, scholarship, and education.

Oxford New York
Auckland   Cape Town   Dar es Salaam   Hong Kong   Karachi   Kuala Lumpur   Madrid
Melbourne   Mexico City   Nairobi   New Delhi   Shanghai   Taipei   Toronto

With offices in
Argentina   Austria   Brazil   Chile   Czech Republic   France   Greece   Guatemala
Hungary   Italy   Japan   Poland   Portugal   Singapore   South Korea   Switzerland
Thailand   Turkey   Ukraine   Vietnam

Copyright © 2008 by Oxford University Press, Inc.

Published by Oxford University Press, Inc. 198 Madison Avenue, New York, New York 10016
www.oup.com

Oxford is a registered trademark of Oxford University Press
Oxford University Press is a registered trademark of Oxford University Press, Inc.

All rights reserved. No part of this publication may be reproduced, stored in a retrieval system, or transmitted, in any form or by any means, electronic, mechanical, photocopying, recording, or otherwise, without the prior permission of Oxford University Press.

Library of Congress Cataloging-in-Publication Data
Kaufman, Roy S.
    Publishing forms and contracts / Roy Kaufman.
      p. cm.
    Summary: "Each chapter provides introductory text concerning a major area of publishing, and each area is accompanied by related forms and agreements with commentary on their use. Covered are: book publishing, periodical publishing, electronic publishing, litigation and litigation avoidance, permissions and subsidiary rights"--Provided by publisher.
    ISBN 978-0-19-536734-8 (pbk. : alk. paper)
1. Authors and publishers--United States. I. Title.
    KF3084.K383 2008
    346.7304'82--dc22

                                                                    2008010216

1 2 3 4 5 6 7 8 9

Printed in the United States of America
on acid-free paper

Note to Readers
This publication is designed to provide accurate and authoritative information in regard to the subject matter covered. It is based upon sources believed to be accurate and reliable and is intended to be current as of the time it was written. It is sold with the understanding that the publisher is not engaged in rendering legal, accounting, or other professional services. If legal advice or other expert assistance is required, the services of a competent professional person should be sought. Also, to confirm that the information has not been affected or changed by recent developments, traditional legal research techniques should be used, including checking primary sources where appropriate.

(Based on the Declaration of Principles jointly adopted by a Committee of the American Bar Association and a Committee of Publishers and Associations.)

You may order this or any other Oxford University Press publication by
visiting the Oxford University Press website at www.oup.com

To my wife, Cindy Derrow, who makes life possible.
To my boys, Jordan and Caleb.
Everything I've done I've done for you.

Contents

Acknowledgments

A book like this can only result from the collaboration of many wonderful people and organizations.

First, I need to thank my employer, John Wiley and Sons, for its unwavering support of my writing projects. I specifically wish to thank members of the legal department who, through providing forms, help, and advice, contributed to this book. These include Gary Rinck, Dick Rudick, Deirdre Silver, Maria Danzilo, Sue Joshua, Peggy Garry, Patrick Murphy, Ray DeSouza, and Angela Briggins.

For allowing me to republish their forms, my gratitude is owed to Ben Strouse, Peter Canelias, Bill Hart, Robert Panzer, Nancy Wolff, Fred Haber, Pieter Bolman, and Ronni Sander.

Recognition also must be extended to my team at Oxford University Press, including Matt Gallaway, Bill Cherry, and Patti Brecht.

Lastly, I wish to thank my family for forgiving the time spent writing. Thank you to Cindy, Jordan and Caleb, my parents Harold and Elaine Kaufman, my sister Michele, my sisters-in-law Paula Derrow and Jo Ellen Fusco, and my in-laws, Joyce and Alfred Derrow.

To the Reader

This book is intended for lawyers, agents, and publishers who possess basic knowledge about publishing contracts and copyright law. Although it is divided into separate chapters, content is content, and readers are encouraged to skim all of the chapters before choosing a form to use in any given situation.

While authors and others should find this book useful, it was designed primarily to represent the viewpoint of publishers. Thus due care is urged when drafting from alternative viewpoints.

About the Author

Roy S. Kaufman is Legal Director of the Wiley-Blackwell business of John Wiley and Sons, Inc., a global multinational publisher. He is a member of the Board of Directors of Copyright Clearance Center, where he belongs to the Rightsholders, Recruiting, and International Committees. A member of the Bar of the State of New York, he currently belongs to the Freedom to Read and Lawyers Committees of the Association of American Publishers, and the Copyright Committee of the International Association of Scientific, Technical and Medical Publishers. Mr. Kaufman has represented and counseled publishing companies in every segment of print, continuity, online and electronic publishing. He is the author of *Drafting Print and Online Publishing Agreements* (Aspen Law & Business 2002), and Editor-in-Chief of *Art Law Handbook: From Antiquities to the Internet* (Aspen Law & Business 2000). He has published and lectured extensively on the subjects of copyright, licensing, anti-piracy, new media, artists' rights, publishing and art law. Prior to joining Wiley, Mr. Kaufman was an associate in the intellectual property and entertainment practice group of the New York office of the law firm Paul, Hastings, Janofsky & Walker.

CHAPTER
1

Book Publishing

§1.01 Background

Chapter 1 is a compendium of materials particularly relevant to traditional book publishing and focuses primarily on the editorial aspects of acquiring books for publication by publishing companies.[1] The chapter begins by highlighting key aspects of the contract drafting and negotiation processes (*see* § 1.02, *infra*). This section is followed by five different types of "book contracts" pursuant to which a publishing company acquires rights from an author/ editor: (1) an educational publishing agreement, (2) a trade publishing agreement, (3) a professional publishing agreement, (4) a multiple-editor edited work agreement (5) a "work for hire" book agreement (Forms 1.1–1.5). I have also included a co-publishing agreement (Form 1.6) and a book packaging agreement (Form 1.7), which are similar to author agreements, but are used for transactions between companies.

---

1 *See* Chapters 3, 4, 5, and 6 *infra*, for forms relating to other aspects of book publishing.

Forms 1.8 and 1.9 are an advisory board member agreement and a series editor agreement. Both of these templates are for outside contractors providing editorial services to a publisher on behalf of its book programs.

Three forms for contributors to edited works follow: (1) a short form contributor agreement for an unpaid contributor, (2) a long form contributor agreement for a paid author, and (3) a contributor agreement specifically designed for use with U.S. government employees (Forms 1.10–1.12).

The chapter ends with a number of short letter agreements and clauses that are used in conjunction with standard author agreements, including a revision letter, a reversion of rights letter, a personal guarantee for authors who sign contracts through closely held corporations, and some sample contract clauses (Forms 1.13–1.19).

§ 1.02 The Core Issues of a Publishing Agreement

There are three fundamental questions for publishers pertaining to publishing agreements:

- What is the work?
- What rights are you getting in the work (including what restrictions have been placed on those rights)?
- How much do the rights cost?

Almost all clauses in a standard publishing agreement, whether it is an agreement for a book, journal, or electronic product, involve one or more of these three issues. For example, in Form 1.1, the educational publishing agreement, each section, with the exception of a few legal boilerplate clauses, pertains to one or more of these questions. Sections 1, 2(c), 3, 7, 8, 9, and 10 all relate, in whole or in part, to the rights acquired by the publisher. Sections 2(a), (b), (c), (d), and 8 relate to the work in which rights are to be acquired, and Sections 4, 5, 6, and 8 relate to the publisher's cost to acquire those rights. Only paragraph 11, "general," is not primarily concerned with one or more of the core issues.

[A] Rights

[1] Publishing Rights

The most important rights to be acquired in a publishing agreement are, naturally, publishing rights. In author agreements, publishing rights can be expressed either as "copyrights," as is typical where all rights in the copyright are to be transferred, or as individual publishing rights, as when only certain express rights are to be licensed.

Rights can fit into two broad categories. The first comprises rights analogous to those rights granted to "authors" under U.S. copyright law. These include the rights to:

- copy/reproduce,
- transmit,
- distribute,
- display,
- prepare derivative works,
- publish, and
- sell.

In a contract with a broad grant of rights, such as a professional publishing agreement, these are typically listed, either explicitly or with language such as "all rights comprised in the copyrights" or "all copyrights," modified by broad qualifiers such as "in all media known or unknown, throughout the world." (*See* Form 1.3.)

The second category of rights includes specific rights for certain markets, territories, or types of publications. In general, the appearance of markets, territories, or specific types of publications in a "rights" clause indicates that some form of limitation exists, or that some rights are subject to negotiation. Accordingly, they are more often listed in trade contracts, where rights are negotiated between agents and publishers, than in those segments such as educational and professional publishing where rights tend to be non-negotiable. Such rights include:

- English-language rights,
- North American rights,
- first serialization rights,
- paperback rights,
- mass-market rights,
- audio rights,
- merchandising rights,
- video and motion picture rights, and
- interactive multimedia rights.

The explicit listing of some of these rights does not mean that such rights are negotiable (in certain countries, such as Germany, all rights must be explicitly listed in order for the publisher to acquire them), or that the contract is per se a contract for limited rights, and one can well imagine a tediously drafted contract listing these and more. However, the mere listing of many such rights implies, in an otherwise "all rights" contract, the willingness of the publisher to negotiate certain rights that are not critical to its business plans.

With respect to listing of the rights, the exact approach to drafting should be dictated in part by the law of the jurisdiction governing the contract. Specifically, although the cases can be reconciled, there's a tendency in the Ninth Circuit to interpret grant of rights narrowly, while the trend in the Second Circuit is to interpret liberally.[2]

[a] Rights to Be Acquired: Professional, Educational, and Trade Publishing Compared

When drafting a contract, it is important to look at the competitive environment, your client's business plans, and the relevant market segment. For both educational and professional publishing, it is customary for the publisher to receive all rights. Consider this example of a typical rights clause from a college textbook contract:

> The Author grants to the Publisher for the full term of copyright and all extensions thereof the exclusive copyright in the Work throughout the world in all languages. The Publisher's exclusive rights will include the right by itself or with others to reproduce, publish, distribute, transmit and sell the Work and derivative works, in whole or in part, in all media and forms of distribution, under the Publisher's name and other imprints or trade-names, together with the exclusive right to license others to do so and to register the copyright in the Work. The title of the Work and any series titles used on or with it will also belong to the Publisher. For purposes of this Agreement, the term "Work" will include any material contributed by the Author to any supplementary or ancillary materials which may accompany the Work.

Because it is typical for the publisher to acquire all rights, insisting on such rights does not place the educational publisher at a competitive disadvantage.

By contrast, consider the following rights-granting language from a trade contract:

> The Author hereby grants to the Publisher during the full term of copyright and all extensions thereof the full and exclusive rights comprised in the copyright in the Work, including any "Supplementary Materials" (as defined in Paragraph 2(a) below) and any revised editions, including but not limited to the right,

---

2 *Compare, e.g.,* S.O.S., Inc. v. Payday, Inc., 886 F.2d 1081, 1088 (9th Cir. 1989) *with* Bartsch v. Metro-Goldwyn-Mayer, Inc., 391 F.2d 150 (2d Cir.), *cert, denied,* 393 U.S. 826 (1968). *Cf.* Random House, Inc. v. Rosetta Books, LLC, 150 F. Supp. 2d 613 (S.D.N.Y. 2001), *aff'd* 283 F.3d 490 (2d Cir. 2002). See generally Paul Goldstein, *Copyright* § 4.6.2.1 (2d ed., Aspen L. & Bus. 2000).

by itself or with others, throughout the world, to print, publish, republish, distribute and transmit the Work and to prepare, publish, distribute and transmit derivative works based thereon, in English and in other languages, in all media of expression now known or later developed, and to license or permit others to do so. The Publisher's rights shall include but shall not be limited to:

(a) The exclusive right to publish and sell the Work in the English language in North America (the United States, its possessions and territories, Canada and Mexico), the Philippines, the British Commonwealth and the Republics of Ireland and South Africa, Europe and all other countries (the "Territory");
(b) Foreign-language rights throughout the world;
(c) Periodical or newspaper rights prior to or following book publication, including syndication rights throughout the world;
(d) Non-dramatic audio recording rights throughout the world;
(e) Motion picture, television, radio, stage dramatic and musical rights throughout the world;
(f) Commercial and merchandising rights throughout the world;
(g) Interactive multi-media rights;
(h) Mass market publication rights.

As you can see, the trade contract, although granting "all rights," is written in a way that invites the author and her agent to strike listed rights that are to be retained by the author (only, of course, after negotiation). Certain rights, such as "electronic rights" generally, are not listed separately, which indicates that the publisher is less flexible with respect to allowing the author to retain electronic rights.[3]

The disparity between the rights reserved in trade contracts and the rights reserved in most other publishing segments is due to several factors. In some market segments, there are only a handful of rights worth having. The rest of the rights are largely irrelevant to both parties, but since the publishers draft the forms, they tend to seek all rights, regardless of value, and no one argues. For example, in legal publishing, for a U.S. legal treatise, the only important

---

3 The trade practice of allowing authors to reserve certain rights led one court to conclude that unnamed rights were also reserved. In *Random House, Inc.* v. *Rosetta Books, LLC*, 150 F. Supp. 2d 613 (S.D.N.Y. 2001), *aff'd*, 238 F.3d 490 (2d Cir. 2002), the trial court, in concluding that a grant of rights to publish a work "in book form" did not extend to the later invented "e-book" format, noted that the authors had retained specific other rights under their contracts. According to the court, the retention of rights provided evidence that the authors intended to transfer only those rights explicitly specified in their contracts. Although the tepid affirmation by the Second Circuit calls the District Court decision somewhat into question, *Rosetta* issues can be avoided simply by adding express language to cover electronic rights, and by adding "all media now known or later developed."

rights are the rights to sell the work in the English language in North America and the rights to include the work in electronic format in databases or on the World Wide Web. There is minimal value in subsidiary rights generally, and no great value to the foreign-language rights, the "rest of world rights," or audiovisual rights, so when the publisher drafts a contract acquiring all rights, the author is not going to waste negotiating strength on rights that have no value. With respect to the primary rights listed above (e.g., electronic rights and the North American rights), all publishers will demand them before signing, so there is no competitive disadvantage inuring to the publisher who demands such rights.

In trade publishing, however, there exists (1) a competitive environment, (2) publishers who have competing business models, and (3) agents who are exploiting the environment and have the ability to sell rights separately. All three factors work in tandem. For example, some vertically integrated entertainment companies that own both publishing houses and film divisions may mandate the acquisition of film rights for each book but may not offer the publishing company adequate additional funds to compete with another company that is willing to give a smaller advance but not acquire the film rights. On the other hand, the vertically integrated company could buy the book rights and an option on the film at a cost that few small publishers would be able to match. None of these competitive differences would matter but for the presence of professional agents, who have the contacts (the author hopes) to sell the reserved rights to other publishers.

For the author, the biggest danger in reserving rights, whether individually or through an agent, is what I call "reserving rights to spite your publisher." As the digital environment has made copyright into a front-page topic, an increasing number of authors and artists are being exhorted to "reserve your rights," and particularly, but not exclusively, electronic, Web, and/or multimedia rights. That this can backfire is illustrated in the following true example. A well-known photographer was told early in her career to "never assign your rights." She was asked to contribute to a book that was going to make headlines, generate a lot of money for her, and would launch her career to the next stage. In the end, she did not assign, but agreed to the license of every right comprised in the copyright, and was left with the moral "victory" of retaining copyright in a meaningless sense, along with a large legal bill.

When an author is not represented by an agent, the author will usually benefit from assigning all rights to the publisher. Publishers, even ones that do not have separate rights and permissions departments, have more money, expertise, and facilities to exploit non-core rights than the authors do themselves, and unless the author really expects to spend time selling these rights, he or she might as well leave it for the publisher. Accordingly, when negotiating on behalf of a publisher directly against an author, the best way to negotiate against allowing a reservation of rights is to ask, "What, specifically do you want to do with the reserved right, other than simply to retain it?" If the authors' response is that they once read somewhere that they should retain it but have no specific plans, a discussion of the publisher's success in exploiting the rights sought to be retained will usually work.

When agents are involved, the risk to the author is that the agent will reserve rights to "show how tough" the agent is. When the agent reserves an unimportant right, such as film rights in a financial planning book, it is harmless, but when the agent reserves a right that the publisher would otherwise exploit, the author will suffer unless the agent actually can exploit it himself or herself. Thus, it is important for authors to ask during negotiations handled by agents what experience the agent has in selling the reserved rights.[4]

[2] The Right to Make Publishing Decisions

Other than publishing rights themselves, the next most important right for the publisher is the right to exercise and exploit the publishing rights without interference from the author. This is typically accomplished with a version of the following language:

> Subject to the terms and conditions herein, the Publisher will publish and market the Work at the Publisher's own expense. It shall be published under the imprint of the Publisher or any other imprint selected by the Publisher, and marketed in the style, media and manner and at the price that the Publisher, in its sole discretion, deems appropriate.

For a publisher who does not desire endless disputes over trivial matters and the concomitant increase in legal bills, some version of this language is critical.

Authors and publishers share a common goal of financial success for each book published. However, there are many points at which their interests diverge. Royalties are not profit-sharing arrangements. If the publisher has a $120 cost of sale for a $100 book, the author is still paid, but it does not do much good for the publisher. Likewise, publishers often release competing works. The appearance, whether real or not, of favoritism with respect to publishing dates, revised additions, and marketing dollars has led to contentious debates between publishers and authors.

Also, as electronic books and new formats have become popular (or, at least, become a popular topic), more authors are asking why their works do or do

---

4 It is also important to remember that rights need not be all or nothing. Form 1.19 presents two intermediate options with respect to rights reservation: (1) specific rights are exclusive to the publisher, but become nonexclusive after a certain time period if the publisher has not exploited such rights (Clause C), and (2) the author and the publisher share certain rights on a nonexclusive basis (Clause D).

not appear in a given format. In the mid-1990s, many professional publishers were rushing to place their books on CD-ROMs or floppy diskettes, only to learn that their library customers hated them. But authors signed at the time still complained. Today, some authors complain when there are no e-book or Internet versions of their works, and others complain when there are.

Notwithstanding the importance of the "publishing decisions" language, there are many publishing matters such as marketing plans, sales materials, and cover designs where there is no obvious conflict between the publisher and the author, and where a responsible publisher will in fact consult with and follow the advice of the author, who should be an expert in the subject of the book. Moreover, there are certainly situations in which individual publishing decisions ought to be subject to the author's approval, such as the cover design for an artistic monograph or where the author is contributing a trademark or other branding to the project. Form 1.19 (miscellaneous clauses L and M) contains appropriate language for author consultation or approval in such cases.

[3] Warranties

Warranties are not technically rights but are rather a guarantee from an author that the publisher is receiving all rights needed to fully exploit the rights granted (or licensed) to the publisher by the author. Few clauses in a contract generate more concern from authors. Standard warranty language follows:

> The Author represents and warrants that: the Work is original except for material for which written third party permissions have been obtained; it has not previously been published and is not in the public domain; the Author has the right to enter into this Agreement and owns and can convey the rights granted to the Publisher; the Work contains no libelous or unlawful material or instructions that may cause harm or injury; it does not infringe upon or violate any copyright, trademark, trade secret or other right or the privacy of others; and statements in the Work asserted as fact are true or based upon generally accepted professional research practices.

Edited works will also include warranties with respect to material prepared by others that involves some form of scienter for liability, such as:

> The Editors will not include in the Work any contribution or material written or illustrated by others that the Editors believe or have reason to know or suspect may not be original or may contain libelous or unlawful statements or instructions that may cause harm or injury or that infringes upon or violates any copyright, trademark, or other right or

the privacy of others, and the Editors shall exercise due care in selecting contributors and reviewing contributions to minimize the risks of such infringements, instructions, and harms.

In book agreements, the warranties are usually backed with an indemnity clause such as the following:

The Author agrees to indemnify and hold harmless the Publisher, its licensees and assignees, from all costs, expenses (including attorneys' fees and expenses), losses, liabilities, damages, and settlements arising out of or in connection with any claim or suit based on allegations which, if true, would constitute a breach of any one or more of the above warranties. Until any claim or suit to which such indemnity may pertain has been resolved, the Publisher may withhold any sums due to the Author under this or any other agreement between the Author and the Publisher. The Author will cooperate fully with the defense or prosecution of any lawsuit between the Publisher and any third party involving the Work.

Authors are often frightened by this language, particularly the indemnity provisions, and authors who are not represented by agents (who understand this to be standard) will often require some coaxing on this issue. In general, the best way to negotiate is to listen to the author's concerns, explain what each clause means, make those clarifications that do not violate the publisher's internal policies, and further explain to authors that it is they, not the publishers, who know the content of their books and whether the books will give rise to liability. For example, when faced with the above-quoted "scienter" language for edited books, many editors are concerned that they will be held responsible if a contributor places infringing matter in their books. The negotiator should explain what it means to "believe or have reason to know or suspect" that material is infringing. Often, the editor will be satisfied with language indicating that the editor has no independent duty to investigate whether a contribution violates any of the warranties if he or she does not "believe or have reason to know or suspect" that it does. Other authors will be more concerned with baseless or "strike" suits. No publisher would survive for long if it sued authors for indemnification when they did nothing wrong, and many publishers will try to find mutually acceptable language to assuage the author's fears.

Sometimes authors will try to (1) limit their liability to the amount of royalties received, (2) strike the indemnity altogether, or (3) seek to be added to the publisher's insurance policy. Most publishers will reject option 1, under the theory that if the publisher's liability to third parties is not limited to its profits, why should the author's be limited to royalties? After all, only the author knows if, for example, the materials infringe third-party copyrights. With respect to striking the indemnity clause, the publisher should remember that if the clause was never in the agreement, it could argue that it was entitled to sue the author for its damages under the warranty, which would be similar to the indemnity. Once it is struck in negotiation, however, that position becomes weaker. With respect to option 3, many large publishers have author liability insurance and can add authors at no cost to their policy. This is beneficial to the author insofar as it may protect the author not only from liability to the publisher but also from direct third-party liability. However, authors are typically held responsible for the deductible, and in actual fact, this sometimes makes the negotiations more difficult. Although it is not rational, many authors find it easier to agree to the unlimited liability as stated in a standard indemnification clause (which is somewhat inchoate) than to agree to a maximum of $300,000 in liability under an insurance policy (which is a concrete number upon which they can fixate).

[4] Other Rights

Other rights that may be found in publishing agreements are:

- the right to use the author's name, likeness, and biographical data;
- the right of first option on the next book by an author; and
- the right to make a revised edition (with or without first requesting the same of the author).

The right to use the author's name, likeness, and biographical data is included in most author agreements but is not a high point of contention. In contrast, the right of first option, which is particularly used in the trade context, will often guarantee difficult negotiations. Following is one version of such language:

> The Author shall submit to the Publisher a book proposal with a table of contents or a complete manuscript for the Author's next book-length work (the "Next Book") before offering rights to the Next Book to any other publisher. The Publisher shall notify the Author within 60 days after receipt of such proposal or manuscript, or within 60 days following the Publisher's first publication of the Work, whichever is later, whether it desires to publish the Next Book. If the Publisher, within such period, notifies the Author that it does wish to publish the Next Book, the parties shall negotiate in good faith with respect to the terms of such publication. If within 30 days thereafter, the Author and the Publisher are unable to agree on such terms, the Author may offer rights to the Next Book to other publishers. If thereafter the Author receives a bona fide offer for the

Next Book from any third party, the Author shall submit the terms of such offer to the Publisher in writing and the Publisher shall have 5 business days thereafter to advise the Author whether it will publish the Next Book on such terms. If the Publisher does so, the Author shall enter into a contract with the Publisher incorporating such terms but otherwise in the form of this Agreement.

The issues with respect to revised editions are discussed in § 1.02[B][4], *infra.*

[B] Editorial Responsibilities/Defining the Work

The book agreement must set forth the editorial responsibilities of the parties. The most important parts are the:

- due date(s),
- length of the book,
- responsibilities of the parties with respect to artwork and permissions clearances,
- right of the publisher to make stylistic and/or substantive edits, and
- rights and obligations of the parties with respect to revised editions.

Some agreements also identify the target level of readership, e.g., middle-school, professional, post graduate.

[1] Length, Components, and Due Date

All book agreements should specify the length of the work, the components of the work (e.g., the index, frontmatter), and the due date:

The Author will prepare and deliver the complete and final manuscript of the Work, satisfactory to the Publisher in organization, form, content and style[5]

---

5 The issue of acceptability of manuscripts generates litigation. In general, a publishing company has broad discretion to reject a work that is not acceptable as to form and content, so long as it acts in good faith. Mark A. Fischer, E. Gabriel Perle and John Taylor Williams, *Perle and Williams on Publishing Law*, § 2.07 (3d ed., Aspen L. & Bus. 2001). *See also* Doubleday v. Curtis, 763 F.2d 495, 496 (2d Cir. 1985). However, a publishing company may not reject a work on form and content grounds if the real reason for termination is marketing concerns. Chodos v. West Publishing Co., 292 F.3d 992 (9th Cir. 2002). *Cf.* Random House, Inc. v. Gold, 464 F. Supp. 1306 (S.D.N.Y. 1979). Also, a publisher must use good faith in deciding whether a manuscript is acceptable. Helprin v. Harcourt, Inc., 277 F. Supp. 2d 327 (S.D.N.Y. 2003). If the ability to terminate an otherwise acceptable manuscript for adverse market conditions is desired, language such as that appearing in Form 1.19, Clause EE should be used.

by _____ (the "Due Date"), time being of the essence. To this end, the Author will complete and deliver the interim materials described on the attached Schedule of Deliverables in the format specified by the Publisher.

The manuscript will consist of text, illustrations, frontmatter and endmatter to convert to approximately _____ printed pages, including any additional material listed on the Schedule of Deliverables. If requested, the Author will also deliver suitable copy for an index when the proofs are returned. The final manuscript will include _____ photographs and clear sketches of line drawings in a form suitable for final production with appropriate labels, captions, and any necessary related materials. The Author will retain a copy of all material delivered to the Publisher. While the Publisher will, on request at the time of publication, make reasonable efforts to return material supplied by the Author, it will not be responsible for any loss or damage.

Where appropriate, the publisher will often attempt to tie the advance, if any, to meeting specified milestones as set forth on a "Schedule of Deliverables." As authors are routinely late, this enables the publisher to exert leverage during the writing process.

[2] Permissions

Typically, authors are responsible for permissions clearance, although the publisher should provide some guidance to the authors:[6]

The Author will, at the Author's expense, obtain written permission, in a form and scope acceptable to both parties, for any third party material included in the Work and will submit the permissions with the final manuscript. If any permissions or other material due from the Author is furnished by or paid for by the Publisher, it may withhold an amount equal to such cost from any sums due to the Author.

Although the author is primarily responsible for permissions clearance, it is very important for the publisher to retain the right to clear permissions and charge them against royalties, particularly for those infringement situations euphemistically referred to as "retroactive permissions."

In some situations, the publisher will perform the clearance function, such as in fine arts publishing for artistic monographs. Even here, however, the deductibility from author's royalties for permissions clearance should be negotiated up front.

---

6 *See generally*, Chapter 6, *infra*.

[3] Editing

The publisher will typically reserve the right to edit the manuscript. This is fine, and it is expected by most authors. In the context of professional or educational publishing, however, the author will usually seek and be granted some form of qualification, such as "the Publisher may edit the Work, provided that it does not materially change the meaning."

[4] Revised Editions

The main issue to decide in revised editions clauses is whether, assuming that the publisher desires to revise the work, it has an obligation to first ask the author. For most works, the answer should be yes. However, for major reference works involving large up-front investments from the publisher, or for works where the publisher develops the concept and then solicits authors or editors to prepare the work, it is not unreasonable for the publisher to reserve the right to use someone else to revise the work. In the following language, the use of the words "shall" or "may" completely changes the rights of the publisher:

> If the Publisher decides to publish a revised edition of the Work (hereinafter called the "Revised Edition(s)"), the Publisher [may] [shall] request the Editor to prepare the Revised Edition and the Editor shall advise the Publisher within 30 days of such request whether he will do so in accordance with the schedule set forth by the Publisher. If the Editor advises the Publisher that he will prepare the Revised Edition, the Editor shall diligently proceed with the revision, keep the Publisher advised of the Editor's progress, and deliver the complete manuscript to the Publisher on the scheduled due date.
>
> If the Editor does not participate in the revision, or if the Editor does not diligently proceed with the revision, the Publisher shall have the right to arrange with others for the preparation of the Revised Edition. In such case, the Publisher may have the revision done and charge any fees and/or royalties paid to the reviser(s) against royalties due or to become due to the Editor. The Editor's royalties shall not, however, be reduced by more than 50% for the first such revised edition and shall not be reduced by more than 75% for the next revised edition. No royalties shall be paid to the Editor with respect to further revised editions. The Revised Editions may be published under the same title and may continue to use the name of the Editor on all editions of the Work, but credit may be given to the reviser(s) in the Revised Edition(s) and in advertising and promotional material with respect thereto, at the Publisher's discretion.
>
> Except as otherwise provided herein, the provisions of this Agreement, including royalty terms, shall apply to each successive Revised Edition as though it were the first edition.

The right to not ask an editor to participate in a revision becomes even more important with multiple editors, who often have disagreements about their work.

[C] Consideration

[1] Royalties

Royalties are obviously key to most book agreements. Historically, royalties have been fairly complicated, with different royalties for different market segments:

> The Publisher shall pay to the Author, as a royalty, the following percentages of the Publisher's "dollar receipts" (as defined below) from sales or licenses of the Work:
>
> (1) from sales of a hardcover edition in the United States, its possessions and territories, and Canada: __%
> (2) (i) from sales of a trade paperback or other softcover edition (except for a mass-market paperback edition) in the United States, its possessions and territories, and Canada: __%
> (ii) from sales of a mass-market paperback edition in the United States, its possessions and territories, and Canada: 7½%
> (3) from sales of a hardcover edition elsewhere: 8%
> (4) from sales of a trade paperback or other soft-cover edition (including a mass-market paperback edition) elsewhere: 7½%
> (5) from sales or licenses of the Work or materials from the Work in electronic form, whether directly by the Publisher or indirectly through or with others: __%
> (6) From sales of any edition through direct-to-consumer marketing (including, for example, direct mail, but not including sales made via the Publisher's Web site): 5%
> (7) from sales of the Work at discounts of 56% or more from list price or sold in bulk for premium or promotional use, or special sales outside the ordinary channels of trade: 5%
> (8) from sales of the Work produced "on demand" when it is not feasible to maintain a normal inventory: 5%
> (9) from sales of non-dramatic audio recording and audio/video adaptations: 7½%
> (10) From sales or licenses by the Publisher of the following subsidiary rights in the Work to third parties: reprint (50%); book club (50%); foreign language (50%); first serial (50%); second serial (50%); condensations (50%); motion picture (50%); non-dramatic audio recording and audio/video adaptation rights (50%); dramatic and ancillary

rights (50%); commercial and merchandising rights (50%); public performance rights (50%); and in any media, permissions for quotations of short excerpts and photocopies (50%); in each case after deduction of the Publisher's out-of-pocket costs, if any, incurred in connection with such licenses.

(11)   should Publisher undertake, either alone or with others, the activities described in (10): 7½%

(12)   from sales or licenses of other, adaptations and other derivative works not specified above: 7½%

(13)   from use of all or a part of the Work in conjunction collectively with other work(s), a fraction of the applicable royalty rate equal to the proportion that the part of the Work so used bears to the entire collective work: pro rata

In an effort to simplify agreements and account for new technological uses not yet invented, some attorneys, including this author, are advocating what I call the "unified royalty theory," which provides a single royalty rate for all revenue streams attributable to a work:

The Publisher shall pay to the Author, as a royalty, ____% of the Publisher's "dollar receipts" (as defined below) from sales or licenses of the Work, and any other revenue attributable directly to the work (such as advertising revenue generated by banner ads included in the online edition, if any) in any media or channel of trade, except that if all or a part of the Work is used in conjunction collectively with other work(s), the Author shall be paid that fraction of the applicable royalty rate equal to the proportion that the part of the Work so used bears to the entire collective work.

When royalties are to be paid to authors on "net receipts" (whether called "receipts," "dollar receipts," "net receipts," "net income," or otherwise) a definition of the revenues upon which the royalty is to be paid is required:

"Dollar receipts" are defined as United States Dollars earned and received by the Publisher less any discounts, taxes, bad debts, customer returns, allowances, and credits and excluding any sums charged separately to the customer for shipping.

This does not apply when royalties are paid on the list price.

[2] Grants

A "grant" is a non-recoupable payment to an author. Grants are less common in book publishing agreements than royalties, but it is not unheard of for a publisher to pay a grant, particularly for reference works where the task of authoring or editing the book will involve significant time commitments and/or may necessitate heavy third-party expenses (e.g., permissions clearance and secretarial staff). Of course, dollars are fungible and contracts with high grants may have lower royalties or lower advances.

[3] Advances

Authors will typically seek a substantial advance. Publishers have an obvious interest in keeping the size of the advance low to minimize the business risk of a failed publication, or worse, an undelivered one.[7]

For an author, lawyer, or agent negotiating an advance, it is useful to ask the publisher the size of the first printing and/or the publisher's first year's projected revenues, and then negotiate the advance based on that number—if the publisher makes the mistake of sharing that information with you.

The publisher should remember that the advance may be used as an effective tool to ensure compliance from an author. Form 1.18 contains examples of language granting the author a higher advance for timely delivery of manuscript (Clause Q) and language assessing a penalty for late delivery (Clause R).

[4] Issues Involving Multiple Authors

Finally, although no author would sign an agreement not specifying the royalties to be received, in the case of multiple-authored works, sometimes they do just that. It is highly recommended that multiple authors divide the spoils and the credit in advance. Arm twisting from the publisher is well worth the effort with stubborn authors, as money disputes can quickly embroil the publisher in a lawsuit or jeopardize the success of the book. If, notwithstanding the best efforts of the publisher to force the authors to reach agreement prior to signing the contract, the authors simply do not know who will be doing what, the following language is recommended:

> The Authors shall notify the Publisher in writing of the division of the royalties among the authors no later than the Due Date specified in Paragraph _____ above. At such time, an addendum shall be issued by the Publisher and must be signed by all Authors. If the Authors disagree as to the appropriate division of the royalties, then the royalties shall be divided equally among them, and the Authors shall jointly and severally indemnify the Publisher from and against any claims challenging such a division.[8]

---

7 Although advances are typically recoverable, few publishers relish the opportunity to chase money from a defaulting author.

8 The following clause, which is more likely to get the publisher involved in a dispute, is a less desirable alternative:

> The Authors shall notify the Publisher of the division of royalties among the Authors no later than the Due Date set forth in Paragraph 2(a). At such time an amendment letter specifying such division of royalties shall be executed by all parties to this Agreement.

Remember also that with any multiple-authored book there should be a basic resolution of disputes clause, as follows:

In the event of any disagreement among the Editors that precludes the timely submission of a complete and satisfactory manuscript, or otherwise interferes with the publication of the Work, the Publisher shall have the right (but not the obligation) to determine how the disagreement will be resolved and its determination shall be final. In addition, in such event the Publisher shall have the right by written notice to terminate this Agreement with respect to one or more of the Editors, pursuant to Paragraph 17(b) below, or to discontinue the participation of one or more of the Editors, in which case the Editor shall not participate in any further efforts with respect to the Work or Revised Editions thereof, and such Editor's share of royalties shall be adjusted to reflect the amount of work actually performed by such Editor in relation to the published Work, as determined by the Publisher in its reasonable judgment.

If the Authors disagree as to the appropriate royalty split, then the royalties will be held in escrow by the Publisher until the Publisher receives written notice signed by all the Authors setting forth the division among them.

Educational Publishing Agreement

The following educational publishing agreement is designed to be "author friendly" in tone. The warranties, revised edition, and general boilerplate clauses have all been compressed for readability (Clauses 7, 8, and 11). The royalty clauses have also been simplified (Clause 4). Note that to reflect the fact that books may now have long lives independent of the print medium, in Clause 10, "out of print" has been replaced with language concerning the work's "availability for purchase."

Educational Publishing Agreement

AGREEMENT made this _____ day of _____20___, between
_____ (the **"Publisher"**) and _____ (the **"Author"**), with respect to a Work tentatively titled: (the **"Work"**).

The Publisher and the Author wish to work together to achieve the professional standards and commercial success that they each desire for the Work, and agree as follows:

1.   Grant of Rights

(a)   The Author grants to the Publisher for the full term of copyright and all extensions thereof the exclusive copyright in the Work throughout the world in all languages. The Publisher's exclusive rights will include the right by itself or with others to reproduce, publish, distribute, transmit and sell the Work and derivative works, in whole or in part, in all media and forms of distribution, under the Publisher's name and other imprints or tradenames, together with the exclusive right to license others to do so and to register the copyright in the Work. The title of the Work and any series titles used on or with it will also belong to the Publisher. For purposes of this Agreement, the term "Work" will include any material contributed by the Author to any supplementary or ancillary materials which may accompany the Work. For purposes of this Agreement, the term "Work" will include any material contributed by the Author to any supplementary or ancillary materials which may accompany the Work.

(b)   The Publisher and its licensees may use the name, likeness and professional credits of the Author on and in connection with any edition or derivative version of the Work.

2.   Manuscript Delivery

(a)   The Author will prepare and deliver the complete and final manuscript of the Work, satisfactory to the Publisher in organization, form, content and style by _____ (the "Due Date"), time being of the essence. To this end, the Author will complete and deliver the interim materials described on the attached Schedule of Deliverables in the format specified by the Publisher. The Work will be written for the [introductory course] level. The manuscript will be the next book-length work delivered by the Author to any publisher, whether alone or with any other party.

(b) The manuscript will consist of text, illustrations, frontmatter and end matter to convert to approximately _____ printed pages, including any additional material listed on the Schedule of Deliverables. If requested, the Author will also deliver suitable copy for an index when the proofs are returned. The final manuscript will include _____ photographs and clear sketches of _____ line drawings in a form suitable for final production with appropriate labels, captions and any necessary related materials. The Author will retain a copy of all material delivered to the Publisher. While the Publisher will, on request at the time of publication, make reasonable efforts to return material supplied by the Author, it will not be responsible for any loss or damage.

(c) The Author will, at the Author's expense, obtain written permission, in a form and scope acceptable to both parties, for any third party material included in the Work and will submit the permissions with the final manuscript. If any permissions or other material due from the Author is furnished by or paid for by the Publisher, it may withhold an amount equal to such cost from any sums due to the Author.

(d) If the Author has not delivered a satisfactory manuscript for the Work by the Due Date, the Publisher may (i) make other arrangements to complete the Work and charge the reasonable costs of such arrangements to any sums due to the Author, or (ii) terminate this Agreement and recover from the Author any monies paid to or on behalf of the Author in connection with the Work and in such event the Publisher will have no further obligation or liability to the Author.

3. Publication of the Work

(a) The Publisher will publish the Work at its own expense in such formats as it deems appropriate for the market, and will determine and implement all aspects of publication such as price, style, quantity, appearance and design, as well as such marketing, distribution and licensing arrangements as it deems appropriate for the successful launch of the Work into the marketplace. The Author may terminate this Agreement by written notice if the Publisher declines to publish the Work following timely submission of a complete and satisfactory final manuscript. Upon such termination: (i) the Publisher will revert all rights to the Author in lieu of any other damages or remedies, (ii) the Author may retain any payments received by the Author from the Publisher with respect to the Work, and (iii) neither party will have any further obligation or liability to the other.

(b)   The Publisher may edit the Work, provided that it does not materially change the meaning. If the Publisher delivers proofs to the Author, the Author will read, correct and return them promptly. If costs of additions, deletions, corrections or alterations (other than those resulting from printer's errors or the Publisher's errors) exceed 15% of typesetting and illustration cost, such excess cost may be charged against any sums due to the Author.

4.   Royalties to the Author

(a)   The Publisher will pay to the Author the following percentages of the Publisher's "dollar receipts" (as defined below) from sales or licenses of the Work, whether directly by the Publisher or indirectly through or with others:

   (i)   in the U.S. and its territories, whether in print or in digital form, (except as provided below): _____;

   (ii)   10% on sales or licenses:
   - outside the U.S. and its territories;
   - outside the U.S. and Canada of special lower-priced paperback editions printed for limited circumstances (for example, a special Asian edition sold in India where the market demands that the sales price be very low);
   - of electronic, audio or video adaptations of the Work or material therefrom (other than direct electronic conversions which will be subject to Section 4(a)(i) above), and/or use in databases and in electronic information storage and retrieval systems or devices; and
   - of any derivative works or licenses not specified elsewhere;

   (iii)   5% in connection with direct-to-consumer marketing (including, for example direct mail but not including sales made via Publisher's Web site) and on-demand editions and 7% on sales or licenses to elementary and high schools;

   (iv)   50% of the applicable royalty rate on sales or licenses at discounts greater than 50%;

   (v)   50% on the license of the following subsidiary rights in the Work to third parties: reprint, book club, foreign language, serial, motion picture, dramatic and ancillary rights; and, in any media, permissions for quotations of short excerpts; in each case after deduction of the Publisher's out-of-pocket costs, if any, incurred in connection with such licenses;

When the Publisher packages or sells the Work or any part of it together with other products, the Publisher will allocate to the Work that portion of the proceeds that is equal to the proportion that the Work or part of it bears to the entire product, and apply the appropriate royalty rate. "Dollar receipts" are U.S. dollars earned and received by the Publisher less discounts, taxes, bad debts, customer returns, allowances and credits and excluding sums charged separately to the customer for shipping.

(b)   If domestic sales fall below 1,000 copies in any calendar year following the year the Work is published, the royalty rate in section 4(a)(i) will be reduced by half.

(c)   No royalties will be paid on copies sold below manufacturing cost, or on ancillary materials that may accompany the Work unless covered by a separate written agreement between the parties.

(d)   With the exception of illustrative material prepared by the Author at the Author's expense and submitted in finished and usable form as part of the final manuscript, all illustrative material created at the Publisher's expense (including material based on preliminary sketches from the Author) will belong to the Publisher and the Publisher may use it in other works without payment to the Author.

5.   Accounting

An accounting of royalties due the Author based on sales for the preceding half year ending June 30 and December 31 will be made semiannually within two months after the close of each royalty period. The Publisher may take credit for any returns for which royalties have been previously paid, and it may retain a reserve for future returns. Any offsets against royalties or sums owed by the Author to the Publisher under this Agreement or any other may be deducted from payments due the Author. If the balance due in any accounting period is less than $10, no accounting or payment will be made until the cumulative amount exceeds $10 for any accounting period. Payments will be sent to the Author at the address set forth at the end of this Agreement unless the Author provides a different address in writing.

6.   Author's Copies

The Publisher will give 10 free copies of the Work to the Author on publication. The Author may purchase, for personal use only, additional copies of the Work and other publications of the Publisher (except journals) at a discount of 25% from the then current U.S. catalog list price.

7.   Warranties

The Author represents and warrants that: the Work is original except for material for which written third party permissions have been obtained; it has not previously been published and is not in the public domain; the Author has the right to enter into this Agreement and owns and can convey the rights granted to the Publisher; the Work contains no libelous or unlawful material or instructions that may cause harm or injury; it does not infringe upon or violate any copyright, trademark, trade secret or other right or the privacy of others; and statements in the Work asserted as fact are true or based upon generally accepted professional research practices. The Author will hold the Publisher and its licensees harmless against all liability, including expenses and reasonable counsel fees, from any claim which if sustained would constitute a breach of the foregoing warranties. Each party will give prompt notice to the other if any claim is made and the Author will cooperate with the Publisher, who will direct the defense thereof. Pending any settlement, final resolution or clear abandonment of a claim, the Publisher may engage counsel of its choice and may withhold in a reasonable amount sums due the Author under this or any other agreement between the parties. The provisions of this paragraph will survive termination of this Agreement.

8.   Revised Editions

The Author agrees to revise the Work if the Publisher considers it in the best interests of the Work. The provisions of this Agreement, including the royalty provisions, will apply to each revised edition as though it were the Work being published for the first time. If the Author is unwilling or unable to provide a manuscript of the revision within the reasonable time stipulated by the Publisher (whether because the Author is deceased, disabled or otherwise), the Publisher may have the revision done and charge any fees and/ or royalties paid to the reviser(s) against royalties due or to become due to the Author. The Author's royalties shall not, however, be reduced by more than 50% for the first such revised edition and shall not be reduced by more than 75% for the next revised edition. No royalties shall be paid to the Author with respect to further revised editions. Revised editions may be published under the same title and may refer to the Author by name, but the Publisher may credit the reviser(s) in the revised edition(s) and in related advertising and promotional material.

9.   Competing Works

Until the Work goes out of print, the Author will not publish, contract to publish or submit for publication any work on the same subject that would, in the Publisher's reasonable judgment, interfere with or injure the sale of the Work. The Author may draw on material contained in the Work in preparing articles and presentations for scholarly and professional journals and meetings, provided that credit is given to the Work and the Publisher.

10.   Available for Purchase

If the Publisher decides that the public demand for the Work no longer warrants keeping it "available for purchase" and the Publisher does not, within six months after receipt of a written request from the Author make it available for purchase or contract to make it available for purchase within a reasonable time, the Publisher will revert all rights to the Author subject to the Publisher's right to continue to publish and sell any derivative works then published or already scheduled for publication, and subject to any outstanding options or licenses to third parties. The Work will be deemed "available for purchase" if any English language version is available from the Publisher or any of its licensees in any format including copies manufactured or electronically transmitted on demand.

11.   General

Except for the right to receive monies, neither this Agreement nor any of the Author's obligations may be assigned without the Publisher's prior written consent. Otherwise, this Agreement will inure to the benefit of the heirs, successors, administrators and permitted assigns of the Author and to the parent, affiliates, subsidiaries and assigns of the Publisher. This Agreement may not be changed in whole or in part except by written agreement of the parties and no waiver of any provision will be deemed a waiver of any other. All notices will be sent in writing, with a copy of any notice to the Publisher sent to the attention of the Vice President & General Manager, College Division, of the Publisher. The provisions of this paragraph will survive termination of this Agreement, and this Agreement will be construed and interpreted according to the laws of the State of New York; any legal action will be instituted in a court of competent jurisdiction in New York County; and each party consents and submits to the personal jurisdiction of such court, waives any objection to venue in such court, and consents to service of process by registered or certified mail, return receipt requested, at such party's last known address.

AGREED AND ACCEPTED

AUTHOR

_____

[*author*]

_____

Social Security Number
(or, for nonresident aliens,
U.S. Taxpayer
Identification Number)

_____

Date of Birth

_____

Citizenship

_____

Address

_____

PUBLISHER

By _____

[*insert name and title of authorized
signatory*]

Trade Publishing Agreement

The following is a basic trade publishing agreement. For those who are unfamiliar with the book industry, "trade publishing" refers to books distributed by the book trade (i.e., books that are purchased by consumers in book stores), and not, as is commonly thought, books for people involved in specific trades (that publishing segment is generically called "professional publishing").

As explained more fully in § 1.02 [A] *supra*, the rights in trade agreements tend to be separately listed so that they can be easily struck if negotiated away (see Clause 1).

Note the strong first option language in Clause 14. This language is more common in trade publishing, where the publisher's investment in an author is an ongoing matter, than in other publishing segments, where authors are less likely to develop followings.[9]

Trade Publishing Agreement

AGREEMENT made this _ day of _____ 20_, between ___, of _____ (the **"Author"**) and **Publisher, Inc.**, address, New York, NY (the **"Publisher"**) with respect to a Work tentatively titled: (the **"Work"**).

The Publisher and the Author wish to work together to achieve the professional standards and success that they each desire from the Work, and agree as follows:

1.   Rights

The Author hereby grants to the Publisher during the full term of copyright and all extensions thereof the full and exclusive rights comprised in the copyright in the Work, including any "Supplementary Materials" (as defined in Paragraph 2(a) below) and any revised editions, including but not limited to the right, by itself or with others, throughout the world, to print, publish, republish, distribute and transmit the Work and to prepare, publish, distribute and transmit derivative works based thereon, in English and in other languages, in all media of expression now known or later developed, and to license or permit others to do so. The Publisher's rights shall include but shall not be limited to:

(a)   The exclusive right to publish and sell the Work in the English language in North America (the United States, its possessions and territories, Canada

---

9 For example, many people eagerly await sequels from certain well-known trade authors, and the publisher is more likely to invest in promoting an author's works if the publisher will be able to benefit from the goodwill in future works. By contrast, few people will buy a given professional book simply because they bought another book by the same author (unfortunately).

and Mexico), the Philippines, the British Commonwealth and the Republics of Ireland and South Africa, Europe and all other countries (the "Territory");

(b)   Foreign-language rights throughout the world;

(c)   Periodical or newspaper rights prior to *or* following book publication, including syndication rights throughout the world;

(d)   Non-dramatic audio recording rights throughout the world;

(e)   Motion picture, television, radio, stage dramatic and musical rights throughout the world;

(f)   Commercial and merchandising rights throughout the world.

2.   Manuscript

(a)   The Author agrees to prepare and submit the final manuscript of the Work, to consist of approximately ____ words not later than ___, unless the Publisher has agreed to extend the time in writing (the "Due Date"). The Author shall submit the first half of the manuscript three months before the Due Date. The Author shall also submit sample chapters from time to time as the Publisher may reasonably request. The final manuscript shall be submitted in computer disk format or other electronic format specified by the Publisher together with two printouts double-spaced on 8½" by 11" white paper printed on one side only with pages numbered consecutively, complete and satisfactory to the Publisher in organization, form, content, and style, accompanied by appropriate illustrative material, a table of contents and any additional material listed below (individually and collectively the "Supplementary Materials"), which shall be considered part of the Work:

Material   *Due Date (if different from above)*

If the Author fails to supply any Supplementary Materials or illustrative material on or before the Due Date, or to supply suitable copy for a final index when the proofs are returned, the Publisher shall have the right, but not the obligation, to obtain them and charge the reasonable cost against any sums due to the Author.

Illustrative material submitted as part of the final manuscript shall be in the form of black and white drawings, photographs or high resolution computer renderings in a form suitable for direct use without redrawing, lettering or retouching by the Publisher.

The Author shall, at the Author's expense, submit with the final manuscript of the Work, written permissions, on a form approved by the Publisher, to use any copyrighted material which the Author incorporates in the Work.

(b)   If the Author delivers the final manuscript on or before the Due Date, the Publisher shall, within 90 days after such delivery, notify the Author whether the manuscript is, in the Publisher's judgment, complete and satisfactory and, if it is not, request changes that would make the manuscript satisfactory to the Publisher. If the Author does not make the changes requested by the Publisher within 30 days after receipt of such request, or if, notwithstanding such changes the manuscript is not, in the Publisher's judgment, complete and satisfactory, the Publisher may terminate this Agreement pursuant to Paragraph 19 below or make such other arrangements as the Publisher deems advisable to make the manuscript complete and satisfactory, in which event the reasonable costs of such arrangements may be charged against any sums due to the Author. In the event the Publisher determines that the necessary revisions would be so extensive and fundamental that a satisfactory and timely revision would not be feasible, the Publisher shall have the right to deem the manuscript unsatisfactory without requesting changes and to terminate the Agreement pursuant to Paragraph 19 below.

(c)   If the Author does not receive the above notice from the Publisher within the prescribed period after timely delivery of the manuscript, the Author may request the Publisher in writing to notify the Author whether the manuscript is complete and satisfactory to the Publisher and, if it is not, to indicate what changes would make it complete and satisfactory. If the Publisher does not respond to the Author's request within 30 days after receipt of such request, the Author may terminate this Agreement pursuant to Paragraph 17 below.

(d)   The Author shall promptly correct and return proofs delivered to the Author for that purpose and provides suitable copy for a final index from such proofs. If Author's Alterations are made to the proofs, the costs incurred as a result thereof shall be borne by the Publisher to the extent of 15% of the cost of composition for the proofs originally submitted to the Author, and the excess, if any, shall be charged against any sums due to the Author. Author's Alterations are defined as deletions, additions, and other revisions made by the Author to the proofs, including any revisions made in the illustrations, other than to correct compositor's and/or proofreader's errors.

(e)   If the Author does not submit the final manuscript on or before the Due Date, the Publisher shall have the exclusive right but not the obligation to publish the Work. In such case, the Author shall submit the final manuscript to the Publisher upon completion and the Publisher shall have 90 days from the date of receipt of the final manuscript to determine, in its sole discretion, whether it will proceed under this Agreement or terminate this Agreement pursuant to Paragraph 19 below.

3. Publication

(a) Subject to the terms and conditions contained herein, the Publisher shall publish the Work in such style and manner as the Publisher deems appropriate, within twenty-four (24) months from the date of the Publisher's acceptance of the final manuscript. Notwithstanding the foregoing, in the event either (i) the Work is significantly longer or shorter than specified in Paragraph 2(a) above; (ii) after the manuscript is accepted for publication, changes to the manuscript are made by the Author with the Publisher's consent, revision of the manuscript is required due to unforeseen events or developments, technical errors require correction, or the Author for any reason does not meet the Publisher's schedule for returning materials; (iii) delays result from acts or conditions beyond the control of the Publisher or its suppliers or contractors, including, but not limited to, war, terrorism, fire, flood, labor disputes, governmental action, shortages of material, riots, civil commotions or other similar causes; or (iv) publication must be delayed to accommodate first serial or book club use, then the Publisher shall publish the Work as soon as the Publisher deems practical.

(b) The Publisher shall promote and sell the Work in such manner and at such prices as it deems appropriate, and make any and all other arrangements it deems appropriate with respect to the Work and the rights thereto granted to it herein.

4. Copyright Notice

The Publisher shall include in each copy of the Work published by it a notice of copyright in the Author's name in conformity with the United States Copyright Act and the Universal Copyright Convention and require its licensees to do the same. The Publisher shall have the right to register the copyright in the Work with the United States Copyright Office. Any textual or illustrative material prepared for the Work by the Publisher at its expense may be copyrighted separately in the Publisher's name.

5. Royalties

(a) The Publisher shall pay to the Author, as a royalty, the following percentages of the Publisher's "dollar receipts" (as defined below) from sales or licenses of the Work:

   (1) from sales of a hardcover edition in the United States, its possessions and territories, and Canada: ___%

(2) (i) from sales of a trade paperback or other soft-cover edition (except for a mass-market paperback edition) in the United States, its possessions and territories, and Canada: __%

    (ii) from sales of a mass-market paperback edition in the United States, its possessions and territories, and Canada: 7½%

(3) from sales of a hardcover edition elsewhere: 10%

(4) from sales of a trade paperback or other softcover edition (including a mass-market paperback edition) elsewhere: 7½%

(5) from sales or licenses of the Work or materials from the Work in electronic form, whether directly by the Publisher or indirectly through or with others: __%

(6) From sales of any edition through direct-to-consumer marketing (including, for example, direct mail, but not including sales made via the Publisher's Web site): 5%

(7) from sales of the Work at discounts of 56% or more from list price or sold in bulk for premium or promotional use, or special sales outside the ordinary channels of trade: 5%

(8) from sales of the Work produced "on demand" when it is not feasible to maintain a normal inventory: 5%

(9) from sales of non-dramatic audio recording and audio/video adaptations: 7½%

(10) From sales or licenses by the Publisher of the following subsidiary rights in the Work to third parties: reprint (50%); book club (50%); foreign language (50%); first serial (50%); second serial (50%); condensations (50%); motion picture (50%); non-dramatic audio recording and audio/ video adaptation rights (50%); dramatic and ancillary rights (50%); commercial and merchandising rights (50%); public performance rights (50%); and in any media, permissions for quotations of short excerpts and photocopies (50%); in each case after deduction of the Publisher's out-of-pocket costs, if any, incurred in connection with such licenses.

(11) should Publisher undertake, either alone or with others, the activities described in (10): 7½%

(12) from sales or licenses of other, adaptations and other derivative works not specified above: 7½%

(13) from use of all or a part of the Work in conjunction collectively with other work(s), a fraction of the applicable royalty rate equal to the proportion that the part of the Work so used bears to the entire collective work: pro rata

(b)   As an advance against all royalties and all proceeds due to the Author pursuant to this Agreement or any other agreement between the Author and the Publisher, the Publisher will pay the Author the following:

This advance shall be nonrefundable except as set forth in Paragraph 19 below.

(c)   "Dollar receipts" are defined as United States Dollars earned and received by the Publisher less any discounts, taxes, bad debts, customer returns, allowances and credits and excluding any sums charged separately to the customer for shipping.

(d)   Royalties shall not be due on any revenues earned abroad, where any foreign government blocks the conversion or transmittal of such monies to the United States, until such revenues can be transmitted.

(e)   No royalties shall be paid in connection with:

   (1)   fees received for the use of illustrative material, if any, prepared by the Publisher or at the Publisher's request, plates, negatives, type, tape or other property of the Publisher;
   (2)   any grant of rights by the Publisher at no charge for transcription into Braille, large type publication or otherwise for use by persons with disabilities;
   (3)   remainder copies and other copies sold below or at cost including expenses incurred, or furnished free to the Author, or for review, advertising, sample or similar purposes which may benefit the sale of the Work;
   (4)   copies donated to charity.

6.   Accounting

Payments to the Author shall be made semiannually, on or before the last day of April and October of each year for royalties due for the preceding half-year ending the last day of February and August respectively and shall be accompanied by an appropriate Statement of Account. The Publisher may take credit for any returns for which royalties have been previously paid. If the balance due the Author for any royalty period is less than $10, no payment shall be due until the next royalty period at the end of which the cumulative balance has reached $10. The Publisher may retain a 20% reserve for future returns for three royalty periods, provided the accounting statements indicate the amount of the reserve and how it has been applied. Any offsets against royalties or sums owed by the Author to the Publisher under this Agreement or any other agreement between the Author and the Publisher may be deducted from any payments due the Author under this Agreement or any other agreement between the Author and the Publisher.

7. Author's Copies

Upon publication the Publisher shall give ten (10) free copies of the Work to the Author, who may purchase, for personal use only, additional copies of the Work at a discount of 40% from the then current United States catalog list price and may purchase, for personal use only, the Publisher's other publications, at a discount of 25% from the then current United States catalog list price.

8. Competing Works

The Author, without the Publisher's prior written consent, shall not publish or permit any third party to publish the Work or any portion thereof or any other version, revision or derivative work based thereon in any media now known or later developed. The Author may, however, draw on and refer to material contained in the Work in preparing articles for publication in scholarly and professional journals and papers for delivery at professional meetings, provided that credit is given to the Work and the Publisher.

The Work shall be the Author's next manuscript for the Author's next book-length work whether under the Author's name or in collaboration with any other author.

The Author shall not, without the Publisher's prior written consent, prepare or assist in the preparation of any other work on the same subject as the Work that might, in the Publisher's reasonable judgment, be directly competitive with the Work.

9. Remainder Copies

When the Publisher determines that the demand for the Work is not sufficient to warrant its continued manufacture and sale, the Publisher may discontinue maintaining an inventory of the Work and may remainder all bound copies and sheet stock.

10. Name/Likeness

The Publisher shall have the right to use the name, likeness and biographical data of the Author on any edition of the Work or on any derivative work thereof, and in advertising, publicity or promotion related thereto and may grant such rights in connection with the license of any subsidiary rights in the Work. The Author shall provide in a timely manner any information reasonably requested by the Publisher for use in promoting and advertising the Work.

11. Title of the Work

The rights in the title of the Work, and any series titles used on or in connection with the Work, including without limitation any trademark, service mark or trade dress rights shall belong solely to the Publisher, and the Author hereby transfers and assigns to the Publisher in perpetuity any rights the Author may have in such titles and trade dress.

12.   Author's Property

The Author shall retain a copy of the manuscript of the Work, including any illustrative material. The Publisher may, after publication of the Work, dispose of the original manuscripts, illustrative material and proofs. The Publisher will, however, on written request made prior to publication, make reasonable efforts to return any original illustrative material supplied by the Author. The Publisher shall not be responsible for loss of or damage to any property of the Author.

13.   Revised Editions

If the Publisher determines that a revision of the Work is desirable, the Publisher shall, unless the Author is deceased, request the Author to prepare the revised edition and the Author shall advise the Publisher within 60 days whether the Author will do so in accordance with the schedule set forth by the Publisher. If the Author advises the Publisher that the Author will prepare the revised edition, the Author shall diligent y proceed with the revision, keep the Publisher advised of the Author's progress, and deliver the complete manuscript to the Publisher on the scheduled due date.

If the Author does not participate in the revision, or if the Author does not diligently proceed with the revision, the Publisher shall have the right to arrange with others for the preparation of the revised edition. In such case, the Publisher shall have the right to deduct from the Author's royalties any fee: or royalties paid to the reviser(s) provided that the Author's royalties shall not be reduced by more than 50% for the first such revised edition. No royalties shall be paid to the Author with respect to further revised editions not prepared by the Author. The revised editions may be published under the same title and may refer to the Author by name, but credit may be given to the reviser(s) in the revised edition(s) and in advertising arid promotional material with respect thereto.

Except as otherwise provided herein, the provisions of this Agreement, including royalty terms (but excluding the advance provided herein), shall apply to each successive revised edition as though it were the first edition.

14.   Option

The Author shall submit to the Publisher a book proposal with a table of contents or a complete manuscript for the Author's next book-length work (the "Next Book") before offering rights to the Next Book to any other publisher. The Publisher shall notify the Author within 60 days after receipt of such proposal or manuscript, or within 60 days following the Publisher's first publication of the Work, whichever is later, whether it desires to publish the Next Book. If the Publisher, within such period, notifies the Author that it does wish to publish the Next Book, the parties shall negotiate in good faith with respect to the terms of such publication. If within 30 days thereafter, the Author and the Publisher are unable to agree on such terms, the Author may offer rights to the Next Book to other publishers. If thereafter the Author receives a bona fide offer for the Next Book from any third party, the Author shall submit the terms of such offer to the Publisher in writing and the Publisher shall have 5 business days thereafter to advise the Author whether it will publish the Next Book on such terms. If the Publisher does so, the Author shall enter into a contract with the Publisher incorporating such terms but otherwise in the form of this Agreement.

15. Warranty

The Author represents and warrants that: the Work is original except for material for which written third party permissions have been obtained; it has not previously been published and is not in the public domain; the Author has the right to enter into this Agreement and owns and can convey the rights granted to the Publisher; the Work contains no libelous or unlawful material or instructions that may cause harm or injury; it does not infringe upon or violate any copyright, trademark, trade secret or other right or the privacy of others; and statements in the Work asserted as fact are true or based upon generally accepted professional research practices. The Author will hold the Publisher and its distributors and licensees harmless against all liability, including expenses and reasonable counsel fees, from any claim which if sustained would constitute a breach of the foregoing warranties. Each party will give prompt notice to the other if any claim is made and the Author will cooperate with the Publisher, who will direct the defense thereof. Pending any settlement, final resolution or clear abandonment of a claim, the Publisher may engage counsel of its choice and may withhold in a reasonable amount sums due the Author under this or any other agreement between the parties. The provisions of his paragraph will survive termination of this Agreement.

16. Infringement

If the copyright in the Work or in any derivative work is infringed, the Publisher shall have the right, but not the obligation, to pursue a claim for infringement in such manner as it deems appropriate. if it does so, the Publisher shall recoup the expenses incurred from any recovery, and the balance of the proceeds, if any, shall be divided equally between the Author and the Publisher. If the Publisher does not pursue such a claim after the Author's request to do so, the Author, at the Author's expense, shall have the right to prosecute an action, and any recovery shall belong solely to the Author.

17. Termination by Author

(a)   The Author may terminate this Agreement by written notice to the Publisher if the Publisher does not reply to the Author's request for required changes pursuant to Paragraph 2(c) above, or if the Publisher does not publish the Work within the time specified in Paragraph 3(a) above, for reasons other than as specified therein.

(b)   The Author may terminate this Agreement prior to publication by written notice to the Publisher if a voluntary petition in bankruptcy under Title 11, United States Code is filed by the Publisher or an involuntary petition under Title 11, United States Code is filed against the Publisher and an order for relief is entered.

(c)   Upon termination of this Agreement by the Author pursuant to subparagraph (a) or (b) above, the Publisher agrees to revert to the Author all rights herein granted and the Author shall retain as liquidated damages in lieu of any other damages or remedies, any payments received by the Author from the Publisher with respect to the Work.

18. Available for Purchase

If the Publisher, in its sole discretion decides that sales of the Work are not sufficiently profitable to keep it "available for purchase" and the Publisher does not, within six months after receipt of a written request from the Author make it available for purchase or contract to make it available for purchase within a reasonable time, all rights granted to the Publisher shall, at the end of the six-month period revert to the Author, subject however, to any option, license, or contract granted to third parties prior to the date of the reversion, and further subject to the Publisher's right to continue to publish and sell any then-existing derivative work based on the Work, all subject to the rights of the Author and the Publisher to their respective shares of the proceeds from such license or use under this Agreement. The Work shall be deemed to be "available for purchase" for this purpose if any English language edition of the Work is on sale or is otherwise available or is under option or contract for publication under the Publisher's or any other imprint, or if the Publisher or its licensee offers for sale copies of the Work to be produced, manufactured or electronically transmitted, upon receipt of orders therefor.

19. Termination by Publisher

(a)   The Publisher may terminate this Agreement prior to publication in the event:

   (1)   the Author fails to deliver a complete and satisfactory manuscript pursuant to Paragraph 2(a) above by the Due Date or fails or refuses

to make the changes requested by the Publisher pursuant to Paragraph 2(b) above; or

(2) the Publisher does not exercise its exclusive right to publish the Work pursuant to Paragraph 2(e) above; or

(3) publication may result in legal liability unacceptable to the Publisher in its reasonable judgment.

(b) Upon termination of this Agreement by the Publisher pursuant to subparagraph (a) above, the Author shall promptly repay to the Publisher any advances or other payments made to the Author hereunder. Upon receipt of such repayment, the Publisher shall revert to the Author all rights herein granted, and the Publisher shall have no further obligation or liability hereunder.

20. General

(a) The engagement of the Author is personal and the rights hereunder granted to the Author are not assignable nor may the obligations imposed be delegated without the prior written consent of the Publisher; provided however, that the Author may assign any sums due to the Author hereunder without the Publisher's consent.

(b) Except as provided in the preceding subparagraph, this Agreement shall inure to the benefit of the heirs, successors, administrators, and permitted assigns of the Author and the subsidiaries, successors, and assigns of the Publisher.

(c) All notices to be given by either party hereunder shall be in writing and shall be sent to the Author at the Author's address as it is set forth in this Agreement unless such address has been changed by proper written notice, or to the Publisher, addressed to the attention of the Vice President & General Manager.

(d) This Agreement shall not be subject to change or modification in whole or in part, unless in writing signed by both parties.

(e) No waiver of any term or condition of this Agreement or of any part thereof shall be deemed a waiver of any other term or condition of this Agreement or of any breach of this Agreement or any part thereof.

(f) This Agreement shall be construed and interpreted pursuant to the laws of the State of California applicable to contracts wholly entered into and performed in the State of California. Any legal action, suit or proceeding arising out of or relating to this Agreement or the breach thereof shall be instituted in a court of competent jurisdiction in Los Angeles County in the State of California and each party hereby consents and submits to the personal jurisdiction of such court, waives any objection to venue in such court and consents to service of process by registered or certified mail, return receipt requested, at the last known address of such party.

(g)   The provisions of Paragraph 15 above and this Paragraph shall survive the termination of this Agreement.

AGREED AND ACCEPTED

AUTHOR   **PUBLISHER, INC.**

By: _____   By: _____

Name: _____   Name: _____

_____   Title: _____

                                   Date: _____

Social Security Number
(or, for nonresident aliens,
U.S. Taxpayer
Identification Number)

Address: _____

Date: _____

Date of Birth:_____

Citizenship: _____

Professional Publishing Agreement (Continuity Book; Single Author)

The following is a professional publishing agreement for a continuity book; specifically, a single work that is updated on an annual basis for shipment to a standing order base. Note that the publisher agrees to pay for permissions, but only as an advance against royalties (Clause 3). Note also that revised editions and updates, which are critical to a continuity book, are offered to the author on a first option basis, with the publisher retaining the right to terminate the author without further payments if he or she does not prepare the update or revised edition as requested (Clause 8).

Although it is a simple author agreement, it expressly contemplates that there may be other contributors to the book (Clause 4).

Publishing Agreement
(Continuity Book; Single Author)

AGREEMENT made this ____ day of _____, 20___ between
_____ (hereinafter called the "Publisher"), a Delaware corporation having its principal place of business at _____ and _____
_____ (hereinafter called the "Author"), for publication of a continuity-based book tentatively titled _____ (hereinafter called the "Work," which term shall include both the Base Volume and any and all Updates and Revisions thereto).

1. Submission of Manuscript

The Author will, at his/her own expense, prepare and deliver to the Publisher a manuscript of the Work in both print and Microsoft Word format (or such other electronic format as may be agreed by the parties). The manuscript will be delivered to the Publisher, along with any and all permissions from other persons as may be required for publication of any copyrighted or other material contained in the Work, on or before _____, 20___. The manuscript for the initial version of the Work (hereinafter called the "Base Volume") will be of sufficient length to yield _____ printed pages, including any table of contents, preface, illustrations, legends, tables, references, appendices, or other supplementary matter that is to appear in the Work. The manuscript and all permissions must be acceptable to the Publisher in form and content.

If the Author has not delivered in form and content acceptable to the Publisher a complete manuscript and all permissions by the delivery date herein agreed to, including any delivery date pursuant to paragraph 8 with respect to any Revisions or Updates of the Work, the Publisher may, if it so chooses, return all of the unpublished materials that have been submitted to the Publisher by the Author and, at its sole option, terminate this Agreement by prior written notice to the Author, without any liability whatsoever on the Publisher's part. Alternatively, the Publisher may, at its sole option, extend the manuscript delivery date or give the Author a reasonable amount of additional time to make changes or revisions acceptable to the Publisher (although the Publisher shall not be required to do so). Should the Author be unwilling or unable to meet the new delivery date or to make changes or revisions acceptable to the Publisher in that time, the Publisher may return all unpublished materials as provided above and, at its sole option, terminate this Agreement by prior written notice to the Author, without any liability whatsoever on the Publisher's part. [In such event, the Author shall return any advance previously paid to the Author.]

If in the Publisher's reasonable judgment the manuscript needs to be retyped or reformatted, the Publisher may retype or reformat the manuscript and deduct the expense from the Author's royalties.

The Author will furnish an index to the Work after delivery of the manuscript to the Publisher, provided, however, that the Author may request that the Publisher arrange indexing on the Author's behalf, in which case the expense will be deducted from the Author's royalties.

2. Rights to the Work

The Author grants the Publisher all right, title, and interest in and to the Work including the copyright thereto. The Author acknowledges that as a result of this grant of ownership, the Publisher has throughout the world the exclusive right, among others, to reproduce the Work in any form or medium (now known or hereafter devised), to prepare derivative works based upon the Work, to distribute copies of the Work in any form or medium (now known or hereafter devised) to the public by sale or other transfer of ownership, or by license, rental, lease, or lending, and to perform and display the Work publicly. The Author further acknowledges that its grant to the Publisher of the ownership of the copyright to the Work includes the copyright to all derivative works based upon the Work and gives the Publisher the sole right to secure or renew copyright registration for the Work and all such derivative works in the Publisher's name in any place in the world where the Publisher chooses to do so.

3. Permissive Materials

The Author will ensure that the Work contains no material from other works without the prior written permission of the owner of such material. Such permissions will be obtained by the Author and/or by his contributors in form and content acceptable to the Publisher and delivered to the Publisher along with the manuscript of the Work. Upon receipt and acceptance by the Publisher as provided in paragraph 1 of this Agreement of a complete manuscript of the Work and any and all permissions, the Publisher will pay up to a total of $_____ for all such permissions taken together, provided that the total amount paid by the Publisher for permission fees will be deducted from the Author's royalties. The Author will notify the Publisher in writing of all materials in the Work that were taken from documents prepared or published by the United States Government.

4.   Warranties

The Author shall be responsible for securing copyright transfer agreements from any other authors contributing to the Work using the Copyright Transfer Form shown as Attachment A hereto and for delivering such agreements to the Publisher along with the manuscript of the Work. Except for materials described in the first and last sentences of paragraph 3 above and except for contributions from other authors covered by a Copyright Transfer Form as shown in Attachment A hereto, the Author warrants that he/she is the sole author and owner of the Work, has full authority to grant to the Publisher the right, title, and interest described in paragraph 2 above, and has neither previously granted any such right, title, or interest to any other party nor otherwise encumbered the Work. Except for contributions from other authors covered by a Copyright Transfer Form as shown in Attachment A hereto, the Author warrants that the Work contain no libelous, obscene, or any other unlawful materials, violates no common law or statutory copyright or any other property or personal right whatsoever of any other person or entity, is original, and is not in the public domain, and further warrants that all statements asserted in the Work as facts are true or based upon reasonable research for accuracy. Upon signing of the Copyright Transfer Form shown as Attachment A, each contributing author will be bound by a warranty similar to that contained in the preceding sentence. The Author will keep all working materials for the manuscript of the Work for a period of two years from the date of first publication of the Work.

The Author agrees to indemnify and hold harmless the Publisher, its licensees and assignees, from all costs, expenses (including attorneys' fees and expenses), losses, liabilities, damages, and settlements arising out of or in connection with any claim or suit based on allegations which, if true, would constitute a breach of any one or more of the above warranties. Until any claim or suit to which such indemnity may pertain has been resolved, the Publisher may withhold any sums due to the Author under this or any other agreement between the Author and the Publisher. The Author will cooperate fully with the defense or prosecution of any lawsuit between the Publisher and any third party involving the Work.

In no event shall the Publisher be obligated to publish anything which in its opinion breaches any one or more of the above warranties. In the event of a breach by the Author of any one or more of the above warranties, the Publisher shall be entitled to terminate this Agreement by prior written notice to the Author, without any liability whatsoever on the Publisher's part. In the event that the Publisher shall have advanced any monies to the Author pursuant to this Agreement, the Author shall return all such monies within ninety (90) days after receipt of a notice of termination pursuant to this paragraph.

5. Competing Works

For the life of this Agreement, the Author agrees not to write, edit, or otherwise contribute to any work that might, in the reasonable opinion of the Publisher, compete directly with or injure the distribution of copies of the Work.

6. Author's Corrections

The Author will promptly read, correct, and return the galley and/or page proofs of the Work. If the Author fails to perform these duties within such reasonable time as the Publisher may specify, the Publisher may proceed as if the Author had performed them. Should the Author make any alterations in the Work in galley and/or page proofs, the Publisher will pay the cost of the alterations up to ten percent (10%) of the cost of the original composition. Alteration charges in excess of this ten percent (10%) allowance will be deducted from the Author's royalties. The Publisher will pay for correction of typographical errors.

7. Publication and Marketing

Subject to the terms and conditions herein, the Publisher will publish and market the Work at the Publisher's own expense. It shall be published under the imprint of the Publisher, and marketed in the style and manner and at the price that the Publisher, in its sole discretion, deems appropriate. The Publisher shall not be liable for delays in publication or marketing caused by circumstances beyond its control. The Author grants to the Publisher the right to use the Author's name and likeness, and relevant information about the Author, in connection with the Publisher's marketing of the Work and shall provide the same to the Publisher upon reasonable request therefor.

8. Revisions and Updates

The Author understands that it is the Publisher's intent to keep the Work continually up to date through Revisions and Updates that will be published on an annual or other periodic basis as the Publisher may determine in its sole discretion. Each Revision shall be a book that replaces the Base Volume or any prior Revision of the Work. Each Update shall consist of updated pages or new materials that are published separately from the Base Volume or from a current Revision and that are designed to be used with, rather than as a replacement for, the Base Volume or Revision.

Provided that this Agreement has not been previously terminated, the Author shall have the right of first refusal with respect to the preparation of each Revision and Update. Such right of first refusal must be exercised in writing within thirty (30) calendar days after the Publisher notifies the Author in writing of its intention to publish a Revision or Update.

In the case of a Revision, if the Author exercises his/her right of first refusal and thereby undertakes to prepare the Revision, all of the provisions of this Agreement, with the exception of the deadline described in sentence two of paragraph 1 and the page specification described in sentence four of paragraph 1, will apply to the Revision of the Work by the Author as though that Revision were the Base Volume being published under this Agreement.

If the Author does not exercise his/her right of first refusal and thereby does not undertake to prepare the Revision, or is unable to exercise such right due to death or any other reason, the Publisher may, at its sole option, terminate this Agreement by prior written notice to the Author, without any liability whatsoever on the Publisher's part, except for the obligation to account for and pay any outstanding royalties due to the Author up to the date of termination. In any event, whether or not the Publisher terminates this Agreement pursuant to the foregoing sentence, the Publisher may prepare the Revision itself or arrange with others for the preparation of the Revision, and the Author shall receive no royalties derived from sales or other distribution of any Revision that he/she did not prepare pursuant to the terms of this paragraph 8. The Publisher may but is not required to continue to use the Author's name and likeness, and relevant information about the Author, in connection with any Revision even if the Author has not participated in the preparation of such Revision. The Publisher's rights under the preceding sentence shall survive termination of this Agreement.

In the case of an Update, if the Author exercises his/her right of first refusal and thereby undertakes to prepare the Update, all of the provisions of this Agreement, with the exception of the deadline described in sentence two of paragraph 1 and the page specification described in sentence four of paragraph 1, will apply to the Update of the Work by the Author as though that Update were the Base Volume being published under this Agreement.

If the Author does not exercise his/her right of first refusal and thereby does not undertake to prepare the Update, or is unable to exercise such right due to death or any other reason, the Publisher may, at its sole option, terminate this Agreement by prior written notice to the Author, without any liability whatsoever on the Publisher's part, except for the obligation to account for and pay any outstanding royalties due to the Author up to the date of termination. In any event, whether or not the Publisher terminates this Agreement pursuant to the foregoing sentence, the Publisher may prepare the Update itself or arrange with others for the preparation of the Update, and the Author shall receive no royalties derived from sales or other distribution of any Update that he/she did not prepare pursuant to the terms of this paragraph 8. The Publisher may but is not required to continue to use the Author's name and likeness, and relevant information about the Author, in connection with any Update even if the Author has not participated in the preparation of such Update. The Publisher's rights under the preceding sentence shall survive termination of this Agreement.

9.   Royalties

Royalties will be based upon the net sales of the Work (including supplements or updates) for all copies of the Work actually distributed by the Publisher in the United States. For the purpose hereof net sales will mean the net cash receipts (gross sales less returns, discounts, and bad debts) of monies reported on the Publisher's books of account from the distribution of copies of the Work (whether by sale or other transfer of ownership, or by license, rental, lease, or lending). The Author shall be entitled to payment in accordance with the following schedule: [*Add rate and escalator*] The royalty rate will be ten per-cent (10%) for net sales occurring outside the United States.

If the Publisher itself exercises its subsidiary rights in the Work, or licenses or transfers them to others, the Author will be entitled to ten percent (10%) of the net sales the Publisher derives from such exercise, or of the net proceeds it receives from the license or transfer of these rights to others. Subsidiary rights include, but are not limited to, translation rights, book club rights, paperback rights, and the right otherwise to exploit the Work by any present or future methods or means now known or hereafter devised (including electronic rights).

No royalties will be paid for copies sold at or below cost, furnished gratis to the Author or contributors, or furnished for review, advertising, sample, or like purposes.

10.   Payments and Statements

The Publisher will mail to the Author semiannual statements of accounts through the 30th of June and the 31st of December stating net sales of the Work (and any net sales and net proceeds from the exercise, license, or transfer of subsidiary rights), and the royalty due thereon, for the previous six months. Such statements will be mailed to the Author within ninety (90) days after the end of the period and will include the payment due to the Author.

11.   Author's Copies

Upon publication, the Publisher will provide the Author, without charge, ten (10) copies of the Work (including supplements or updates) for personal use and not for resale. Additional copies may be purchased by the Author at a thirty-three percent (33%) discount for personal use and not for resale.

12.   Contributors' Copies

All contributors to the Base Volume or to a Revision will receive one complimentary copy of the Base Volume or of such Revision, as the case may be. Contributors to Updates will receive one complimentary copy of the Base Volume or Revision with which the Update is designed to be used, provided they have not already received a complimentary copy of such Base Volume or Revision, and one copy of the Update to which they have contributed. In the case of multiple contributors to an Update or to a chapter within an Update, only the senior contributors will be provided complimentary materials.

13.   Right to Discontinue Publication

When, in the sole judgment of the Publisher, the public demand for the Work is not sufficient to produce profitable distribution of the Work or to warrant its continued publication, the Publisher may, at its sole discretion, discontinue the distribution of the Work and allow the Work to go out of print.

14.   Complete Understanding

This Agreement contains the entire understanding and agreement of the parties with respect to the Work and supersedes all prior understandings or agreements. This Agreement may not be modified except by a writing executed by the parties.

15.   Assignment

The Author may not assign or otherwise transfer any of the Author's rights or obligations hereunder without the express prior written consent of the Publisher, except that the Author may without the Publisher's consent assign any revenues due to Author hereunder. The Agreement is binding on the heirs, legal representatives, successors, and permitted assignees of the Author, and on the successors and assignees of the Publisher.

16.   Licenses Survive Termination

Termination of the Agreement for any reason shall not affect the licenses previously granted by the Publisher.

17.   Sums Due and Owing

Any sum due and owing from the Author to the Publisher may be deducted from any sum due, or to become due hereunder, from the Publisher to the Author.

18. Governing Law

The Agreement shall be construed according to, and all rights and liabilities of the parties shall be governed by, the internal laws of the State of _____.

AGREED

AUTHOR   PUBLISHER

_____   _____
Author   Date   Acquisitions Editor   Date

_____   _____
Social Security Number   Publisher   Date

FORM 1.4
Multiple-Editor Edited Work Agreement

The following is an example of an edited work agreement for two or more editors. It contains the important warranty distinction between material authored
by the editors themselves, for which they are absolutely liable in the event
of an infringement, and material authored by others, for which they are only
liable if they believe, have reason to know, or suspect that it infringes prior to
including such material in the work.

This agreement also contains the critical language concerning editors'
credit (i.e., name order), resolution of disputes among the editors (the publisher
decides and its decision is final), and the division of royalties. (See Clauses 15,
16, and 5(e) respectively.) These issues should be addressed in advance in any
multiple editor or multiple author agreement.

Multiple-Editor Edited Work Agreement

AGREEMENT made this ____ day of _____, between ____ (individually
an "Editor" and collectively the "Editors"), and _____ (the
"Publisher"), for the purpose of publishing a collective work in print and/or
electronic form tentatively titled:

[*Title*]

(hereinafter referred to as the "Work"), commissioned by the Publisher.

In consideration of the promises set forth in this Agreement, the Editors and
the Publisher agree as follows:

1. Editors' Duties

(a)   The Publisher hereby commissions the Editors to edit the Work and to
perform the following services, subject to the Publisher's approval:

  (i)   prepare an outline of the scope of the Work, including without
        limitation the number and title of the contributions to be included
        therein, select suitable contributors (the "Contributors"), fix the length
        and scope of each contribution, and arrange for each Contributor
        to prepare and promptly submit the contribution in accordance
        with a schedule consistent with the Manuscript Due Date set forth
        in Paragraph 1(a)(v) below, and as set forth in the schedule (if any)
        attached hereto and made a part hereof (the "Schedule");

  (ii) prepare and submit to the Publisher a detailed table of contents of the
        Work on or before ____ and a sample chapter (not an introductory
        chapter) on or before____;

  (iii) review each contribution, make or request the Contributor to make
        such revisions as the Editors or the Publisher thinks appropriate,

and reject any contribution deemed unsatisfactory by the Editors or the Publisher;

(iv) advise each Contributor that each contribution must be accompanied by a Contributor Agreement in the form attached hereto as Addendum A (the "Contributor Agreement"), which all Contributors will be required to sign and deliver with the manuscript by the Manuscript Due Date;

(v) submit to the Publisher the complete final manuscript of the Work (including any material to be written by an Editor) and all signed Contributor's Agreements not later than _____ unless the Publisher has agreed to extend the time in writing (the "Manuscript Due Date"). The final manuscript shall consist of approximately _____ printed book pages (approximately 500 words per printed page of text) or _____ words. The final manuscript shall be submitted on computer disk in a format specified in the Publisher's instructions (made available to the Editors by the Publisher) with one double-spaced computer printout, and shall be satisfactory to the Publisher in organization, form, content, and style, accompanied by appropriate illustrative material in the format(s) specified by the Publisher, a table of contents, and suitable copy for a final index, all of which shall be considered part of the Work.

If the Editors fail to supply any of these materials, the Publisher shall have the right to obtain such materials and charge the cost against any sums due to the Editors hereunder;

(vi) obtain, at the Editors' expense, and submit with the final manuscript of the Work, written permissions, on a form approved by the Publisher, to reprint and reuse in all formats, worldwide, any copyrighted material which the Editors or any Contributor incorporates in the Work. If the Editors fail to supply such written permissions, the Publisher shall have the right, but not the obligation, to obtain them and to charge the cost against any sums due to the Editors hereunder;

(vii) promptly correct and return proofs and/or edited manuscripts delivered to the Editors for that purpose. If "Editors' Alterations" are made to the proofs, the costs incurred as a result thereof shall be borne by the Publisher to the extent of 15% of the cost of typesetting the proofs originally submitted to the Editors, and the excess, if any, shall be charged against royalties payable to the Editors. "Editors' Alterations" are defined as deletions, additions, and other revisions made by the Editors to the proofs, including any revisions made in the illustrations, other than to correct printer's errors; and

(viii) in general, assume editorial responsibility for the preparation and timely submission to the Publisher of the complete final manuscript of the Work, in accordance with the Manuscript Due Date.

(b) If the Editors do not submit the complete final manuscript on or before the Manuscript Due Date, unless the time for submission has been extended in writing by the Publisher, this Agreement shall be converted into an option to the Publisher to publish the Work. In such case, the Editors shall submit the final manuscript to the Publisher upon completion and the Publisher shall have 90 days from the date of receipt of the manuscript to determine whether it will proceed under the terms of this Agreement, or terminate this Agreement pursuant to Paragraph 17(b) below.

(c) If the Editors do not deliver a manuscript which is, in the Publisher's judgment, complete and satisfactory and/or do not make the changes requested by the Publisher within a reasonable time set by the Publisher, or if, notwithstanding such changes, the manuscript is not, in the Publisher's judgment, complete and satisfactory, the Publisher may terminate this Agreement with respect to one or more of the Editors pursuant to Paragraph 17(b) below or make such other arrangements as the Publisher deems advisable to make the manuscript complete and satisfactory, in which event the reasonable costs of such arrangements may be charged against any sums due to the Editors. In addition, disagreements among the Editors may be resolved pursuant to Paragraph 16 below.

2. Publication

Subject to the terms and conditions contained herein, the Publisher, at its own expense, shall manufacture, publish, promote, sell, transmit and distribute the Work in such manner and at such prices as the Publisher deems appropriate, and make any and all other arrangements it deems advisable with respect to the Work and the rights thereto granted to it herein.

3. Ownership of the Work

The Work and the separate contributions contained therein, and any Revised Editions, whether or not prepared by the Editors, shall be considered a work made for hire and the copyright and the full and exclusive rights comprised in the copyright, and all other right, title and interest in and to the Work and the material contained therein, shall vest initially in and shall thereafter belong to the Publisher. To the extent, if any, that the Work or any contribution or other material contained in the Work or any Revised Edition thereof does not qualify as a work made for hire or copyright therein might otherwise vest in the Editors, the Editors hereby grant, transfer and assign to the Publisher for the full term of copyright and all extensions thereof the full and exclusive rights comprised in the copyright in and to the Work and the material and contributions contained therein, any Revised Editions thereof and all derivative works based thereon, and all other proprietary rights thereto, in all languages and forms, and in all media of expression now known or later developed, throughout the world.

4.   Copyright Notice and Registration

The Publisher shall reproduce in each copy of the Work published by it a notice of copyright in the Publisher's name in conformity with the U.S. Copyright Act and the Universal Copyright Convention and require its licensees to do the same. The Publisher may, at its discretion, register the copyright in the Work with the U.S. Copyright Office after first publication. In the event of a prior publication of a portion of the Work, the Editors shall provide the Publisher with all necessary information about such publication and obtain any assignments required to ensure that the Publisher has the full and complete right, title and interest in and to the Work and its copyright and may properly register the copyright in the Publisher's name.

5.   Editors' Compensation

(a)   In full payment for all services to be performed and any rights transferred hereunder, the Publisher shall pay the Editors, as royalties, the following percentages of the Publisher's "dollar receipts" (as defined below) from the following sales or licenses of the Work published hereunder:

   (i) from sales of the original edition of the Work whether in hardcover, paperback or other medium (the "regular edition") in the United States, its possessions and territories, and Canada: ___%
  (ii) from sales of the regular edition elsewhere: ___%
 (iii) from sales of lower priced paperback editions throughout the world: ___%
  (iv) from sales of the Work directly to the consumer through Publisher-owned book clubs, through direct mail campaigns or solicitation by telephone, radio or television: 5%
   (v) from sales of any edition at discounts of 50% of more from list price or sold in bulk for premium or the promotional use, or special sales outside the ordinary domestic applicable channels of trade: 50% of the applicable royalty rate
  (vi) from sales of copies of the Work produced "on demand" upon receipt of orders therefor, when it is not feasible to maintain a normal inventory: 5%
 (vii) from sales or licenses of software and electronic adaptations (including e-Books), audio and video adaptations, and/or use of the Work in databases and in electronic information storage and retrieval systems or devices and, to the extent attributable to the Work, from licenses for photocopying: ___%
(viii) from sales of condensations, adaptations, and other derivative works not specified elsewhere: ___%

(ix) from sales or licenses by the Publisher to third parties of book club, reprint, serial and translation rights, permission grants other than for photocopying and any other rights not enumerated above, excluding any reimbursement of production or other expenses made to third parties: 50%

(x) from use by the Publisher of all or part of the Work in conjunction collectively with other work(s), a fraction of the applicable royalty rate equal to the proportion that the part of the Work so used bears to the entire collective work: pro rata

(b) "Dollar receipts" are defined as United States Dollars received by the Publisher net of discounts and excluding any excise, sales or use or other domestic or foreign tax (except for income taxes), bank fees for foreign currency payments, any transportation, shipping and handling charges applicable thereto and less bad debts, customer returns, allowances and credits as well as any taxes withheld.

(c) Royalties shall not be due on any revenues earned abroad where any foreign government blocks the conversion or transmittal of such monies to the United States until such revenues can be transmitted.

(d) No royalties shall be paid in connection with:

(i) fees received for the use of illustrative material, if any, prepared by the Publisher, plates, negatives, type, tape, or other property of the Publisher;

(ii) any grant of rights made by the Publisher at no charge for transcription into Braille, large type publication or otherwise for use by persons with disabilities;

(iii) remainder copies or other copies sold below or at cost including expenses incurred, or furnished free to the Editors or the Contributors, or for review, advertising, sample or similar purposes which may benefit the sale of the Work;

(iv) revenues which cannot reasonably be attributed to the Work; and

(v) copies donated to charity.

(e) The royalties accruing to the Editors hereunder shall be divided as follows:

(f) Any fees, honoraria or other sums paid by the Publisher to the Contributors to the Work shall be considered an advance against all royalties and proceeds due to the Editors pursuant to this Agreement.

6. Payment and Accounting

(a) Payments to the Editors shall be made semiannually, on or before the last day of April and October of each year for royalties due for the preceding half-year ending the last day of February and August, respectively, and shall be accompanied by an appropriate Statement of Account. The Publisher may take credit for any returns for which royalties have been previously paid. If the balance due any Editor for any royalty period is less than $10, the Publisher will make no payment to that Editor until the next royalty period at the end of which the cumulative balance due such Editor has reached $10.

(b)   The Publisher may retain a reserve for future returns provided the Statements of Account indicate the amount of the reserve and how it has been applied. Any reserve held shall be based on the Publisher's reasonable expectation of sales and returns at the time the Statement of Account is prepared. Any offsets against royalties or sums owed by any Editor to the Publisher under this Agreement or any other agreement between such Editor and the Publisher may be deducted from any payments due such Editor under this Agreement or any other agreement between such Editor and Publisher.

7.   Editors' Copies

Upon publication, the Publisher shall give free copies of the Work to each Editor. The Editors may purchase, for personal use only, additional copies of the Work at a discount of 25% from the United States catalog list price and may purchase, for personal use only, the Publisher's other publications at a discount of 20% from the United States catalog list price.

8.   Related and Competing Works

No Editor, without the Publisher's prior written consent, shall publish or permit any Contributor or other third party to publish the Work or any portion thereof or any other version, revision, or derivative work based thereon in any media of expression now known or later developed. An Editor may, however, after giving written notice to the Publisher, draw on and refer to material contained in the Work in preparing articles for publication in scholarly and professional journals and papers for delivery at professional meetings, provided that credit is given to the Work and the Publisher.

The Work shall be each Editor's next manuscript for such Editor's next book-length work whether under such Editor's name or in collaboration with any other author.

No Editor shall, without the Publisher's prior written consent, contribute to or work as an editor on or prepare or assist in the preparation of any other work that might, in the Publisher's judgment, interfere with or injure the sale of the Work.

9.   Title of the Work

The rights in the title of the Work, and any series titles used on or in connection with the Work, including without limitation any trademark, service mark, or trade dress rights shall belong solely to the Publisher, and the Editors hereby transfer and assign to the Publisher in perpetuity any rights the Editors may have in such titles and trade dress.

10. Revised Editions

If the Publisher decides to publish a revised edition of the Work (hereinafter called the "Revised Edition(s)"), the Publisher may, at its option, request one or more of the Editors to prepare the Revised Edition and the Editors shall advise the Publisher within 30 days of such request whether they will do so in accordance with the schedule set forth by the Publisher. If the Editors advise the Publisher that they will prepare the Revised Edition, the Editors shall diligently proceed with the revision, keep the Publisher advised of the Editors' progress, and deliver the complete manuscript to the Publisher on the scheduled due date.

If an Editor does not choose to participate in the revision, or if the Publisher does not elect to have an Editor prepare the Revised Edition, or if an Editor does not diligently proceed with the revision (a "non-participating Editor"), the Publisher shall have the right to arrange with any remaining Editor(s) and, at the Publisher's option, with others for the preparation of the Revised Edition. In such case, no royalties shall be paid to a non-participating Editor with respect to any Revised Edition not prepared by such Editor. The Revised Editions may be published under the same title and may continue to use the names of all the Editors on all editions of the Work, but credit may be given to the reviser(s) in the Revised Edition(s) and in advertising and promotional material with respect thereto, at the Publisher's discretion.

Except as otherwise provided herein, the provisions of this Agreement, including royalty terms, shall apply to each successive Revised Edition as though it were the first edition.

11. Remainder Sales

When the Publisher determines that the demand for the Work is not sufficient to warrant maintaining an inventory of the Work, the Publisher may remainder or otherwise dispose of all bound copies and sheet stock.

12. Illustrative Material

All illustrative material shall be and remain the property of the Publisher and may be used by the Publisher in any other work without payment to the Editors.

13. Editors' Property

The Editors shall retain a copy of the Work, including any illustrative material. The Publisher may, after publication of the Work, dispose of the original manuscripts, illustrative material and proofs. The Publisher will, however, on written request made prior to publication, make reasonable efforts to return any original material supplied by an Editor. The Publisher shall not be responsible for loss of or damage to any property of the Editors or of any Contributor.

14.   Name and Likeness

The Publisher shall have the right to use the name, likeness and biographical data of the Editors on any edition of the Work or in any derivative work thereof, and in advertising, publicity or promotion related thereto and may grant such rights in connection with the license of any subsidiary rights in the Work. The Editors shall provide, in a timely manner, any information reasonably requested by the Publisher for use in promoting and advertising the Work.

15.   Credit

The Editors' names shall be listed on the cover and title page in the order set forth on the first page of this Agreement unless otherwise set forth below:
   [set forth order of names and titles, if different]

16.   Resolution of Disagreements

In the event of any disagreement among the Editors that precludes the timely submission of a complete and satisfactory manuscript, or otherwise interferes with the publication of the Work, the Publisher shall have the right (but not the obligation) to determine how the disagreement will be resolved and its determination shall be final. In addition, in such event the Publisher shall have the right by written notice to terminate this Agreement with respect to one or more of the Editors, pursuant to Paragraph 17(b) below, or to discontinue the participation of one or more of the Editors, in which case the Editor shall not participate in any further efforts with respect to the Work or Revised Editions thereof, and such Editor's share of royalties shall be adjusted to reflect the amount of work actually performed by such Editor in relation to the published Work, as determined by the Publisher in its sole judgment.

17.   Termination

(a)   The Editors may jointly terminate this Agreement prior to publication by written notice to the Publisher if a petition in bankruptcy is filed by the Publisher, or a petition in bankruptcy is filed against the Publisher and such petition is finally sustained, or a petition for reorganization is filed by or against the Publisher, and an order is entered directing the liquidation of the Publisher as in bankruptcy, or if the Publisher makes an assignment for the benefit of creditors.

(b)   The Publisher may terminate this Agreement with respect to one or more Editors in the event:

   (i)   an Editor resigns or fails to fully and satisfactorily perform such Editor's duties hereunder, whether as a result of disability, death, or otherwise; or

   (ii)   the Editors fail to deliver a complete and satisfactory final manuscript on or before the Manuscript Due Date or fail or refuse to make the changes requested by Publisher pursuant to the terms of Paragraph 1(a) above; or

   (iii)   the Publisher does not exercise its exclusive option pursuant to Paragraph 1(b) above; or

   (iv)   the Publisher exercises its right to terminate pursuant to Paragraph 16 above; or

   (v)   publication may result in legal liability unacceptable to the Publisher in its sole judgment; or

   (vi)   in the Publisher's judgment there have been adverse changes in economic or market conditions which would affect the Publisher's ability to market the Work.

(c)   In the event of termination with respect to one or more of the Editors pursuant to sections (i), (ii) or (iv) of subparagraph (b) above, the Publisher shall have the right to appoint a new editor or otherwise complete the publication of the Work, and the Publisher shall have no further obligation or liability to the terminated Editor(s) hereunder. In such event, the terminated Editor(s) or the Editor(s)' personal representative shall promptly turn over to the Publisher all Contributor manuscripts in the Editor(s)' possession and all other material relating to the Work including the Editor(s)' materials relating thereto, which the Publisher shall own pursuant to Paragraph 3 above. In the event of termination as to an Editor pursuant to sections (i), (ii) or (iv) of subparagraph (b) above, the terminated Editor shall promptly repay to the Publisher any advances or other payments, if any, made to or on behalf of such Editor under this Agreement.

(d)   In the event of termination pursuant to sections (iii), (v) or (vi) of subparagraph (b) above, the Publisher agrees to transfer to the Editors all rights herein granted to the Publisher in any discrete chapters contributed solely by the Editors, in lieu of any other damages or remedies, and the Editors may retain any advances or other payments, if any, made to the Editors under this Agreement, and the parties shall have no further obligation or liability to one another hereunder.

18.   Warranties and Indemnities

(a)   The Editors jointly and severally warrant and represent that:

   (i)   with respect to any material prepared by the Editors for the Work, such material shall be original, except for such excerpts and illustrations from copyrighted works for which the Editors have obtained written permission from the copyright owners on a form approved by the Publisher, and such material shall not contain libelous or unlawful statements or instructions that may cause harm or injury and shall not infringe upon or violate any copyright, trademark, trade secret or other right or the privacy of others;

(ii) the Editors will not include in the Work any contribution or material written or illustrated by others that the Editors believe or have reason to know or suspect may not be original or may contain libelous or unlawful statements or instructions that may cause harm or injury or that infringes upon or violates any copyright, trademark, or other right or the privacy of others, and the Editors shall exercise due care in selecting contributors and reviewing contributions to minimize the risks of such infringements, instructions, and harms;

(iii) to the best of the Editors' knowledge all statements asserted as fact in the Work are either true or based upon generally accepted professional research practices;

(iv) the Editors have the full power and authority to enter into this Agreement and to perform the services required herein; and

(v) any compensation to any other party who assists the Editors in performing services required of the Editors hereunder shall be the responsibility of and shall be paid by the Editors.

(b)   The Editors jointly and severally agree to indemnify the Publisher against all liability and expense, including counsel fees, arising from or out of any breach or alleged breach of these warranties.

(c)   The Editors' warranties and indemnities hereunder shall not be affected by the Publisher's failure to exercise its rights pursuant to Paragraph 17(b)(v) above or by any changes made in the Work on the advice of the Publisher or its counsel.

(d)   Each party shall promptly inform the others of any claim made against any of them which, if sustained, would constitute a breach of any of the Editors' warranties. The Publisher shall have the right to defend any such claim, action or proceeding with counsel of its own choice and, after consultation with the Editors, to settle any such claim. The Editors shall fully cooperate with the Publisher in such defense and any Editor may join in such defense with counsel of such Editor's selection, at such Editor's expense.

(e)   If any such claim is made, the Publisher may withhold payments due to the Editors under this Agreement or any other agreement to cover the Editors' indemnity stated above; provided however, that any sums so withheld, less any costs or expenses already incurred in defense of the claim, shall be remitted to the Editors after the successful disposition of the claim or after the claim has, in the Publisher's opinion, been abandoned.

19.   General

(a)   The engagement of the Editors is personal and the rights hereunder granted to the Editors are not assignable nor may the obligations imposed be delegated without the prior written consent of the Publisher; provided however, that an Editor may assign any sums due to such Editor hereunder without the Publisher's consent.

(b)   The relationship between the Editors and the Publisher shall be that of independent contractors. No payments under this Agreement shall be or be deemed to be compensation or salary to the Editors providing or entitling the Editors (or any employee of an Editor) to any employment benefits from the Publisher. The Editors are not authorized to make any commitments on behalf of the Publisher without the Publisher's prior written consent. Only the Publisher may accept contributions for publication.

(c)   Except as provided herein, this Agreement shall inure to the benefit of the heirs, successors, administrators, and permitted assigns of the Editors and the subsidiaries, successors, and assigns of the Publisher.

(d)   This Agreement shall not be subject to change or modification in whole or in part, unless in writing signed by both parties.

(e)   All notices to be given by any party hereunder shall be in writing and shall be sent to an Editor at the Editor's address as it is set forth in this Agreement unless such address has been changed by proper written notice, or to the Publisher addressed to the attention of the Vice President & General Manager.

(f)   No waiver of any term or condition of this Agreement or of any part thereof shall be deemed a waiver of any other term or condition of this Agreement or of any breach of this Agreement or any part thereof.

(g)   This Agreement shall be construed and interpreted as if wholly entered into and performed in the State of New York. Any legal action, suit or proceeding arising out of or relating to this Agreement or the breach thereof shall be instituted in a court of competent jurisdiction in New York County in the State of New York and each party hereby consents and submits to the personal jurisdiction of such court, waives any objection to venue in such court and consents to service of process by first class mail at the last known address of such party.

(h)   The provisions of Paragraphs 14 and 18 above and this Paragraph shall survive termination of this Agreement.

ACCEPTED AND AGREED   PUBLISHER

By: _____   By: _____
　　　　[*name*]   [*name*]

_____
Social Security Number

By: _____
　　　　[name]

_____
Social Security Number

By: _____
　　　　[name]

_____
Social Security Number

By: _____
　　　　[name]

_____
Social Security Number

"Work for Hire" Book Agreement

Although as a technical matter most books prepared by independent contractors do not qualify as "works made for hire" under the U.S. Copyright Act,[10] "work for hire" is used as industry shorthand for books written on a flat fee (no royalty) basis, where all rights are transferred to the publisher. These agreements are fairly simple. The main issues are delivery requirements, rights transfers, and payment terms. Note that these agreements must include back-up assignment language (see Paragraph 4(a)) specifying that if the work does not qualify as a work made for hire, all rights are transferred to the publisher. In the absence of such language, the publisher may be held to have received only a license.

Work for Hire Book Agreement

[WRITER

AND

ADDRESS]

Contract #_____   **Dated:**_____

Dear [Writer]:

This letter, when executed by the parties, will constitute an agreement between Book Publishing, Inc. ("BPI," "we," or "us") and you ("you") with respect to the following:

1.   BPI hereby commissions you to conduct original research for and to prepare a previously unpublished manuscript for our book tentatively titled _____ (the "Work"). You accept such commission and undertake to produce the Work in accordance with BPI's instructions and under our editorial supervision and guidelines.

2.   (a) You agree that no later than the Final Due Date specified in subparagraph (c)(iii) below, you will deliver to us the complete and final manuscript of the Work, (the "Manuscript") and related materials, including without limitation the bibliography, third party permissions, captions, charts, drawings, excerpts, graphics, illustrations, notes, photographs, quotes, screen shots, software, indexes, tables, case studies, glossary, table of contents, and titles (collectively, the "Materials") in the electronic format specified by BPI or in the Word template supplied by BPI.

The written third party permissions to use any copyrighted material you incorporate in the Manuscript shall be obtained at your own expense, and

---

10 *See* 17 U.S.C. § 101 (definition of "work made for hire").

submitted with the Manuscript. The Manuscript must be complete and satisfactory, and acceptable to BPI in organization, form, content and style, and ready for the printer and of a length that corresponds with the book template, if provided by BPI.

(b)   The Work is described as follows: [preliminary outline for each chapter to be provided by BPI]:

(c)   You agree to deliver the Manuscript and the Materials on the following schedule:

(i)   The [_____] chapter(s) of the Manuscript and related Materials no later than _____.

(ii)   The index, the next ____ chapter(s) of the Manuscript and related Materials no later than _____.

(iii)   The complete and final Manuscript by _____("Final Due Date").

(iv)   All additional materials that BPI deems necessary to publish the Work by _____. BPI will promptly notify you of any necessary additional Materials by _____.

3.   (a) If you deliver the final, complete Manuscript on or before the Final Due Date, BPI shall, within _____ days after such delivery, notify you whether the final Manuscript as delivered is satisfactory and acceptable, and, if it is accepted by BPI, you will be paid pursuant to Paragraph 6 below.

(b)   If you fail to timely create and deliver the acceptable Manuscript (including the Materials) on or before the Final Due Date specified in Paragraph 2 above, BPI may engage another writer to assist in completing the Work or make other arrangements as we deem acceptable to keep the Work on schedule or make the Manuscript complete and satisfactory. In such event the reasonable cost of such arrangements may be charged against any sums due to you hereunder.

(c)   If the final Manuscript and the Materials as delivered are not acceptable to BPI in its sole discretion, BPI will specify the deficiencies in its notice to you. If BPI advises you of unacceptability, within ten (10) days after such notice you will submit either (i) revised, acceptable Manuscript and Materials, or (ii) a proposed plan and delivery schedule for revising the Manuscript and Materials. Acceptance of such revised Manuscript and Materials or proposed plan and delivery schedule will be at BPI's sole discretion. If BPI rejects such Manuscript and Materials or plan and schedule, BPI may terminate this Agreement pursuant to Paragraph 8 below.

(d)   Although BPI and/or its reviewers will review and edit the Manuscript and Materials you are ultimately responsible for their accuracy and completeness including making all changes pursuant to such Manuscript review as per BPI's instructions. Within five (5) days after BPI's delivery of review pages to you, you will return them proofed for accuracy and completeness together with thorough response to any queries of questions BPI has communicated to you with respect thereto. If you fail to timely return the review pages, BPI may at its sole option (i) extend the delivery time, (ii) hire a third party to provide answers to any queries or questions unanswered by you and charge any sums due to you hereunder, or (iii) make other appropriate arrangements and proceed with publication.

4.   (a) You agree that the Work will be prepared and delivered by you as an independent contractor, and all Materials contained therein (including preliminary drafts and other content) and all derivative works based thereon shall be "works made for hire" (as that term is defined in the United States Copyright Law) for BPI. You further agree that all research for the Work will be done by you and not sub-contracted to any third parties without BPI's prior written consent. You acknowledge that BPI will own all right, title and interest, including copyright and all other intellectual property and proprietary rights in and to the Materials and Work and the content contained therein and updates and revised editions thereof, throughout the world and that you will have no right, title or interest in the Materials, the Work or any derivative works based thereon, or in the copyright thereto, which shall be BPI's sole property. To the extent such rights do not vest in BPI as a "work made for hire," you hereby grant, assign and transfer to BPI during the full term of copyright and all extensions thereof all of your right, title and interest in and to the Work and the content contained therein and all Materials contained in or prepared for the Work, and the results and proceeds thereof, throughout the universe, in all media now known or hereafter devised. BPI shall have the right to alter, modify or expand the Work submitted by you and to combine it with other works, to make derivative works therefrom, and to publish or not publish the Work furnished by you, at its sole discretion.

(b)   You further acknowledge that BPI shall retain in perpetuity the sole and exclusive right to print, publish, republish, display, transmit, distribute, sell, advertise, promote and/or license the sale of the Work and the Materials, or any derivative works based thereon throughout the world in all languages and all media now known or hereinafter devised. BPI shall have the right, but shall not be obligated, to use your name, likeness, biographical data or professional credits on and in connection with the publication of the Work or some or all of the Material produced hereunder, or any derivative Work, and in advertising, publicity or promotion related to, and may grant such rights in connection with the license to third parties of any rights in the Work or the Materials.

(c)   You agree to execute such other assignments and instruments as BPI may from time to time deem necessary or desirable to evidence, establish, maintain and protect the aforementioned copyrights and all such other rights, title and interest in or to all such Material.

(d)   You may draw on your research for the Work for use in other works on similar topics but you cannot use such research or any material contained in or produced for the Work in a work which, in BPI's judgment, would be directly competitive with the Work without BPI's prior written consent.

5.   The rights in the title of the Work, and any series titles, trademarks, service marks, "look and feel," and trade dress used on or in connection with the Work (hereinafter collectively referred to as the "Brand"), shall belong solely to BPI, and you hereby transfer and assign to BPI in perpetuity, any rights of ownership including without limitation copyright and/or any other intellectual property or other rights you might have therein. BPI shall have the exclusive right to use the Brand in all formats and media throughout the world in perpetuity or to license such rights or otherwise exploit the Brand, in any media, by itself or in arrangements with third parties, separate and apart from the Work or in combination with the Work.

6.   In full and final consideration for all services you provide, and for all rights granted or relinquished by you hereunder, and upon the condition that you shall fully perform all your obligations hereunder, BPI shall pay you a total of $_____ as follows:

> $_____ on execution of this Agreement; and
> $_____ on timely delivery (on or before the Final Due Date) of one hundred percent (100%) of the complete Manuscript, including the Materials, and acceptance of such Manuscript in BPI's sole discretion pursuant to Paragraph 2 above.

7.   (a) You warrant and represent the following:

   (i)   You have the right to enter into this Agreement and to perform as required herein and to grant BPI the rights herein granted.
   (ii) The Work has not been previously published, is wholly original, is not copied in whole or in part from any other work, except for excerpts and illustrations from copyrighted works for which you have obtained written permission from the copyright owners on a form approved by BPI, and is not in the public domain.
   (iii) The Work is not (and shall not be) libelous or obscene and it does not violate the right of privacy, infringe upon or violate any copyright, trademark, trade secret or other right of any other party, or infringe any common law or statutory copyright.

(iv) All statements asserted as fact in the Work are either true or based upon generally accepted professional research practices.

(b)   You agree to hold BPI, its licensees and any seller of the Work harmless from any liability, loss or damage (including reasonable attorneys' fees) arising out of any claim, action, or proceeding which, if finally sustained or settled, would be inconsistent with or in breach of the above warranties or representations.

8.   (a) BPI may terminate this Agreement prior to publication in the event: (i) you fail to deliver a complete, satisfactory Manuscript pursuant to Paragraph 2 above by the Final Due Date or fail or refuse to make the changes or edits requested by the Publisher in a timely manner pursuant to Paragraphs 3, or (ii) publication may result in legal liability unacceptable to the Publisher in its reasonable judgment.

(b)   If the Manuscript, as revised, remains unacceptable to BPI for editorial reasons, you may keep the amounts paid to you in accordance with the terms set forth herein, but shall not receive the final payment due on delivery and acceptance. In the event of termination for non-delivery or for legal reasons, you shall repay to BPI all amounts previously paid hereunder.

(c)   Upon such repayment, if any, and termination of this Agreement, BPI's obligations to you will also terminate and all liability between the parties shall terminate. You understand and agree that BPI shall own all material delivered by you hereunder as well as any work in progress and BPI shall have the absolute rights of ownership of such material pursuant to Paragraph 4 above.

9.   Upon first publication of the Work, we will provide you with (_____) free copies of the Work. You shall be permitted to purchase further copies for personal use (not for resale) at a discount of forty percent (40%) from the retail list price.

10. (a) This Agreement sets forth the entire understanding of the parties and may not be modified except by a writing signed by both parties. This Agreement shall be construed and interpreted pursuant to the laws of the State of New York applicable to contracts wholly entered into and performed in the State of New York. Any legal action, suit or proceeding arising out of or relating to this Agreement or the breach thereof shall be instituted in a court of competent jurisdiction in New York County in the State of New York and each party hereby consents and submits to the personal jurisdiction of such court, waives any objection to venue in such court, and consents to the service of process by registered or certified mail, return receipt requested, at the last known address of such party.

(b)   This Agreement is personal to you and is not assignable without BPI's prior written consent. This Agreement may not be modified, except in writing and signed by both parties. The provisions of paragraphs 4, 5, and 7 shall survive expiration or termination of this Agreement.

(c)   You are not an employee of BPI as a result of this Agreement, and you are not entitled to any benefits (including, without limitation, pensions, medical, health, holiday or disability). You are an independent contractor and shall be solely responsible for any unemployment or disability insurance payments, or any social security, income tax or other withholdings, deductions or payments which may be required by federal, state or local law with respect to any sums paid to you hereunder. You shall indemnify and hold BPI harmless against any loss or damage resulting from a claim, demand, suit or proceeding brought or made against BPI by reason of your failure to pay the foregoing taxes or other sums.

Please sign below to confirm that this Agreement is in accordance with your understanding, and then return all copies to us for our countersignature. We will remit a fully executed copy to you for your files.

ACCEPTED AND AGREED	BOOK PUBLISHING, INC.
By: _____	By: _____
Name:	Name:
Social Sec. #_____	Title: _____
Date: _____	Date: _____
Citizenship: _____	
Date of Birth: _____	

Co-Publishing Agreement

"Co-publishing" is a generic term describing any one of a variety of publishing arrangements involving two or more parties. The following is an example of one such negotiated arrangement for a limited-rights co-publication between two experienced and prestigious publishing companies; one relatively small publisher ("Publisher 1"), that is primarily responsible for editorial development, and one relatively large publisher ("Publisher 2"), that is accepting the co-publication rights. This arrangement is somewhat unusual in that it allows the two companies to compete against each other in the same territory. This happens where both parties have strengths in different marketing channels but cannot as a practical matter prevent their efforts from spilling over into other channels. The agreement calls for a dual imprint, but separate ISBNs (Clause III (c)). The separate ISBNs make it easier to track and credit returns to the party making the sale. Because of the dual imprint, it is prudent for Publisher 2 to demand and receive strong editorial input rights, and termination rights if the input is not addressed sufficiently (Clauses III (a) and (b)). This contract also allows both parties to take advantage of the unit cost efficiencies of a large print run (Clause III(d)).

Co-Publishing Agreement—Print Rights
Only—Limited Territory

This Co-Publishing Agreement ("Agreement") is executed by and between Publisher 1 [address] and Publisher 2 [address] and shall be in effect from August _____, 20__.

WHEREAS, Publisher 1 is a publisher of books and desires to co-publish with Publisher 2 one such book currently titled _____ (the "Title");

WHEREAS, Publisher 2 is a publisher of books, and desires to co-publish the Title with Publisher 1 and to sell copies of the Title in the United States and Canada (the "Territory").

NOW, THEREFORE, the parties do hereby agree as follows:

I.   Incorporation of Recitals
The recitals above are incorporated herein by reference.

II.   Term and Termination
A.   This Agreement shall commence as of the date first written above and, unless earlier terminated as provided herein, shall continue in effect while the Title remains in print.

B.   Either party may terminate this Agreement immediately upon written notice in the event that the other party fails to make payments or to perform any other substantial obligations required under this Agreement and such failure is not corrected within thirty (30) days after written notice thereof is sent by the other party. Further, any party may terminate this Agreement immediately upon written notice to the other if a voluntary petition in bankruptcy under Title 11, United States Code, is filed by the other or an involuntary petition under Title 11, United States Code, is filed against the other and an order for relief is entered.

C.   Upon expiration or termination of this Agreement:

1.   Publisher 2 may continue to sell and distribute all copies of the Title currently in stock, subject to the royalty obligations set forth herein. Except as set forth in the preceding sentence, Publisher 2 shall not thereafter use names, trademarks or colophons of Publisher 1 or names, trademarks or colophons likely to cause confusion therewith or like-sounding or appearing names or marks in any manner whatsoever.

2.   For the maximum period of time allowed by law, the terms of subsection II.C, Section IV, subsections XI.A, XI.B, XI.C, XI.D, and Section XII shall continue in full force and effect.

III.   Co-Publication of the Title

A.   Publisher 2 shall have the opportunity to cooperate in the editorial process with respect to the Title, including but not limited to review of intermediate drafts and the final draft of the Title. Publisher 2 shall have thirty (30) days from receipt of any drafts to review the same and to either: (i) accept the draft in writing; (ii) advise Publisher 1 of any recommended modifications; or (iii) terminate this Agreement without further liability. Upon the expiration of Publisher 2's review period for any drafts, Publisher 1 shall have thirty (30) days to either: (i) accept Publisher 2's modifications in writing; (ii) propose to Publisher 2 an alternate set of modifications; or (iii) terminate this Agreement without further liability. If Publisher 1 proposes an alternate set of modifications, Publisher 2 shall have fifteen (15) days from receipt of such modifications to review the same and to either: (i) accept the modifications in writing; or (ii) terminate this Agreement without further liability. All time periods provided in this subsection III.A may be modified by mutual agreement in writing by Publisher 1 and Publisher 2. Any termination of this Agreement pursuant to this subsection III.A, Publisher 1 retains full copyright in the Title and may proceed with publication of same. Notwithstanding any other provision herein to the contrary, the Agreement relates solely to the publication of the Title in paper format. Publisher 1 reserves all rights to the Title in all other media, whether now in existence or hereafter invented.

B.   Publisher 1 will perform all production work on the Title and will use reasonable efforts to deliver a final camera-ready manuscript, including cover art and indexing, to Publisher 2 by one hundred twenty (120) days from the date that all modifications to the final draft are agreed upon by Publisher 2 and Publisher 1 in writing. Publisher 2 may, in its sole discretion, terminate this Agreement if the manuscript is delivered more than thirty (30) days after the period set forth in this subsection III.B. All time periods provided in this subsection III.B may be modified by mutual agreement in writing by Publisher 1 and Publisher 2.

C.   Publisher 2 shall arrange for printing of the copies of the Title in two editions: one edition bearing an ISBN identifying Publisher 2 as the publisher of the Title and one edition bearing an ISBN identifying Publisher 1 as the publisher of the Title. Publisher 2 shall be responsible for ensuring that the printing of both editions of the Title shall be in accordance with the printing specifications agreed in writing between the parties and in accordance with the following: (i) each copy of the Title shall bear a notice of copyright in the name of Publisher 1; and (ii) each copy of the Title shall bear a dual imprint containing the colophons of both Publisher 2 and Publisher 1.

D.   Publisher 1 and Publisher 2 will each be responsible for the costs of printing their respective editions of the Title, and Publisher 2 will direct the printer to invoice Publisher 1 for the cost of Publisher 1's edition. Publisher 2 shall notify Publisher 1, in writing, at least sixty (60) days before it plans to order any print run of the Title, and Publisher 1 shall notify Publisher 2, in writing, of the number of copies it wants printed for its editions and shall provide such notification at least thirty (30) days prior to the date of the proposed print run.

E.   Except as expressly set forth herein, Publisher 2 is not granted any rights in the Title or in the co-publication of the Title, including but not limited to copyright, and shall therefore not have the right to register any copyright in the Title or in the co-publication of the Title. Publisher 1 may, in its sole discretion, publish future numbered editions of the Title and may elect, in its sole discretion, to co-publish one or more of such future editions with Publisher 2 pursuant to a separate, mutually agreeable written agreement.

IV.   Limited Reprint Rights; No Subsidiary Rights; No Translation or Adaptation

Publisher 2 shall have no right to reprint the Title except in its entirety, and may not license other parties to reprint all or any part of the Title. Publisher 2 shall have no right to use all or any part of the Title, or to license others to do the same, for any purpose whatsoever, including but not limited to use of portions of the Title in anthologies or other collective works. Any subsidiary use rights and any further reprint rights shall be the subject of a separate agreement between Publisher 1 and Publisher 2. Publisher 2 shall not translate or adapt all or any part of the Title without entering into a separate agreement with Publisher 1 regarding such translation or adaptation.

V.   Marketing

A.   Subject to the terms and conditions contained herein, Publisher 2 shall share Publisher 1's otherwise exclusive right to publish, promote, market, sell, and distribute the Title in the Territory. Publisher 2 agrees not to market or sell copies of the Title outside the Territory. It is expressly agreed that Publisher 2 shall have no further publishing, marketing or distribution rights with respect to the Title upon the expiration or termination of this Agreement, except as expressly set forth herein.

B.   Each party shall be responsible for the costs of marketing and distributing its copies of the Title. Each party shall make its own pricing decision with respect to its copies of the Title.

C.   Pursuant to the terms of subsection XI below, each party shall, solely for the purposes of this Agreement, have the right to use the other party's name and trademarks.

VI.   Royalties

A.   Publisher 2 shall pay to Publisher 1 royalties consisting of (a) _____ per cent (___%) of Publisher 2's Net Billings from its sales attributable to the Title for the first [number] _____ copies of the Title sold by Publisher 2, (b) ____ percent (___%) of Publisher 2's Net Billings from its sales attributable to the Title for the second [number] copies of the Title sold by Publisher 2, and (c) ____ percent (___%) of Publisher 2's Net Billings from its sales attributable to the Title for all additional copies of the Title sold by Publisher 2. For purposes of this Agreement, "Net Billings" shall be defined as the amount in United States Dollars received by Publisher 2 net of applicable discounts and excluding any excise, sales, use or other taxes (except for income taxes), any transportation, shipping and handling charges applicable thereto, any bad debts or credits applicable thereto, including credits for returned copies of the Title, and any taxes withheld.

B.   No royalties shall be paid in connection with copies sold below or at cost including expenses incurred, or furnished without charge either to the author or for review, advertising, sample or similar purposes which are reasonably calculated to benefit the sale of copies of the Title.

C.   Publisher 1 shall be solely responsible for payment of any royalties due to authors or to editors of the Title.

VII. Sales Reports

Publisher 2 will provide Publisher 1 with a sales report for copies of the Title no less frequently than twice per year, detailing the author, title, publication date, units in stock, units and dollars sold during a fiscal year, and total life units from publication date. Publisher 2 will provide any reasonable information requested by Publisher 1 regarding sales and marketing of Publisher 2's copies of the Title, and will provide Publisher 1 with copies of all marketing and promotional literature related to the Title.

VIII. Payment and Accounting

Publisher 2 will make royalty payments semiannually to Publisher 1, on or before the last day of April and October of each year for royalties due for the preceding six months ending the last day of February and August, respectively. An appropriate Statement of Account shall accompany such payments in the form attached hereto as Attachment A. Publisher 2 may take credit for any returns for which royalties have previously been paid. Publisher 2 may, based on its reasonable expectation of sales and returns at the time the Statement of Account is prepared, retain a reserve, provided that the Statement of Account indicates the amount of the reserve and how it has been applied.

IX. Audits

Publisher 1 shall have the right, at its own expense and upon at least two (2) weeks prior notice to Publisher 2, to have its representative inspect Publisher 2's financial accounting records concerning the Title. Such inspection shall occur at Publisher 2's offices during normal business hours, and shall occur not more often than once per year.

X. Author's Name and Likeness

Publisher 1 shall obtain for Publisher 2 the right to use the name of the Title's author(s) and shall use reasonable efforts to obtain for Publisher 2 the right to use the likeness and biographical data of the Title's author(s) in connection with the co-publication of the Title and in advertising, publicity or promotional material related thereto. Further, Publisher 1 shall use reasonable efforts to obtain from the author(s) any reasonable information requested by Publisher 2 for use in promoting and advertising the Title. Direct contact between Publisher 2 and the author(s) will be initiated only upon mutual agreement by Publisher 1 and Publisher 2.

XI. Protection of Intellectual Property

A.   Publisher 2 shall not do or fail to do any act which will impair Publisher 1's intellectual property rights in the Title, nor shall Publisher 2 challenge in any way Publisher 1's ownership of the Title or of the intellectual property rights therein.

B.   Neither party will remove, mask, modify or otherwise alter any of the other party's proprietary notices, including but not limited to trademarks, publisher identifications, or colophons which appear on copies of the Title, or change their placement. Further, neither party will remove, mask, modify or otherwise alter the other party's notices which appear on copies of the Title, or change their placement.

C.   The parties acknowledge and agree that each shall retain the sole and exclusive ownership of its respective trademarks and service marks (collectively referred to as "Trademarks") and all goodwill and rights related thereto; that use of the other party's Trademarks pursuant to this Agreement shall inure to the benefit of the other party; and that neither party shall acquire any rights in the other party's Trademarks, goodwill or rights related thereto as a result of such use.

D.   Each party acknowledges and agrees that it may not at any time, during the term of this Agreement or after the termination or expiration thereof, register, seek to register, or challenge or impede the other party's registration of any of the other party's Trademarks, nor attack, dispute or infringe upon the validity, ownership or enforceability of any of the other party's Trademarks within the Territory or any other country.

E.   Each party agrees that its use of the other party's Trademarks shall be limited to the publication and/or marketing of the Title pursuant to the terms of this Agreement. If either party wants to use the Trademarks of the other, it must submit the proposed use to the Trademark owner in written form for approval. Any use not rejected in ten (10) business days shall be deemed approved.

F.   In any use of the Trademarks pursuant to this Agreement, neither party will combine the other party's Trademarks any other trademark, name, appellation or marking, nor may either party use any marks which are confusingly similar to the other party's Trademarks. Each party further agrees to abide by the guidelines as provided by the other party from time to time for use of its Trademarks. Each party reserves the right to prohibit the use of or to modify any materials containing its Trademarks which do not comply with the terms of this Agreement.

XII.   Warranty and Indemnification

A.   Publisher 1 represents and warrants that it has the right to convey all the rights herein conveyed; that the Title does not infringe copyrights or other proprietary rights; that Publisher 1 will pay any royalties or fees necessary to enable Publisher 2 to co-publish the Title hereunder; that the Title does not, to Publisher 1's knowledge, violate the rights and privacy of, or libel, other persons; and that Publisher 1 has complied with and obtained all consents, licenses and authorities necessary to publish the Title in the Territory.

B.   Publisher 2 shall promptly notify Publisher 1 in writing of any claim made against Publisher 2 which, if sustained, would constitute a breach of Publisher 1's representations and warranties in subsection XII.A above. Publisher 2 shall allow Publisher 1 to control the defense or settlement of any such claim, action or proceeding; and Publisher 1 shall take control of such defense or settlement, in consultation with Publisher 2. Publisher 2 shall have the right, at its own expense, to cooperate in the defense or settlement of any such claim, action or proceeding. If Publisher 2 elects not to exercise this right, Publisher 1 may at its option and expense, require that Publisher 2 provide Publisher 1 with complete cooperation as well as all information necessary for such defense or settlement. Subject to the provisions of this subsection XII.B, Publisher 1 agrees to indemnify Publisher 2 by paying any settlement approved by Publisher 1, or any judgment, costs or attorneys' fees finally awarded against Publisher 2 which are directly attributable to breach of Publisher 1's representations and warranties. If any proposed settlement under this Section XII.B. will adversely affect the rights granted to Publisher 2 under this Agreement, Publisher 1 will obtain Publisher 2's approval on such settlement, which approval shall not be unreasonably withheld.

C.   THE FOREGOING STATES THE ENTIRE LIABILITY OF PUBLISHER 1 WITH RESPECT TO THE WARRANTIES SET FORTH IN SUBSECTION XII.A ABOVE.

XIII.   No Assignment or Delegation

Neither party may assign or transfer this Agreement or delegate its rights or obligations hereunder (except the right to receive payments), including any assignment or delegation to a parent, subsidiary or affiliated corporation, without the prior written consent of the other party. Notwithstanding the previous sentence, either party may assign this Agreement in connection with a sale of substantially all of its publishing assets. Subject to the provisions of this Section XIII, this Agreement shall inure to the benefit of the parties and their permitted assigns.

XIV.   Miscellaneous

A.   This Agreement constitutes the entire understanding and agreement between the parties hereto. All prior negotiations and agreements between the parties hereto are superseded by this Agreement, and there are no representations, warranties, understandings or agreements other than those expressly set forth herein. This Agreement may not be modified or amended, in whole or in part, except by a written agreement hereafter signed by both of the parties hereto. No waiver of any term or condition of this Agreement or of any part thereof shall be deemed a waiver of any other term or condition of this Agreement or any part thereof. A party's failure for any period of time to enforce any of its rights hereunder shall not be construed as a waiver of such rights.

B.   The headings in this Agreement are included for convenience only and in no way define or limit any of the provisions of this Agreement or otherwise affect their construction or effect.

C.   This Agreement creates neither a corporate affiliation between the parties nor a joint venture. At no time may either party represent itself as an agent or representative of the other without the express written consent of the other party.

D.   This Agreement shall be construed and interpreted according to laws of the State of New York.

E.   Any notice to be given hereunder shall be made in writing and shall be mailed, certified or registered, return receipt requested, or delivered by hand or courier service addressed to the other party as follows:

FOR PUBLISHER 2   FOR PUBLISHER 1

[*address*]   [*address*]

with a copy to:

[*lawyer's address*]   [*lawyer's address*]

F.   Any suit or legal action arising out of or relating to this Agreement shall be commenced in a court of competent jurisdiction in the State of, County of; and each party consents to the jurisdiction and venue of such forum. Each party hereby consents to service of process by first class mail at the last known address of such party.

G.   If the performance of this Agreement or of any obligations hereunder is prevented, restricted or interfered with by reason of fire or other casualty or accident; strikes or labor disputes; inability to procure raw materials, equipment, power, or supplies; war, revolution, or other violence; plague, proclamation, regulation, ordinance, demand or requirement of any governmental agency or intergovernmental body; order of a court having jurisdiction over the parties or this Agreement; or any other act or condition whatsoever beyond the reasonable control of the parties hereto, the party so affected, upon giving prompt notice to the other party, shall be excused from such performance to the extent of such prevention, restriction or interference; and shall be under no liability for any loss, damage, injury or expense, whether direct or consequential, suffered by the other party due to the affected performance; provided that the party so affected shall use reasonable efforts under the circumstances to avoid or remove such causes of non-performance and shall continue performance hereunder with the utmost dispatch whenever such causes are removed.

IN WITNESS HEREOF, the parties hereto have caused this Agreement to be executed by their duly authorized representatives.

ACCEPTED BY

PUBLISHER 1

_____

Authorized Signature

_____

Name (type or print)

_____

Title

_____

Date

PUBLISHER 2

_____

Authorized Signature

_____

Name (type or print)

_____

Title

_____

Date

Book Packaging Agreement[11]

A "book packager" is a party who performs all or most of the editorial functions in the preparation of a book to be published by another party. For example, the following agreement between a packager and a publisher calls for
the delivery to the publisher of a camera-ready major reference work (e.g., an
encyclopedia or dictionary), with the packager providing all editorial functions
other than cover design and preparation of marketing material.

This agreement was drafted by the publisher, is un-negotiated, and leaves
nothing to chance. Structurally, it is not all that different from a detailed author
agreement, with added duties. The complexities of using a packager to prepare
a major reference work account for the extremely detailed delivery language.
For simpler works, a simpler agreement could be used.

Agreement

AGREEMENT made this ___ day of June 20___, between **Book Packager,
Inc.**, a New York corporation with offices at _____ New York, NY (hereinafter,
"**Packager**") and **The Publisher, Inc.**, a California corporation with offices at
_____ CA (hereinafter, "**Publisher**").

Packager and Publisher agree as follows:

1. Definitions

Whenever used in this Agreement, the following terms and expressions,
whether used in the singular or in the plural, shall have the meaning set forth
in this Article 1, except where the context clearly otherwise requires:

1.1 "Advances" shall mean the advances paid against royalties as set forth
in Section 6.2.
1.2 "Affiliate" shall all mean present and future foreign subsidiary and
affiliated companies of Publisher.
1.3 "Articles" shall have the meaning specified in Section 2.1(a).
1.4 "Contributions" shall mean the Articles and the Supplementary
Works, collectively.
1.5 "Contributors" shall mean all writers, artists, and other contributors of
original works of authorship created or prepared for the Work.
1.6 "Deliverables" shall mean the items specified in Section 5.1 to be
delivered by Packager to Publisher in the format required, as specified
in Section 5.2.

---

11 This form was developed by Ronni Sander of Bluestein and Sander and is included herein
with permission.

1.7 "E-Books" shall mean reproductions of the verbatim text of, and pictorial and graphic works in, the Work or portions thereof (in complete, condensed, adapted or abridged versions), in an electronic, digital, optical or other machine-readable form or medium, now known or later conceived or developed (whether or not permanently affixed in such medium), from which the contents of the Work can be made available in visual form for reading with the same arrangement contained in the Work in its printed book form, the result of which serves as a substitute for sales of copies of the Work in printed book form.

1.8 "Editor" shall mean the editor-in-chief of the Work.

1.9 "Final Deliverables" shall have the meaning specified in Section 5.1(g).

1.10 "Net Receipts" shall mean all amounts actually received by Publisher in U.S. dollars, or when convert into U.S. dollars, excluding excise, sales, use, value added, and similar domestic or foreign taxes, and shipping and similar charges reimbursed by customers, less discounts, credits, rebates, allowances, and refunds for returns

1.11 "Permission Materials" shall mean copyrighted pictorial and graphic materials and excerpts from copyrighted literary works that are contained in Contributions and owned or controlled by third parties (i.e., other than Publisher, Packager, and independent contractors retained by Packager for the Project) from whom permission or clearance must be obtained to reproduce such materials in the Work.

1.12 "Production Fees" shall mean the non-recoupable payments payable to Packager in respect of services and functions performed and materials provided by Packager for the Project (as described in Article 4) in the amount specified in Section 6.1.

1.13 "Project" shall mean the undertaking of the creation and preparation of the Work by Packager for Publisher pursuant to this Agreement.

1.14 "Supplementary Works" shall have the meaning, generally, as set forth in §101 of the Copyright Act of 1976, as amended, and, specifically, those works identified in Section 2.1(b).

1.15 "Work for Hire Agreements" shall have the meaning specified in Section 4.4.

1.16 "Work Product" shall mean all text, graphic, and other materials created, generated, prepared or obtained for the Work by Packager during the Project, in whatever form or medium, whether finished or in any preliminary stage of completion, including all literary, pictorial and graphic works in progress and in finished form, drafts, edited and unedited manuscripts, artwork, proofs, digital files, and all other parts, elements, and things constituting or relating to the Articles, the Supplementary Works, and Deliverables, excepting only pre-existing copyrighted materials; and, all Work for Hire Agreements, copyright transfers, permissions, and other rights transfer documents for Publisher's benefit.

1.17 The "Work" shall have the meaning specified in Section 2.1.

2. The Work

2.1 <u>Specially Ordered or Commissioned</u>. Publisher hereby specially orders or commissions Packager to create and prepare for Publisher, in the form and manner hereinafter set forth, a collective reference work on the subject of _____, tentatively entitled _____, to be composed of:

   (a) 250 separate and independent original literary works, totaling approximately 302,000 words ("Articles"); and

   (b) 20 pictorial and graphic works, a bibliography, a detailed name, place and concept index, a headword list, in-margin cross references, and editorial materials (such as an introduction, a foreword, commentaries and/or editorial notes) (collectively, "Supplementary Works").

sufficient to constitute 420 printed 8.5"x11" pages (collectively, "the Work").

2.2 <u>Excluded Material</u>. The foregoing order or commission to Packager does not include the design, artwork, creation, or preparation of the cover of the Work or any promotional materials for the Work.

3. Rights in the Work

3.1 <u>Works Made for Hire</u>. The Work, as a collective whole and each Article and Supplementary Work therein, and all Work Product shall be considered works made for hire for Publisher under the Copyright Act of 1976, as amended, and the copyrights and all of the exclusive rights comprised therein, and all other rights, title, and interest throughout the world in and to the Work, the Contributions, and the Work Product shall vest initially in and be owned by Publisher. Publisher shall have the sole and exclusive right to obtain all copyright registrations for the Work and the Contributions as may be appropriate, and any extensions and renewals thereto.

3.2 <u>Assignment of Copyrights</u>. To the extent that the copyright in any original work of authorship created for the Work does not, by operation of law, vest in Publisher as a work made for hire, Packager hereby irrevocably transfers and assigns, or shall cause to be irrevocably transferred and assigned, to Publisher all right, title and interest of every kind and nature in and to such work and the copyright and all exclusive rights comprised therein, free and clear of any and all rights and claims of Packager any other party, including, without limitation, the right to register the copyright in the said work in the name of Publisher and the sole and exclusive right throughout the world to do and to authorize any of the following:

   (a) to reproduce copies of such work or portions thereof, by any method and in any format and medium, now known or later conceived or developed, from which the work can be perceived or communicated either directly or with the aid of a machine or device, such as printed book forms and optical, digital, electronic, mechanical, and other machine-readable formats embodied on any storage medium;

(b) to prepare derivative works based upon such work, such as foreign language translations, abridgements, condensations, adaptations, digitized forms, multimedia works, interactive works, dramatizations, sound recordings, motion picture and other audiovisual works; and to reproduce copies of such derivative works by any method and in any format and medium, now known or later conceived or developed, from which the derivative work can be perceived or communicated either directly or with the aid of a machine or device; and

(c) to publish, distribute through any channel of distribution, transmit, sell, license, market, merchandise, and publicly perform and display copies of, and excerpts from, such work and derivative works based thereon, by any method, device, or process now known or later conceived or developed, including distribution, publication, performance, and display by electronic, wireless, or other transmission system now known or later conceived or developed.

3.3 Additional Documents. Packager shall execute and deliver, or cause to be executed and delivered, to Publisher such documents and instruments of transfer and assignment as Publisher may reasonably request from time to time to perfect the rights defined in Section 3.2, [at *Publisher's expense.*]

3.4 Use of Names and Likenesses. Packager hereby grants to Publisher the right [*but not the obligation*] to use its name, and the names, likenesses, biographical materials, and professional credits of those of its employees who contribute material to or provide services for the Work: (a) on copies of the Work and derivative works based thereon, and in the publication, distribution, display, and performance thereof, and (b) subject to Packager's prior consent, [*not to be unreasonably withheld or delayed*] in connection with the marketing, advertising, and promotion of the Work and derivative works based thereon.

3.5 Revisions. If the Work is published under this Agreement and Publisher thereafter desires to revise the Work to create a second or subsequent revised edition, it shall so notify Packager. At its option, Packager may undertake to revise the Work and, in such event, the provisions of this Agreement will apply to such revised edition, except for the amount of Production Fees, Advances, and bonus payment, if any, applicable to that revised edition, which the parties will negotiate in good faith. If Packager declines or is unwilling to undertake such revisions, then Publisher will have the right to make whatever arrangements for the preparation of such revisions as it, in its sole discretion, may determine and Publisher and Packager will have no obligation to each other whatsoever with respect to such or any subsequent revised edition of the Work, and Packager shall have no claim or interest whatsoever therein.

4. Services and Functions to be Performed by Packager

4.1 <u>Project Management Services</u>. Packager shall perform the following management services and functions for and during the Project, at its expense:

(a) Subject to Section 4.4, retaining the services of:
   (i) an Editor, who shall be subject to Publisher's approval. It is acknowledged that Publisher has approved [*name*] to serve as Editor;
   (ii) an assistant to the Editor, and other editorial staff and assistants as needed;
   (iii) a Project designer; and
   (iv) all Contributors;
(b) Managing and supervising the Contributors to develop appropriate material of high quality for the Work;
(c) Subject to Section 4.5, obtaining, processing, and paying for permissions and clearances to reproduce and use Permission Materials in the Work;
(d) Trafficking and coordinating materials from Contributors, sub-contractors, and other sources;
(e) Contract administration and related financial tasks, such as payments to, and preparation and filing of tax forms for, the Editor, editorial staff, Project designer, Contributors, sub-contractors and other third parties;
(f) Supervising quality control of the Project;
(g) Consulting with Publisher regarding editorial and design development of the Work and regularly advising as to the status of the Project; and
(h) Providing support and information for Publisher's marketing staff regarding the Project.

4.2 <u>Editorial Services</u>. Packager shall perform or provide the following editorial services and functions for and during the Project, at its expense:

(a) development, creation, and preparation of:
   (i) a headword list;
   (ii) in-margin cross references;
   (iii) a bibliography; and
   (iv) a detailed name, place, concept index;
(b) structural and content editing;
(c) line editing and copyediting of manuscripts;
(d) photograph and other illustration research and editing; and
(e) editorial consultation and design.

4.3 <u>Graphic and Production Services</u>. Packager shall perform or provide the following graphic and production services and functions for and during the Project, at its expense:

(a) design development and refinement;
(b) photo scanning, cropping, retouching and other processing;

(c)   creation of original non-photographic illustrations;

(d)   page composition and layout; and

(e)   generation of laser proofs and proofreading.

4.4   Work for Hire Agreements. Packager will enter into a written agreement with the Editor, the Project designer, each Contributor, and each other provider of original work(s) of authorship for the Work who is not an employee of Packager, which agreements shall provide that: (a) all original works of authorship prepared by such person for the Work shall be deemed specially ordered or commissioned for use as a contribution to the Work and shall be considered works made for hire for Publisher, as designee of Packager, under the Copyright Act of 1976, as amended, and the copyrights and all of the exclusive rights comprised therein, and all other rights, title and interest throughout the world in and to such works, shall vest initially in and be owned by Publisher; and (b) such individual's name and professional credits may be used by Publisher on copies, and in connection with the publication, distribution, marketing, and promotion, of the Work and derivative works based thereon ("Work for Hire Agreements"). All Work for Hire Agreements shall be delivered to Publisher as provided in Section 5.1.

4.5   Permissions and Clearances. Packager shall not include any Permission Material in a Contribution unless Packager has obtained prior written permission or clearance from the copyright owner thereof for Publisher to use such Permission Material in the Work to the fullest extent contemplated herein. Accordingly, such permissions and clearances to be obtained by Packager shall grant to Publisher a nonexclusive, perpetual, irrevocable, worldwide license to:

(a)   reproduce the Permission Material in the Work, any revision of the Work, and any derivative works based on the Work or revisions thereof, by any method and in book, E-Book, and any other form or medium, now known or later conceived or developed, from which Permission Material can be perceived or communicated either directly or with the aid of a machine or device, including optical, digital, electronic, mechanical and other machine-readable formats embodied on any storage medium; and

(b)   to distribute, publish, transmit, sell, license, market, merchandise, publicly perform and display copies of, and excerpts from, the Permission Material as part of the Work, any revision of the Work, and any derivative works based on the Work or revisions thereof, by any method, device, or process now known or later conceived or developed, including distribution, publication, performance and display by electronic, wireless or other transmission system now known or later conceived or developed.

Acceptance of any permission or clearance that does not grant to Publisher the foregoing scope of rights will be subject to Publisher's prior approval. All permissions and clearances shall be delivered to Publisher as provided in Section 5.1.

5. Delivery and Approval of Deliverables

5.1 <u>Deliverables and Delivery Dates</u>. Packager shall deliver to Publisher, in the required format specified in Section 5.2, each Deliverable listed below, satisfactory to Publisher in form and content, on or before the delivery date indicated:

	Deliverable	*Delivery Date*
(a)	Final headword list	__/__/20__
(b)	Manuscript of the text of the 1st quarter of Articles (i.e., 60–65 Articles)—content, structural and line editing complete	__/__/20__
(c)	Manuscript of the text of the 2nd quarter of Articles—content, structural and line editing complete	__/__/20__
(d)	Manuscript of the text of the 3rd quarter of Articles—content, structural and line editing complete	__/__/20__
(e)	Manuscript of the text of the 4th quarter of Articles and of all editorial materials, if any—content, structural and line editing complete	__/__/20__
(f)	First proofs—composed pages of the complete and final text of all Articles and editorial materials previously approved by Publisher, with pictorial and graphic works, headwords and in-margin cross references—copyediting and first stage proofreading complete	__/__/20__
(g)	Final proofs—composed pages of the complete and final text of all Articles, editorial materials, and pictorial and graphic works previously approved by Publisher, and the index, bibliography and all other Supplementary Works—, copyediting and final stage proofreading complete, artwork in camera-ready form; electronic files containing the text and graphics of all Articles and Supplementary Works in digital form; and all Work for Hire Agreements, permissions and clearances (the "Final Deliverables").	__/__/20__

5.2 <u>Format of Deliverables</u>. Packager shall deliver to Publisher the respective Deliverable in the applicable format, as follows:

(a) Final headword list—one (1) complete hard copy, double-spaced on 8.5″ by 11″ paper; and one (1) complete digital file;

(b) Manuscript Deliverables—one (1) complete hard copy, double-spaced on 8.5″ by 11″ paper; and one (1) complete digital file;

(c) First proofs—one (1) complete digital copy;

(d) Final proofs—one (1) complete camera-ready digital copy; one (1) complete camera-ready hard copy, all ready for the printer.

5.3 <u>Time of the Essence</u>. Timely delivery of Deliverables, satisfactory to Publisher in form and content, is of the essence of this Agreement.

5.4 <u>Approval of Deliverables; Failure to Deliver</u>.

(a) If Publisher, in it sole judgment, deems a Deliverable satisfactory in form and content, then it will approve such Deliverable and so notify Packager in writing and, within ten (10) business days after the date of such approval, remit to Packager the applicable Production Fee or Advance payment set forth in Article 6. The approval of each Deliverable shall be determined solely by Publisher and based upon its evaluation of the quality, editorial merit, and marketability of the Deliverable.

(b) If Publisher does not, in it is sole judgment, deem a Deliverable satisfactory in form and content, then it will so notify Packager in writing, setting forth in reasonable detail the reasons for its dissatisfaction and specifying the revisions required to be made to said Deliverable in order to make it satisfactory to Publisher. If, within fifteen (15) business days after the date of such written notice or such other period as may be set forth therein (whichever is longer), Packager revises and re-delivers said Deliverable and Publisher, in its sole judgment, deems it now satisfactory in form and content, then the provisions of Section 5.4(a) shall apply thereto. If, however, within such time period, Packager does not make the specified revisions as required by Publisher and re-deliver said Deliverable or, notwithstanding such revisions said Deliverable, as revised and re-delivered, is still not, in Publisher's sole judgment, satisfactory in form and content, then Publisher shall have the right to terminate this Agreement by written notice to Packager and, in such event, the provisions of Section 8.2(b) shall apply.

(c) If Packager fails to deliver a Deliverable within thirty (30) business days after the delivery date therefor, Publisher shall have the right, unless it extends such delivery date in writing, to terminate this Agreement by written notice to Packager, and, in such event, the provisions of Section 8.2(b) shall apply.

5.5 <u>Publication</u>. Notwithstanding the approval of any or all of the Deliverables, Publisher shall have no obligation whatsoever to manufacture, sell and/or distribute the Work and may publish or decline to proceed with the publication of the Work as Publisher, in its sole discretion, may decide.

6. Consideration

6.1 <u>Production Fees</u>. Publisher will pay Packager Production Fees in the amount of ____ Thousand ($___.00) Dollars, payable as follows:

(a) $___.00 within ten (10) business days after the full execution of this Agreement;

(b) $___.00 within ten (10) business days after the date of Publisher's approval of the Deliverable specified in Section 5.1(a) (i.e., final headword list);

(c) $___.00 within ten (10) business days after the date of Publisher's approval of the Deliverable specified in Section 5.1(b) (i.e., manuscript of the text of the 1st quarter of Articles);

(d) $___.00 within ten (10) business days after the date of Publisher's approval of the Deliverable specified in Section 5.1(c) (i.e., manuscript of the text of the 2nd quarter of Articles); and

(e) $___.00 within ten (10) business days after the date of Publisher's approval of the Deliverable specified in Section 5.1(d) (i.e., manuscript of the text of the 3rd quarter of Articles).

6.2 <u>Advances</u>. Publisher will pay Packager Advances in the total amount of ____ Thousand ($____.00) Dollars, payable as follows:

(a) $____.00 within ten (10) business days after the date of Publisher's approval of the Deliverable specified in Section 5.1(e) (i.e., manuscript of the text of the 4th quarter of Articles and editorial materials, if any);

(b) $____.00 within ten (10) business days after the date of Publisher's approval of the Deliverable specified in Section 5.1(f) (i.e., first proofs, etc.); and

(c) $____.00 within ten (10) business days after the date of Publisher's approval of the Final Deliverables specified in Section 5.1(g).

Each Advance shall be charged against and recoupable at any time from any and all royalties accruing to Packager hereunder.

6.3 <u>Bonus</u>. If Packager completes and delivers to Publisher the Final Deliverables on or before ____, 20 ____, in form and content satisfactory to Publisher, then, within ten (10) business days after the date of Publisher's approval thereof, Publisher will pay Packager a non-recoupable production bonus in the amount of ____ Thousand ($____.00) Dollars; provided, however that such bonus payment shall not apply if the Final Deliverables are required to be revised and re-delivered, in accordance with Section 5.4(b), unless such revised Final Deliverables are re-delivered to Publisher on or before ____, 20 ____.

6.4 <u>Royalties</u>. If and when Publisher publishes the Work, Publisher will pay Packager, in the manner provided in Article 7, royalties at the following rates:

    (a) On all copies of the Work in hardcover book form sold by Publisher:
        (i) 10% of Net Receipts from the first 1,500 copies sold;
      (ii) $12^1/_2$% of Net Receipts from the next 1,500 copies sold; and
     (iii) 15% of Net Receipts from all copies sold in excess of 3,000.
    (b) On all copies of the Work in E-Book form sold by Publisher:
        (i) 10% of Net Receipts from the first 1,500 copies sold;
      (ii) $12^1/_2$% of Net Receipts from the next 1,500 copies sold; and
     (iii) 15% of Net Receipts from all copies sold in excess of 3,000.
    (c) On quantity sales of 100 copies or more of the Work sold by Publisher to a single buyer at a discount of more than 50% of the retail list price, one-half (1/2) of the otherwise applicable royalty rate set forth in Sections 6(a) and (b);
    (d) 10% of Net Receipts from all copies of the Work in printed book form sold by Publisher to book clubs;
    (e) 10% of Net Receipts from the licensing or other exploitation of rights in the Work; and
    (f) On all copies of the Work sold by Affiliates, 8% of each such Affiliate's Net Receipts from such sales.
    (g) No royalty shall be payable on copies of the Work furnished gratis for review, advertising, promotion, bonus, sample, or like purposes.

6.5 <u>Complimentary Copies</u>. If and when Publisher first publishes the Work, Publisher will provide Packager with 25 complimentary copies, and the Editor and the Contributors each with 1 complimentary copy, of the Work in hardcover book form. [*If published in electronic form only, Publisher will provide the Editor and each Contributor* _____]. Packager, the Editor, and the Contributors shall be entitled to purchase copies of the Work in hardcover book form at a 40% discount of the list price, provided such copies are not resold.

6.6 <u>Comprehensive</u>. The consideration specified in this Article 6 is comprehensive and is intended to, and shall be, inclusive of all amounts due or payable by Publisher to Packager in connection with the Project and the Work. Unless expressly agreed by Publisher in writing, Publisher shall have no monetary obligation whatsoever to the Editor; the assistant to the Editor and other editorial staff; the Project designer; the Contributors; sub-contractors; and other persons and entities employed or retained by Packager to render services, supply materials, or grant, transfer or assign rights in connection with the Project or Publisher's exercise of its rights in the Works and the Contributions.

7. Accounting and Payment

7.1 Annual Statements. If and when Publisher publishes the Work, royalties earned hereunder will be accrued annually as of December 31st of each year, commencing with the year of publication. Royalties payable hereunder shall be subject to reasonable reserves against future returns established by Publisher. On or before each March 1st, Publisher will issue an annual statement of account to Packager for the preceding calendar year. Each state- ment rendered hereunder by Publisher shall be conclusive and binding on Packager for any reason unless specific written objection thereto is made by Packager within two (2) years from the date of such statement. Publisher shall not be required to issue an annual statement of account for any year in which there are no royalties earned.

7.2 Payment of Royalties. Payment of all royalties earned, less Advances and deductions (if any), as shown to be due and payable on each annual statement will be remitted to Packager within sixty (60) days after the statement date; provided, however, that if the amount of royalties shown to be payable for the reported period total less than $25.00, then payment thereof will be deferred until the cumulative accrued and payable royalties exceed $25.00. State, federal and foreign taxes on royalties payable to Packager which Publisher is required by law to withhold shall be proper deductions from royalties other- wise due and payable to Packager hereunder.

8. Termination

8.1 Circumstances Warranting Termination. This Agreement may be terminated:

(a) by Publisher pursuant to Section 5.4(b) or Section 5.4(c);
(b) by Publisher at any time upon ninety (90) days prior written notice to Packager, in the event that Publisher, in its sole discretion, decides to cancel the Project and the development and publication of the Work for any reason whatsoever; or
(c) by either party, at its option, upon written notice if the other party: (i) makes a general assignment for the benefit of its creditors; (ii) is adjudged bankrupt or insolvent, or a receiver or trustee in bankruptcy is appointed for such party, which is not discharged or terminated within sixty (60) days; or (iii) becomes the subject of a bankruptcy or insolvency proceeding under United States laws, which pro- ceeding is not discharged or terminated within sixty (60) days after commencement.

8.2 <u>Events Upon Termination</u>. In the event of the termination of this Agreement by either party for any reason, Packager shall immediately deliver to Publisher the Work, all Articles, all Supplementary Works, and all Work Product of any nature whatsoever in the possession or control of Packager. In addition:

(a) If the Agreement is terminated by Publisher pursuant to Section 8.1(b) or by Packager pursuant to Section 8.1(c), then, provided Packager has delivered the Work, Contributions and Work Product to Publisher as required:

   (i) Packager shall have the right to retain all monies previously paid to it hereunder in respect of Deliverables delivered and accepted prior to the date of termination;

   (ii) Packager shall be entitled to receive and Publisher shall be obligated to make the payments in respect of Deliverables delivered and accepted by Publisher for which payment remains outstanding on the date of termination; and

   (iii) Publisher shall be obligated to compensate Packager for the reasonable value of the services performed and materials provided by Packager for Deliverables in progress but not delivered as of the date of termination. Packager shall submit to Publisher a detailed invoice of the value of such services and materials, which shall not be binding upon Publisher; however, approval of such invoice shall not be unreasonably withheld. In no event shall the total invoiced amount for such services and materials exceed the amount of the payment which would have been due for the next scheduled Deliverable.

Payment by Publisher of the amounts set forth in Sections 8.2(a)(i), (ii) and (iii) above shall constitute full and final compensation to Packager for all services performed and materials provided for the Project, and Packager shall have no claim or interest whatsoever in the Work, the Contributions, and the Work Product.

(b) If the Agreement is terminated by Publisher pursuant to Section 8.1(a) or (c), then, provided Packager has delivered the Work, Contributions and Work Product to Publisher as required, Packager shall have the right to retain all monies previously paid to it hereunder in respect of Deliverables delivered and accepted prior to the date of termination of this Agreement. Such sums shall constitute full and final compensation to Packager for all services performed and materials rendered for the Project, and Packager shall have no claim or interest whatsoever in the Work, the Contributions, and the Work Product. Publisher shall be wholly free to make such arrangements as it may decide for the completion of the Work and any sale, license, or disposition of any rights therein, free of any claim of Packager. In addition to any and all rights and remedies of Publisher in law or at equity, Publisher shall be entitled to offset its damages in completing the Work against any payment in respect of Deliverables delivered and accepted by Publisher for which payment remains outstanding on the date of termination.

8.3 No Waiver of Remedies. The election of either party to terminate this Agreement pursuant to Section 8.1 hereof shall not serve to waive, limit, bar or otherwise extinguish any rights that party may have to pursue and recover any damages that party may have suffered or incurred due to the breach of any term or condition of this Agreement.

8.4 Survival. In the event of termination of this Agreement for any reason whatsoever, the provisions of Article 3, Article 8, Article 9, Article 10, Article 11, and Article 12 shall survive.

9. Warranties, Representations, Indemnification

9.1 Warranties and Representations of Packager. Packager warrants and represents that:

(a) all actions required to be taken by or on the part of Packager necessary to authorize it to enter into this Agreement have been duly and properly taken, and that the person executing this Agreement on its behalf is authorized to do so;

(b) it has the full power and authority to enter into this Agreement and to fully perform the services and functions hereunder, and that it is financially competent to fulfill its obligations hereunder and agrees that any change in such status shall be immediately communicated in writing to Publisher;

(c) the Contributions and all portions thereof shall be developed solely by Packager through the use of Packager's employees or through the services of independent contractors pursuant to the provisions of Section 4.4 hereof, who have executed and provided such services pursuant to a Work for Hire Agreement, and Packager shall make all payments to such independent contractors when due and payable;

(d) the Articles and Supplementary Works and other materials prepared for the Work and delivered to Publisher by Packager will be original (except for material in the public domain or Permission Materials for which permission has been obtained), and will not contain any libelous or otherwise unlawful material or infringe any copyright, or any personal or proprietary right of any person or entity.

9.2 Warranties and Representations of Publisher. Publisher warrants and represents that all actions required to be taken by or on the part of Publisher necessary to authorize it to enter into this Agreement have been duly and properly taken; and, that the person executing this Agreement on Publisher's behalf is authorized to do so.

9.3 <u>Indemnification</u>. Packager shall indemnify, defend, and hold Publisher, its Affiliates, and their successors, assigns, officers, directors, employees, agents, and licensees, harmless from and against any and all liabilities, losses, damages, judgments, settlements, costs and expenses of every kind whatsoever (including reasonable attorneys' fees and expenses and court costs) (collectively "damages") arising out of or relating to any claim, demand, action, suit or proceeding of any kind (a "claim"), based on facts which, if true, would constitute a breach of any representation or warranty by Packager set forth in Section 9.1, or arising out of Packager's failure to obtain permissions or clearances required for Permission Materials. Publisher will give Packager prompt written notice of the existence of every claim for which Publisher intends to demand indemnification hereunder. The costs and attorneys' fees for defending such claim shall be borne by Packager; however, Publisher shall have the right to elect to control the defense of such claim, with counsel of its own choice, and may settle the claim on terms it deems advisable, subject to Packager's prior written consent, which shall not be unreasonably withheld. Packager shall cooperate and provide reasonable assistance to Publisher. If Publisher does not elect to control the defense of such claim, Packager shall conduct such defense, and Publisher shall have the right to participate in the defense of the claim with counsel of its choice, at its own expense. Publisher shall have the right to withhold its reasonable estimate of the total damages from sums otherwise payable to Packager hereunder, and to apply such sums to payment of such damages.

9.4 <u>No Remedy Exclusive</u>. The rights of indemnification of Publisher, its Affiliates, and their successors, assigns, officers, directors, and employees shall not be limited to the provisions of this Article, and the provisions of this Article shall be in addition to, and shall not be exclusive of, any other rights or remedies which may accrue to Publisher, its Affiliates, and its successors, assigns, officers, directors, and employees.

10.   Relationship of Parties; Taxes

10.1 <u>Relationship</u>. Packager is appointed by Publisher only for the specific purposes and only to the extent set forth in this Agreement, and Packager's relation to Publisher hereunder will be that of an independent contractor. Packager shall perform all services and functions hereunder in good faith, and shall avoid any conflicts of interest in the performance of its obligations hereunder. Packager does not have the right, power, or authority to bind Publisher or to assume or to create any obligation or responsibility, express or implied, on behalf of Publisher. Packager, its employees, and the independent contractors and sub-contractors retained by Packager for the Project are not agents or employees of Publisher and shall not represent themselves as such. The parties do not intend hereby, and nothing contained herein shall be construed, to create any joint venture, partnership, or fiduciary relationship between Packager and Publisher, and neither party shall be responsible for the acts or omissions of the other.

10.2 <u>Payments to Contractors</u>. Packager assumes full responsibility for those hired or retained by it for the Project and, unless otherwise agreed in writing by Publisher, is responsible for any and all payments of any nature whatsoever which become due and payable to the Editor; the assistant to the Editor and other editorial staff; the Project designer; Contributors; sub-contractors; and other persons and entities employed or retained by Packager to render services, supply materials, or grant, transfer or assign rights in connection with Project and the Work. Packager shall promptly pay when due any and all payments to any such person or entity in connection with the Project or as a result of the exercise by Publisher of its rights in the Work or the Contributions.

10.3 <u>Taxes</u>. Packager shall be solely responsible for the payment of all federal, state and local taxes and payments on amounts paid to it hereunder. Packager shall meet all of its obligations and responsibilities as an employer to its own employees under any federal, state or local laws or regulations, including, without limitation, those relating to the withholding and/or payment of federal, state and local taxes and payments for those hired or retained by Packager to render services or provide materials for the Project.

11. Resolution of Disputes

11.1 <u>Mediation</u>. If a dispute arises from or relates to this Agreement or the breach hereof, and if the dispute cannot be settled by the parties through direct negotiation, the parties agree first to try in good faith to settle the dispute by mediation before resorting to arbitration, litigation, or some other dispute resolution procedure. The place of mediation shall be New York County, New York. The parties shall mutually select a mediator and, in the event the parties cannot agree upon a mediator, each party will chose a representative who will confer and select a mediator to hear the dispute. The parties shall equally share the mediation administrative costs and mediator's fees. The requirements of filing a notice of claim with respect to the dispute submitted to mediation shall be suspended until the conclusion of the mediation process.

11.2 <u>Arbitration</u>. If the parties' dispute is not resolved within sixty (60) days after initiation of the mediation process described in Section 11.1 above, any unresolved controversy or claim arising out of or relating to this Agreement or breach hereof shall be settled by arbitration administered by the American

Arbitration Association under its then current Commercial Arbitration Rules, and judgment on the award rendered by the arbitrator may be entered in any court having jurisdiction thereof. The place of arbitration shall be New York County, New York. The arbitrator shall determine how the administrative fees and arbitrator's compensation will be allocated between the parties, and, in his or her discretion, may award the prevailing party all or part of its costs and fees. For purposes of this provision, "costs and fees" means all reasonable pre-award expenses of the arbitration, including the arbitrator's fees, administrative fees, travel expenses, out-of-pocket expenses such as copying and telephone, stenographer, court costs, witness fees, and reasonable attorneys' fees.

12. General Provisions

12.1 <u>Notices</u>. All notices required or which may be given hereunder shall be in writing and may be delivered in person, or by overnight courier service or express mail addressed as set forth below or to such other address or person as a party may designate in writing. At the time of dispatch, a courtesy copy of each notice given hereunder shall be simultaneously given by facsimile transmission. A notice shall be deemed given and effective at the time delivered, if personally delivered; or on the date recorded as delivered by receipt or equivalent record of delivery, and in the absence of such record it shall be presumed to have been delivered three (3) business days after dispatch. Notwithstanding the foregoing, notices of change of address will be deemed given and effective upon actual receipt by the party to whom directed.

(a) Publisher: (b) Packager:

12.2 <u>Force Majeure</u>. Neither party shall be deemed in default of this Agreement to the extent that performance of its obligations or attempts to cure any breach are delayed or prevented by reason of any act of God, fire, natural disaster, accident, riots, acts of government, shortage of materials or supplies, or any other cause beyond the reasonable control of such party; provided, that the party interfered gives the other party prompt written notice of any such event or occurrence.

12.3 <u>Assignments, Binding Agreement</u>. Neither party shall be entitled to assign its rights or delegate its duties and obligations under this Agreement, without the prior written consent of the other, except that Packager shall have the right to assign its right to receive payments hereunder and Publisher shall have the right to assign the rights herein granted and delegate the performance of its obligations to any successor in interest. Any other assignment or delegation made without such prior consent shall be null and void. Upon full execution, this Agreement shall be binding upon the parties hereto and their permitted assigns and successors.

12.4 <u>Waiver</u>. The waiver by either party, or the failure of either party to claim a breach, of any provision of this Agreement shall not operate or be construed as a waiver of such provision, a waiver of any continuing or subsequent breach of such provision, or a waiver of any other provision of this Agreement or breach thereof. The failure of either party at any time to require performance of any provision of this Agreement shall in no way affect the right of such party to thereafter require performance of that provision.

12.5 <u>Severability</u>. If any provision of this Agreement is found by any arbitral tribunal or by a court of competent jurisdiction to be invalid, illegal, or otherwise unenforceable, such provision shall be deemed to be severed from this Agreement and shall not affect the validity or enforceability of any other provision of this Agreement, which shall continue to be in full force and effect.

12.6 <u>Headings and Grammar</u>. Article and Section headings contained in this Agreement are for reference purposes only and shall not be deemed to be a part of, or to affect the meaning or interpretation of, this Agreement. Wherever used in this Agreement, the words "including" and "such as" are illustrative and not limiting. Any grammatical variation of any defined term shall have the same meaning.

12.7 <u>Governing Law</u>. This Agreement shall be construed, interpreted, governed, and enforced in accordance with the laws of the State of New York and of the United States as interpreted by the U.S. federal district and appeal courts of the Second Circuit, applicable to agreements entered into and wholly performed within New York and without reference to New York's choice of law rules. Subject to Article 11, each party hereby consents to the jurisdiction and venue of the courts of the State of New York located in New York County and of the U.S. District Court for the Southern District of New York.

12.8 <u>Amendments, Modifications</u>. No amendment or modification of any provision of this Agreement shall be valid or binding unless made in writing and signed by the parties hereto.

12.9 <u>Entire Agreement</u>. This Agreement constitutes the entire agreement between the parties with respect to the subject matter hereof, and supersedes all prior agreements, understandings, representations, and warranties, written or oral, between the parties in such regard.

12.10 <u>Counterparts</u>. This Agreement may be executed in two or more counterparts, each of which shall be deemed an original, but all of which together shall constitute one and the same instrument.

IN WITNESS WHEREOF, each party has caused this Agreement to be executed by its duly authorized officer as of the date first written above.

THE BOOK PACKAGER, INC.   THE PUBLISHER, INC.

By: _____   By: _____

Name: _____   Name: _____

Title: _____   Title: _____

Fed Tax ID# _____

Date: _____   Date: _____

FORM 1.8

Advisory Board Member Agreement

The following agreement is designed for advisory board members who are specifically retained by the publisher to review and solicit manuscripts for their areas of expertise. There are a variety of reasons why a publisher would retain such a board, including (1) lack of in-house editorial expertise in a given field, (2) the desire to affiliate with "big names" in a given field, and (3) the desire to increase acquisitions without a major increase in overhead (i.e., new personnel). This type of arrangement is particularly useful in professional and scientific publishing, which are segments that do not typically use agents. For a small finder's fee, the publisher can sign more books and use the imprimatur of well-known experts. The experts, for their part, can help friends and colleagues get published, increase their visibility, and make a reasonable amount of money for modest effort.

Advisory Board Member Agreement

AGREEMENT, made this _____ day of _____, 20__, between of _____ (the "Advisory Board Member"), and, located at _____ (the "Publisher"), for the purpose of publishing works (the "Works") in the field of _____.

1.   Performance of Services

The Publisher shall retain the services of _____ as Advisory Board Member. The Advisory Board Member shall perform such services at such place or places as the Advisory Board Member may reasonably determine. Unless otherwise agreed to in writing by the Publisher, the Publisher shall not be required to provide the Advisory Board Member with office space, supplies, clerical or stenographic assistance.

2.   The Advisory Board Member's Duties

The Advisory Board Member agrees to:

(a) Recommend to the Publisher, from time to time, and advise the Publisher of subject matter, programs and developments suitable for Works.

(b) Review, upon request by the Publisher, proposals for Works and manuscripts for purposes of determining suitability for publication.

(c) Meet periodically with the Publisher' editorial staff to discuss and review the progress of publication of Works.

3.   The Works

All decisions as to which Works shall be published, the format of publication, the acceptability of manuscripts, and the manner of production, promotion, and sale of the Works shall be at the sole discretion of the Publisher.

4.   Ownership

All material prepared and services performed by the Advisory Board Member hereunder shall be considered a work made for hire to the Publisher, and, as between the Advisory Board Member and the Publisher, the Publisher shall own the copyright and all of the rights comprised in the copyright. To the extent any material does not qualify as a work made for hire, the Advisory Board Member hereby transfers to the Publisher during the full term of copyright and all extensions thereof the full and exclusive rights comprised in the copyright in such material and any revisions thereof, including but not limited to the right, by itself or with others, throughout the world, to print, publish, republish, transmit and distribute such material and to prepare, publish, transmit and distribute derivative works based thereon, in all languages and in all media of expression now known or later developed, and to license or permit others to do so. The terms of this paragraph shall survive termination of this Agreement for any reason.

5.   Compensation

In full consideration of the Advisory Board Member's services under this Agreement (or other rights herein granted to the Publisher), the Publisher shall pay the Advisory Board Member:

(a)   A reviewing fee of $_____ per written review for the reviewing of a Work undertaken by the Advisory Board Member with the advance written agreement of the Publisher for the purpose of determining the suitability of the Work for publication. The reviewing fee will be payable within a reasonable time after the Publisher's receipt of the written review.

(b)   A finder's fee of $_____ for any Work that the Publisher publishes whose manuscript was originally solicited by the Advisory Board Member. The finder's fee shall be payable in two installments: $____ upon signing of a contract by the author of a Work; and $____ upon acceptance of a complete and satisfactory final manuscript by the Publisher.

6.   Copies

The Publisher shall furnish the Advisory Board Member, without charge, one copy of each Work published under the Advisory Board Member's Advisorship. The Advisory Board Member may purchase, for personal use only, additional copies of these and other publications of the Publisher, except journals, at a discount of 25% from the then current United States catalog list price.

7. Related Work

The Advisory Board Member shall not serve as advisor, author, editor, contributor or consultant for a competitive publishing program in the field of _____ _____ for another publishing company during the term of the Agreement, without the written permission of the Publisher.

8. Use of Name and Likeness

The Publisher shall have the right (but not the obligation) to use the name, likeness, and biographical data of the Advisory Board Member on the Works, and in advertising or sales promotion efforts relating thereto. After termination or expiration of this Agreement, the Publisher may continue to use the name of the Advisory Board Member on all Works then published or contracted for under this Agreement and, at the Publisher's discretion, on revisions of any Works, after which time the Publisher agrees to delete such name, likeness, and/or biographical data from future Works upon the Advisory Board Member's written request.

9. Confidential Information

The Advisory Board Member hereby agrees that the Advisory Board Member shall keep in confidence and shall not disclose to any third party or parties any Confidential and/or Proprietary Information ("Confidential Information") or any work done for the Publisher in connection with the Works.

Confidential Information is defined as any information disclosed to or learned by the Advisory Board Member as a consequence of the Advisory Board Member's performance of services under this Agreement (including without limitation, any information conceived, originated, discovered, or developed by the Publisher during the term of this Agreement) not generally known to the public and relating to the Works, including any related information, to which the Advisory Board Member may have access during the term of this Agreement. Without limiting the generality of the foregoing, publishing plans and schedules for unpublished works are deemed "Confidential Information."

10. Independent Contractors

The relationship between the Advisory Board Member and the Publisher shall be that of independent contractors. No payments under this Agreement shall be or be deemed to be compensation or salary to the Advisory Board Member providing or entitling the Advisory Board Member to any employee benefits from the Publisher. The Advisory Board Member is responsible for the payment of all taxes relating to the compensation paid to the Advisory Board Member under this Agreement. The Advisory Board Member acknowledges and agrees that the Advisory Board Member may not make any commitment on behalf of the Publisher, and is not authorized to conduct negotiations with or extend formal invitations to potential authors or editors on behalf of the Publisher.

11. Term and Termination

The term of this Agreement shall be for an initial period of _____ years from the date of this Agreement, and shall be automatically renewed thereafter for additional one-year periods unless either party gives written notice of termination not less than three months before the expiration of the applicable period.

Notwithstanding anything to the contrary hereinabove, if, at any time, the Advisory Board Member shall die or become disabled, or shall otherwise be unable or fail to perform the duties hereunder to the satisfaction of the Publisher, the Publisher shall have the right to terminate this Agreement by written notice at any time.

12. Warranty

The Advisory Board Member warrants that no action taken in the performance of the Advisory Board Member's duties as specified herein shall violate any law or the rights of any third parties. The Advisory Board Member warrants that any material prepared by the Advisory Board Member shall be original on the Advisory Board Member's part except for such excerpts and illustrations from copyrighted works which may be included with the written permission of the copyright owners, to be obtained by the Advisory Board Member on a form approved by the Publisher, such permission to be submitted to the Publisher with the respective material. The Advisory Board Member further warrants that such material shall contain no libelous or unlawful material, shall contain no instructions that may cause harm or injury and shall not infringe upon or violate any copyright, trademark, trade secret or other rights or the privacy of others, and that all statements asserted as fact in the material are either true or based upon generally accepted professional research practices. The Advisory Board Member agrees to indemnify and hold the Publisher and any licensee of any subsidiary right granted by the Publisher harmless against any and all liability and expense, including counsel fees, arising from or out of any breach or alleged breach of the above warranties, and arising out of or in connection with the services provided hereunder. The terms of this paragraph shall survive termination of this Agreement for any reason.

13. General

(a) The engagement of the Advisory Board Member is personal and the rights hereunder granted to the Advisory Board Member are not assignable nor may the obligations imposed by delegated without the Publisher's prior written consent; provided however, that the Advisory Board Member may assign any sums due to the Advisory Board Member hereunder without the Publisher's consent.

(b)   Except as provided in the preceding subparagraph, this Agreement shall inure to the benefit of the heirs, successors, administrators and permitted assigns of the Advisory Board Member and the subsidiaries, successors and assigns of the Publisher.

(c)   This Agreement shall not be subject to change or modification in whole or in part, except by a written instrument signed by both parties. Any waiver in one or more instances by either of the parties of any breach by the other of any terms or provisions contained in this Agreement shall not constitute a waiver of any such succeeding or preceding breach.

(d)   This Agreement shall be construed and interpreted pursuant to the laws of the State of New York applicable to contracts wholly entered into and performed in the State of New York. Any legal action, suit or proceeding arising out of or relating to this Agreement or the breach thereof shall be instituted in a court of competent jurisdiction in New York County in the State of New York and each party hereby consents and submits to the personal jurisdiction of such court, waives any objection to venue in such court and consents to service of process by registered or certified mail, return receipt requested, at the last known address of such party.

(e)   The parties hereto are independent contractors and the Advisory Board Member has no authority to bind the Publisher. The provisions of Paragraph 12 and this Paragraph shall survive termination of this Agreement for any reason.

ACCEPTED AND AGREED

ADVISORY BOARD MEMBER   PUBLISHER

By: _____   By: _____

Name: _____   Name: _____

SS#: _____   Title: _____

FORM 1.9
Series Editor Agreement

In many ways, a series editor is like an advisory board member (*see* Form 1.8). Both provide expert support to a publishing program in a specific area, both recommend titles, and both review works. The major differences are the degree of editorial involvement, and of course, the fact that you cannot have a series editor if you do not have a "series." In recognition of the series editor's role in planning the publishing program, the series editor receives a royalty on books he or she acquires for the series. For the publisher, it is crucial to set forth in the contract that (1) the publisher alone makes the final decision as to inclusion or exclusion of works in a series (and the final decision with respect to all other publishing matters) (Clause 2), and (2) if the publisher acquires works on its own for the series, without the involvement of the series editor, there is no royalty payable on those works (Clause 5(c)).

Series Editor Agreement

AGREEMENT made this _____ day of _____20___, between _____ (the "Series Editor") and **PubCo, Inc.**, (the "Publisher") for the purpose of publishing a series of works in printed and/or electronic form (the "Works") commissioned by the Publisher, tentatively known as the **PubCo Series On** _____ (the "Series").

1. Series Editor's Duties
The Series Editor agrees to provide the following services:

(a) Provide the Publisher with a detailed logical structure for the Series, so that a consistent set of interrelated Works may be developed.

(b) Recommend to the Publisher, from time to time, subject matter, programs and developments suitable for Works in the Series and individuals who may be suitable to serve as authors or editors for Works in the Series.

(c) In cooperation with the Publisher, solicit potential Series authors or editors and work with such authors or editors to develop Works suitable for the Series.

(d) Meet periodically with the Publisher's editorial staff to plan and review the progress of publication of Works in the Series.

(e) Review proposals for Works and manuscripts for purposes of determining suitability for publication in the Series, and upon their acceptance by the Publisher, review them for scholarly content, and suggest suitable reviewers to the Publisher. For proposed Works, the review shall be in writing and shall assess the following:

(i) The overall scope and scholarly content of the Work.

(ii) The expertise of the individuals involved.

(iii) The expected audience and market potential for the Work.

(iv) The relationship of the project to other existing and planned related Works on the topic.

(v) The overall merits of publishing the Work.

(vi) The appropriateness of the Work for publication in the Series.

The Series Editor will make every effort to provide such written assessment to the Publisher within 30 days after the Series Editor's receipt of the materials for review. The Publisher may, at its option, secure additional reviews by others, before commissioning a Work or accepting it for publication.

2.　The Series

All decisions as to which Works shall be included in the Series, the date, order, and format of publication, the acceptability of manuscripts, and the manner of production, promotion, pricing, and sale of the Series shall be at the sole discretion of the Publisher. All new or revised Works in the Series acquired in whole or in substantial part through the efforts of the Series Editor will be included in the Series, if contracted for and accepted by the Publisher as part of the Series. The Publisher, at its sole discretion, shall have the right to publish a revised edition of a Work initially published in the Series without including it in the Series.

Any Work, or revised edition thereof as provided in Paragraph 3 below, to be included in the Series for which compensation shall be paid to the Series Editor as provided in Paragraph 5 below shall be designated in a written memorandum, in the form annexed hereto as Exhibit "A," to be signed by both parties.

3.　Revised Editions

All decisions as to whether or not to undertake a revision of a Work, whether the Series Editor shall participate in the revision of such Work and whether such revised edition shall be considered part of the Series shall be at the sole discretion of the Publisher.

4.　Ownership

Any contributions made by the Series Editor to the Series (other than a Work prepared under a separate publishing agreement as provided in Paragraph 5 below) shall be considered a work made for hire, and the Publisher shall own the copyright and all rights comprised in the copyright. To the extent any such material does not qualify as a work made for hire, the Series Editor hereby transfers to the Publisher, during the full term of copyright and any extension thereof, the full and exclusive rights comprised in the copyright in any such material and any revisions thereof, including but not limited to the right, by itself or with others, throughout the world, to print, publish, republish, transmit and distribute the Works, the Series and derivative works based thereon, in all languages, in all media of expression now known or later developed, and to license and permit others to do so. The provisions of this paragraph shall survive termination of this Agreement for any reason.

5. Series Editor's Compensation

(a)   The Series Editor shall receive compensation as set forth below on new or revised Works included in the Series in whole or in substantial part through the Series Editor's efforts, provided such Works fall within the scope of the Series as determined by the Publisher and are confirmed in writing in the form annexed hereto as Exhibit "A." The Publisher reserves the right to publish outside of the Series a Work previously confirmed as a Series Work, but in such case the Series Editor shall nevertheless be entitled to receive compensation with respect to such Work. Works identified in writing as qualifying for compensation and placed under contract during the term of this Agreement, but published after its expiration, shall also qualify for such compensation. If the Series Editor, by agreement with the Publisher, authors or edits a Work for inclusion in the Series, the Series Editor will first sign a standard publishing agreement with the Publisher for that purpose. A Work authored or edited by the Series Editor under such separate publishing agreement and included in the Series shall not qualify for compensation under this Series Editor Agreement. The compensation is as follows:

A royalty of _____% of the Publisher's dollar receipts on all copies sold or licensed in the United States and its dependencies and territories, the Commonwealth of Puerto Rico, and Canada.

A royalty of _____% of the Publisher's dollar receipts on all copies sold or licensed elsewhere.

No royalties shall be earned on sales or licenses of subsidiary rights.

"Dollar receipts" are defined as United States Dollars received by the Publisher net of any discounts excluding any excise, sales or use or other domestic or foreign tax (except for income taxes), any transportation, shipping and handling charges applicable thereto, and less bad debts, customer returns, allowances and credits as well as any taxes withheld.

(b)   If the Series Editor is requested by the Publisher and agrees to participate in the preparation of a revised edition of any Work, the parties shall confirm such understanding in the form set forth in Exhibit "A" and the Series Editor shall be entitled to compensation as set forth in this Paragraph 5. No compensation shall be payable to the Series Editor on revised editions of any Works in the Series unless the Series Editor has participated in the revision in the same manner as for new Works in the Series, and such participation is confirmed in writing in the form set forth in Exhibit "A."

(c)   If the Publisher places any of its existing works in the Series, either on its own initiative or at the recommendation of the Series Editor, no compensation shall be paid to the Series Editor on such works. No compensation shall be paid to the Series Editor for works included in the Series by the Publisher without substantial involvement from the Series Editor, including works acquired by the Publisher after the date of this Agreement.

(d)   No royalties shall be paid in connection with sales or licenses not included in the categories set forth above.

(e)   No royalties shall be paid in connection with remainder copies and other copies sold below or at cost including expenses incurred, or furnished free to the author(s), editor(s), contributor(s) or the Series Editor, or for review, advertising, sample, or other similar purposes which may benefit the sale of Works published in the Series.

(f)   The Series Editor shall be paid a reviewing fee of $____ per written review for the reviewing of a potential work with the advance written agreement of the Publisher for the purpose of determining whether it should be included in the Series. The reviewing fee will be payable within a reasonable time after the Publisher's receipt of the written review. However, once a Work has been included in the Series and is subject to the royalties set forth above, reviewing the Work will constitute a part of the Series Editor's normal duties and will not entitle the Series Editor to additional compensation.

(g)   The Publisher will provide the Series Editor with appropriate stationery for use in the Series Editor's capacity as Series Editor. During the term of this Agreement and any renewal or extension thereof, the Publisher shall make available to the Series Editor a drawing account of up to $____ per year to defray office or travel expenses incurred in the course of the Series Editor's duties enumerated herein. Funds from the drawing account will be payable to the Series Editor upon the Publisher's approval of the Series Editor's written request for reimbursement, accompanied by appropriate receipts.

6.   Payment and Accounting

Payments to the Series Editor shall be made semiannually, on or before the last day of April and October of each year, for royalties due for the preceding half-year ending the last day of February and August respectively and shall be accompanied by an appropriate Statement of Account. The Publisher may take credit for any returns for which royalties have been previously paid. If the balance due the Series Editor for any royalty period is less than $10, no payment shall be due until the next royalty period at the end of which the cumulative balance has reached $10. The Publisher may retain a reserve for future returns for three royalty periods, provided the accounting statements indicate the amount of the reserve and how it is applied. Any offsets against royalties or sums owed by the Series Editor to the Publisher under this Agreement or any other agreement between the Series Editor and the Publisher may be deducted from any payments due the Series Editor under this Agreement or any other agreement between the Series Editor and the Publisher.

7. Series Editor's Copies

The Publisher shall furnish the Series Editor, without charge, _____ copies of each Work published under the Series Editor's Series Editorship. The Series Editor may purchase, for personal use only, additional copies of these and other publications of the Publisher, except journals, at a discount of 25% from the then current United States catalog list price.

8. Related Work

The Series Editor shall not serve as advisor, author, editor, contributor or consultant for a competitive series or individual work in this field for another publishing company during the term of the Agreement, without written permission of the Publisher.

9. Use of Name

The Publisher shall have the right to use the name, likeness, and biographical data of the Series Editor on Works in the Series, and in advertising or sales promotion efforts relating thereto. After termination or expiration of this Agreement, the Publisher may continue to use the name of the Series Editor on all Works then published or contracted for under this Agreement and, at the Publisher's discretion, on revisions of any Works in the Series, after which time the Publisher agrees to delete such name, likeness, and/or biographical data from future Works in the Series upon the Series Editor's written request.

10. Confidential Information

The Series Editor hereby agrees that the Series Editor shall keep in confidence and shall not disclose to any third party or parties any Confidential and/or Proprietary Information ("Confidential Information") or any work done for the Publisher in connection with the Series.

Confidential Information is defined as any information disclosed to or learned by the Series Editor as a consequence of the Series Editor's performance of services under this Agreement (including without limitation, any information conceived, originated, discovered, or developed by the Publisher during the term of this Agreement) not generally known to the public and relating to the Series, including any related information, to which the Series Editor may have access during the term of this Agreement. Without limiting the generality of the foregoing, publishing plans and schedules for publication of unpublished Works are deemed "Confidential Information."

11.   Independent Contractors

The relationship between the Series Editor and the Publisher shall be that of independent contractors. No payments under this Agreement shall be or be deemed to be compensation or salary to the Series Editor providing or entitling the Series Editor to any employee benefits from the Publisher. The Series Editor is responsible for the payment of all taxes relating to compensation or royalties paid to the Series Editor under this Agreement. The Series Editor acknowledges and agrees that the Series Editor may not make any commitment on behalf of the Publisher, and is not authorized to conduct contract negotiations with or extend formal invitations to potential authors or editors on behalf of the Publisher.

12.   Term of Agreement

The term of this Agreement shall be for an initial period of _____ years from the date of this Agreement, and shall be automatically renewed thereafter for additional one-year periods unless either party gives written notice of termination not less than three months before the expiration of the applicable period.

Notwithstanding anything to the contrary hereinabove, if, at any time, the Series Editor shall die or become incapacitated, or shall otherwise be unable or fail to perform the duties hereunder to the satisfaction of the Publisher, the Publisher shall have the right to terminate this Agreement by written notice at any time.

After termination of this Agreement, royalties shall be payable only on Works or revised editions specifically covered above.

13.   Warranty

The Series Editor warrants that the Series Editor is skilled in the services required herein and will perform them to the best of the Series Editor's ability and that no action taken in the performance of the Series Editor's duties as specified herein shall violate any law or the rights of any third parties. The Series Editor warrants that any material prepared by the Series Editor shall be original on the Series Editor's part except for such excerpts and illustrations from copyrighted works as may be included with the written permission of the copyright owners, to be obtained by the Series Editor at the Series Editor's expense on a form approved by the Publisher, such permission to be submitted to the Publisher with the final manuscript of the respective Work. The Series Editor further warrants that such material shall contain no libelous or unlawful material, shall contain no instructions that may cause harm or injury and shall not infringe upon or violate any copyright, trademark, trade secret or other rights or the privacy of others, and that all statements asserted as fact in the material are either true or based upon generally accepted professional research practices. The Series Editor agrees to indemnify and hold the Publisher and any licensee of any subsidiary right granted by the Publisher harmless against any and all liability and expense, including counsel fees, arising from or out of any breach or alleged breach of the above warranties, and arising out of or in connection with the services provided hereunder. The foregoing warranty, which shall survive termination of this Agreement, does not apply to material contained in the Series which was not prepared by the Series Editor.

14.   General

(a)   The engagement of the Series Editor is personal and the rights hereunder granted to the Series Editor are not assignable nor may the obligations imposed be delegated without the prior written consent of the Publisher; provided however, that the Series Editor may assign any sums due to the Series Editor hereunder without the Publisher's consent.

(b)   Except as provided in the preceding sentence, this Agreement shall inure to the benefit of the heirs, successors, administrators and permitted assigns of the Series Editor and the subsidiaries, successors, and assigns of the Publisher.

(c)   This Agreement shall not be subject to change or modification in whole or in part, except by a written instrument signed by both parties. Any waiver in one or more instances by either of the parties of any breach by the other of any terms or provisions contained in this Agreement shall not constitute a waiver of any

(d)   This Agreement shall be construed and interpreted pursuant to the laws of the State of New York applicable to contracts wholly entered into and per-formed in the State of New York. Any legal action, suit or proceeding arising out of or relating to this Agreement or the breach thereof shall be instituted in a court of competent jurisdiction in New York County in the State of New York and each party hereby consents and submits to the personal jurisdiction of such court, waives any objection to venue in such court and consents to service of process by registered or certified mail, return receipt requested, at the last known address of such party.

(e)   The Provisions of Paragraph 13 and this Paragraph shall survive termination of this Agreement.

ACCEPTED AND AGREED   PubCo., INC.

By: _____   By: _____
[*series editor*]

Name: _____

_____

Social Security Number   Title: _____

EXHIBIT A

Memorandum of Agreement

TO: [*Series editor*] FROM: PubCo., Inc. DATE: [*date*]

RE: [*title of work by (author'(s) or editor'(s) name(s))*]

This memorandum will confirm that the above work has been contracted for publication by the Publisher under a separate agreement executed with the author(s)/editor(s) of the work. It is the intention of the Publisher and the Series Editor that this work shall be published as part of the Series titled:

PubCo Series On _____

If the manuscript is delivered to the Publisher in accordance with the terms and conditions set forth in the publication agreement for the work, and is deemed suitable for publication in organization, form, content and style by the Publisher, the Series Editor will be entitled to compensation as set forth in the Series Editor Agreement dated [*date of agreement*].

ACCEPTED AND AGREED   **PubCo., INC.**

By: _____   By: _____

[*series editor*]

Name: _____

_____

Social Security Number

Title: _____

Copyright Transfer Agreement for Chapter Author—No Money (Short Form)

In contrast to Form 1.11, the following is a short copyright transfer agreement, with warranty and biographical information language, for use with book chapter contributors.

Copyright Transfer Form

Dear _____:

Upon your acceptance, and in exchange for a complementary copy of [PUBLICATION TITLE], this letter will constitute a transfer from you to Publishers, Inc., of full ownership of the copyright, and all of the rights comprised therein, in this and all other media throughout the world, to the work entitled:

[*Please insert ARTICLE TITLE(s)*]:
[*Please insert CHAPTER TITLE(s)*]:
[*Please insert PUBLICATION TITLE*]:

Your acceptance of this letter will further signify that you represent and warrant that you are the sole author(s) and sole proprietor(s) of all rights in and to the aforementioned work; that the work is original and not in the public domain; that it has not been previously published; that it does not violate or infringe on any copyright or any other personal or property rights of others, whether common law or statutory; that it contains nothing libelous, obscene, or otherwise contrary to law; that all statements asserted in the work as facts are true or based on reasonable research for accuracy; that if you are using material owned by your employer, company, or organization, you have notified them; and that you have full power to enter into this agreement.

Your acceptance of this letter will also constitute your agreement that the work contains no material from other copyrighted or unpublished works that has been used without the written consent of the copyright owner and/ or of the owner of any other rights to or in such other works and that you will obtain any such written consent as may be required and deliver it to us.

Your acceptance of this letter will further constitute your agreement to the use of your name and relevant biographical information in connection with the marketing of the work or any publication containing the work.

Your signature at the place marked below will indicate your acceptance of this letter.

PUBLISHERS. INC.

By: _____

Accepted: [Please SIGN below.]

_____   _____
Author   Date   Social Security Number

_____   _____
Author   Date   Social Security Number

_____   _____
Author   Date   Social Security Number

Copyright Transfer/Contributor Agreement for Chapter Author—Money Paid (Long Form)

Most contributors to professional books are not compensated, except for a free copy of the book or volume of the work in which their contribution appears. This agreement is for use when the contributor is also going to receive a cash payment. Note that the Contributor Copies clause (Clause 7) offers electronic access for a limited duration as an option for books published both on the Web and in print. If the contributor is a U.S. Government employee, *see* Form 1.12, *infra*.

Contributor Agreement

AGREEMENT, dated _____, by and between _____ (the "Contributor(s)") and _____ (the "Publisher").

This will confirm that the Publisher has commissioned the Contributor to prepare an original and previously unpublished contribution (the "Contribution") on the subject of _____ for inclusion in the forthcoming work tentatively entitled _____ (the "Work"), authored/edited by _____, to be published by the Publisher. The terms are as follows:

1. The Contribution
[IF THE CONTRIBUTION HAS NOT YET BEEN DELIVERED, USE THE FOLLOWING LANGUAGE]

The Contribution shall consist of approximately [*insert number of pages*] printed pages (a printed page of text consists of approximately 500 words) including illustrations, figures and tabular materials and shall be submitted not later than [*insert delivery date*], unless the Publisher has agreed to extend the time in writing (the "Due Date").

The final manuscript shall be submitted in an agreed electronic format complete and satisfactory to the Publisher in organization, form, content and style. It shall be submitted as the following address: [*insert name and address of person to whom the contribution should be delivered*].

If the Contributor delivers the final manuscript on or before the Due Date, the Publisher shall, within 90 days after such delivery, notify the Contributor whether the manuscript is, in the Publisher's judgment, complete and satisfactory and acceptable for publication. If the Contribution is not submitted on or before the Due Date or is not complete and satisfactory to the Publisher, the Publisher shall either terminate this Agreement or request changes that would make the Contribution complete and satisfactory. If the Contributor does not make the changes requested by the Publisher within a reasonable time set by the Publisher, or if, notwithstanding such changes, the Contribution is not in the Publisher's judgment, complete and satisfactory, then the Publisher may terminate this Agreement.

[IF THE CONTRIBUTION HAS ALREADY BEEN DELIVERED AND ACCEPTED, USE THE FOLLOWING LANGUAGE INSTEAD OF THE ABOVE LANGUAGE]

The Publisher acknowledges that the Contributor has submitted the Contribution to the Publisher, in organization, form, content and style acceptable to the Publisher.

2. Ownership

The Contribution, including all illustrations, figures, tabular and other materials, shall be considered a work made for hire to the Publisher, and the Publisher shall own the copyright and all of the rights comprised in the copyright. To the extent the Contribution or any material contained therein or attached thereto does not qualify as a work made for hire, the Contributor hereby transfers to the Publisher during the full term of copyright and all extensions thereof the full and exclusive rights comprised in the copyright in the Contribution and any revisions thereof, including but not limited to the right, by itself or with others, throughout the world, to print, publish, republish, transmit and distribute the Contribution and to prepare, publish, transmit and distribute derivative works based thereon, in all languages and in all media of expression now known or later developed, and to license or permit others to do so.

The Publisher shall have the right to make such revisions, deletions or additions to the Contribution that the Publisher may deem advisable in the interest of space and uniformity of style and presentation, provided that the accuracy of the text is not impaired.

3. Contributor Use

The Contributor may draw on and refer to material in the Contribution in preparing other articles for publication in scholarly and professional journals and papers for delivery at professional meetings, provided that credit is given to the Work and to the Publisher.

4. Warranty

The Contributor represents and warrants that: the Contribution is original except for excerpts and illustrations from copyrighted works for which the Contributor has obtained written permission from the copyright owners at the Contributor's expense on a form approved by the Publisher; the Contribution has not been previously published and is not in the public domain; the Contributor owns and has the right to convey all the rights herein conveyed to the Publisher; the Contribution contains no libelous or unlawful material, contains no instructions that may cause harm or injury and does not infringe upon or violate any copyright, trademark, trade secret or other right or the privacy of others; and all statements asserted as fact in the Contribution are either true or based upon generally accepted professional research practices. The Contributor agrees to indemnify the Publisher and any licensee of any subsidiary right, against all liability and expense, including counsel fees, arising from or out of any breach or alleged breach of these warranties.

5. Use Of Name

The Publisher shall have the right to use the Contributor's name, likeness, biographical data or professional credits on any edition of the Work or in any derivative work thereof, and in advertising, publicity or promotion related thereto and may grant such rights in connection with the license of any sub-sidiary rights in the Work.

6. Compensation

In full consideration of the rights in the Contribution granted to the Publisher herein, the Publisher shall pay the lead Contributor the following: $_____.

Payment shall be made within 60 days after the Publisher's initial publication of the Work.

7. Contributor Copies

The lead Contributor shall receive without charge one free copy of the pub-lished Work in which the Contribution appears, or a two-year subscription to the Web version of the Work. The Contributor (or all Contributors, in the event there are more than one) may purchase, for personal use only, additional print copies of the Work at a discount of 25% from the then current United States catalog list price.

8. Updates and Revised Editions

In the event the Contributor modifies or otherwise changes or enhances the Contribution for any update or revised edition of the Work, the terms of this Agreement (excluding Paragraph 6) shall apply to said update and/or revision.

9. Termination

The Publisher may terminate this Agreement in the event:

(i)   the Contributor does not deliver the final manuscript on or before the Due Date pursuant to Paragraph 1 above, or fails or refuses to make changes requested by the Publisher pursuant to Paragraph 1 above; or

(ii) the Publisher, in its sole judgment, chooses not to publish the Contribution.

In such event this Agreement shall terminate, the Publisher shall return the Contribution to the Contributor as soon as practicable and shall simultaneously revert all rights in the Contribution to the Contributor, and thereafter neither party shall have any further obligation or liability to the other hereunder.

10. General

This Agreement shall be construed and interpreted pursuant to the laws of the State of New York applicable to contracts wholly entered into and performed in the State of New York. Any legal action, suit or proceeding arising out of or relating to this Agreement or the breach thereof shall be instituted in a court of competent jurisdiction in New York County in the State of New York and each party hereby consents and submits to the jurisdiction of such court, waives any objection to venue in such court and consents to service of process by registered or certified mail, return receipt requested, at the last known address of such party.

AGREED AND ACCEPTED

CONTRIBUTOR   **PUBLISHER**

By: _____   By: _____

                                   Title: _____

_____   Date: _____

Social Security Number

By: _____

_____

Social Security Number

By: _____

_____

Social Security Number

By: _____

_____

Social Security Number

Contributor Agreement for Chapter Author—U.S. Government Works

United States government employees are subject to a common set of rules governing publishing agreements between the employees and publishing (and other) companies. These common rules, however, tend to be interpreted differently by different branches, offices, and departments of the government, as well as by the attorneys who represent them.

This contributor agreement attempts to include the major common rules; specifically (1) that the work is in the public domain in the United States, (2) that the employee cannot be compensated personally, and (3) that the federal government cannot submit to the jurisdiction of a particular state's courts. Even within these principles, variations can occur. For example, some government employees are allowed to receive a complimentary copy, some are allowed to receive them "for their departments," and others are not allowed to receive them at all. The practical way to deal with this issue is either to prepare a generic "government work" like the example below or to simply send your standard form. Either way, you will be asked to make changes that you were not able to anticipate. This latter approach is suggested for foreign government works, as it is easier than trying to learn the laws of every country with which your client does business.

Contributor Agreement [U.S. Government Works]

AGREEMENT, dated [*insert date*], by and between [*insert contributor's name*], of [*insert contributor's address*] (the "Contributor") and _____ (the "Publisher").

This will confirm that the Contributor has prepared an original and previously unpublished contribution (the "Contribution") on the subject of [*insert description of contribution*] for inclusion in the forthcoming collective work tentatively entitled [*insert title of work*] (the "Work"), to be edited by [*insert name(s) of editor(s)*] (the "Editor(s)"), to be published by Publisher. The terms are as follows:

1. The Contribution

[IF THE CONTRIBUTION HAS NOT YET BEEN DELIVERED, USE THE FOLLOWING LANGUAGE]

The Contribution shall consist of approximately [*insert number of pages*] printed pages (a printed page of text consists of approximately 500 words) including illustrations, figures and tabular materials and shall be submitted not later than [*insert delivery date*], unless the Publisher has agreed to extend the time in writing (the "Due Date").

The final manuscript shall be submitted in an agreed electronic format complete and satisfactory to the Publisher in organization, form, content and style. It shall be submitted as the following address: [*insert name and address of person to whom the contribution should be delivered*].

If the Contributor delivers the final manuscript on or before the Due Date, the Publisher shall, within 90 days after such delivery, notify the Contributor whether the manuscript is, in the Publisher's judgment, complete and satisfactory and acceptable for publication. If the Contribution is not submitted on or before the Due Date or is not complete and satisfactory to the Publisher, the Publisher shall either terminate this Agreement or request changes that would make the Contribution complete and satisfactory. If the Contributor does not make the changes requested by the Publisher within a reasonable time set by the Publisher, or if, notwithstanding such changes, the Contribution is not in the Publisher's judgment, complete and satisfactory, then the Publisher may terminate this Agreement.

[IF THE CONTRIBUTION HAS ALREADY BEEN DELIVERED AND ACCEPTED, USE THE FOLLOWING LANGUAGE INSTEAD OF THE ABOVE LANGUAGE]

The Publisher acknowledges that the Contributor has submitted the Contribution to the Publisher, in organization, form, content and style acceptable to the Publisher.

2. Ownership

The Contribution is a "United States Government Work" as described in the U.S. Copyright Act and was or will be written as part of the Contributor's official duties as a Government employee. As such, the Publisher acknowledges that the Contribution is not subject to copyright protection in the United States and the Contributor acknowledges that the Contribution is freely available to the Publisher for publication in the United States without restriction, in all languages and media of expression now known or later developed. The Publisher shall have full dissemination rights outside the United States.

The Publisher shall have the right to make such revisions, deletions or additions to the Contribution that the Publisher may deem advisable in the interest of space and uniformity of style and presentation, provided that the accuracy of the text is not impaired.

3. Warranty

The Contributor represents and warrants that: the Contribution is original except for excerpts and illustrations from copyrighted works for which the Contributor has obtained written permission from the copyright owners at the Contributor's expense on a form approved by the Publisher; the Contribution has not been previously published as a contribution to a collective work; the Contributor has the right to convey all the rights herein conveyed to the

Publisher; the Contribution contains no libelous or unlawful material, contains no instructions that may cause harm or injury and does not infringe upon or violate any copyright, trademark, trade secret or other right or the privacy of others; and all statements asserted as fact in the Contribution are either true or based upon generally accepted professional research practices.

4. Use of Name

The Publisher shall have the right to use the Contributor's name, likeness or professional credits on any edition of the Work or in any derivative work thereof, and in advertising, publicity or promotion related thereto and may grant such rights in connection with the license of any subsidiary rights in the Work.

5. Copies

The Contributor's department shall receive, without charge, one free copy of the published Work in which the Contribution appears, which shall be sent to the attention of the Contributor. The Contributor may purchase, for personal use only, additional copies of the Work at a discount of 25% from the then current United States catalog list price.

6. Revised Editions

In the event the Contributor modifies or otherwise changes or enhances the Contribution for any revised edition of the Work, the terms of this Agreement shall apply to said revision.

7. Termination

The Publisher may terminate this Agreement in the event:

(i)   the Contributor does not deliver the final manuscript on or before the Due Date pursuant to Paragraph 1 above, or fails or refuses to make changes requested by the Publisher pursuant to Paragraph 1 above; or

(ii) the Publisher, in its sole judgment, chooses not to publish the Contribution.

In such event this Agreement shall terminate, the Publisher shall return the Contribution to the Contributor as soon as practicable and shall simultaneously revert all rights in the Contribution to the Contributor, and thereafter neither party shall have any further obligation or liability to the other hereunder.

8. General

This Agreement shall be construed and interpreted pursuant to the laws of the United States of America.

ACCEPTED AND AGREED

Contributor

[or authorized contracting officer]	**Publisher**
_____	By _____
[insert contributor's name]	*[insert name of publisher]*
	Publisher
	[insert name of division]
Date _____	Date _____
_____	
Social Security Number	

Revision Agreement

Many publishing agreements contain language regarding revised editions that allows the revised editions to be prepared pursuant to the original contract. In practice, those publishers often want authors to sign a separate document confirming that the authors will prepare the new edition. Moreover, the advances and page budgets for revised editions are seldom the same as for the original work. The following letter is used in such circumstances to confirm the author's agreement to prepare the revised edition, and to set a new page budget, due date, and advance.

Revised Agreement

Dated: _____

   This Revision Agreement, when signed by you (the "Author") and by us (the "Publisher"), shall serve to amend the agreement between us, dated [*insert date of original agreement*] (the "Agreement"), concerning the work entitled [*insert title of work*] (the "Work").

1. The Author agrees to prepare and submit the final manuscript of the ____ _____ edition of the Work, to consist of approximately _____ words, not later than [*insert due date*], unless the Publisher has agreed in writing to extend the time (the "Due Date"). The final manuscript shall be submitted in computer disk format, together with two printouts double-spaced on 8-1/2" x 11" white paper printed on one side only with pages numbered consecutively, complete and satisfactory to the Publisher in organization, form, content and style, accompanied by appropriate illustrative material, a table of contents and any additional material agreed upon between the Author and the Publisher.

2. As an additional advance against all royalties and all proceeds due to the Author under the Agreement and this Revision Agreement, the Publisher will pay the Author the following:

[insert advance amount]

3. Except as expressly set forth in this Revision Agreement, the rights and obligations of the Author and the Publisher with respect to the edition shall be as set forth in the original Agreement, which shall remain in full force and effect except for Paragraphs [*insert the numbers of any provisions relating to advances and grants, as well as any other special provisions which were* *negotiated specifically for the previous edition only*], which shall not apply to this or any subsequent edition of the Work.

AGREED AND ACCEPTED   PUBLISHER

_____   By: _____

[*author*]   Name: _____

                                                   Title: _____

Termination Agreement—Author has Repaid Monies (Short Form)

Termination Agreement

Dated: _____

The Agreement, dated [*insert date of publishing agreement*], between [*insert name of author*] (the "Author") and _____ (the "Publisher"), with respect to the work tentatively entitled [*insert title of work*] (the "Work") is hereby terminated.

The Publisher acknowledges that the Author has repaid to the Publisher the advance against royalties of $[*insert amount received*] and the grant-in-aid of $[*insert amount received or delete if no grant was paid*] paid to date to the Author pursuant to the Agreement.

The Author and the Publisher shall have no further obligation or liability to each other in connection with the Work or the Agreement.

AGREED AND ACCEPTED   PUBLISHER, INC.

_____   By: _____

[author]   [publisher]

Letter Extending Due Date

Letter Extending Due Date

[*date*]

[*author*]
[c/o *agent, if applicable*]
[*author's address, or agent's address, if applicable*]

Dear [*author*]:

This letter, when signed by you (the "Author") and by us (the "Publisher"), shall serve to amend the agreement between us, dated [*insert date of original agreement*], as amended [*insert date(s) of any amendment(s) to the original agreement*] (collectively, the "Agreement"), concerning the work [*tentatively*] entitled [*insert title of the work*] (the "Work"). Except as provided herein, all defined terms have the same meaning as in the Agreement. The parties hereby agree as follows:

1. Paragraph of the Agreement shall be amended to reflect that the Due Date is [*insert new due date*].
2. Except as herein expressly modified, the Agreement is hereby ratified and affirmed.

Please sign in the space provided below to indicate your acceptance of the foregoing.

PUBLISHER, INC.

By: _____

Publisher

AGREED AND ACCEPTED

_____
[*author*]

Sample Letter—Requesting that Author Agree to a Lower Royalty Rate

[*date*]

[*author*]
[c/o *agent, if applicable*]
[*author's address, or agent's address, if applicable*]

Dear [*author*]:

I am writing to request your consideration of an amendment to the royalty provisions contained in our publishing agreement dated [*date of agreement*] for your book entitled [*title*] covering sales of a [new format] edition of your book. We believe that your book would be very suitable for publication in [new format], and that this publication could lead to greater visibility for your book.

The royalty percentage of _____ % of our dollar receipts contained in the publishing agreement is not a royalty rate that would make it economically feasible for us to publish a [new format] edition. However, with your agreement to modify the royalty percentage to _____ % of our dollar receipts on regular sales of a [new format] edition in the U.S., its territories and possessions and Canada; and a royalty of _____ % of our dollar receipts on regular sales of it elsewhere, we will be in a position to publish a [new format] edition.

If you approve of this royalty modification, please countersign the enclosed copy of this letter and return it to me. We look forward to including your book in our publishing program.

Very truly yours,
PUBLISHER, INC.

By: _____

Publisher

AGREED AND ACCEPTED

_____

[*author*]

FORM 1.17
Reversion Letter

Most publishing agreements provide for reversions of rights when a book is no longer available for purchase (also known as "out of print"). With some agreements the reversion is automatic, while others require affirmative steps from the author, such as a written demand. This letter is usable for either situation.

Reversion Letter

VIA FAX—(212) 555-1212

[*date*]

[*author*]
[c/o *agent, if applicable*]
[*author's address, or agent's address, if applicable*]

Re: <u>Book Title</u>

Dear _____:

This is to confirm that Publisher's rights in the above-referenced work have reverted to you pursuant to that certain publishing agreement between you and the publisher for the aforementioned book, subject to any outstanding licenses previously granted. I have been advised that there is an outstanding license with _____, and I have asked our Subsidiary Rights Department to take the necessary steps to terminate that license. For further information on the license, you may contact _____ in our Subsidiary Rights Department, at [*phone number*].

Enclosed for your file are copies of the Certificate of Copyright Registration and Certificate of Renewal Registration for the work.

Now that rights in the work have reverted to you, you may wish to register the work with the Copyright Clearance Center (CCC), a not-for-profit clearinghouse which provides photocopy permissions to a wide range of users and charges the users a fee. For further information, you may contact the CCC directly at 222 Rosewood Drive, Danvers, MA 01923; by telephone at (508) 750-8400; and by fax at (508) 750-4744.

Please feel free to contact me at [*phone number*] if you have any questions or if I can be of further assistance.

Very truly yours, [*name*]

FORM 1.18

Guarantee

There are a variety of tax, trust and estate, employee benefits, and liability reasons for an author to transfer all copyrights to a closely held corporation and to have the corporation sign all publishing agreements as author.[12] For a publisher, there are two primary concerns with this arrangement. The first can be a difficult issue: that the individual will have limited liability and the corporation, in the event of a dispute, will have few assets. The second concern is also important, but not controversial: that the publisher needs the right to use the name of the individual, not the company, as "author" on the book. The following personal guarantee addresses both of these issues.

Guarantee

GUARANTEE given this ___ day of ___, ___ to _____ (the "Publisher").

WITNESSETH

WHEREAS, the Publisher and [name] (the "Company"), a corporation, will be executing simultaneously herewith a publishing agreement (the "Agreement") regarding publication of a manuscript tentatively entitled [name] (the "Work"); and

WHEREAS, the Guarantor desires to induce the Publisher to enter into the Agreement;

NOW, THEREFORE, in consideration of the foregoing, the Guarantor agrees as follows:

1.   The Guarantor unconditionally guarantees to the Publisher, its subsidiaries, successors and assigns, the prompt performance of the Company of each and every obligation, duty and liability as and when due to the Publisher pursuant to the Agreement and otherwise, as though the Guarantor was the party designated as "Author" in the Agreement.

2.   The obligations of the Guarantor pursuant to this Guarantee shall be irrevocable, continuing, and absolute; may not be assigned by the Guarantor; shall not be subject to any counterclaim, set-off, or defense based upon any claim the Guarantor may have against the Company or the Publisher; and shall remain in full force and effect. The Guarantor's obligations shall not be released, discharged or in any way affected by any circumstance or condition

---

12 For a detailed exposition on some of the advantages of transferring copyrights to an entity, and the tax consequences thereof, *see* Richard Halperin, "Structures for Holding and Transferring Copyrights," *Art Law Handbook*, Ch. 15 (Roy Kaufman ed., Aspen L. & Bus. 2000).

(whether or not the Guarantor shall have any knowledge or notice of same), including without limitation:

(a) any amendment, modification of, or supplement to the Agreement between the Company and the Publisher;

(b) any assignment or transfer of the Agreement by the Publisher;

(c) any waiver, consent, or other action pursuant to the Agreement, or any exercise or non-exercise of any right, remedy, power or privilege pursuant to the Agreement or this Guarantee;

(d) any bankruptcy, insolvency, reorganization, arrangement, readjustment, composition, liquidation, dissolution or similar occurrence or proceeding by, against, or with respect to the Company; and

(e) any limitation on the liability of the Company other than in accordance with the terms of the Agreement, or any invalidity or unenforceability, in whole or in part, of the Agreement or any part thereof.

3. The Publisher shall have the right to use the name, likeness and biographical data of the Guarantor on any edition of the Work or in any derivative work thereof, and in the advertising, publicity and promotion related thereto and may grant such rights in connection with the license of any subsidiary rights in the Work. The Guarantor shall provide in a timely manner any information reasonably requested by the Publisher for use in promoting and advertising the Work.

4. The Guarantor unconditionally waives:

(a) notice of default or breach on the part of the Company pursuant to the Agreement or this Guarantee;

(b) notice of any of the matters set forth in Paragraph 2 above;

(c) demand upon the Company for any obligation, duty and liability pursuant to the Agreement or this Guarantee; and

(d) all notices which may be required by statutes, rule of law or otherwise to preserve any rights against the Guarantor hereunder, including without limitation, any notice of any failure on the part of the Company to perform or comply with any terms of the Agreement.

5. This Guarantee may not be modified, changed, waived, discharged, or terminated except in writing signed by both parties. The terms of this Guarantee shall be binding upon and inure to the benefit of and be enforceable by the heirs, successors, and administrators of the Guarantor and by the subsidiaries, successors and assigns of the Publisher.

6. This Guarantee shall be construed and interpreted pursuant to the laws of the State of New York applicable to contracts wholly entered into and performed in the State of New York. Any legal action, suit or proceeding arising out of or relating to this Guarantee or the breach thereof shall be instituted in a court of competent jurisdiction in New York County in the State of New York and each party hereby consents and submits to the personal jurisdiction of such court, waives any objection to venue in such court and consents to service of process by registered mail or certified mail, return receipt requested, at the last known address of such party.

IN WITNESS WHEREOF, the Guarantor has caused this Guarantee to be executed as of the date set forth above.

_____

Guarantor

Miscellaneous Clauses

A. Third-Party Contributors

It is understood and agreed that certain material shall be supplied by third-party contributors to be selected by the Author subject to the Publisher's approval. The Author shall obtain from each such contributor a signed Contributor's Agreement in a form acceptable to the Publisher and shall submit each such Contributor's Agreement with the final manuscript of the Work. The Author shall remain solely responsible for the performance of the Author's obligations pursuant to this Agreement including without limitation the delivery of a complete and satisfactory manuscript pursuant to Paragraph.

B. New Contract for Same Book

This Agreement supersedes the agreement, dated _____, between the Publisher and _____ with respect to the Work.

C. Rights Reservation Language—Nonexclusive if Non-Use

In the event that the Publisher has not exercised, licensed or optioned a third party to exercise [*insert the rights that the author wants to retain*] rights within [*insert time frame*] after initial publication of the Work, the Author shall have the right to give the Publisher notice that unless the Publisher notifies the Author of its intent to exercise, or enters into an agreement (or commences negotiations therefor) for the license or option of such rights, within 90 days of the Publisher's receipt of such notice, then at the expiration of such 90-day period both the Author and the Publisher shall have the nonexclusive right to exercise, license or option such rights; and in the event the Publisher does not notify the Author of its intent to exercise, or does not enter into an agreement (or commence negotiations therefor) for the license or option of such rights within such 90-day period, such rights shall automatically become nonexclusive at the expiration of such 90-day period. After such rights become nonexclusive, both parties shall supply each other with prior written notice of any plans to exercise such rights, or negotiations to license or option such rights, and neither party shall exercise or license such rights without the other party's prior written approval, which shall not be unreasonably withheld. If the responding party fails to respond to the requesting party's request for approval within 30 days following the responding party's receipt of notice, then the requesting party's proposed exercise, license or option shall be deemed approved. In the event the Author exercises, licenses or options such rights after such rights become nonexclusive pursuant to this paragraph, the Author shall pay to the Publisher [*insert publisher's share of proceeds*]% of all amounts received by the Author pursuant to any such exercise, license or option. In the event the Publisher exercises, licenses or options such rights after such rights become nonexclusive pursuant to this paragraph, the Publisher shall pay to the Author the appropriate royalty or share of the proceeds as set forth in Paragraph 5 of the Agreement. Each party shall supply the other with a copy of all fully executed agreements for any licenses or options of such rights.

D. Rights Reservation Language—Nonexclusive

The Publisher and the Author shall each have the nonexclusive right to exercise, license or option a third party to exercise [*insert the rights that the author wants to retain*] rights. Both parties shall supply each other with prior written notice of any plans to exercise such rights, or negotiations to license or option such rights, and neither party shall exercise or license such rights without the other party's prior written approval, which shall not be unreasonably withheld. If the responding party fails to respond to the requesting party's request for approval within 30 days following the responding party's receipt of notice, then the requesting party's proposed exercise, license or option shall be deemed approved. In the event the Author exercises, licenses or options such rights, the Author shall pay to the Publisher [*insert publisher's share of proceeds*]% of all amounts received by the Author pursuant to any such exercise, license or option. In the event the Publisher exercises, licenses or options such rights, the Publisher shall pay to the Author the appropriate royalty or share of the proceeds as set forth in Paragraph ____ of the Agreement. Each party shall supply the other with a copy of all fully executed agreements for any licenses or options of such rights.

E. Reserved Rights are Retained

Those rights stricken from Paragraph ____ are hereby reserved to the Author.

F. Index—Publisher Prepares and Charges Against Advance

If the Publisher determines that an index to the Work is desirable, the Publisher shall prepare or engage a third party to prepare the index in such manner as the Publisher deems appropriate and charge the cost thereof against any sums due to the Author.

G. Index—Publisher Prepares

If the Publisher determines that an index to the Work is desirable, the Publisher shall prepare or engage a third party to prepare the index in such manner as the Publisher deems appropriate and the Publisher shall pay the cost thereof.

H.   Author Maintains Companion Web Site

The Author agrees to create and maintain, at the Author's sole cost and expense, a World Wide Web site relating to the Work (the "Web Site"). The Web Site shall include (but shall not be limited to) [*insert description of materials*]. The initial design and contents of the Web Site shall be subject to the Publisher's prior written approval, which shall not be unreasonably withheld. The Web Site shall be housed on the Author's World Wide Web site at the Author's sole cost and expense, and the Author shall arrange to have the Web Site up and running no later than [*insert date*]. The Author shall make disclosure, in an appropriate and prominent place in the Web Site, that the Web Site has been created and is maintained solely by the Author and not by the Publisher and the Author agrees to include any other disclaimer language provided by the Publisher. The Author shall maintain and update the contents of the Web Site for so long as the Work is in print. Upon the Publisher's request, the Publisher shall have the right to approve the contents of the updates. The Author shall be under no obligation to maintain or update the contents of the Web Site after the Work ceases to be in print; provided however, that if the Author chooses not to maintain or update the Web Site after such time then the Author shall take all reasonable and necessary steps to ensure that the Web Site is deleted from the Internet. The Author may make reference in the Web Site to the fact that the Work is published by the Publisher. The Author shall not have any other right to use any of the Publisher's trademarks, service marks or trade dress in or in connection with the creation and maintenance of the Web Site and the Author shall not disparage the Publisher or the Publisher's trademarks on the Web Site.

I.   Author Prepares Companion Web Site for Publisher

As part of the complete and satisfactory final manuscript, the Author shall prepare and submit to the Publisher, at the Author's sole cost and expense, material for a World Wide Web site relating to the Work (the "Web Site"). The material for the Web Site shall be submitted in an appropriate Web-ready format as specified by the Publisher suitable for direct use by the Publisher without correction, no later than [*insert date*]. The Web Site shall include (but shall not be limited to) [*insert description of materials*]. If the Web Site materials are acceptable to the Publisher and in accordance with this Agreement, the Web Site shall be housed on the Publisher's server in such manner and for such duration as deemed appropriate by the Publisher in its discretion, at the Publisher's sole cost and expense. The Author agrees to maintain and update the contents of the Web Site for so long as the Work is in print. Thereafter, the Author shall be under no obligation to maintain or update the contents of the Web Site.

J. Author Provides Software with Book

In addition to the preparation of a final manuscript of the text of the Work as set forth in Paragraph _____ of the Agreement, the Author shall prepare and submit to the Publisher electronic material consisting of the following:

> *[Insert appropriate description of the content of the Electronic Component]* (hereinafter referred to as the "Electronic Component").

The Author shall prepare and deliver complete copies of the source code for the Electronic Component in machine readable form on master disks suitable for reproducing high quality [disks/CD-ROMs] for distribution to end-users, and suitable for electronic transmission including but not limited to Internet-based electronic delivery and use in information storage and retrieval systems or devices, complete and satisfactory to the Publisher in organization, form, content, style and technical development (the "Final Deliverables"), on or before [*insert due date*] (the "Electronic Due Date"). The Author shall, at the Author's expense, submit with the Final Deliverables, written licenses and/or permissions, on a form approved by the Publisher, to include any proprietary material which the Author incorporates in the Electronic Component.

If the Final Deliverables are not free of programming defects or errors in accordance with industry standards, not installable on Windows and/or Macintosh platforms, or not otherwise acceptable to the Publisher in organization, form, content, style and technical development, the Publisher may reject the Final Deliverables. In the event that the Publisher deems it appropriate in light of the Publisher's scheduling requirements, the Publisher shall have the right (but not the obligation) to permit the Author to revise the Final Deliverables to address the Publisher's concerns and the Author agrees to revise and resubmit the Final Deliverables to the Publisher in accordance with the schedule set forth by the Publisher. If the Author does not deliver the Final Deliverables by the Electronic Due Date or the revised Final Deliverables within the time required by the Publisher, or if the Publisher rejects the revised Final Deliverables because they are unacceptable, then the Publisher may, in addition to any other rights it may have under this Agreement: (i) give the Author written notice of termination of this Agreement, upon which notice the Author shall promptly repay to the Publisher any advances or other payments made to the Author under this Agreement and this Agreement shall terminate without further obligation or liability to the Author; (ii) require the Author to make additional corrections to the Final Deliverables; (iii) notify the Author that it wishes to make other arrangements for the completion of the Electronic Component in which case the Author shall promptly deliver to the Publisher all work in progress, including without limitation, the source code, which the Publisher may reasonably require to complete the Electronic Component; or (iv) elect, in its discretion, to proceed with publication of the Work without inclusion of the Electronic Component.

If the Publisher elects option (iii), then the Publisher may make such other arrangements with respect to the Electronic Component as it deems appropriate and shall deduct from any sums due to the Author the cost of such arrangements. If the Publisher permits the Author to revise the Final Deliverables and acceptable revised Final Deliverables are not delivered to the Publisher by the extended Due Date, then the Publisher may, in addition to any other rights it may have under the Agreement, exercise either option (i) or option (iii) or option (iv) or require the Author to make additional corrections to the Final Deliverables under option (ii).

The Publisher shall have the right (but not the obligation) to make editorial and/or programming changes to the Final Deliverables and to the Electronic Component as the Publisher deems appropriate, and the Author agrees to review and test such changes.

The Author acknowledges that time is of the essence with respect to all Due Dates under this Agreement, including but not limited to the Electronic Due Date set forth above. In the event the Publisher gives the Author the opportunity to revise the Final Deliverables, such opportunity shall not postpone or otherwise affect any other Due Dates under this Agreement unless the Publisher expressly agrees in writing to extend such Due Dates.

Any errors identified after acceptance of the Final Deliverables, including without limitation errors regarding the proper functioning of the interface, buttons and navigation links, will be corrected by the Author at no cost to the Publisher. Following acceptance of the Final Deliverables, the Publisher shall be responsible for providing routine technical support to end users. The Author will, however, provide technical support related to any interface or navigation problems at no cost to the Publisher.

The Author shall cause to be displayed via code contained in the Electronic Component, and on the title/copyright screen of the Final Deliverables, a notice of copyright in [the publisher's/the author's] name, together with an appropriate disclaimer, in a form approved by the Publisher.

Upon the Publisher's request, the Author shall supply the Publisher with any materials necessary for registration of the copyright in the Electronic Component.

The Electronic Component shall be considered a part of the Work under this Agreement.

K. Developmental Editor

The Publisher shall have the right, but not the obligation, to obtain the services of a third-party developmental editor to assist in connection with the Work, on terms and conditions deemed advisable by the Publisher in its sole discretion. The Author agrees to make her/himself available to respond to queries from the developmental editor and to assist the developmental editor in other ways reasonably requested by the Publisher or the developmental editor. The

Author acknowledges and agrees that any monies paid to the developmental editor may be charged against any sums due to the Author (including but not limited to the advance payable on acceptance of the final manuscript), and such sums may be paid directly to the developmental editor by the Publisher. Notwithstanding the engagement of the developmental editor, the Author shall remain responsible for the delivery of a complete and satisfactory final manuscript pursuant to Paragraph _____.

L. Publishing Decisions—Consultation Right

The Publisher shall consult with the Author regarding the [*insert appropriate description of specific matters, e.g., title*] of the Work, but the final decision as to such matters shall be made by the Publisher in its sole judgment and discretion.

M. Publishing Decisions—Approval Rights

The Author shall have the right to approve the [*insert appropriate description of specific matters (e.g., cover design, title)*] of the Work, such approval not to be unreasonably withheld. Any [*insert appropriate description of specific matters (e.g., cover design, title)*] not disapproved by the Author in writing setting forth the reasonable basis for such disapproval within three business days of submission by the Publisher to the Author, shall be deemed approved by the Author.

N. Copyright Registration—Author May Register in Foreign Countries

Any agreement made by the Publisher to dispose of any rights in and to the Work shall require the licensee or grantee to take all necessary and appropriate steps to protect the copyright in the Work. The Publisher may take such steps as it deems appropriate to register the copyright in the Work in countries other than the United States, but the Publisher shall be under no obligation to procure registration in any such countries, and shall not be liable to the Author for any acts or omissions by it in connection therewith. The Author may register the copyright in the Work in any foreign country if the Publisher fails to take steps to obtain such a registration within 30 days after receiving a written request from the Author to do so.

O. Royalties—Escalator Exclusions

Sales of the Work as set forth in sections ___ through ___ of Paragraph ___ are not included in the calculation of units sold for purposes of escalating royalties.

P. Subsidiary Rights—Notice to Author

The Publisher shall make reasonable efforts to notify the Author of any subsidiary rights licenses granted to third parties. Inadvertent failure to so notify the

Author shall not be deemed a breach of this Agreement. Upon written request by the Author, the Publisher shall provide the Author with copies of subsidiary rights licenses granted to third parties.

Q. Additional Advance for Early Delivery

In addition to the advance specified in Paragraph ____, in the event the Author delivers the complete and satisfactory final manuscript of the Work on or before [*insert date, usually a date earlier than the due date in paragraph* ____], then the Publisher shall pay the Author an additional advance of $_____ upon acceptance of the final manuscript.

R. Lower Advance for Late Delivery

As an advance against all royalties and all proceeds due to the Author pursuant to this Agreement or any other agreement between the Author and the Publisher, the Publisher will pay the Author the following: $_____, payable as follows:

$_____ upon signing of this Agreement; and $_____ upon acceptance of the final manuscript of the Work, complete and satisfactory to the Publisher, provided that the final manuscript is delivered in complete and satisfactory form no later than the Due Date provided in Paragraph ___ above. In the event the final manuscript of the Work, complete and satisfactory to Publisher, is delivered later than the Due Date provided in Paragraph ____ of the Agreement, and the Publisher elects, in its sole discretion, to waive its right to terminate this Agreement pursuant to Paragraph ____, the portion of the advance due on such acceptance shall be reduced to $_____. The advance shall be nonrefundable except as set forth in Paragraph ____.

S. Multiple Authors—Unclear Division of Royalties—Money Held in Escrow

The Authors shall notify the Publisher of the division of royalties among the Authors no later than the Due Date set forth in Paragraph _____. At such time an amendment letter specifying such division of royalties shall be executed by all parties to this Agreement. If the Authors disagree as to the appropriate royalty split, then the royalties will be held in escrow by the Publisher until the Publisher receives written notice signed by all the Authors setting forth the division among them.

T. Multiple Authors—Unclear Division of Royalties—Money Divided Evenly

The Authors shall notify the Publisher in writing of the division of the royalties among the authors no later than the Due Date specified in Paragraph ____ above. At such time, an addendum shall be issued by the Publisher and must be signed by all Authors. If the Authors disagree as to the appropriate division of the royalties, then the royalties shall be divided equally among them, and the Authors shall jointly and severally indemnify the Publisher from and against any claims challenging such a division.

U.   Multiple Authors—Designation of Representative

Any one of the Authors may be designated in writing to act on behalf of all the Authors jointly, and the Publisher may rely on the acts or decisions of the author so designated as representative and binding upon all the Authors. In the absence of such designation in the event of a disagreement, the Publisher shall have the right but not the obligation to terminate this Agreement.

V.   Audit Right

Upon written request by the Author made reasonably in advance, the Author's designated accountant may examine the Publisher's royalty records relating to the sale and licensing of the Work, for the 24 months immediately preceding such examination. Any such examination shall be at the Author's expense, and no more than one such examination may be made within any 12-month period and must be conducted at a reasonable time during the Publisher's normal business hours. The Publisher is not required to retain royalty records for a period of more than two years following the issuance of any Statement of Account, such statement being deemed conclusive after the elapse of such two-year period.

W.   Required Author Buy-Back

The Author acknowledges that part of the consideration for the Publisher's obligations contained in this Agreement is the Author's commitment to purchase not less than [*insert minimum quantity*] copies of the Work, at a discount of [*insert agreed upon discount*]% from the U.S. list price, plus shipping and handling and any applicable taxes, in accordance with the following schedule: [*insert agreed-upon schedule*, e.g., at the time of the first printing, during the first year following publication; within two years following initial publication]. After the initial required purchase the Author may purchase additional copies in incremental quantities of no less than [*insert minimum required quantity for future purchases*] copies per order, at a discount of [*insert agreed upon discount*]% from the U.S. list price, plus shipping and handling and any applicable taxes. No royalty shall be paid on copies purchased under this paragraph. The Author agrees that (i) such copies are non-returnable; (ii) such copies may not be resold or distributed through traditional retail and wholesale book trade channels for works of this type; and (iii) such copies are to be used in connection with the Author's own ongoing business and promotional activities. The Author agrees to make payment upon receipt of the Publisher's invoices, which will be sent as follows: 25% at the time copies are ordered (including at the first printing of the Work, if appropriate); and the balance on shipment. [In the event the Author fails to place the required order or to make payment for an order when due, in addition to all other remedies available to the Publisher, it may charge the invoice amount for such copies against any sums due to the Author under this Agreement or any other agreement between the Author and the Publisher.] All purchases are subject to credit approval. In the event the Publisher accepts an order to purchase copies under this clause from a third party on the Author's behalf, the Author shall remain personally obligated for such purchases under the terms hereof.

X. Discretionary Author Buy-Back

The Author may purchase copies of the Work directly from the Publisher at the time of the initial print run or thereafter, subject to the Publisher's inventory requirements, it being understood that the Publisher shall not be obligated to arrange for a printing of the Work to fill an order for the Author if such a printing cannot be done on terms deemed economically feasible by the Publisher in its discretion. It is understood that all orders shall be in mini-mum quantities of [*insert minimum required quantity for future purchases*] copies, at a discount of [*insert agreed upon discount*]% from the U.S. list price, plus shipping and handling and any applicable taxes. No royalty shall be paid on copies purchased under this paragraph.[13] The Author agrees that (i) such copies are non-returnable; (ii) such copies may not be resold or distributed through traditional retail and wholesale book trade channels for works of this type; and (iii) such copies are to be used in connection with Author's own ongoing business and promotional activities.[14] The Author agrees to make payment upon receipt of the Publisher's invoices which will be sent as follows: 25% at the time copies are ordered (including at the first printing of the Work, if appropriate); and the balance on shipment. [In the event the Author fails to make payment for an order when due, in addition to all other remedies available to the Publisher, may charge the invoice amount for such copies against any sums due to the Author under this Agreement or any other agreement between the Author and the Publisher.] All purchases are subject to credit approval. In the event the Publisher accepts an order to purchase copies under this clause from a third party on the Author's behalf, the Author shall remain personally obligated for such purchases under the terms hereof.

---

13 If the author will receive royalties on the copies then delete this sentence.

14 Item (iii) may vary depending upon the nature of the author's activities.

Y. Use of Work in Author's Business

The Publisher acknowledges that the ideas and concepts contained in the Work are utilized by the Author in the normal course of the Author's regular day-to-day business, and the use of such ideas and concepts in the Author's day-to-day business shall not be deemed in violation of this Agreement. In addition, notwithstanding anything to the contrary contained in the Agreement and without limiting the rights granted to the Publisher hereunder, the Publisher agrees that the Author may use nominal amounts of verbatim material from the Work (not to exceed a total of [*insert quantity*] [words/ pages] of the Work in total) in the normal course of the Author's regular day-to-day business (including in consulting, training, seminar and course materials), provided that (i) credit is given to the Work and to the Publisher; and (ii) the Author shall not use the material in such a way as to interfere with, compete with, or injure the sale of the Work.

Z. Author Notice of Remaindering

Prior to remaindering bound copies (and sheet stock), the Publisher shall use reasonable efforts to notify the Author of the availability of such copies and stock at such price and quantities as determined by the Publisher. The Author may purchase all or any portion of such copies and stock upon written notice to the Publisher exercisable within two weeks after the Publisher's notice. Inadvertent failure to offer such copies and stock to the Author shall not be deemed a breach of this Agreement.

AA. Approval Over Use of Name and Likeness

The Author shall have the right to approve the likeness and biographical data of the Author which the Publisher intends to use in the advertising, publicity and promotion of the Work, such approval not to be unreasonably withheld. Any material not disapproved by the Author in writing setting forth the reasonable basis for such disapproval within 10 business days of submission by the Publisher to the Author shall be deemed approved by the Author. Thereafter, the Publisher shall have the right to use the approved material without further approval thereof.

BB. Use of Title in Connection with Reserved Rights

The Author shall have the right to use the title of the Work in connection with any rights reserved to the Author hereunder. In addition, in the event of a reversion of rights to the Author, the Author shall have the right to use the title of the Work in connection with the exercise or license of such reverted rights.

CC.   Warranties—Interest on Withheld Sums/Abandonment of Claim

Any sums withheld hereunder shall be reasonably related to the size of the claim, shall be held by the Publisher in an interest-bearing account, and if the withheld funds are paid to the Author, then the Author shall be entitled to the interest on the portion of the sums paid to the Author. Notwithstanding the foregoing, in the event the Publisher shall have been notified of a claim or demand, if the claim or demand shall not result in a suit or proceeding within one year of notice to the Publisher, and the Publisher shall have incurred no expenses therefor, then the Publisher shall release the withheld funds, except that the Publisher may in its sole discretion continue to withhold funds if the Publisher has a reasonable basis to believe that a suit or proceeding shall be commenced within a reasonable time thereafter, and except that the Publisher may again commence withholding funds should a suit or proceeding be commenced after any release of withheld funds.

DD.   Out of Print—Notice to Author

The Publisher shall use reasonable efforts to notify the Author in the event the Work goes out of print; provided however, that inadvertent failure to so notify the Author shall not be deemed a breach of this Agreement.

EE.   Publisher Termination for Adverse Changes in Market

Notwithstanding anything contained in this Agreement to the contrary, the Publisher shall not be obligated to publish the Work if, in its sole judgment to be reasonably exercised, whether before or after acceptance of the final manuscript, supervening events or circumstances have adversely changed the economic expectations of the Publisher in respect to the Work at the time of the making of this Agreement, and in such event all of the Publisher's rights in and to the Work shall terminate and revert to the Author on the giving by the Publisher to the Author of notice of its decision, and in such event the Author shall be entitled as liquidated damages and in lieu of all damages and remedies, legal or equitable, to retain all payments theretofore made to the Author under this Agreement.

CHAPTER

2

Periodical Publishing

§ 2.01 Background

Chapter 2 presents form agreements for use in nonbook continuity (i.e., periodical) publishing. The specific types of publications addressed are journals, newsletters, magazines, and newspapers.

"Journals" are typically scholarly publications, such as law reviews or research publications like *The New England Journal of Medicine*. Although varied, journals are usually subject to some form of peer review, often provided by an editorial board comprising experts in the field. Some journals are published by or in affiliation with well-known universities or professional societies (*see* Form 2.1, *infra*). Journals, unless they are self-published by an institution or a society, are often edited by an outside expert retained for the specific journal by the publisher (*see* Form 2.2 *infra*). For larger journals, assistant or associate editors may be retained (*see* Form 2.5, *infra*). The contributors whose material is published in journals are experts in the subject matter, who publish for reasons of professional advancement and are seldom compensated beyond a nominal amount (*see* Forms 2.7 and 2.8, *infra*).

Articles that appear in journals and other publications are often cited in "newsletters," which provide summaries with citations indicating the sources for further research. Newsletters tend to be summary reviews of newly available literature or recent events in a given field. Newsletters may publish peer-reviewed material under editorial board oversight, but more often they are simply prepared by the editor based on his or her review of activities in the field (*see* Forms 2.3 and 2.4, *infra*).

Newspapers and magazines tend to use fewer outside editors than journals and newsletters, but do rely on professional independent contractors who write commissioned articles on a freelance basis. The relationship between the freelancers and publishers is often contentious.[1] Form 2.9, which is a standard agreement drafted by a publisher, is very different from the agreements drafted for authors (Form 2.10), and careful attention is required when using another party's agreement.

In addition to the editorial contracts discussed above, an advertising representative agreement for use with outside sales representatives is included as Form 2.6, as is a form (2.11) for use with subscription agencies. Other form agreements of interest for periodical publishers can be found in Chapters 3, 4, 5 and 6, *infra*.

---

1 *See, e.g.*, New York Times Co., Inc., et al. v. Tasini et al., 533 U.S. 483, 121 S. Ct. 2381, 150 L. Ed. 2d 500 (2001); Greenberg v. National Geographic Society, 488 F.3d 1331 (11th Cir. 2007); Faulkner v. Natural Geographic Enterprises, 409 F. 3d 26 (2d Cir 2005).

FORM 2.1

Society Affiliation Agreement

The following is an affiliation agreement between a publisher and a scholarly society for a new journal, which is to be launched and owned by the publisher. It outlines a standard relationship model between societies and publishers for publisher-owned journals: the publisher provides editorial office support, the society performs the editorial functions through an appointed editor and editorial board, and the society's members all receive a subscription to the journal as part of their annual dues. The society purchases the member subscriptions from the publisher at a steep discount from the institutional price (Clause 5(c)). Because this contract is for a new journal and the parties are entering into a five-year agreement, the contract provides special language allowing the publisher to terminate the agreement if the journal is not economically viable and allowing the society to assume publication in such event for an assumption of the liabilities relating thereto (Clause 7(b)).

Agreement

Agreement made this _____ day of _____, 20__ between Publisher, Inc., (hereinafter called the "Publisher") and Society, Inc., _____ (hereinafter called "Society"), with respect to the Publisher's journal tentatively entitled _____ (hereinafter called the "Journal").

1. Responsibilities of Society

(a)   Society, in joint cooperation with the Publisher, is responsible for editorial policy and control. It will exercise this responsibility by drafting a statement of the editorial aims and scope of the Journal and by appointing _____ as editor-in-chief (hereinafter called the "Editor"). Changes in the editorial policy will be made with the approval of the Publisher. The Editor shall sign an Editor's agreement with the Publisher.

(b)   Society shall have the responsibility of supervising the Editor, ensuring the implementation of editorial policy and procedures and standards for acceptance of manuscripts. Decisions about the inclusion or exclusion of manuscripts shall be vested in the Editor.

(c)   If the Editor is unable or unwilling to perform routine duties related to the Journal's publication for any extended period of time, Society shall ensure that the Publisher can rely on another authorized individual for day-to-day decisions regarding the operation of the editorial office. In the event the Editor is not performing his obligations and duties to the reasonable satisfaction of the Publisher, the Publisher shall so inform Society, specifying in detail the areas of unsatisfactory performance. If the Editor is unable to improve his performance as provided in the Editor's Agreement with the Publisher, the Editor's Agreement shall be terminated and Society shall appoint an interim editor and initiate a search for a successor, all in consultation with, and subject to the approval of, the Publisher.

(d) During the initial Term and any renewal Term of this Agreement, Society shall not publish, affiliate with, or sponsor any other journal reasonably deemed by the Publisher to be competitive with the Journal. Cooperation of Society with its Members who may serve in editorial or advisory capacities on other journals shall not be deemed in violation of this Agreement.

(e) Society will provide a membership mailing list to the Publisher for each issue.

2.   Use of Society's Name, Logo and Seal

Society hereby grants to the Publisher a nonexclusive, non-transferable, world-wide limited license to use the name, logo, and seal of Society in connection with the publication, sale, and marketing of the Journal during the term of this Agreement. Society retains full ownership of its trade name and logo. Each issue of the Journal shall contain the following on its cover: "The Official Journal of [Society]."

3.   Publisher's Responsibilites

All publishing activities of the Journal shall be the responsibility of the Publisher, including but not limited to the following:

(a) The Publisher shall produce the Journal in 8.5" by 11" trim size with single color (black) printing internally and at least two-color heavy stock on the cover. Single issues shall be at least _____ pages in length, with a goal of _____. The Publisher shall determine all other matters of form and style of the Journal and arrange for the copyediting, typesetting, proofreading, printing, binding, publication, sale and distribution, promotion, and advertising of the Journal. [The Publisher shall obtain Society's and the Editor's approval on the substantive content of any third-party advertising and promotional materials concerning the Journal. Any advertising or promotional materials not rejected within ten (10) business days of the mailing of the request for approval shall be deemed approved. Specific advertising and promotion materials only need to be approved for use by Society before the first use.]

(b) The Publisher shall, in its sole discretion, set the subscription rates (except for member rates set forth in 5(c)); online access fees; single, back-issue, and reprint prices; all fees for grants of subsidiary rights (to the extent the Publisher has been granted subsidiary rights under this Agreement); and all other terms for sale of the Journal through any medium, and may modify all such terms from time to time. The Publisher directly or through its representatives shall solicit subscriptions for the Journal in any manner that the Publisher elects.

(c)   The Publisher directly or through its representatives may solicit advertising for the Journal and shall set rates for advertising space in the Journal. [The editorial policy for the Journal, however, shall be to minimize the inclusion of advertising as befitting a scholarly publication. The Editor shall set a maximum limit for the amount of advertising that may be included.]

(d)   The Publisher is under no obligation to publish any Contribution from a Contributor who does not return a signed copy of the Copyright Transfer Agreement or to publish any Contribution that may, in the judgment of the Publisher, result in liability unacceptable to the Publisher, or otherwise be inappropriate.

(e)   The Publisher reserves the right to copyedit the Contribution, provided that the meaning of the text is not altered. The Publisher will in a timely manner provide the Editors and the Contributors with final edited Contributions prior to publication of any edited Contribution, for approval of the Publisher's modifications.

(f)   Color plates, if any, must be paid for by the Contributor at rates set by the Publisher.

(g)   The Publisher will distribute published copies of the Journal to the subscription list, including the Society membership list. The Publisher will make a reasonable effort to distribute copies to all members within three (3) weeks of publication. The non-member subscription list shall be the sole property of the Publisher.

4.   Ownership of the Journal

The Publisher is the sole and exclusive owner of the Journal and the material contained therein in all formats and media now known or hereafter devised, and all derivative works based thereon; the title, trademark and trade name, if any, of the Journal (except for the name, logo or seal of Society included therein which shall remain the sole property of Society); and all rights in and to the Journal, including its subscription list, copyright and renewals and extensions of copyright; and Society acknowledges that it has no rights in the Journal except as expressly provided herein.

All material in the Journal and the results of the services provided by Society shall, upon creation, vest in and be solely owned by the Publisher and shall constitute "a work made for hire" under the U.S. Copyright Act. To the extent, if any, that any rights, inclusive of the copyright, in the Journal or any portion thereof, do not qualify as "a work made for hire" or might otherwise vest in Society, Society hereby assigns and transfers such rights to the Publisher.

5. Compensation

In full consideration of the services to be provided hereunder and the transfer of rights contained herein:

(a) The Publisher agrees to pay to the Editor an editorial office expense grant of _____ per year, except that for the remainder of calendar year _____, the Editor will receive an editorial expense grant of $ _____. The grant for _____ shall be paid within thirty (30) days after the signing of this Editor's Agreement. Thereafter, the grant shall be paid in four equal advance installments of $ _____ each on January 1, April 1, July 1 and October 1 of each year, provided that the Agreement remains in effect for the quarter following payment. Should the Agreement be terminated within a quarter, the Editor may retain the editorial expense grants already paid. The Editorial office expense grant may be adjusted in future years by mutual agreement, subject to the editorial workload and economic requirements of the Journal.

(b) The Publisher shall give to the Editor and to each member of the Editorial Board a complimentary subscription to the Journal, for personal use only.

(c) Society agrees to pay a per-member publications fee of $_____ entitling each member to a subscription to the Journal. Society agrees to pay an additional annual $_____ mailing charge for each non-U.S. subscription. Society guarantees [a minimum of subscriptions] [a minimum payment of $_____] payable to the Publisher in quarterly advance installments on January 1, April 1, July 1, and October 1 of each year of the Term, provided that the Agreement remains in effect for the quarter following payment. The Publisher shall be entitled to the member publications fee even if the member elects not to receive the Journal. New members will be added retroactively on a calendar-year basis.

(d) Society shall have the right to purchase up to _____ additional copies of each issue for Society use at the same price as member subscriptions.

6. Term of Agreement

(a) This Agreement shall commence on the date this Agreement is signed by both parties and shall remain in effect for five (5) calendar publication years (hereinafter called the "Term"). Thereafter, the Term of the Agreement shall be automatically renewed on the same terms and conditions herein for succeeding five (5) calendar publication year periods unless either party notifies the other in writing that it does not wish to renew the Agreement, such notification to be given at least six (6) months prior to scheduled expiration of the initial Term or each five-year extension thereof.

(b)   Upon termination of this Agreement, the duties and obligations of each party shall terminate, except for the warranties in Paragraph 8 which shall survive such termination. The Editor or Society shall promptly turn over to the Publisher all Contributor manuscripts, subscription lists, other lists, records and documents, and all other materials relating to or in connection with the publication of the Journal. The Publisher shall have the right to appoint a new Editor or to otherwise continue the publication of the Journal as it sees fit without further duty or obligation to the Editor or Society provided, however, that the Publisher shall not use Society's name and logo on or in connection with any issues published after termination.

7.   Early Termination

(a)   During the Term, should the Publisher determine either (i) that there has not been a sufficient flow of quality manuscripts to permit a timely publication of two consecutive issues, or (ii) that the Journal is insufficiently profitable to justify its continued publication with Society, the Publisher shall notify Society in writing to this effect. Should Society, working with the Publisher, be unable to rectify the situation within a one hundred eighty (180) day period following this notice, then the Publisher may send a subsequent written notice to Society to this effect and the Publisher shall have the right to terminate this Agreement pursuant to Paragraph 6 above. Additionally, either party may terminate this Agreement (1) in the event of a material breach of this Agreement which is not cured within sixty (60) days of written notice, or (2) in the event the other party is or becomes bankrupt or insolvent.

(b)   In the event that the Publisher decides in its sole discretion that continued publication of the Journal is not economically viable, Society shall have the option to purchase the Journal from the Publisher in exchange for an assumption by Society of all of the subscription and contractual liability relating to the Journal, which liabilities must be explicitly explained to Society prior to any assumption by Society of the liabilities. Any revenue or other benefit attaching to any liabilities assumed by Society shall belong solely to Society.

8.   Warranties and Indemnities

(a)   Society warrants and represents that:

(i)   Society has full power and authority to make this Agreement and to perform its obligations hereunder; and

(ii)   any material prepared by or originating with Society for inclusion in the Journal shall be original, shall not infringe upon or violate any copyright, trademark, obligation of confidentiality or any other right or the privacy of others, or contain any libelous matter or material or matter or instructions that may cause harm or injury.

Society shall indemnify and hold the Publisher harmless from any and all claims, damages, liabilities, costs, and expenses (including counsel fees) that the Publisher incurs or sustains arising out of any breach by Society of the foregoing warranties.

(b)   The Publisher warrants and represents that:

(i)   the Publisher has full power and authority to make this Agreement and to perform its obligations hereunder; and

(ii)   any material prepared by or originating with the Publisher for inclusion in the Journal shall be original, shall not infringe upon or violate any copyright, trademark, obligation of confidentiality or any other right or the privacy of others or contain any libelous matter or material or matter or instructions that may cause harm or injury.

The Publisher shall indemnify and hold Society harmless from any and all claims, damages, liabilities, costs, and expenses (including counsel fees) that the Publisher incurs or sustains arising out of any breach by the Publisher of the foregoing warranties.

(c)   All representations, warranties and indemnities shall survive the termination of this Agreement.

9.   Notices

Any notice to be given hereunder shall be in writing and shall be mailed, certified or registered, return receipt requested, or delivered by hand or courier service addressed to the other party as follows:

For the Publisher: For Society:
[*address*]   [*address*]

With a copy to:
[*address*]   [*address*]

or to such new address for the Publisher or Society as shall become effective by written notification.

10.   General

(a)   The relationship between the parties is that of independent contractors and does not constitute a partnership or employment relationship, and neither party shall have any authority to bind the other in any way.

(b)   This Agreement shall inure to the benefit of the subsidiaries, successors, and assigns of the parties.

(c)   This Agreement constitutes the complete understanding of the parties. No modification or waiver of any provision shall be valid unless in writing and signed by both parties. Any waiver in one or more instances by either of the parties of any breach by the other of any terms or provisions contained in this Agreement shall not be considered a waiver of any succeeding or preceding breach.

(d)   This Agreement shall be construed and interpreted pursuant to the laws of the State of Virginia applicable to contracts wholly entered into and performed in the State of Virginia. Any legal action, suit, or proceeding arising out of or relating to this Agreement or the breach thereof shall be instituted in a court of competent jurisdiction in the state where the defendant resides and each party hereby consents and submits to the personal jurisdiction of such court, waives any objection to venue in such court, and consents to service of process by first-class mail at the last-known address of such party.

(e)   Paragraph headings are for convenience only and, being no part of this Agreement, shall not be used to modify, interpret, or change it.

AGREED AND ACCEPTED

SOCIETY

By: _____

Name: _____

Title: _____

Date: _____

PUBLISHER

By: _____

Name: _____

Title: _____

Date: _____

Journal Editor Agreement (No Royalty)

The following is a standard third-party journal editor agreement for a pub-lisher-owned journal, with optional clauses in brackets. All work performed by the editor is done on a "work-made-for-hire" basis (Clause 7). The agreement stipulates that the publisher will provide the editor with editorial office grants and an annual honorarium. If royalties are to be paid to the editor, appropriate language will have to be added.

Agreement

AGREEMENT made this _____ day of _____, 20__, by and between _____ (hereinafter referred to as the "Editor") and _____ (hereinafter referred to as the "Publisher") with respect to the editing of the Publisher's journal entitled _____ (hereinafter referred to as the "Journal").

The Parties hereto agree as follows:

1.   Editor's Duties

The Editor agrees to perform the following services with respect to the Journal, conscientiously, expeditiously, and to the best of his or her ability:

(a)   in consultation with the Publisher, to establish editorial policy and define the aims and scope of the Journal, decide upon procedures and standards for the acceptance of manuscripts, and obtain the Publisher's written approval of any material changes therefrom;

(b)   in consultation with the Publisher, to select an Editorial Board of up to _____ members which shall advise the Editor with respect to editorial policy and assist in reviewing Contributions, and to ensure that each such Editorial Board member shall authorize the use of his or her name as specified in Paragraph 12 below;

(c)   to solicit the submission of high quality contributions to the Journal (hereinafter referred to as the "Contribution(s)"), to invite review articles, select supplements, and to oversee any other special features of the Journal (book reviews, letters and so forth) as appropriate;

(d)   to evaluate submitted Contributions, in accordance with the editorial policy, and to select suitable Contributions for the review process for the Journal;

(e)   to arrange for and supervise the independent peer review of Contributions by [two or more reviewers who are] members of the Editorial Board or *ad hoc* reviewers, and to make or request the Contributor to make such revisions as the Editor and/or reviewers deem appropriate, and to reject any Contribution the Editor deems unsatisfactory;

(f) to ensure that each Contributor of an accepted Contribution transfers his or her copyright to the Publisher by sending each Contributor a Copyright Transfer Agreement in the form attached hereto as Exhibit A and incorporated herein, which, among other things, transfers to the Publisher the copyright in the Contribution(s), and by requiring that all Contributors sign and return to the Editor such Copyright Transfer Agreement; and to instruct each Contributor to obtain written permissions, on a form specified by the Publisher, to reprint or reproduce in all formats worldwide any copyrighted material which the Contributor incorporates in the Contribution(s);

(g) to assume editorial responsibility for the timely submission to the Publisher of the final Contributions in the English language in form, content and style satisfactory to the Publisher in accordance with the Publisher's current "Information for Authors" and in accordance with the annual production schedule to be set by the Publisher and agreed upon by the Editor. Illustrations shall be provided in a form suitable for direct use without redrawing, lettering, or retouching, [(color plates will be included when paid for separately by the author or by a separate subvention)];

(h) to correct page proofs received from the Publisher. The Publisher may charge Contributors for alterations after type has been set to the extent that the cost thereof is in excess of 10% of the original cost of composition. The Publisher will provide page proofs to the Editor for information purposes and for corrections within the same limits as for Contributors;

(i) to meet and confer with the Publisher's personnel at such times as the Publisher reasonably requests;

(j) to make best efforts to ensure the currency and accuracy of the contents of each Contribution provided to the Publisher for each issue of the Journal as of the date on which the issue's contents are forwarded to the Publisher and to perform all other editorial services usually performed by journal editors; and

(k) to provide office services at the Editor's own office for the receipt of Contributions, routing them to members of the Editorial Board and *ad hoc* referees and preparing final manuscripts. Such office will maintain records and statistics regarding the status of Contributions submitted to the Journal and will provide the Publisher with annual status reports.

2.   Publisher's Responsibilites

All publishing activities of the Journal in any medium shall be the responsibility of the Publisher, including but not limited to the following:

(a)   The Publisher shall determine the typography, format, frequency of publication and style of the Journal and shall arrange for the typesetting, proofreading, printing, binding, publication, manufacture and packaging, sale and distribution, transmission, promotion and advertising of the Journal. The Publisher shall have the exclusive right to exercise any or all of these functions itself or to enter into any contracts or subcontracts with third parties to perform some or all of these functions.

(b)   The Publisher shall, in its sole discretion, set the subscription rates, single, back issue, and reproduction and reprint prices, all fees for grants of subsidiary rights, and all other terms of sale or license for the exploitation of all rights in and to the Journal and the material contained therein in any medium, and may modify all such terms from time to time. The Publisher directly or through its representatives shall solicit subscriptions for the Journal and all other sales and licenses hereunder in any manner that the Publisher elects.

(c)   The Publisher directly or through its representatives may solicit advertising for the Journal.

(d)   The Publisher is under no obligation to publish any Contribution from a prospective Contributor [including material contributed by the Editor] who does not return a signed copy of the Copyright Transfer Agreement, or any Contribution which is not of literary quality reasonably acceptable to the Publisher or in form and content satisfactory to the Publisher in its sole discretion for inclusion in the Journal or which may result in liability unacceptable to the Publisher in its judgment.

(e)   The Publisher reserves the right to edit, alter or add to Contributions, provided the scientific meaning of the text is not altered. The Publisher will notify the Editor or the Contributor, as appropriate, prior to publication of any edited Contribution, if any editing of a substantive nature is undertaken.

(f)   The Publisher will maintain an online system for the submission and review of manuscripts.

3.   Frequency of Issues and Number of Pages

(a)   The Journal will be published [_____] times per year, with an average of approximately [_____] printed editorial text pages in each issue, in an $8^1/_2$" by 11" format. Any subsequent changes in the size of the Journal or the number of volumes, issues, pages or format will be made by the Publisher after due consultation with the Editor at least six (6) months in advance of the publication year in which the change is introduced.

(b)   Supplemental issues, or pages in excess of the annual page budget established by the Publisher in consultation with the Editor, may be included in the Journal, subject to the Publisher's prior approval and taking into account the editorial and economic requirements of the Journal. Such requests for supplemental issues or pages to appear in the Journal should be submitted to the Publisher by the Editor not later than June 1st of the year preceding that calendar year in which the material would be scheduled to appear as part of the subscription plan for the Journal. Requests for supplemental issues or pages received after that date will be considered by the Publisher for publication in later years, or within a given calendar year if costs can be covered by a separate subvention from outside sources, at costs set by the Publisher.

4.   Editorial Office Budget

The Publisher, after consultation with the Editor, shall establish an annual budget to provide the Editor with the following:

(a)   reasonable office expenses, approved in advance in the annual budget, not to exceed _____ to cover telephone, fax, postage, office supplies, and other reasonable expenses connected with the Editor's responsibilities herein which shall be reimbursed only upon submission to the Publisher of adequate invoices or receipts by the Editor therefor in a form acceptable to the Publisher; and the Publisher agrees to reimburse such expenses within thirty (30) days of submission;[2] and

(b)   letterhead stationery for the Editor and other printed forms for the operation of the Journal's editorial office without cost to the Editor. [*;and*]

[(c)   The Publisher agrees to help support an annual meeting of the Editorial Board of the Journal.]

Any editorial support staff employed by the Editor shall be for the Editor's own account and in no event shall any editorial support staff be deemed to have been employed by the Publisher or engaged by the Editor for the account or on behalf of the Publisher.

---

2 Authors note: Many Publishers prefer to pay a set fee on a predetermined schedule to avoid the hassle of reimbursements.

5. Honorarium and Grant

(a)   In consideration of the services to be provided hereunder and the transfer of rights contained herein, the Publisher shall pay the Editor an annual honorarium in the amount of $_____ in equal quarterly installments.

(b)   The Publisher shall provide additional annual grants to defray start-up costs and other expenses, including journal-related travel, payable as follows:

6. Complimentary Subscriptions; Offprints

(a)   The Publisher shall give to the Editor and to each member of the Editorial Board a complimentary subscription to the Journal, for personal use only. In addition, the Publisher shall, upon request, supply the Editor with a reasonable number of complimentary copies of selected issues of the Journal for discretionary use in the solicitation of manuscripts and the like.

(b)   The Publisher shall offer Contributors the opportunity to order offprints of their articles in quantities of one hundred (100) or multiples thereof, at the Publisher's standard rates, and will send them order forms in advance of publication of their articles.

7. Ownership and Copyright of the Journal

(a)   The Publisher is the sole and exclusive owner of the Journal, including the title, trademark, tradename, its subscription or circulation lists, copyrights and renewals or extensions of copyright, the Contributions, all inventory and all other materials and all rights of any nature whatsoever relating to the Journal. The Publisher has the full and exclusive rights comprised in the copyright of the Journal and the material contained therein, and all other rights pertaining thereto, throughout the world, in perpetuity, including but not limited to the rights to publish, manufacture, distribute, transmit, promote and sell the Journal and derivative works based thereon, in all forms and media whether presently in existence or later developed and to sell or license the exercise of any of these rights including, but not limited to, the right to grant or license any reprint, subsidiary, electronic and other rights in and to the Journal throughout the world.

(b)   The Journal and all material contained therein and the work product of the Editor and the Editor's staff produced hereunder shall constitute a "work-made-for-hire" under the U.S. Copyright Act and all rights comprised therein shall automatically, upon creation, vest in and thereafter be solely owned by the Publisher. To the extent, if any, that the Journal and/or any Contribution or other material contained therein do not qualify as a "work-made-for-hire" or copyright or other proprietary rights thereto might otherwise vest in the Editor, the Editor hereby grants, assigns and transfers all such rights exclusively and in perpetuity to the Publisher, in all languages and formats, in all media of expression now known or later developed, throughout the world.

(c) If either the Publisher or the Editor believes that the copyright of any issue of the Journal has been infringed, the party so believing shall notify the other thereof. The Editor shall, at the sole cost and expense of the Publisher, render reasonable assistance to the Publisher in any infringement proceedings which the Publisher chooses to bring. Such assistance may consist of aiding the Publisher or its representative in determining the nature of the infringement, testifying as a witness, or other assistance.

8. Term and Termination

Unless sooner terminated as provided below, this Agreement shall commence on the date first above written and remain in effect for [___] [calendar publication years] [until _____]. Thereafter, the Agreement shall be automatically renewed on the same terms and conditions contained herein on a calendar publication year basis for succeeding one-year periods unless either party notifies the other in writing that it does not wish to renew the Agreement, such notification to be given at least six months prior to scheduled expiration of the initial term or each annual extension thereof.

9. Early Termination

Notwithstanding the above, this Agreement may be terminated early,

(a)   upon the Editor's death or incapacity;

(b)   by the Publisher if, in the Publisher's judgment, the Editor is not meeting his/her obligations or performing his/her duties as outlined in this Agreement, including but not limited to the Editor's failure to obtain sufficient acceptable manuscript material in time to permit publication of two consecutive issues of the Journal on schedule, provided, however, that (1) the Publisher has given the Editor written notice setting forth his/her unsatisfactory performance, and (2) the Editor has not improved such performance to the Publisher's reasonable satisfaction within ninety (90) days of receipt of such notice;

(c)   by resignation of the Editor upon six (6) months prior written notice to the Publisher; or

(d)   by either party for breach of any material provision of this Agreement (i) for which written notice is given to the breaching party, and (ii) such breach is not corrected within ninety (90) days.

10. Post-Termination

(a)   The Publisher, within ninety (90) days after termination of this Agreement, shall pay to the Editor all expense reimbursements due him/her which have accrued as of such termination date.

(b)   Upon termination of this Agreement, the Publisher shall have the right to appoint a new Editor or to otherwise continue the publication of the Journal as it sees fit without further duty or obligation to the Editor. The Editor or the Editor's personal representative shall promptly return to the Publisher all Contributor manuscripts, lists, records and documents and all other materials relating to or in connection with the publication of the Journal.

11. Warranties and Indemnities

(a)   The Editor warrants and represents that:

  (i)   the Editor has full power and authority to make this Agreement and to perform his or her obligations hereunder;

  (ii)   no organization for which the Editor works as a regular salaried employee shall have any rights in or control over the Editor's work in the Journal, and the Editor's personal services on behalf of the Journal as set forth herein do not violate any agreement between the Editor and any employer of the Editor;

  (iii)   any material written by the Editor for the Journal shall be original, shall not infringe upon or violate any copyright, trademark, trade secret, obligation of confidentiality or any other right or the privacy of others or contain any libelous matter or material or matter or instructions that may cause harm or injury;

  (iv)   the Editor will not include in the Journal any Contribution(s) that the Editor believes or has reason to know or suspect may infringe upon or violate any copyright, trademark, trade secret or obligation of confidentiality or other right or the privacy of others or contain any libelous matter or contain such material or matter or instructions that may cause harm or injury;

  (v)   to the best of the Editor's knowledge all statements asserted as fact in the Journal are either true or based upon generally accepted professional research and any advice, recipe, formula or instruction contained in it will not, if followed accurately, cause any injury, illness or damage to the user.

(b)   The Editor agrees to indemnify and hold the Publisher harmless from any and all claims, damages, liabilities, costs and expenses (including legal fees) that the Publisher incurs or sustains arising out of any breach or alleged breach by the Editor of the foregoing warranties or out of the use of any materials prepared by the Editor hereunder.

(c)   Each party shall promptly inform the other of any claim made against either which, if sustained, would constitute a breach of any of the Editor's warranties. The Publisher shall have the right to defend any such claim, action or proceeding with counsel of its own choice and, after consultation with the Editor, to settle any such claim. The Editor shall fully cooperate with the Publisher in such defense and may join in such defense with counsel of the Editor's selection, at the Editor's expense.

All representations, warranties and indemnities shall survive the termination of the Agreement.

12.   Name and Likeness

The Publisher shall have the right and may grant to others the right to use, in any medium, the Editor's name, likeness, biographical information and professional credits, in connection with the Journal or the promotion or advertising thereof, and the Editor shall obtain for the Publisher the same rights with respect to Editorial Board members.

13.   Noncompetition

During the term of this Agreement, the Editor, without the Publisher's written consent, shall not perform services as Editor, advisor or consultant for any other journal that might, in the Publisher's judgment, be directly competitive with the Journal.

14.   Notices

Any notice, request, statement or other communication to be given hereunder to any party shall be in writing addressed to the party as follows:

For the Publisher:

with a copy to:

For the Editor:

with a copy to:

and any such notice, request, statement or other communication, shall be deemed to have been given when received, except that if mailed by registered or certified mail, return receipt requested, or by overnight courier service, it shall be deemed to have been given when mailed as aforesaid.

15.   General

(a)   The relationship between the parties is that of independent contractors and does not constitute a partnership or employment relationship, and the Editor shall have no authority to bind the Publisher in any way. No payments under this Agreement shall be deemed to be compensation or salary to the

Editor entitling the Editor or the editorial support staff to any employee benefits from the Publisher. [The Editor is not authorized to make any commitments on behalf of the Publisher without the Publisher's prior written consent. Only the Publisher may accept Contributions for publication.]

(b)   The engagement of the Editor is personal and the services to be performed by the Editor are special and unique and, therefore, the rights hereunder granted to the Editor are not assignable nor may the obligations or duties imposed be delegated without the prior written consent of the Publisher.

(c)   Except as provided in subparagraph (b) above, this Agreement shall inure to the benefit of the heirs, successors, and permitted assigns of the Editor and the subsidiaries, successors, and assigns of the Publisher.

(d)   This Agreement constitutes the complete understanding of the parties. No modification or waiver of any provision shall be valid unless in writing and signed by both parties. Any waiver in one or more instances by either of the parties of any breach by the other of any terms or provisions contained in this Agreement shall not be considered a waiver of any succeeding or preceding breach.

(e)   This Agreement shall be construed and interpreted pursuant to the laws of the State of New York applicable to contracts wholly entered into and performed in the State of New York. Any legal action, suit or proceeding arising out of or relating to this Agreement or the breach thereof shall be instituted in a court of competent jurisdiction in New York County in the State of New York and each party hereby consents and submits to the personal jurisdiction of such court, waives any objection to venue in such court and consents to service of process by first class mail at the last known address of such party.

(f)   Paragraph headings are for convenience only and, being no part of this Agreement, shall not be used to modify, interpret or change it.

AGREED AND ACCEPTED

EDITOR   **PUBLISHER**

By: _____   By: _____

Date: _____   Title: _____

SS#: _____   Date: _____

Newsletter Editor Agreement—Multiple Scholarly Newsletters

The following newsletter editor agreement is for an editor who is preparing two newsletters. The agreement contemplates that the editor will actually write all of the content published in the newsletters (Clause 2(b)), but incorporates language for the possibility of material being contributed by others (e.g., Clause 2(c)). Because these newsletters are scholarly, the agreement also contains more detailed language regarding an editorial board (Clauses 2(e), 2(h), 6(b), 7, and 12) than is provided in Form 2.4.

Agreement

AGREEMENT dated _____, 20__, by and between _____ (hereinafter referred to as the "Editor") and _____ (hereinafter referred to as the "Publisher") with respect to the editing of the Publisher's newsletters _____ and _____ (hereinafter referred to as the "Newsletters").

The Parties hereto agree as follows:

1. Ownership and Copyright of the Newsletters

(a)   The Publisher is the sole and exclusive owner of the Newsletters including their titles, trademarks, tradenames, and the goodwill related thereto, subscription or circulation lists, copyrights and renewals or extensions of copyright, Contributions as defined below, all inventory and all other materials and rights of any nature whatsoever relating to the Newsletters. The Publisher has the exclusive right in perpetuity to publish, manufacture, distribute, promote and sell the Newsletters in all forms and media whether presently in existence or later developed, throughout the world and to sell or license the exercise of any of these rights including, but not limited to, the right to grant or license any reprint, subsidiary and other rights in and to the Newsletters throughout the universe.

(b)   The Newsletters and all material contained therein and the work product of the Editor and the Editor's staff produced hereunder shall constitute a "work-made-for-hire" under the U.S. Copyright Act and all rights comprised therein shall automatically, upon creation, vest in and thereafter be solely owned by the Publisher. To the extent, if any, that any rights, inclusive of the copyright, in and to the Newsletters, the material contained therein or any portion thereof, do not qualify as a "work-made-for-hire" or might otherwise vest in the Editor, the Editor hereby assigns and transfers all such rights in perpetuity throughout the universe to the Publisher.

(c)   If either the Publisher or the Editor believes that the copyright of any issue of the Newsletters has been infringed, the party so believing shall notify the other thereof. The Editor shall, at the sole cost and expense of the Publisher, render reasonable assistance to the Publisher in any infringement proceedings which the Publisher chooses to bring. Such assistance may consist of aiding the Publisher or its representative in determining the nature of the infringement, testifying as a witness, or other assistance.

2.   Editors's Duties

The Publisher hereby commissions the Editor and the Editor agrees to perform the following services with respect to the Newsletters, conscientiously, expeditiously, and to the best of her ability, subject to the Publisher's overall direction:

(a)   in consultation with the Publisher, establish editorial policy and define the aims and scope of the Newsletters, decide upon procedures and standards for the acceptance of manuscripts, and obtain the Publisher's approval of any material changes therefrom;

(b)   write and edit all content for both Newsletters in a form and style acceptable to the Publisher;

(c)   although the parties currently intend that the Editor shall continue to write and edit all content for the Newsletters, should the Publisher decide in the future to include in the Newsletters material written by others, the Editor shall solicit the submission of high quality contributions to the Newsletters (hereinafter referred to as "Contribution(s)"), invite articles, and oversee any other special features of the Newsletters (book reviews, letters, and so forth) as appropriate, and shall have each author of a Contribution (hereinafter referred to as "Contributor(s)") execute and deliver a Copyright Transfer Agreement or Work for Hire Agreement in a form provided by the Publisher. Any fees paid to Contributor(s) shall be paid by the Publisher as agreed to in advance by the Publisher;

(d)   assume editorial responsibility for the timely submission of camera ready copy of each final newsletter manuscript in the English language in form, content and style satisfactory to the Publisher and in accordance with the annual schedule to be set by the Publisher and agreed upon by the Editor. Illustrations shall be provided in a form suitable for direct use without redrawing, lettering, or retouching;

(e)   in consultation with the Publisher, select an Editorial Board which shall advise the Editor with respect to editorial policy and content and secure from each such member the authorization for use of his or her name as specified in Paragraph 12 below;

(f) meet and confer with the Publisher's personnel at such times as the Publisher reasonably requests;

(g) make best efforts to ensure the currency and accuracy of the contents of each manuscript provided to the Publisher for each issue of the Newsletters as of the date on which the issue's contents are forwarded to the Publisher and perform all other editorial services usually performed by Newsletters editors; and

(h) provide office services at her own office for the receipt of Contributions, if any, route them to members of the Editorial Board and *ad hoc* referees and prepare final manuscripts. Such office will maintain records and statistics regarding the status of Contributions submitted to the Newsletters and will provide the Publisher with annual status reports, in accordance with the Publisher's regular practices.

3. Publisher's Responsibilities

All publishing activities of the Newsletters shall be the responsibility of the Publisher, including but not limited to the following:

(a) The Publisher shall determine the typography, format, frequency of publication and style of the Newsletters and shall arrange for the typesetting, proofreading, printing, binding, publication, sale and distribution, promotion and advertising of the Newsletters. The Publisher shall have the exclusive right to do so, subject only to Paragraph 4 below, and to enter into any contracts or subcontracts with third parties to perform some or all of these functions.

(b) The Publisher shall, in its sole discretion, set the subscription rates, single, back issue, and reprint prices, all fees for grants of subsidiary rights, and all other terms of sale for the Newsletters through any medium, and may modify all such terms from time to time. The Publisher directly or through its representatives shall solicit subscriptions for the Newsletters in any manner that the Publisher elects.

(c) The Publisher directly or through its representatives may solicit advertising for the Newsletters.

(d) The Publisher is under no obligation to publish any Contribution from a prospective Contributor who does not return a signed copy of the Copyright Transfer Agreement, or any Contribution which is not of literary quality reasonably acceptable to the Publisher or in form and content satisfactory to the

Publisher in its sole discretion for inclusion in the Newsletters or which may result in liability unacceptable to the Publisher in its judgment.

(e)   The Publisher reserves the right to edit, alter or add to Contributions or the text of the Newsletters, provided the meaning of the text is not altered. The Publisher will notify the Editor or the Contributor, as appropriate, prior to publication of any edited Contribution, if any editing of a substantive nature is undertaken.

4.   Frequency of Issues and Number of Pages

(a)   The Newsletters each will be published _____ times per year with an average of approximately _____ printed editorial text (i.e., non-advertising) pages in each issue in $8^{1}/_{2}''$ by 11″ format. Any subsequent changes in the size of the Newsletters or the number of volumes, issues, pages or format will be made by the Publisher.

(b)   Supplemental issues or pages in excess of the annual page budget established by the Publisher in consultation with the Editor may be included in the Newsletters, subject to the Publisher's prior approval and taking into account the editorial and economic requirements of the Newsletters.

5.   Editorial Office Budget

(a)   The Editor shall be paid $_____ per year, paid quarterly, to cover all costs associated with the performance of this Agreement including but not limited to office expenses and subcontractors as the Editor deems necessary.

(b)   The Publisher will provide the Editor with stationery for correspondence relating to the Newsletters and with all forms and agreements necessary for the operations of the Newsletters.

6.   Compensation

In addition to the money for the editorial office budget, as consideration for the services to be provided hereunder and any transfer of rights contained herein:

(a)   The Publisher shall pay to the Editor a royalty of ___% of net income received by the Publisher. "Net income" shall be defined as the moneys received and earned by the Publisher in U.S. dollars from all sources, including advertisements and subscriptions less any relevant discounts to subscription agents, bank charges for processing payments from foreign countries, sales tax, postal surcharge or handling, commissions, credits, and excise or similar taxes.

(b)   No royalties shall be paid on subscriptions to the Newsletters furnished free to the Editor or Editorial Board, to advertisers and potential advertisers, to abstracting and indexing services, or to others.

(c)   Payments to the Editor of the royalties set forth herein shall be made semi-annually, on or about June 30 and December 31st, for royalties due for the preceding six months ending April 30 and October 31 and shall be accompanied by an appropriate Statement of Account. The Publisher may take credit for royalties paid on bad debts, or debts incurred and owing to Publisher by the Editor. If the balance due the Editor for any royalty period is less than $10, the Publisher will make no accounting payment until the next royalty period at the end of which the cumulative balance has reached $10.

(d)   Upon written request by the Editor made reasonably in advance, the Editor's designated certified public accountant may examine the Publisher's royalty records relating to any Statement of Account for the Newsletters, for the twenty-four months immediately preceding such examination. No more than one such examination may be made within any twelve-month period and must be conducted at a reasonable time during the Publisher's normal business hours. The Publisher is not required to retain royalty records for a period of more than two (2) years following any Statement of Account, such Statement being deemed conclusive after the lapse of such two-year period.

7.   Complimentary Subscriptions

The Publisher shall give to the Editor ten complimentary subscriptions to the Newsletters for personal use only, and the Publisher shall give to each member of the Editorial Board one complimentary subscription to the relevant Newsletter for personal use only. In addition, the Publisher shall, upon request, supply the Editor with a reasonable number of complimentary copies of selected issues of the Newsletters for discretionary use in the solicitation of manuscripts and the like.

8.   Term and Termination

Unless sooner terminated as provided below, the Agreement shall commence on the date first above written and remain in effect for five (5) years from that date. Thereafter, the Agreement shall be automatically renewed on the same terms and conditions herein for successive one year terms unless either party notifies the other in writing that it does not wish to renew the Agreement, such notification to be given at least six months prior to expiration of the initial Agreement or each renewal thereof.

9. Early Termination

(a)   Notwithstanding the above, if, in the Publisher's reasonable judgment, the Editor is not substantially meeting her obligations or performing her duties as outlined in the Agreement, provided, however, that (1) the Publisher has given the Editor thirty (30) days written notice setting forth in detail her unsatisfactory performance and (2) the Editor has not improved such performance to the Publisher's reasonable satisfaction; then, in any such case, the Publisher, at its sole discretion, shall have the option to terminate the Agreement or to appoint a co-editor whose remuneration shall be paid out of the royalties and fees due to the Editor hereunder.

(b)   The Agreement shall terminate immediately upon the death or incapacity of the Editor.

(c)   Subject to subsection 9(a) above, the Agreement may be terminated early by either party for breach of any material provision of this Agreement, provided written notice is given to the breaching party, and such breach is not corrected to the reasonable satisfaction of the non-breaching party within ninety (90) days.

(d)   The Agreement may be terminated early by either party upon three (3) months prior written notice to the other party.

10. Post-Termination

(a)   The Publisher, within ninety (90) days after termination of this Agreement, shall pay to the Editor all fees, royalties and reasonable expense reimbursements due her which have accrued as of such termination date, apportioned for those issues of the Newsletters that are published as of the termination date.

(b)   Upon termination of the Agreement, the Publisher shall have the right to appoint a new Editor or to otherwise continue the publication of the Newsletters as it sees fit without further duty or obligation to the Editor. The Editor or the Editor's personal representative shall promptly return to the Publisher all manuscripts, lists, records and documents and all other materials relating to or in connection with the publication of the Newsletters.

(c)   If notice of termination is given by the Publisher pursuant to subparagraphs 9(a) or (c) above or by the Editor or Publisher pursuant to subparagraph 9(d) above, the Editor shall not edit any competing Newsletters for a period of one year after such termination.

11.   Warranties and Indemnities

(a)   The Editor warrants and represents that:

   (i)   the Editor has full power and authority to make the Agreement and to perform her obligations hereunder;

  (ii)   no organization for which the Editor works as a regular salaried employee shall have any rights in or control over the Editor's work in the Newsletters, and the Editor's personal services on behalf of the Newsletters as set forth herein do not violate any agreement between the Editor and any employer of the Editor;

 (iii)   any material written by the Editor for the Newsletters shall be original, and shall not infringe upon or violate any copyright, trademark, obligation of confidentiality or any other right or the privacy of others or contain any libelous matter or material or matter or instructions that may cause harm or injury; and

 (iv)   The Editor will not include in the Newsletters any Contribution(s) that the Editor believes, or has reason to suspect, infringes upon or violates any copyright, trademark or obligation of confidentiality or other right or the privacy of others or contain any libelous matter or contain such material or matter or instructions that may cause harm or injury.

(b)   The Editor shall indemnify and hold the Publisher harmless from any and all claims, damages, liabilities, costs and expenses (including reasonable counsel fees) that the Publisher incurs or sustains arising out of any breach by the Editor of the foregoing warranties or out of the use of any materials prepared by the Editor hereunder; and

(c)   All representations, warranties and indemnities shall survive the termination of the Agreement for any reason.

12.   Name and Likeness

The Publisher shall have the right and may grant to others the right to use, in any medium, the Editor's name, likeness and professional credits, in connection with the Newsletters or the promotion or advertising thereof, and the Editor shall obtain for the Publisher the same rights with respect to Editorial Board members.

13.   Noncompetition/Confidentiality

During the term of this Agreement and for the additional time set forth in Paragraph 10, the Editor shall not own, manage, operate, control, serve as an advisor, author, editor, employee, partner, officer, director or consultant for any business entity, other than the Publisher, engaged in competition with the Newsletters.

14. Notices

Any notice, request, statement or other communication to be given hereunder to any party shall be mailed, certified or registered, return receipt requested, or delivered by hand or overnight courier service addressed to the other party as follows:

For the Publisher:	For the Editor:
[address]	[address]
with a copy to:	with a copy to:
[address]	[address]

15. General

(a)   The relationship between the parties is that of independent contractors and does not constitute a partnership or employment relationship, and the Editor shall have no authority to bind the Publisher in any way. No payments under the Agreement shall be deemed to be compensation or salary to the Editor entitling her editorial support staff to employee benefits from the Publisher.

(b)   The engagement of the Editor is personal and the services to be performed by the Editor are special and unique and, therefore, the rights hereunder granted to the Editor are not assignable nor may the obligations or duties imposed be delegated without the prior written consent of the Publisher.

(c)   Except as provided in subparagraph 15(b) above, the Agreement shall inure to the benefit of the heirs, successors, and permitted assigns of the Editor and the subsidiaries, successors, and assigns of the Publisher.

(d)   The Agreement constitutes the complete understanding of the parties. No modification or waiver of any provision shall be valid unless in writing and signed by both parties. Any waiver in one or more instances by either of the parties of any breach by the other of any terms or provisions contained in this Agreement shall not be considered a waiver of any succeeding or preceding breach.

(e)   The Agreement shall be construed and interpreted pursuant to the laws of the State of New York and of the United States Courts located in the State of New York without reference to the State of New York's choice of law rules. Any legal action, suit or proceeding arising out of or relating to this Agreement or the breach thereof shall be instituted in a court of competent jurisdiction in the county in which the defendant maintains its principal place of business and each party hereby consents and submits to the personal jurisdiction of such court, waives any objection to venue in such court and consents to service of process by first class mail at the last known address of such party.

(f)   Paragraph headings are for convenience only and, being no part of the Agreement, shall not be used to modify, interpret or change it.

AGREED AND ACCEPTED

EDITOR   **PUBLISHER**

By: _____   By: _____
                                              [name]
                                              [title]

SS#: _____

Newsletter Editor Agreement

The following newsletter editor agreement is similar in scope to Form 2.3 but has a slightly different "feel." In addition to the obvious difference that this agreement is for only one newsletter, the agreement contemplates that more material in the newsletter will be written by people other than by the editor (e.g., Clause 2). The agreement is also more publisher-biased, in that the publisher may terminate without cause on 30 days' written notice, but the editor must provide at least 90 days' notice to terminate (Clause 19). The agreement also contains strict, concrete penalties for late delivery of manuscripts (Clause 14), which are lacking in Form 2.3.

Newsletter Editor Agreement

AGREEMENT made this _____ day of _____, 20__, between _____ (hereinafter called the "Publisher"), a Delaware corporation having its principal place of business at _____, and _____ (hereinafter called the "Editor"), for the services of the latter as editor of Publisher's monthly newsletter tentatively titled _____ (hereinafter called the "Work").

The rights and responsibilities of Publisher and the Editor are as follows:

1. The Editor shall assess the field of _____ for appropriate material for publication in the Work.

2. The Editor shall write and/or acquire original articles (or, on occasion, previously published material for reprinting, when mutually agreed by Publisher and the Editor) on behalf of Publisher for publication in the Work. All authors are subject to Publisher's prior written approval. All articles and materials must be acceptable to the Publisher in form and content. Any compensation to authors shall be the sole responsibility of the Editor.

3. The Editor shall deliver to Publisher no later than thirty (30) days prior to the publication date specified by Publisher for each issue of the Work one copy of a complete manuscript for that issue, along with any and all permissions from other persons as may be required for publication of any copyrighted or other material contained in the issue. The manuscript (as well as all permissions) shall be submitted in designated electronic format and must be acceptable to Publisher in form and content, and the manuscript shall be ready for editing and composition, and of sufficient length to yield an eight-page, typeset newsletter (approximately thirty (30) typed manuscript pages) including all charts, tables, graphs, or other types of art, which must, to the greatest extent possible, be camera ready. Final specifications for length and format will be furnished the Editor by the Publisher.

It is understood that the submitted manuscript shall be the Editor's final draft, and that the manuscript shall be clean and can be edited without retyping. The Editor will be available for consultation with the Publisher upon Publisher's receipt of the manuscript.

4. The Work shall be considered a work made for hire, and all articles written and/or acquired by the Editor pursuant to this Agreement shall be considered as works made for hire and as contributions to a collective work (except for previously published materials reprinted in the Work by mutual agreement between the Publisher and the Editor where an element of the permission to republish granted by the copyright owner is that the copyright shall not belong to the Publisher). The Publisher shall thus have all right, title, and interest in and to the Work and all articles contained therein including, but not limited to, the copyright thereto. Such copyright shall cover, without limitation, the right to create any rendition of the Work in print, electronic, or other media of any kind whatsoever now known or hereafter developed. In the event that the Work or any article contained therein is not deemed a work made for hire, the Editor hereby grants to the Publisher all right, title, and interest in the Work and all articles contained therein including, but not limited to, the copyright thereto worldwide, in all media now known and hereafter devised.

5. The Editor shall also be responsible for securing copyright transfer agreements from all authors contributing to each issue of the Work (including guest editors) and for delivering such agreements to the Publisher along with the manuscript for the issue. The Editor shall use the Copyright Transfer Form shown as Attachment A hereto to secure the copyright transfers described in the preceding sentence.

6. The Editor shall see to it that each issue of the Work contains no material from other works without the prior written permission of the owner of such material where such other work is copyrighted or where such permission is otherwise required. Such permissions will be obtained by the Editor in form and content acceptable to the Publisher and delivered to the Publisher along with the manuscript for each issue of the Work. The Editor will notify the Publisher in writing of all materials in each issue of the Work that were taken from documents prepared or published by the United States Government.

7. Except for materials described in the first and last sentences of the preceding paragraph, the Editor warrants that the articles submitted for publication in the monthly issues of the Work will be original works of authorship and that to the best of the Editor's knowledge, the authors thereof have full authority to grant to the Publisher all right, title, and interest in and to them pursuant to paragraph 4 of this Agreement. The Editor warrants to the best of his/her knowledge that the Work contains no libelous, obscene, or any other unlawful materials, violates no common law or statutory copyright or any other property or personal right whatsoever of any other person or entity, and is not in the public domain, and further warrants that all statements asserted in the Work as facts are true or based upon reasonable research for accuracy.

The Editor further warrants that he/she has full power and authority to enter into this Agreement.

8. The Editor agrees to indemnify and hold harmless the Publisher, its licensees and assignees, from all costs, expenses (including attorneys' fees and expenses), losses, liabilities, damages, and settlements arising out of or in connection with any claim or suit based on allegations which, if true, would constitute a breach of any one or more of the above warranties. Until any claim or suit to which such indemnity may pertain has been resolved, the Publisher may withhold any sums due to the Editor under this or any other agreement between the Editor and the Publisher. The Editor will cooperate fully with the defense or prosecution of any lawsuit between the Publisher and any third party involving the Work.

In no event shall the Publisher be obligated to publish anything which in its opinion breaches any one or more of the above warranties. In the event of a breach by the Editor of any one or more of the above warranties, the Publisher shall be entitled to terminate this Agreement by prior written notice to the Editor, without any liability whatsoever on the Publisher's part. In the event that the Publisher shall have advanced any monies to the Editor pursuant to this Agreement, the Editor shall return all such monies within ninety (90) days after receipt of a notice of termination pursuant to this paragraph.

9. The first issue of the Work will be published on _____, 20___. Publisher will set, in writing, all publication dates for subsequent issues and any additional production deadlines for all issues. Publisher may alter, in writing, any and all publication dates and production deadlines upon request or as it deems necessary.

10. The Editor shall promptly read, correct, and return the copyedited manuscripts in accordance with the production deadlines prescribed in writing by Publisher, or any authorized alteration of such deadlines. If the Editor fails to perform these duties on schedule, Publisher may proceed as if the Editor had performed them.

11. Subject to the terms and conditions herein, the Publisher will publish and market the Work at the Publisher's own expense. It shall be published under the imprint of the Publisher, and marketed in the style and manner and at the price that the Publisher, in its sole discretion, deems appropriate. The Publisher shall not be liable for delays in publication or marketing caused by circumstances beyond its control.

12. The Editor grants to the Publisher the right to use the Editor's name and likeness, and relevant information about the Editor (including, without limitation, the Editor's affiliation), in each issue of the Work, in connection with the Publisher's marketing thereof, and in any promotional material distributed on its behalf, and the Editor shall provide the same to the Publisher upon reasonable request therefor. The Editor will cooperate with promotional campaigns and other marketing activities by promptly completing an Author Questionnaire and by providing, upon request, lists of upcoming topics and input for reader surveys.

13. The Editor understands and agrees that if a guest editor performs any services for any issue of the Work, the Editor nonetheless remains fully responsible for all of the Editor's obligations under this Agreement.

14. Upon delivery of the complete and acceptable manuscript for each monthly issue of the Work according to the deadline set pursuant to paragraph 3 (or any authorized alteration of such deadline pursuant to paragraph 9), Publisher agrees to pay the Editor the sum of $____ (the "Monthly Fee"). It is understood that the annual total of such fees shall be considered an advance against royalties due the Editor under the terms of this Agreement. Should royalties due the Editor be less than the total advanced, the Editor will retain the fees advanced with no sum due Publisher. The Editor will also be provided with a monthly stipend of $____ for expenses incurred in preparation of the Work. This amount shall not be considered an advance against royalties.

Missing any deadline for any issue of the Work as set forth in paragraphs 3 or 9 will result in the following penalty schedule of amounts to be deducted from the Monthly Fee.

Up to five business workdays late	225% penalty of Editor's fee
Six to ten business workdays late	250% penalty of Editor's fee
Eleven to fifteen business workdays late	275% penalty of Editor's fee
Twenty business workdays late	2100% penalty of Editor's fee

Should the Editor fail to deliver the Work twenty-one or more business workdays late, the Publisher may terminate this Agreement at will.

15. Publisher agrees to pay the Editor, as a royalty, a designated percentage of net subscription revenues actually received by Publisher, based upon the number of paid subscriptions to the Work, according to the following schedule:
   [*add royalty schedule*]
   The number of paid subscriptions to the Work shall be determined for each calendar year by dividing the audited net subscription revenue for the Work for that year (as recorded on the Publisher's books as of December 31 of that year) by the prevailing average subscription rate for the Work during that year (as provided in Attachment B which is hereby incorporated into this Agreement).

Net subscription revenue means gross subscription revenue less returns, discounts, shipping and handling, sales and similar taxes and bad debt.

16. Publisher shall mail to the Editor an annual statement covering the net subscription revenues of the Work, the prevailing average subscription rate for the Work, and the royalty due thereon for the previous calendar year. Such statements shall be mailed to the Editor within ninety (90) days after the end of the calendar year and shall include the royalty payment due the Editor.

17. Upon publication, the Publisher shall provide the Editor, without charge, with ten (10) copies of each issue of the Work. The Editor and contributing authors may purchase additional copies of each issue of the Work at a 66.6% discount off the list price of an individual issue. Publisher shall furnish each official member of the editorial advisory board for the Work with one complimentary subscription to the Work during his/her term of service. All copies furnished or sold by Publisher pursuant to this paragraph shall be for Personal use and not for resale.

18. For the life of this Agreement, and for one (1) year from the date of termination by either party, the Editor agrees not to participate in the development of, contribute writing to, edit or publish, any other newsletter that might, in the reasonable opinion of the Publisher, compete directly with or injure the sales of the Work.

19. This Agreement may be terminated by the Publisher with or without cause upon thirty (30) days prior written notice. This Agreement may be terminated by the Editor with or without cause upon ninety (90) days prior written notice. Should the Editor terminate this Agreement, the Editor will deliver to the Publisher a complete and acceptable manuscript, according to the specifications contained in this Agreement, for one additional issue of the Work to be published subsequent to the date the termination becomes effective, provided that Publisher requests the Editor to do so.

20. The Editor may not assign or otherwise transfer this Agreement or any of the Editor's rights or obligations thereunder without the prior written consent of Publisher. The Publisher may freely assign or otherwise transfer this Agreement and any and all of its rights and obligations thereunder. The Agreement is binding on the heirs, legal representatives, successors, and permitted assignees of the Editor, and on the successors and assignees of Publisher.

21. This Agreement contains the entire understanding and agreement of the parties with respect to the Work and supersedes all prior understandings or agreements. It may not be modified except by a writing executed by the parties.

22. This Agreement shall be construed according to, and all rights and liabilities of the parties shall be governed by, the laws of the State of Delaware, notwithstanding any conflicts of law or other provision of the laws of Delaware or any other state that would otherwise result in the application of the laws of any other jurisdiction.

AGREED

EDITOR   PUBLISHER

_____   _____
Editor   Date   Acquisitions Editor   Date

_____   _____
Social Security Number   Publisher   Date

Associate Editor Agreement

The following is an extremely detailed associate editor agreement for a scholarly journal. It is modeled on an agreement pursuant to which the associate editor was to be responsible for over 1,000 pages of text per year. For an associate editor with fewer responsibilities, the form can be abbreviated by cutting or shortening language from the associate editor's duties, the publisher's responsibilities, the termination, and the post-termination sections.

Associate Editor Agreement

AGREEMENT made this _____ day of _____ by and between _____ (hereinafter referred to as the "Associate Editor ") and _____ (hereinafter referred to as the "Publisher") with respect to the editing of the Publisher's journal entitled _____ (hereinafter referred to as the "Journal").

The Parties hereto agree as follows:

1. Ownership and Copyright of the Journal

(a)   The Publisher is the sole and exclusive owner of the Journal, including the title, trademark, tradename, its subscription or circulation lists, copyrights and renewals or extensions of copyright, Contributions as defined below, all inventory and all other materials and rights of any nature whatsoever relating to the Journal. The Publisher has the exclusive right in perpetuity to publish, manufacture, distribute, promote and sell the Journal in all forms and media whether presently in existence or subsequently devised and to sell or license the exercise of any of these rights including, but not limited to, the right to grant or license any reprint, subsidiary and other rights in and to the Journal throughout the world.

(b)   The Journal and all material contained therein and the work product of the Associate Editor and the Associate Editor's staff produced hereunder shall constitute a "work-made-for-hire" under the U.S. Copyright Act and all the rights comprised in the copyright of the Journal shall automatically, upon creation, vest in and thereafter be solely owned by the Publisher. To the extent, if any, that any rights, inclusive of the copyright, in and to the Journal, the material contained therein or any portion thereof, do not qualify as a "work-made-for-hire" or might otherwise vest in the Associate Editor, the Associate Editor hereby assigns and transfers such rights in perpetuity to the Publisher.

(c)   If either the Publisher or the Associate Editor believes that the copyright of any issue of the Journal has been infringed, the party so believing shall notify the other thereof. The Associate Editor shall, at the sole cost and expense of the

Publisher, render reasonable assistance to the Publisher in any infringement proceedings which the Publisher chooses to bring. Such assistance may consist of aiding the Publisher or its representative in determining the nature of the infringement, and testifying as a witness.

2. Associate Editor's Duties

The Publisher hereby commissions the Associate Editor and the Associate Editor agrees to perform the following services with respect to the Journal, conscientiously, expeditiously and to the best of his ability:

(a)   in consultation with the Publisher and the Editor-in-Chief and other Journal Editors, to follow editorial policy and the aims and scope of the Journal, and decide upon procedures and standards for the acceptance of manuscripts and obtain the Publisher's approval of any material changes therefrom;

(b)   solicit the submission of high quality articles to the Journal (hereinafter referred to as "Contribution(s)"), and oversee any other special features of the Journal (book reviews, mini-review articles, pro and con forums, letters, etc.) as appropriate;

(c)   evaluate submitted Contributions, in accordance with the editorial policy, and select suitable Contributions for the review process for the Journal;

(d)   arrange for and supervise the independent peer review of Contributions by members of the Editorial Board or ad hoc reviewers and make or request the Contributors to make such revisions as the Associate Editor(s) and/or reviewers deem appropriate; and reject any Contribution the Associate Editor deems unsatisfactory;

(e)   arrange for each Contributor of an accepted Contribution to transfer his or her copyright to the Publisher by signing a Copyright Transfer Agreement in the form attached hereto as Exhibit A and incorporated herein, which, among other things, transfers to the Publisher the copyright in the Contribution(s) and is signed by all Contributors, and to obtain written permissions, on a form approved by the Publisher, to reprint any copyrighted material incorporated in the Contribution(s);

(f)   assume editorial responsibility for the timely submission to the Publisher, for each issue of the Journal, of the final Contributions in the English language in form, content and style satisfactory to the Publisher in accordance with the Publisher's current "Information for Authors" and in accordance with the annual schedule to be set by the Publisher and agreed upon by the Associate Editor. Illustrations shall be provided in a form suitable for direct use without redrawing, relettering or retouching;

(g)   in consultation with the Publisher and the Editor-in-Chief and other Associate Editors, select an Editorial Board which shall advise the Associate Editor with respect to editorial policy, and assist in reviewing Contributions and promoting the Journal. Each member of the board shall authorize the use of his or her name as specified in Paragraph 11 below;

(h) report regularly to the Publisher, Editor-in-Chief, other Journal Editors, and Editorial Board Members on editorial operations;

(i)   meet and confer with the Publisher's personnel at such times as the Publisher reasonably requests;

(j)   make best efforts to ensure the currency and accuracy of the contents of each Contribution provided to the Publisher for each issue of the Journal as of the date on which the issue's contents are forwarded to the Publisher and perform all other editorial services usually performed by journal Associate Editors; and

(k)   provide office services at his own office for the receipt of Contributions, routing them to members of the Editorial Board and ad hoc referees and preparing final manuscripts. Such office will maintain records and statistics regarding the status of Contributions submitted to the Journal and will provide the Publisher with regular status reports, in accordance with the Publisher's regular practices.

3.   Publisher's Responsibilities

All publishing activities of the Journal shall be the responsibility of the Publisher, including but not limited to the following:

(a)   The Publisher shall determine the typography, format and style of the journal and arrange for the typesetting, proofreading, printing, binding, publication, sale and distribution, promotion and advertising of the journal.

(b)   The Publisher shall, in its sole discretion, set the print and electronic subscription rates, single, back issue and reprint prices, all fees for grants of subsidiary rights, advertising rates, and all other terms of sale for the Journal and may modify all such terms from time to time. The Publisher directly or through its representatives shall solicit subscriptions for the Journal in any manner that the Publisher elects.

(c)   The Publisher is under no obligation to publish any Contribution from a prospective Contributor who does not return a signed copy of the Copyright Transfer Agreement, or any Contribution which is not of literary quality reasonably acceptable to the Publisher or in form and content satisfactory to the Publisher in its sole discretion for inclusion in the Journal or which may result in liability unacceptable to the Publisher in its judgment.

(d) The Publisher reserves the right to edit, alter or add to the Contribution, provided that the meaning of the text is not altered. The Publisher will notify the Associate Editor or the Contributor, as appropriate, prior to publication of any edited issue, if any editing of a substantive nature is undertaken.

4.   Frequency of Issues and Number of Pages

(a)   The Journal will be published _____ times per year in one volume of _____ issues, with an average of approximately printed editorial text pages per annum, in an $8^{1}/_{2}''$ by 11" format. Any changes in the size of the Journal or the number of pages or format will be made by the Publisher after due consultation with the Editor-in-Chief and Associate Editors in advance of the publication year. The Associate Editor shall be responsible for acquiring _____ printed editorial pages each year.

(b)   Supplemental pages in excess of the annual page budget established by the Publisher in consultation with the Editor-in-Chief and the Associate Editors may be included, subject to the Publisher's prior approval and taking into account the editorial and economic requirements of the Journal.

5.   Editorial Office Budget and Compensation

The Publisher shall provide monies to the Associate Editor to help support editorial operation of the Journal for each year as detailed in payment schedule Attachment A. Stationery for the Associate Editor's use in connection with his duties will be supplied by the Publisher.

6.   Complimentary Subscription

The Publisher shall give to the Associate Editor a complimentary subscription to the Journal, for personal use only. In addition, the Publisher shall, upon request, supply the Associate Editor with a reasonable number of complimentary copies of the Journal for discretionary use in the solicitation of manuscripts and the like.

7.   Term and Termination

Unless sooner terminated as provided below, this Agreement shall commence on the date first above written and remain in effect until December 31, 20__. Thereafter, the Agreement shall be automatically renewed annually on the same terms and conditions herein unless either party notifies the other in writing that it does not wish to renew the Agreement, such notification to be given at least six months prior to expiration of the initial Agreement or extension thereof.

8.   Early Termination

Notwithstanding the above, this Agreement shall be terminated early,
(a)   automatically, upon the Associate Editor's death or incapacity;

(b)   at the Publisher's sole discretion:

   (i)   if, in the Publisher's judgment, the Associate Editor is not meeting
        his obligations or performing his duties as outlined in this Agreement,
        including but not limited to the Associate Editor's failure to obtain
        sufficient acceptable manuscript material in time to permit publication
        of two consecutive issues of the Journal on schedule, provided, how-
        ever, that (1) the Publisher has given the Associate Editor written
        notice setting forth his unsatisfactory performance, and (2) the
        Associate Editor has not improved such performance to the Publisher's
        reasonable satisfaction within ninety (90) days of receipt of such
        notice; or
   (ii) on not less than sixty (60) days prior written notice to the Associate
        Editor if the Publisher decides, in its sole judgment, to discontinue
        publication of the Journal. The Associate Editor shall keep the money
        advance for editorial office expenses, if any, for the year in which
        termination takes place; or
   (iii) in the event of any disagreements between or among the Associate
        Editor and other Associate Editors or the Editor-in-Chief that interfere
        with publication of the journal.

(c)   at the discretion of the non-breaching party, for breach of any material
provision of this Agreement:

   (i)   for which written notice is given to the breaching party; and
   (ii) such breach is not corrected within ninety (90) days.

9.   Post-Termination

(a)   The Publisher, within ninety (90) days after termination of this
Agreement, shall pay to the Associate Editor all fees and expense reimbursements due him which have accrued as of such termination date, for those
volumes of the Journal that are published or ready for publication as of the
termination date.

(b)   Upon termination of this Agreement, the duties and obligations of
the Associate Editor shall terminate, except for the warranties in Paragraph 10
which shall survive such termination. The Publisher shall have the right
to appoint a new Associate Editor or to otherwise continue the publication
of the Journal as it sees fit without further duty or obligation to the Associate
Editor. The Associate Editor or his personal representative shall promptly return
to the Publisher all Contributor manuscripts, lists, records and documents
and all other materials relating to or in connection with the publication of the
Journal.

(c)   If notice of termination is given by the Associate Editor under Paragraph 7 or by the Publisher under Paragraph 8(c)(i) above, he shall not edit any competing journal for a period of one year after such termination.

10.   Warranties and Indemnities

The Associate Editor warrants and represents that:

(a)   the Associate Editor has full power and authority to make this Agreement and to perform his obligations hereunder;

(b)   no organization for which the Associate Editor works as a regular salaried employee shall have any rights in or control over the Associate Editor's work in the Journal, and the Associate Editor's personal services on behalf of the Journal as set forth herein do not violate any agreement between the Associate Editor and any employer of the Associate Editor;

(c)   any material prepared by the Associate Editor for the Journal shall be original, shall not infringe upon or violate any copyright, trademark, obligation of confidentiality or any other right or the privacy of others or contain any libelous material or instructions that may cause harm or injury; and

(d)   the Associate Editor will not include in the Journal any Contribution that the Associate Editor believes may infringe upon or violate any copyright, trademark, obligation of confidentiality or other right or the privacy of others or contain any libelous material or instructions that may cause harm or injury.

The Associate Editor shall indemnify and hold the Publisher harmless from any and all claims, damages, liabilities, costs and expenses (including counsel fees) that the Publisher incurs or sustains arising out of any breach by the Associate Editor of the foregoing warranties or out of the use of any materials prepared by the Associate Editor hereunder.

All representations, warranties and indemnities shall survive the termination of the Agreement.

11.   Name and Likeness

The Publisher shall have the right and may grant to others the right to use, in any medium, the Associate Editor's name, likeness and professional credits, and the names, licenses and professional credits of the Editorial Board, in connection with the Journal or the promotion or advertising thereof.

12.   Noncompetition

During the Term, the Associate Editor, without the Publisher's written consent, shall not perform any editorial services for any other journal that might, in the Publisher's judgment, be competitive with the Journal.

13.   Notices

Any notice to be given hereunder shall be in writing and shall be mailed, certified or registered, return receipt requested, or delivered by hand or courier service addressed to the other party as follows:

For the Publisher: For the Associate Editor:

14.   General

(a)   The relationship between the parties is that of independent contractors and does not constitute a partnership or employment relationship, and the Associate Editor shall have no authority to bind the Publisher in any way.

(b)   The engagement of the Associate Editor is personal and the services to be performed by the Associate Editor are special and unique and, therefore, the rights hereunder granted to the Associate Editor are not assignable nor may the obligations or duties imposed be delegated without the prior written consent of the Publisher.

(c)   Except as provided in subparagraph (b) above, this Agreement shall inure to the benefit of the heirs, successors, and permitted assigns of the Associate Editor and the subsidiaries, successors, and assigns of the Publisher.

(d)   This Agreement constitutes the complete understanding of the parties. No modification or waiver of any provision shall be valid unless in writing and signed by both parties. Any waiver in one or more instances by either of the parties of any breach by the other of any terms or provisions contained in this Agreement shall not be considered a waiver of any succeeding or preceding breach.

(e)   This Agreement shall be construed and interpreted pursuant to the laws of the State of New York applicable to contracts wholly entered into and performed in the State of New York. Any legal action, suit or proceeding arising out of or relating to this Agreement or the breach thereof shall be instituted in a court of competent jurisdiction in New York County in the State of New York and each party hereby consents and submits to the personal jurisdiction of such court, waives any objection to venue in such court and consents to service of process by first class mail at the last known address of such party.

(f)   Paragraph headings are for convenience only and, being no part of this Agreement, shall not be used to modify, interpret or change it.

AGREED AND ACCEPTED

PUBLISHER

By: _____

Name: _____

Title: _____

Date: _____

EDITOR

By: _____

Name: _____

Social Security Number: _____

Date: _____

Advertising Representative Agreement

The following is an agreement for a third-party representative to provide services on a commissioned basis with respect to advertising sales.[3] This agreement was designed for a scholarly journal, and so has language that may be superfluous for use with non-scholarly publications (e.g., the provisions of 2(a)(i) concerning the Editorial Board).

This contract contemplates a long-term exclusive relationship for the periodical. To minimize the publisher's risk for such a venture, the language of Attachment A, Paragraph 4 was added, providing a termination right for the publisher if specific revenue targets are not met by the representative.

Advertising Representative Agreement

This Agreement, including Attachments A and B hereto, is made as of _____, between _____, with principal offices at _____ (hereinafter referred to as "Publisher"), and _____ (hereinafter referred to as "Representative").

1.   Publisher hereby appoints Representative, and Representative hereby accepts its appointment, as Publisher's exclusive agent in connection with the promotion and sale of product-display, classified, and online advertising to appear in the joural of (the "Periodical").

2.   Representative agrees to use its best efforts to perform the following:

a)   sell advertising space in, and provide adequate sales representation for, the Periodical; including the following:

   i.   At the discretion of Publisher and at Representative's expense, Representative will attended an Annual Meeting of Periodical Editorial Board to review industry trends, projected advertising for ensuing year, and overall advertising policies.
   ii. Representative will prepare written reports, at request of Publisher, analyzing sales efforts, call reports, account status, results and projections.
   iii. Representative will provide information regularly about conditions in the advertising marketplace.

---

3 For a review of legal issues regarding advertising, see Mark A. Fischer, E. Gabriel Perle and John Taylor William, *Perle and Williams on Publishiing Law*, § 3.02 (3d ed., Aspen L. & Bus. 2001)

b)   to perform, at its sole cost and expense, the following advertising production and billing functions for the Periodical:

i.   Maintaining of current files for each advertiser. Such files will reflect the number of insertions in each issue, insertion orders and contracts, monthly record on each product, agency contact and ad frequency.

ii.   Forwarding of all new ads for copy approval by the Publisher and, when required, the Editor-in-Chief.

iii.   Suggesting advertising layouts in coordination with editorial material, with due consideration to rotation of advertising based on previous placements, multiple product advertisers and sales of premium positions.

iv.   Suggesting banner advertisements and placement of other online advertisements.

v.   Developing and updating advertiser's complimentary subscription list.

vi.   Providing all billing functions, if required, including:
a) Updating frequency rates for issuance of short rates.
b) Assisting in the collection of outstanding invoices.

vii.   Maintaining of current information Standard Rate and Data Service.

viii.   Providing of office space and staff to perform the above functions.

ix.   Selling, developing and maintaining all advertising within the classified/recruitment section of the Periodical.

3.   The services specified in Paragraph 2(a), Publisher agrees to pay Representative a commission of _____ (___%) percent for sales of all paid advertising in the Periodical, including online advertisements, and in supplements thereto (both display and classified). In calculating the total amounts due hereunder, there shall be deducted from the Publisher's net billing all normal agency discounts.

4.   No commission will be due representative if the account debtor defaults in the full payment of the Publisher's invoice, and Representative will either reimburse Publisher for any such payment previously made on account thereof, or Publisher will make an appropriate deduction as herein provided. Collection actions, or litigation to enforce payment of any unpaid invoice, will be at the sole discretion of the Publisher.

5.   The territory assigned to Representative under the terms of this Agreement is North America, but international ads will be accepted and commissionable.

6. This Agreement shall commence on _____, and shall continue for a period of (3) years until _____. In the absence of notice of termination having been given in writing by either party to the other at least three (3) months prior to the end of the initial term, this Agreement shall automatically be renewed for an additional period of two (2) years, in accordance with the terms and conditions in effect on the last day of the then current agreement.

7. At any time during the term of this Agreement, Publisher and Representative can agree to include additional publications under the terms of this Agreement, in which event a Supplemental Agreement shall identify such additional publications.

8. Representative agrees to participate at Publisher's request in meetings arranged by Publisher to analyze advertising sales in competitive publications, identify potential new advertisers, review methodologies for generating sales leads, and propose activities required to promote and maximize advertising sales.

9. Representative shall have no power or authority to make any binding agreement, or incur any obligation, on behalf of Publisher.

10. This Agreement, and any renewals or extensions thereof, shall inure to the benefit of, and be binding upon, the successors and assigns of the parties, provided that no Assignment shall be binding upon either party without the other party's written consent.

11. The relationship between the parties is that of independent contractors and does not constitute a partnership or employment relationship, and neither party shall have any authority to bind the other in any way.

PUBLISHER   REPRESENTATIVE

_____   _____

By: _____   By: _____

Title: _____   Title: _____

Date: _____   Date: _____

Attachment A

1. All Advertising to be placed in the Publication will be subject to the approval of the Publisher, which shall be the sole judge of the suitability of proposed advertising or advertisement, for any reason or for no reason, at its discretion.

2. Both parties agree to keep confidential any information obtained by the other in connection to performance under this Agreement. This shall extend to the advertising complimentary list as well as the list(s) of advertisers, their ad agencies and prospective clients, business operations and all other matters pertaining to the Periodical. The confidentiality imparted by this Agreement shall survive the termination of this Agreement for any reason.

3. Representative agrees not to solicit advertising for a new client where such client would in the Publisher's reasonable judgment be competitive with the Periodical without prior written approval of the Publisher. Competitive will mean any journal, periodical, newspaper, newsletter, magazine or publication whether in print of electronic format, with more than 51% of its annual content relating to _____.

4. This Agreement may be terminated by either party for a material breach by the other so long as the written notice is sent by certified mail to the breaching party and the breach is not corrected within 90 days of receipt of such notice to the satisfaction of the non-breaching party. For the purposes of this paragraph, "breach" is defined to include net revenue, which is more than 25% below target goals set forth in Attachment B. A waiver by either party of any default or breach of this Agreement will not deprive or prevent that party of any right to terminate this Agreement arising out of any later, unrelated breach or default.

5. Either party may terminate this Agreement upon giving of written notice to the other in the event that the other party enters into voluntary or involuntary bankruptcy proceedings or otherwise becomes insolvent.

6. The Agreement will terminate automatically in the event that the Publisher ceases to publish the Publication.

7. A commission of ___% will be paid to the Representative on the direct sale of supplements to the Periodical, bulk subscription or issue sales and reprints of specific articles and any other special sales assigned to the Representative by the Publisher. The Representative's right to solicit the types of sales set forth in this paragraph shall be nonexclusive.

8.   This Agreement contains all the terms and conditions agreed upon by the parties and constitutes the only Agreement in force and effect between the parties for the sale of advertising in the Periodical. This Agreement may only be changed by a written instrument signed by all parties.

9.   This Agreement will be construed and interpreted pursuant to the laws of the State of New York applicable to contracts wholly entered into and performed in the State of New York. Any legal action, suit or proceeding arising out of or relating to this Agreement or the breach thereof shall be instituted in a court of competent jurisdiction in New York County in the State of New York and each party hereby consents and submits to the personal jurisdiction of such court, waives any objection to venue in such court and consents to service of process by first class mail at the last known address of such party.

10. The Representative may not assign or otherwise transfer this Agreement or any of its rights or obligations hereunder, either expressly or by operation of law, without the prior written consent of the Publisher.

Attachment B

Target goals are agreed upon by the Publisher and Representative. Net revenue (total revenue less any agency or frequency discounts) from the sale of advertising space in the Periodical, sponsorships, online revenue, supplements, reprints, and bulk subscription deals will be combined towards reaching target goals.

Year 1	_____	**Target Goal**	$_____
Year 2	_____	**Target Goal**	$_____
Year 3	_____	**Target Goal**	$_____

Copyright Transfer Agreement for Academic Journal

The following Copyright Transfer Agreement for an academic journal is a publisher-friendly form which tries to balance a number of competing interests, and is thus long. In recognition of the desire of some institutions to collect in articles written by faculty in "institutional repositories," and of the desire in some disciplines to post early drafts of papers in "preprint servers," the publisher allows the authors to place the article online, but in the form in which the paper was submitted (*see*, Section C.1.). The final article may be reused in more constrained ways, but cannot be placed online (*see* Section C.3.). The post peer reviewed version, which contains a lot of the "value add" from the publisher, may only be used by separate agreement (*see* Section C.2.).

It is important when drafting a document like this to consider your own processes, standards, and workflows. For example, if you routinely grant little or no fee reuse permissions to authors for their figures and tables (as is typical), why not just allow it in your agreement with them? (*see* C.4.b.) Surprisingly, many publishers fail to consider such author-friendly language, even where the transaction costs of another policy outweigh the benefits.

This form can be contrasted with the "SPARC Author Addendum"[4] which reserves broad online use rights in final articles. Most publishers, fearful of the loss of control and recognizing that final versions posted on the web will be found by search engines and used in lieu of the authoritative version, reject such amendments.

This form can also be compared with Form 2.8, which is friendlier in tone, but less liberal with its grant-backs.

Agreement

Date:

Contributor name:

Contributor address:

Re: Manuscript entitled

_____

_____ (the "Contribution")

for publication in _____(the "Journal")

published by _____ ("Publisher").

---

4 *See*, http://www.arl.org/sparc/author/addendum.html. This document in turn has inspired similar addenda at institutions such as MIT. Permission to include the SPARC Author Addendum in this book was requested but not granted.

Dear Contributor(s):

Thank you for submitting your Contribution for publication. In order to expedite the editing and publishing process and enable Publisher to disseminate your Contribution to the fullest extent, we need to have this Copyright Transfer Agreement signed and returned to us as soon as possible. If the Contribution is not accepted for publication, or if the Contribution is subsequently rejected, this Agreement shall be null and void.

A.   Copyright

1.   The Contributor assigns to Publisher, during the full term of copyright and any extensions or renewals, all copyright in and to the Contribution, and all rights therein, including but not limited to the right to publish, republish, transmit, sell, distribute and otherwise use the Contribution in whole or in part in electronic and print editions of the Journal and in derivative works throughout the world, in all languages and in all media of expression now known or later developed, and to license or permit others to do so.

2.   Reproduction, posting, transmission or other distribution or use of the final Contribution in whole or in part in any medium by the Contributor as permitted by this Agreement requires a citation to the Journal and an appropriate credit to Publisher as Publisher, suitable in form and content as follows: (Title of Article, Author, Journal Title and Volume/Issue, Copyright © [year], copyright owner as specified in the Journal). Links to the final article on Publisher's Web site are encouraged where appropriate.

B.   Retained Rights

Notwithstanding the above, the Contributor or, if applicable, the Contributor's Employer, retains all proprietary rights other than copyright, such as patent rights, in any process, procedure or article of manufacture described in the Contribution.

C.   Permitted Uses by Contributor

1.   **Submission version**. Publisher licenses back the following rights to the Contributor in the version of the Contribution as originally submitted for publication:

 a.   The right to self-archive on the Contributor's personal Web site, place in a subject matter archive, or in the Contributor's institution's/employer's institutional repository or archive. This right extends to both intranets and the Internet. The Contributor may not update the submission version or replace it with the published Contribution.

 b.   The right to transmit, print and share copies with colleagues.

2. **Version as accepted**. Re-use of the accepted and peer-reviewed (but not final) version of the Contribution shall be by separate agreement with Publisher. Publisher has agreements with certain funding agencies governing reuse of this version. For details of those relationships, contact the editorial office.

3. **Final Published Version**. Publisher hereby licenses back to the Contributor the following rights with respect to the final published version of the Contribution:

   a. Copies for colleagues. The personal right of the Contributor only to send or transmit individual copies of the final published version in any format to colleagues upon their specific request provided no fee is charged, and further-provided that there is no systematic distribution of the Contribution, e.g., posting on a listserv, Web site or automated delivery.

   b. Reuse in other publications. The right to reuse the final Contribution or parts thereof for any publication authored or edited by the Contributor where such reused material constitutes less than half of the total material in such publication. In such case, any modifications should be accurately noted.

   c. Teaching duties. The right to include the Contribution in teaching or training duties at the Contributor's institution/place of employment including in course packs, e-reserves, presentation at professional conferences, in-house training, or distance learning. The Contribution may not be used in seminars outside of normal teaching obligations (e.g., commercial seminars). Electronic posting of the final published version in connection with teaching/training at the Contributor's institution/place of employment is permitted subject to the implementation of reasonable access control mechanisms, such as user name and password. Posting the final published version on the open Internet is not permitted.

   d. Oral presentationos. The right to make oral presentations based on the Contribution.

4. **Article Abstracts, Figures, Tables, Data Sets, Artwork and Selected Text (up to 250 words).**

   a. Contributors may re-use unmodified abstracts for any non-commercial purpose. For online uses of the abstracts, Publisher encourages but does not require linking back to the final published versions.

   b. Contributors may re-use figures, tables, data sets, artwork, and selected text up to 250 words from their Contributions, provided the following conditions are met:

      (i) Full and accurate credit must be given to the Contribution.
      (ii) Modifications to the figures, tables and data must be noted. Otherwise, no changes may be made.

    (iii)The reuse may not be made for direct commercial purposes, or for financial consideration to the Contributor.

    (iv)Nothing herein shall permit dual publication in violation of journal ethical practices.

D.   Contributions Owned by Employer

1.   If the Contribution was written by the Contributor in the course of the Contributor's employment (as a "work-made-for-hire" in the course of employment), the Contribution is owned by the company/employer which must sign this Agreement (in addition to the Contributor's signature), in the space provided below. In such case, the company/employer hereby assigns to Publisher, during the full term of copyright, all copyright in and to the Contribution for the full term of copyright throughout the world as specified in paragraph A above.

2.   In addition to the rights specified as retained in paragraph B above and the rights granted back to the Contributor pursuant to paragraph C above, Publisher hereby grants back, without charge, to such company/employer, its subsidiaries and divisions, the right to make copies of and distribute the final published Contribution internally in print format or electronically on the Company's internal network. Although copies so made shall not be available for individual re-sale, they may be included by the company/employer as part of an information package included with software or other products offered for sale or license or included in patent applications. Posting of the final published Contribution by the institution on a public access website may only be done with Publisher's written permission, and payment of any applicable fee(s). Also, upon payment of Publisher's reprint fee, the institution may distribute print copies of the published Contribution externally.

E.   Government Contracts

In the case of a Contribution prepared under U.S. Government contract or grant, the U.S. Government may reproduce, without charge, all or portions of the Contribution and may authorize others to do so, for official U.S. Government purposes only, if the U.S. Government contract or grant so requires. (U.S. Government, U.K. Government, and other government employees: see notes at end.)

F.   Copyright Notice

The Contributor and the company/employer agree that any and all copies of the final published version of the Contribution or any part thereof distributed or posted by them in print or electronic format as permitted herein will include the notice of copyright as stipulated in the Journal and a full citation to the Journal as published by Publisher.

G.   Contributor's Representations

The Contributor represents that the Contribution is the Contributor's original work, all individuals identified as Contributors actually contributed to the Contribution, and all individuals who contributed are included. If the Contribution was prepared jointly, the Contributor agrees to inform the co-Contributors of the terms of this Agreement and to obtain their signature to this Agreement or their written permission to sign on their behalf. The Contribution is submitted only to this Journal and has not been published before, except for submission versions as permitted above. (If excerpts from copyrighted works owned by third parties are included, the Contributor will obtain written permission from the copyright owners for all uses as set forth in Publisher's permissions form or in the Journal's Instructions for Contributors, and show credit to the sources in the Contribution.) The Contributor also warrants that the Contribution contains no libelous or unlawful statements, does not infringe upon the rights (including without limitation the copyright, patent or trademark rights) or the privacy of others, or contain material or instructions that might cause harm or injury.

Check One Box

[____] Contributor-ownoed work

_____   _____
Contributor's signature   Date

_____
Type or print name and title

_____   _____
Co-contributor's signature   Date

_____
Type or print name and title

ATTACH ADDITIONAL SIGNATURE PAGES AS NECESSARY

[____] Company/Institution-owned work (made-for-hire in the course of employment)

_____   _____
Company or Institution   Date
(Employer-for-Hire)

_____   _____
Authorized signature   Date
of Employer

[_____] U.S. Government work

Note to U.S. Government Employees

A contribution prepared by a U.S. federal government employee as part of the employee's official duties, or which is an official U.S. Government publication, is called a "U.S. Government work," and is in the public domain in the United States. In such case, the employee may cross out Paragraph A.1 but must sign and return this Agreement. If the Contribution was not prepared as part of the employee's duties or is not an official U.S. Government publication, it is not a U.S. Government work.

[_____] U.K. Government work (Crown Copyright)

Note to U.K. Government Employees

The rights in a Contribution prepared by an employee of a U.K. government department, agency or other Crown body as part of his/her official duties, or which is an official government publication, belong to the Crown. In such case, Publisher will forward the relevant form to the Employee for signature.

[_____] Other Government work

Note to Non-U.S., Non-U.K. Government Employees

If your status as a government employee legally prevents you from signing this Agreement, please contact the editorial office.

Copyright Transfer Agreement—Scholarly Publishing
(Informal Letter)

This "informal" copyright transfer agreement is designed to look less legal and frightening to the unpaid contributors to whom it is sent than Form 2.7, with which it can be contrasted. Interestingly, although this letter appears friendly, it is actually stronger than Form 2.7; its length and word choice just make it appear less so. Also, the fact that it comes as a letter from the editor, as opposed to the publisher, helps to encourage the authors to sign.

Letter of Agreement

Dear _____:

I am pleased that you are contributing an article to [*publication name*], volume number _____ (the "Periodical"), of which I am the editor. The Periodical is published by _____ (the "Publisher"). A first draft of your article is due to me on _____ [*describe what happens next, e.g., "the article will then be sent for peer review"*] and the final draft is due [*on* _____] [*within* [*30*] *days of being returned to you*].

So that there are no misunderstandings, I would like to define the publishing arrangement in detail:

1. You will supply an original manuscript of an article for inclusion in the Periodical.

2. You guarantee that the article you will furnish will be original and prepared especially for the Periodical, except for excerpts and illustrations for which you will receive permission to republish on a form attached hereto; that the article will not have been and will not be registered for copyright and/or published elsewhere; and that you have not and will not release it for any purpose prior to publication in the Periodical.

3. You guarantee that the article will not infringe any copyright, violate any proprietary rights, contain any libelous, or unlawful material, or material that might cause harm or injury.

4. The Publisher and editor will have the right to make changes in the article (including its title) for clarity, brevity, and conformity to style. You will be contacted about your article before it is set in type only if substantive changes are made in the editing process. You will not receive proofs; the Publisher and I will do the proofreading.

5. You agree that your article will be published, and distributed by the Publisher, in its own name or any other name throughout the world. You hereby assign to the Publisher all copyrights in and to the article during the full term of copyright in all media to enable the Publisher to fully distribute your work. Notwithstanding the foregoing, the Publisher hereby grants back the following:

(a) The right, without charge, to photocopy or to transmit online or to download, print out and distribute to a colleague a copy of the published article in whole or in part, upon the colleague's specific request. Systematic redistribution, posting to a listserv or on the Internet is specifically forbidden.

(b) The right to republish, without charge, in any format, all or part of the material from the published article in a book written or edited by you.

(c) The right to include the article in a compilation for classroom use (course packs) to be distributed to students at your institution free of charge in print or electronic format (subject to reasonable access controls), the right to post it electronically on your employer's secure internal network, and the right to make oral presentations based on the article.

(d) The right to use brief excerpts (up to 250 words) and illustrations for any purpose whatsoever.

Any reuse of the article requires proper attribution to the Periodical. You will retain all other rights, and remain free to use any ideas or data contained in the article for any purpose.

6. If the article is not published for any reason, this Agreement will be void and you are free to use your article for any purpose you desire.

7. In appreciation for your contribution, the Publisher will send you [*five (5) complimentary copies of the issue in which your article appears.*]

I trust the above points meet with your approval. Please sign one copy of this letter and return it to me, along with the information requested below. I look forward to reading your article.

Sincerely,

_____   _____

[*name*]   Date
Editor

Agreed to and accepted:

_____   _____

Signature   Date

PRINT name exactly as it is to appear in the magazine:

_____

List your title and affiliation as you wish it to appear:

_____

Telephone: _____ FAX: _____

Business Address:

_____

Home Address:

_____

Home Telephone:

_____

Please send my complimentary copies to my **business or home** address (circle one). Deliveries cannot be made to post office boxes.

Standard Journalism Contract
(Publisher's Form with Alternative Clauses)

The following agreement for a freelance contribution to a magazine by a professional author was prepared for use by publishers. In contrast to Form 2.10, which was written from the author's perspective and contains narrow grants of rights, this agreement contains options with respect to ownership and licenses for use of the material with no additional fee paid to the author, as well as language for use with limited grants allowing the publisher to make other, unspecified uses of the material for an additional fee. The first version of the rights language (which is bracketed in Clause 1 but not boldfaced or italicized) allows the article to be used in a single edition of the magazine, plus on the related Web site and for promotional purposes. The second version, which is used in conjunction with the first and appears in italics, additionally permits the publisher to license the magazine including the article for database uses, so long as the license between the publisher and the database publisher is a blanket license for the entire magazine.[5] With either of the above-referenced versions, the publisher should also include Clause 2, which clears the rights for any other use subject to an obligation to pay the writer. As an alternative, the boldfaced language in Clause 1 provides that the article is a "work made for hire" under the U.S. Copyright Act, and the publisher owns all rights therein. With this language, Clause 2 becomes unnecessary.

Freelance Agreement

This will confirm our purchase of the rights specified below in and to the literary material entitled: ("Article Title") by author. The general specifications for submission of this project were delivered to the author by Publisher, Inc. ("Publisher"). The author agrees to deliver the article in a form and on or before the due date as have been set forth in the general specifications.

1. In consideration of the of $____ to be paid after receipt and acceptance by Publisher of the article described herein, [the author grants to Publisher, its licensees and assigns, the exclusive first right to reproduce, publish or use the article in the U.S. edition of _____ (the "magazine"), as well as the right to reproduce, publish and use the article: (a) to promote the magazine; (b) on microfilm and microfiche containing the issue of the magazine in which the article is published; [and] (c) in electronic media on the magazine's primary

---

5 This language addresses the uses that were found, in the absence of an agreement, to be in infringement in *New York Times Co., Inc., et al. v. Tasini et al.*, 533 U.S. 483, 121 S. Ct. 2381, 150 L.ED. 2d, 500 (2001).

website maintained by Publisher or a licensee, assignee or service provider of Publisher, sponsored by Publisher, or of which Publisher is a primary content contributor [*and (d) in electronic media published by Publisher or licensed by Publisher, including without limitation database uses in which the article is licensed as part of a collection of articles and in which the article will appear in an aggregated or disintermediated format, so long as the article is not licensed separately.*] [**the author shall prepare the article as a "work made for hire" under the U.S. Copyright Act and all rights comprised therein shall automatically, upon creation, vest in and thereafter be solely owned by Publisher. To the extent, if any, that the article does not qualify as a "work made for hire" or copyright or other proprietary rights thereto might otherwise vest in the author, the author hereby grants, assigns and transfers all such rights exclusively and in perpetuity to Publisher, in all languages and formats, in all media of expression now known or later developed, throughout the world.**] If the Publisher has not scheduled the article for publication within one year of acceptance, unless such time has been changed by mutual agreement, all rights to the article shall revert to the author.

2.   In addition to the uses set forth in paragraph 1 above, Publisher may use, publish or reproduce the article as set forth below:

   (a)   Publisher may syndicate, license or otherwise grant or license rights to the article for any purpose to any third party to reproduce, publish and use the article throughout the world in any media with payment to the author for each such use of fifty percent (50%) of the revenue received by Publisher for such rights. If Publisher exploits these rights itself, it shall pay the author the lesser of fifty percent of the then-prevailing third-party rate for any such exploitation or fifty percent of the fee set forth above.
   (b)   Publisher may produce paper reprints of the text throughout the world with payment to the author for each such use of thirty percent (30%) of the revenue received by Publisher for such rights. Illustrations and photographs in the work, if any, are to be licensed separately.
   (c)   Upon no further payment to author, Publisher may reproduce, publish and use the article or license others, for no fee, to reproduce, publish or use the article for educational or charitable purposes, where no revenue is paid to Publisher for the use, including, but not limited to, the Library of Congress and the service for the blind and physically handicapped.

[This language is not needed if contract is performed on a "work made for hire" basis.]

3.   Author agrees to not exercise the rights retained by author for a period of sixty days after the first day of the month on the cover of the issue containing

the article. After such date, the author shall have the right on a nonexclusive basis to syndicate or otherwise license, assign or sell the article subject to Publisher's rights hereunder, and author may retain one hundred percent of the revenue received. Author shall use author's best efforts to ensure that the magazine receives credit as the original publisher of the article. [This paragraph not needed if contract is performed on a "work for hire" basis.]

4.   Publisher may illustrate, title, edit or revise the article, as it deems appropriate. Author reserves the right to withdraw his/her name from the article upon sufficient advance notice to Publisher and such withdrawal shall not affect the rights of either party hereto or change the terms of this Agreement. Unless author shall withdraw his/her name from the article, Publisher may use the name, likeness and/or biography of the author to promote the magazine.

5.   All source contact information must be submitted to Publisher with submission of the article. All factual information contained in the materiel must be documented and the documentation submitted to Publisher at its request. Author shall retain such documentation for at least one year from the date of publication of the article in the magazine unless Publisher requests an extension of that period in writing.

6.   The author warrants, that he or she is the author of the article; that it is original and has never been published in any form, that the article is accurate and complete; that, to the best of author's knowledge, it contains no matter that is unlawful or violates the rights of any third party and the rights granted hereunder are free and clear of all claims, security interests or liens. The author shall cooperate fully with employees, agents and attorneys of Publisher in the event any complaint, claim, dispute or cause of action arises out of or in connection with the article. The author shall indemnify and hold Publisher harmless for all claims and causes of action arising from a breach or alleged breach of the author's warranties as set forth herein.

7.   Publisher shall reimburse the author for any expenses incurred by the author provided that such expenses have been pre-approved in writing by Publisher and are fully documented by the author.

8.   The author shall make reasonable revisions to the article as requested by Publisher. In the event that the article is submitted within the specifications and otherwise within the terms of this Agreement and is not acceptable to Publisher because of content, style, logic or research, Publisher may, at its option, pay a kill fee of _____ percent of the purchase price of the article (in which case this Agreement shall be otherwise void and the author may sell the article elsewhere), or request that the author make changes to the article which will render it acceptable to the Publisher.

9. The author is an independent contractor and not an employee or agent of Publisher. This Agreement does not create an employer-employee relationship between the parties for any tax, insurance or other purpose, nor is any agency or other form of joint enterprise created hereby. The author shall not state nor imply, either directly or indirectly, that the author is authorized to commit or bind Publisher. The author shall not incur any expenses (unless specifically authorized by Publisher in writing) on behalf of Publisher nor enter into any oral or written Agreement on behalf of or in the name of Publisher.

10. This Agreement sets forth the entire understanding of the parties hereto with respect to the subject matter hereof and supercedes any prior Agreements. This Agreement may not be modified or changed except in a writing signed by the parties hereto. The services of the author are personal, and this Agreement may not be transferred or assigned, in whole or part, by the author to any other party without Publisher's prior written consent.

11. This Agreement shall be governed by the laws of the State of New York applicable to contracts entered into and performed entirely in the State of New York.

AGREED AND ACCEPTED

Publisher, Inc.

By: _____

Name: _____

Title: _____

Date: _____

Author

By: _____

Address: _____

SSN: _____

Standard Journalism Contract
(Writer's Form—Limited Print Rights)

The following agreement for a freelance contribution to a magazine by a professional author was prepared for use by authors, and should be contrasted with Form 2.9. Admittedly, it is usually publishers who determine the form, but this is included to show how it could look from the other side.

Freelance Agreement

This will confirm that _____ ("Writer") has been commissioned by ___ ("Publisher") to write an article on __ (the "Article"). The Article will be approximately __ words long, and will be delivered to Publisher by ___ (the "Due Date").

1. In consideration of the fee of $_____ to be paid after receipt of the Article by Publisher, and the addition fee of $___ to be paid on publication, Author grants to Publisher the exclusive first right to reproduce, publish or use the article in the U.S. print edition of _____ (the "Magazine"). Other uses, including microfilm and microfiche, website, foreign language, and third-party licenses are specifically reserved to Author, and may only be made by Publisher by separate agreement and the payment of a fee.

2. Publisher agrees to publish the Article within ___ days of delivery by Author. If the Article is not published within that period, all rights shall revert to the Author, and the author may retain any fee paid.

3. Publisher may illustrate, title, edit or revise the article, subject to the prior approval of Author. Author will have the opportunity to review and approve any edits to the Article prior to publication, not to be unreasonably withheld.

4. Publisher will provide a credit line for Author in a manner consistent generally with credit lines in the Magazine.

5. Author warrants, that he or she is the author of the Article, that it is original and has never been published in any form, and that the best of Author's knowledge, it contains no matter that is unlawful or violates the rights of any third party and the rights granted hereunder are free and clear of all claims, security interests or liens.

6. Publisher shall reimburse Author within 15 days for any expenses incurred by Author provided that such expenses have been pre-approved in writing by Publisher.

7. Author shall make reasonable revisions to the article as requested by Publisher. In the event that the Article is submitted on time and in the length designated, but Publisher chooses not to publish because of content, style, logic, research, or any other reason, Publisher may, at its option, pay a kill fee of _____ percent of the price set forth above, in which case this Agreement shall be otherwise void and Author may sell the Article elsewhere.

8. This Agreement sets forth the entire understanding of the parties hereto with respect to the subject matter hereof and supersedes any prior Agreements. This Agreement may not be modified or changed except in a writing signed by the parties hereto. The services of the author are personal, and this Agreement may not be transferred or assigned, in whole or part, by the author to any other party without Publisher's prior written consent.

9. This Agreement shall be governed by the laws of the State of New York applicable to contracts entered into and performed entirely in the State of New York.

AGREED AND ACCEPTED

Publisher, Inc.

By: _____

Name: _____

Title: _____

Date: _____

Author

By: _____

Address: _____

SSN: _____

FORM 2.11

Academic Journal Subscription Agency Agreement

Academic and scholarly journals often have tiered pricing. At the high end, full rate subscriptions are sold to libraries, corporations, and other institutional purchasers. These often cost thousands of dollars, reflecting the fact that they will be used by many individuals. These institutions often use "subscription agents" to ease the otherwise substantial burden of having to transact business with hundreds of different publishers each year.

To make journals more affordable to individuals, publishers will often offer "personal rate" subscriptions for as little as one tenth of the full price. Moreover, thousands of learned societies own journals and provide a personal use subscription to their journals as part of membership dues.

There is great temptation for subscription agents, who are supposed to buy full rate journals for institutions at usually single digit discount, to fraudulently procure personal rate and member subscriptions for arbitrage.

In recent years, publishers have increasingly collaborated in bringing lawsuits against such practices, and are reviewing internal practices to prevent the abuse. The following agreement for use with agents can be part of such efforts. It is designed to work alongside terms and conditions in standard price lists. It specifies illegal activities, and enables the publisher to seek liquidated damages in the forum of its choice. It also provides encouragement for the agent to admit to prior acts.

Agreement

This Agreement between Publisher, Inc., its affiliates and subsidiaries ("Publisher"), and _____ ("Agent"), constitutes certain terms and conditions by which Agent shall be allowed to purchase products and services offered by Publisher on behalf of Agent's third-party customers (the "Customers").

WHEREAS, Publisher has in the past been harmed by subscription agents engaging in practices that have been found by courts to constitute fraudulent and racketeering activities (see *American Chemical Society, Inc., et al. v. Commax Technologies, Inc., et al.*, No. 06-04414 JW (N.D. Cal.)); and

WHEREAS, Publisher and Agent wish to clearly establish which practices are allowed and which are not allowed;

NOW THEREFORE, the parties agree as follows:

1.   Agent acknowledges that it agrees to and will abide by the terms and conditions set forth herein and any terms and conditions set forth in any Publisher price lists, including without limitation the obligations of Agent to provide full, complete and accurate details of end-user Customers and their IP addresses.

2.   Agent acknowledges that Publisher may choose in its sole discretion whether to accept personal and member-rate subscriptions to its journals and other products, and may also choose in its sole discretion whether to accept such subscriptions through agents in general, and Agent specifically.

3.   Agent will only purchase personal and member-rate subscriptions on behalf of Customers with the express consent of Publisher. Such consent may be given specifically, or generally as indicated on price lists. These orders must be placed with the name of the Agent clearly indicated. Agent shall provide Publisher with full end-user Customer details on all such orders, and Publisher may, in its sole discretion, choose to ship those orders, and any claimed lost or damaged copies, directly to the end-user Customers so identified. For all such subscriptions, Agent will make reasonable inquiry from the Customer to confirm that such subscriptions are for bona fide personal, and not institutional, use. Agent will, within ten (10) business days of request, provide Publisher with accurate and complete copies of Agent's invoices to such Customers.

4.   Agent acknowledges that institutional subscriptions must be ordered at the institutional rate.

5.   Agent acknowledges that resale of personal, individual and member-rate subscriptions to anyone not in that category harms Publisher and the societies for which it publishes. Agent agrees not to engage in the following practices (collectively "Abusive Practices"):

    A.   Resale to institutions of personal and member-rate subscriptions.
    B.   Use of IP addresses, user names, passwords, or other access control mechanisms other than for the Publisher's Customer of record.
    C.   Distribution of any discounted copies, such as discounted print copies, to any entity other than the Customer in whose name it has been ordered.
    D.   Ordering discounted copies under the account of one Customer for another customer.
    E.   Claiming "lost" or "damaged" copies on the account of one Customer, and providing them to another customer.
    F.   Purchasing personal or member subscriptions without the express consent of Publisher, or without clearly indicating Agent's involvement as set forth in clause 3 above.

G. Photocopying and reproducing of journal issues, or distributing copies unlawfully reproduced by others.

6.   In the event Agent is found to have been engaged in any Abusive Practices, Agent consents to the entry of damages as follows. In the event of a violation of clauses 5(A), (C), (D) and (F), Agent agrees to pay as liquidated damages the amount of three times the difference between the amount paid and full institutional rate for each such subscription. In the event of a violation of clause 5(B), Agent agrees to pay as liquidated damages the amount of three times the full institutional rate for a subscription to any journal accessed through such Abusive Practices, multiplied by the number of distinct institutions accessing through such method. In the event Agent is found to have been engaged in activities described in clause 5(E), Agent agrees to pay as liquidated damages three times the single issue cost of such issues. In the event that Agent is found to have engaged in activities described in clause 5(G), Publisher may elect to pursue statutory damages, or liquidated damages in an amount equal to three times the full institutional price for any material so copied or distributed.

7. Agent represents and warrants that neither it, nor its subsidiaries or affiliates, or any company or agent owned or controlled by its officers or directors, have engaged in Abusive Practices, except as disclosed to Publisher within thirty (30) days of the date of this Agreement. Publisher agrees to settle voluntarily disclosed past Abusive Practices for an amount equal to Publisher's actual damages. In the event Agent fails to disclose any Abusive Practices within thirty (30) days of the date of this Agreement, Publisher's damages for any prior Abusive Practices violations shall be as set forth in clause 6.

8. Publisher reserves the right to accept or reject business from any agent, including Agent, in its sole discretion. Accordingly, while not required, prior approval of bids by Agent is highly recommended.

9. The term of this Agreement shall be two (2) years and it shall automatically renew for additional one (1) year periods unless either party notifies the other of its desire to terminate, which notice must be given at least sixty (60) days prior to the end of the thencurrent term.

10. In the event of a dispute between Agent and Publisher, Publisher may in its sole discretion choose to commence litigation in the State of New York, County of New York, or in the judicial district in which Agent maintains its principal place of business. Agent consents to the jurisdiction of any such court and waives any objections to venue therein.

11. This Agreement shall be governed and interpreted according to the internal laws of the State of New York.

AGREED AND ACCEPTED

Publisher, Inc.

By:_____

Name:_____

Agent, Inc.

By:_____

Name:_____

CHAPTER
3

Electronic Publishing

§ 3.01 Background

The distinctions between "print" and "electronic" publishing are becoming increasingly artificial. Any contract for a publication should address electronic rights, whether directly or implicitly. A professional book agreement involving the transfer of all rights is as much an electronic publishing agreement as it is a print agreement, and many publishers, particularly of major reference works, are choosing to publish exclusively in electronic format. That said, there are clearly rules, agreements, and practices to be addressed by a publisher involved in the dissemination of content in electronic formats.

The forms and materials in this chapter all relate to what is commonly referred to as electronic publishing.

The chapter breaks roughly into three main subsets. The first subset is forms and materials relating to the development of exclusively electronic publishing content. In this subset, I have included negotiating guidelines for use with software developers (§ 3.02), and a corresponding software agreement form (3.1). I have also included short agreements to use with individuals who are moderating Web forums and blogs (Forms 3.2 and 3.3), and a simple "for hire" agreement to use with a programmer (Form 3.4).

The second subset in this chapter is form agreements for use with electronic publishing customers, who are either end-users of content or site licensees providing content to end users. These documents are "shrink wraps," site licenses, user terms of use, and subscriber agreements. (Forms 3.5–3.8).

The last subset comprises three agreements allowing third-party dissemination of published content: an e-book distribution agreement, an authorized dealer agreement for the distribution of software products, and a brief OEM license to include databases in third-party equipment. (Forms 3.9–3.11)

Given that publishing is about content more than media, readers are urged to skim chapters for forms also relevant to electronic publishing.

§ 3.02 Negotiating Software Development Contracts

[A] General Comments

The following guidelines were developed for use by new media and acquisitions editors in the publishing context, primarily for the development of electronic products. The issues discussed herein are generally relevant to all forms of software, including CD-ROMs, diskettes, Web sites, and component software.

[B] Introduction to Guidelines for Negotiating Software Development Contracts

These guidelines have been prepared as an overview for drafting and negotiating software development contracts. They have been written from the point of view of the party commissioning the work and are meant as a companion to the software development agreement (Form 3.1).

The basis for contract negotiations with a new media developer will usually be a developer proposal responding to a client request for proposal (RFP). In evaluating a proposal, the commissioning party should make sure that there is a clear meeting of the minds among all parties involved in the development of the software (including, for example, the commissioning party, any third-party content supplier, and the software developer) regarding the nature and purpose of the software as well as the parties' respective responsibilities for its development and the associated expenses. To this end, the commissioning party should carefully discuss all the issues set forth below.

[1] Product Description and Functional Specifications

Early in the negotiation process, the commissioning party and the developer should agree on a detailed description of the final software, which can be appended to the contract as an exhibit. In addition, the commissioning party should attempt, where possible, to secure a functional specification for the software, as required by the RFP, prior to entering into the contract. In some cases, however, it will not be possible to obtain the document in advance because of the labor involved in preparing comprehensive functional specifications. In such cases, the functional specifications should be the first contract deliverable.

A comprehensive product description and functional specifications are enormously helpful in crystallizing all parties' expectations and obligations. In addition, these documents will often become the primary standards against which subsequent performance will be measured. Accordingly, the commissioning party should take pains to develop these documents carefully during the negotiation process. In so doing, the commissioning party should answer the following questions:

- Is the software description (which will be attached to the contract) sufficiently detailed and specific to describe the purpose and features? The goal is to develop a detailed and unambiguous document that will safeguard against any disagreements as the development process evolves.
- If the commissioning party plans for its software to be portable within a variety of competing technological platforms, does the software description specifically refer to them?

All components of the finished software must be considered. If the developer will be providing the user's guide, documentation, or help files, these items must be identified in the description.

During negotiations the commissioning party should also discuss how any changes to the description or functional specifications during the development of the product will be handled.

[2] Ownership

Ownership can mean many things: ownership of the software as a compilation; ownership of the content; or ownership of all copyrights, trade secret rights, or patents in the software. Software may incorporate an existing software engine owned by the developer or off-the-shelf software licensed for use in the software. Accordingly, the commissioning party must pay particular attention to the question of ownership early in its negotiations. Although obtaining the entire copyright may be more expensive, ownership will ensure complete exclusivity as well as the unfettered right to update and revise the software and prepare derivative works. In cases where ownership is not feasible, the commissioning party must take great care to ensure that it obtains all necessary distribution and development rights as well as the degree of exclusivity necessary to preserve its investment.

If the developer wishes to reserve any rights in software that the commissioning party is paying to have developed, the commissioning party should consider the feasibility of owning the copyright and licensing back to the developer the specific rights the developer wants. For example, if necessary the commissioning party could license back the rights to prepare and publish the developer's own derivative works or improvements, provided that all the commissioning party's content is removed. The commissioning party might also require the developer to provide free source code updates and/or a royalty-free license to use such developer-owned works.

If it is clear, however, that the developer must own the copyright, the commissioning party must resolve the following issues:

- Will the commissioning party's rights be exclusive or nonexclusive?
- Will the commissioning party's rights be limited to a particular market segment?
- Will the commissioning party's rights be limited to a fixed term (e.g., limited to three years)?
- Will the commissioning party have the right to modify the software or develop platform conversions? Is it obliged to work with the original developer or may it use a third-party developer? Does it have access to needed source code?
- Will the commissioning party have access to the source code for any purpose? Is it in a usable, annotated format? Will the developer provide support in using the source code?

- What rights will the developer retain? Will these rights affect the commissioning party's ability to compete in a given market? Has the commissioning party negotiated the best possible noncompete provisions, if necessary?

[3] Hardware and Software Specifications

The commissioning party must investigate the programming environment. Are there hardware specifications to use the commissioning party's product? More bells and whistles may require more computing capacity. Will the software require "plug-ins" that are difficult to load? The commissioning party must understand its market and the market's sophistication.

[4] Delivery and Acceptance

The commissioning party must negotiate a clear, explicit schedule for the delivery of work in progress as well as the finished software. It is advised that the commissioning party require delivery of complete functional specifications, a prototype, and a beta version in advance of the final version. The schedule should take into account the time necessary for the commissioning party to evaluate deliverables and the time reasonably required for the developer to accommodate any changes proposed by the commissioning party as well as its target release date for the software. If the commissioning party will be supplying any content or other components of the product, the schedule should address this process as well. Finally, the commissioning party may wish to include in the schedule a requirement for regular status reports or face-to-face meetings.

The commissioning party must negotiate appropriate acceptance standards. Wherever possible, the commissioning party should require that all deliverables be "complete and satisfactory" to it. If the commissioning party simply cannot persuade a developer to accept these terms (for example, by explaining that it is the commissioning party's standing policy to insist upon a "complete and satisfactory" standard and that the law, as well as its own principles, require it to exercise good faith in the evaluation process even when making subjective judgments), the commissioning party may have to accept some objective constraints on the acceptance process.

Developers sometimes insist, for example, that deliverables that conform to functional specifications be deemed acceptable. This is not unreasonable, particularly for software that is not critical to your business. In cases in which the functional specifications will not be agreed upon until after the contract is signed, however, the commissioning party should reserve the right to evaluate these subjectively even if the commissioning party agrees that subsequent deliverables will be deemed acceptable if they conform in all respects to the functional specifications. Bear in mind that any such constraints may hinder the commissioning party's ability to reject a product and that the commissioning party should do as much as it possibly can to avoid paying for work it cannot use. At a bare minimum, it should reserve the right to contract with third parties to "fix" software that it is required to accept but cannot use in its present form. In any event, if the commissioning party does agree to such constraints on its acceptance criteria, it is particularly important to negotiate a "no-fault" termination provision that limits exposure (*see* § 3.02[B][6], *infra*).

[5] Financial Terms

A developer's compensation may consist of an hourly fee (in which case the commissioning party should insist upon a maximum or "cap" on fees for completion of the project), a fixed development fee (which may be paid out in stages tied to acceptance, not merely delivery, of interim deliverables), royalties, or a combination thereof. In negotiating fees, the commissioning party should try to minimize "front-loading" or payment of large amounts in advance of delivery of the finished product. Any amounts paid up front should also be taken into account when negotiating termination provisions including "kill" fees and "no-fault" termination rights. In addition, the commissioning party may wish to structure the development fee to include incentives or penalties with respect to timely delivery.

If the commissioning party is going to pay a royalty to the developer, the commissioning party should try to structure some or all of the development fee as an advance against those royalties. The commissioning party should try to establish the proper balance between the projected royalties and the size of the advance, remembering that its own risk increases and the developer's risk declines as the amount of the advance increases. In formulating a royalty structure, the commissioning party must take into account the ways in which the software will actually generate revenue. Is the software:

- A specific product, such as an executable database?
- A Web site that enables e-commerce?
- A potential venue for the sale of advertising space?
- A free add-on to a saleable product?

Obviously, not all situations are appropriate for royalties.

Finally, if the software will incorporate any third party or "off-the-shelf" software, the commissioning party should consider whether it or the developer will negotiate and pay for the necessary licenses. Often, developers receive volume discounts that can be passed on to the commissioning party. If the licenses in question are of fixed duration, be sure to negotiate an adequate term. The commissioning party should also consider whether such licenses will allow it to revise the software as needed.

[6] Termination Rights

Although no one wishes to dwell on the possibility of disappointment at the outset of promising negotiations, it is essential that the commissioning party agree on appropriate termination provisions with the developer. A carefully negotiated, well-drafted contract can enable the commissioning party to dissolve an unsuccessful relationship without rancor and, better yet, without involving lawyers and legal threats.

The commissioning party will certainly need to reserve the right to terminate the agreement in the event the developer fails to deliver timely and acceptable deliverables (*see* § 3.02[B][4], *supra*). The commissioning party must consider, however, whether it will be required to give the developer an opportunity to correct deficiencies before it can terminate the agreement. If the commissioning party does agree to such an arrangement, the developer must agree on a reasonable time limit for delivery of corrected materials. The commissioning party should also consider whether the delivery dates for subsequent deliverables will be extended in view of the time spent to cure an earlier deficiency. If the commissioning party does allow such an extension, however, it should set a fixed period of time beyond which the final delivery date for the completed project will not be extended.

The commissioning party must consider the financial consequences of termination for failure to deliver timely and acceptable materials. The developer may be required to refund all or part of the fees paid to date, depending on the payment schedule for the project (*see* § 3.02[B][5]). The more money the developer receives up front, the greater the obligation to refund money should be.

From a practical standpoint, however, it may be more important to focus on the commissioning party's rights to complete or correct work in progress as of the time of termination. Even where there is a legal right to a refund, it may be difficult to obtain cash from a disgruntled or insolvent developer. In such cases, the right to complete a work in progress may be the best means of salvaging investment in a project.

Finally, the commissioning party should consider demanding a "no-fault" termination provision, which will enable it to terminate a project even if the developer has met all of its obligations. This is particularly useful where the development process is likely to be lengthy; in such cases, the anticipated market needs may change during the development process and termination may become quite attractive. The financial consequences of "no-fault" termination are often quite different from those of termination for cause. In some instances, the commissioning party may even agree to pay a "kill" fee (for example, a percentage of the balance due the developer upon completion of the next deliverable or of the final project) in exchange for the opportunity to walk away from a project that no longer looks promising.

[7] Warranties and Liabilities

The limitations on liability are often the hardest part of a negotiation with a developer. As a general rule, developers have their own form agreements designed to protect their interests. For the commissioning party, it is always better to prepare a new draft. The warranty and liability clauses provide a good example of the truth of this statement. Developer's contracts are notoriously deficient (from the commissioning party's perspective, of course) with respect to warranties. A typical developer's form agreement will contain virtually no warranties and many disclaimers. The commissioning party, on the other hand, should require reasonable warranties of

- Non-infringement;
- No harmful statements or instructions;
- No viruses, time bombs, trojan horses, etc.;
- Full and complete source code;
- Full performance in accordance with specifications; and
- Full authority to sign agreement.

A responsible developer will usually agree to most of these warranties but will often require a disclaimer of warranties of fitness for a particular purpose. Developers will also often try to limit their liability for a breach of warranty to the contract value (or less). Whether to accept this limitation requires an evaluation of the risks involved. Consideration should be given to whether the developer has been sued before, and of course, how much money is involved. For a million-dollar contract, $1 million might be adequate to compensate for any loss, although, as a practical matter, it is easier to get concessions from a developer in a million-dollar contract. Additionally, different limits on liability can sometimes be negotiated with respect to different warranties.

[8] Other Development Issues

Authoring system and programming language. It is important to ascertain in advance what authoring system and programming language the developer proposes to use. These issues bear directly on the ability to modify, correct, or complete the project itself in the event the relationship with the developer breaks down. Access to the source code for the product will be meaningless if the programming language or authoring system is arcane. The choice of authoring system may also limit the ability to modify the finished software.

Licenses and fees. Are there any licensing fees for the authoring system and other tools used to develop this product, or any other permissions required? If so, who is responsible for obtaining the licenses and paying the fees?

Content. Who will obtain any required multimedia assets, such as video, audio, and animations, and who will pay for them?

Beta testing. Will the developer be responsible for complete beta testing? Will beta test reports be submitted? Does the beta testing include evaluation of network compatibility?

Errors and bugs. The commissioning party should be sure that the developer will provide a warranty that the final version of the product will be free of error and programming bugs for an adequate term (generally at least 12 months). Confirm that error corrections will be done in a timely manner at no cost.

Technical support. Negotiations should also address the subject of technical support. How will the developer support the completed software? Does the developer maintain telephone support services? Will there be a charge for technical support? Who will support any third-party software used?

Confidentiality. Be certain that the developer understands that work in progress must be treated as highly confidential.

Software Development Agreement

The following form is recommended as the form of first resort for publishers negotiating with software developers. It can be used for any type of software development, although for Web sites it is recommended that the word "software" be replaced with "Web site," and the whereas clauses should be modified as appropriate.

Substantively, this form contains the key elements of any publishing agreement (e.g., rights, compensation, acceptability, and warranties). As such, it differs from most standard developer agreements by containing language for

- Strong pro-commissioning party acceptability standards;
- Full ownership of the copyright in the commissioning party;
- Full intellectual property and related warranties with no disclaimers or express limits on liability;
- Source code ownership by the commissioning party;
- Post-delivery error correction and support obligations;
- Noncompetition from the developer; and
- No fault termination by the commissioning party.

As compared to the "no fault/no liability" form agreements often prepared by developers, this form shifts the balance of power to the party paying to have the work done, and as such it is particularly appropriate to use for key projects. For a short-form programmer agreement, see Form 3.4.

Software Development Agreement

This SOFTWARE DEVELOPMENT AGREEMENT is entered into as of the _____ day of _____ by and between [name], a [state] corporation, with offices at [address] ("Developer") and [name], a [state] corporation, with offices at [address] (the "Commissioning Party").

WITNESSETH

WHEREAS Developer is an expert in the field of creating and programming software;

WHEREAS the Commissioning Party wishes to retain Developer to perform the services described in this Agreement relating to the development of a software program for _____ (the "SOFTWARE"); and

WHEREAS Developer desires to perform these services in accordance with the terms and conditions of this Agreement;

NOW THEREFORE, in consideration of the premises, conditions, covenants and warranties herein contained, the parties agree as follows:

1. The Software

Developer agrees to prepare the SOFTWARE which is more fully described in Exhibit A attached hereto and incorporated herein by reference, and which shall be complete and satisfactory to the Commissioning Party in organization, form, content, style, performance and technical development. The SOFTWARE is to be designed in a manner which is fully portable within the designated environment, PC and Macintosh compatible, and which may be modified by the Commissioning Party should the Commissioning Party, in its sole discretion, choose to prepare such modifications by itself, with third parties or, if the Commissioning Party and the Developer so agree, with the Developer. [Developer will supply _____ ("Third Party Material") for the SOFTWARE at its sole expense and will deliver to the Commissioning Party with the Final Deliverables (as defined in Section 3 below) the nonexclusive, worldwide, perpetual, royalty-free, fully paid-up license for the Commissioning Party to use any and all such Third Party Material in the SOFTWARE and in derivative works based thereon, in all media of expression now known or later developed.] It is understood and agreed that the Commissioning Party will supply artwork, text, information for customers, terms of use, and other content to be determined by the Commissioning Party (the "Commissioning Party Material") for the SOFTWARE at its sole expense.

2. Development Fee

For the timely and satisfactory completion and delivery of the SOFTWARE, including complete copies of the source code for the SOFTWARE in machine readable form and in hard copy (the "Final Deliverables") by the due date specified in Section 3 below and for the other rights granted to the Commissioning Party herein, the Commissioning Party agrees to pay Developer the fees set forth on Exhibit B which is attached hereto and incorporated herein by reference. As an advance against timely delivery of the complete and satisfactory Final Deliverables by the due date, the Commissioning Party will pay Developer [25%/50%] of the Development Fee upon execution of this Agreement.

3. Development and Approval Process

3.1 Preparation of the Final Product Specification. A development team from Developer has met with representatives of the Commissioning Party. From these meetings, Developer has developed and delivered to the Commissioning Party a product specification (the "Final Product Specification") including hardware specifications, story boards, functional specifications and a full description of the SOFTWARE, which has been attached hereto as Exhibit A.

3.2 <u>Preparation of Deliverables</u>. In accordance with the Final Product Specification, Developer will prepare and deliver the Deliverables for the SOFTWARE set forth on Exhibit B which is attached hereto and incorporated herein by reference, complete and satisfactory to the Commissioning Party in organization, form, content, style and technical development by the respective due dates set forth therein (individually the "Due Date" and collectively the "Due Dates").

If any Deliverable is not free of programming defects or errors, or is not otherwise acceptable to the Commissioning Party in organization, form, content, style, performance and technical development, the Commissioning Party may reject such Deliverable, specifying the reasons for such rejection. Developer shall have five (5) working days thereafter to revise the Deliverable to address the Commissioning Party's concerns and resubmit the Deliverable to the Commissioning Party. If Developer does not deliver the Deliverable by the Due Date or the revised Deliverable within the five working day period, or if the Commissioning Party rejects the revised Deliverable on the basis that it is unacceptable as set forth above, the Commissioning Party may, in addition to any other rights it may have: (i) give Developer written notice of termination of this Agreement, after which no further payments shall be due Developer from the Commissioning Party and this Agreement shall terminate; (ii) require Developer to make additional corrections to the Deliverable; or (iii) notify Developer that it wishes to make other arrangements for the completion of the SOFTWARE in which case Developer shall promptly deliver to the Commissioning Party all work in progress, including without limitation, the source code, which the Commissioning Party may reasonably require to complete the SOFTWARE. If the Commissioning Party elects option (iii), the Commissioning Party may make other arrangements with respect to the SOFTWARE as it deems appropriate and shall deduct from the Development Fee the cost of such arrangements. If the cost of such arrangements exceeds the unpaid balance of the Development Fee, no further payments shall be due Developer hereunder.

Upon acceptance of a Deliverable, the Commissioning Party shall pay the Developer the amount identified on Exhibit B as due upon acceptance of said Deliverable. It is understood and agreed, however, that Exhibit B may include deliverables for which no payment is due upon acceptance.

3.3 <u>Time of Essence</u>. Developer acknowledges that time is of the essence with respect to all delivery dates. In the event the Commissioning Party gives Developer the opportunity to revise a rejected Deliverable, such opportunity shall not postpone or otherwise affect the Due Dates for subsequent Deliverables unless the Commissioning Party expressly agrees in writing to extend such Due Dates.

3.4 <u>Error Correction and Technical Support</u>. Any errors identified within one year following [*publication/use/acceptance*] of the SOFTWARE, including without limitation errors regarding the proper functioning of the coding, interface, buttons, graphical user interface and navigation links will be corrected promptly by Developer at no cost to the Commissioning Party. Following acceptance of the Final Deliverables, the Commissioning Party shall be responsible for providing routine technical support to its end-users. Developer will, however, provide technical support related to any interface or navigation problems or any other queries to which the Commissioning Party cannot adequately respond, at no cost to the Commissioning Party, for a period of one-year following [*publication/use/acceptance*] of the SOFTWARE.

4. Proprietary Rights and Credits

4.1 <u>Ownership of Rights</u>. [The Commissioning Party shall be the exclusive owner of the physical copies of the source code as well as the copyright and all other proprietary rights in the SOFTWARE, including without limitation in the source code, and Developer hereby grants, transfers and assigns to the Commissioning Party all rights, including the copyright, in and to the SOFTWARE, and all revisions thereof, in all forms and languages, in all media of expression now known or later developed, for the full term of the copyright, and all renewals and extensions thereof, throughout the world. Developer acknowledges that it acquires no right of any kind or nature whatsoever in the SOFTWARE including but not limited to any rights in any content or other materials supplied by the Commissioning Party and included in the SOFTWARE. Notwithstanding the foregoing, it is understood and agreed that the SOFTWARE incorporates certain Third Party Material identified in Section 1 above for which Developer has only obtained and conveyed to the Commissioning Party the nonexclusive, worldwide, perpetual, royalty-free, fully paid up license to the Commissioning Party to use such material in the SOFTWARE and in derivative works based thereon.

The Commissioning Party shall have the exclusive right, in its sole discretion and without obligation to Developer, to publish, use or otherwise exploit the SOFTWARE and derivative works based thereon.

The Commissioning Party shall be the exclusive owner of the copyright and all other proprietary rights in the "look and feel" of the SOFTWARE including, but not limited to, the graphical user interface and navigation links. [Neither the source code nor any material portion of the "look and feel" for the SOFTWARE may be used by Developer without the Commissioning Party's prior written permission.] [Developer is and shall be the exclusive owner of the physical copies of the source code as well as the copyright and all other proprietary rights in the SOFTWARE. Developer hereby grants to the Commissioning Party the non-exclusive, worldwide, perpetual, royalty-free, fully paid up license to use the SOFTWARE and the source code and to made derivative works based thereon. Additionally, it is understood and agreed that the SOFTWARE incorporates certain Third Party Material identified in Section 1 above for which Developer has obtained and hereby conveys to the Commissioning Party the non-exclusive, worldwide, perpetual, royalty-free, fully paid up license to use such material in the SOFTWARE and in derivative works based thereon.]

4.2 Limited License. The Commissioning Party hereby grants Developer the nonexclusive, nontransferable right, free of charge to use the Commissioning Party Material identified in Section 1 above solely for the purpose of develop-ing the SOFTWARE as set forth in this Agreement.

4.3 Copyright Notice. Developer shall cause to be displayed on the SOFTWARE, in such locations as the Commissioning Party may designate a notice of copyright in the Commissioning Party's name in a form approved by the Commissioning Party.

5. Beta Testing

Developer shall at its sole expense thoroughly beta test the final beta version of the SOFTWARE and shall deliver to the Commissioning Party a complete beta test report, including without limitation testing methodologies, programming and navigational errors, and corrections therefor, with the next deliverable.

6. Related and Competing Works

Developer, without the Commissioning Party's prior written consent, shall not nor shall it permit anyone else to prepare, reproduce or publish any portion of the SOFTWARE, or any version of the SOFTWARE, revision or other derivative work based thereon. In addition, until such time as the Commissioning Party shall decide to no longer to use SOFTWARE or any version thereof, Developer, without the Commissioning Party's prior written consent, shall not nor shall it permit anyone else to prepare, reproduce or use any other software or other product that might in the Commissioning Party's reasonable judgment interfere or compete with its use of the SOFTWARE.

7. Representations and Indemnification

7.1 Developer's Representations and Warranties. Developer represents and warrants that (i) the Final Product Specification, each subsequent Deliverable and the SOFTWARE itself (excluding any materials supplied by the Commissioning Party and any Third Party Material) are original on Developer's part and have not been previously published; (ii) Developer owns and has the right to convey all rights herein conveyed to the Commissioning Party; (iii) the Final Product Specification, each subsequent Deliverable and the SOFTWARE itself contain no libelous or unlawful material, contain no instructions that may cause harm or injury, do not infringe upon or violate any copyright, trade secret, trademark, patent or other right or the privacy of others; (iv) all statements asserted as fact in any content contributed by Developer to the SOFTWARE are either true or based upon generally accepted professional research practices; (v) the SOFTWARE will perform in accordance with its specifications; (vi) the SOFTWARE contains no so-called "viruses," "time bombs," "Trojan horses," "worms," "drop-dead devices," or other software routines designed to permit unauthorized access or to disable, functionally impair or erase software, hardware or data; and (vii) the source code for the SOFTWARE will be delivered complete and accurate and will be updated promptly in the event of any changes or corrections made by Developer.

7.2 Developer's Indemnification. Developer agrees to indemnify the Commissioning Party against all liability and expense, including reasonable counsel fees, arising from or out of any breach or alleged breach of the foregoing representations and warranties.

7.3 Procedures. Each party shall promptly inform the other of any claim made against either which, if sustained, would constitute a breach of any of the foregoing representations and warranties. The Commissioning Party shall have the right to defend or settle any such claim, action or proceeding with counsel of its own choice. Developer shall fully cooperate with the Commissioning Party in such defense and may join the defense with counsel of its choice at its sole expense.

7.4 Survival. The representations and indemnities stated in this section shall survive the expiration or termination of this Agreement.

8. Termination

8.1 Termination Without Cause. In addition to the Commissioning Party's right to terminate this Agreement under Section 3 in the event any Deliverable is not accepted, the Commissioning Party shall have the right to terminate this Agreement without cause or reason at any time, upon thirty days written notice to Developer. Upon receipt of such notice, Developer shall immediately discontinue preparing the SOFTWARE and return all materials to the Commissioning Party. In the event of early termination by the Commissioning Party without cause, Developer shall, in lieu of any other damages or remedy, retain all payments made to Developer up to the date of notice of termination, and Developer may be entitled to an additional payment for its documented and reasonable expenses incurred in performing additional services to the extent the value of such services exceed the total payments made previously, not to exceed the amount that Developer would have received upon acceptance of the next Deliverable due following termination.

8.2 Termination by Developer. Developer shall have the right to terminate this Agreement upon the Commissioning Party's material breach of the Agreement, if such breach is not cured within thirty (30) days following receipt of written notice from Developer to the Commissioning Party setting forth in reasonable detail the nature of the alleged breach. In the event of any such termination by

Developer, Developer shall, in lieu of any other damages or remedy, retain all payments made or due to Developer for deliverables already accepted by the Commissioning Party as of the date of notice of termination, and Developer may be entitled to an additional payment reflecting its damages in connection with such termination for its documented and reasonable expenses incurred in performing additional services to the extent the value of such services exceed the total payments made previously, not to exceed the amount that Developer would have received upon acceptance of the next Deliverable due following termination.

8.3 Rights Upon Termination. In the event of any termination of this Agreement, by either party for any reason whatsoever, the Commissioning Party shall own all work completed or then in development by Developer for which the Commissioning Party has paid and, in such event, Developer shall immediately deliver to the Commissioning Party any and all materials related to the SOFTWARE, including without limitation source code and any documentation for the SOFTWARE.

8.4 Survival. Termination of this Agreement shall not extinguish any of the Commissioning Party's or Developer's rights and obligations under this Agreement which by their terms continue after the date of termination.

9. Confidentiality

In performing its obligations under this Agreement, Developer may receive confidential information from the Commissioning Party, which may be oral or written. Such information, if written, shall be marked "Confidential" by the Commissioning Party and includes, but is not limited to, information pertaining to the terms and conditions of this Agreement, marketing plans and business plans, and all information that by the nature of the circumstances surrounding the disclosure ought in good faith to be treated as confidential. Confidential information shall be used solely to prepare the SOFTWARE and for no other purpose whatsoever. Developer shall protect all such information from disclosure to other parties with the same degree of care as that which is accorded to its own proprietary information. Developer shall limit access to such confidential information to only those of Developer's employees, agents and subcontractors who have need of such access for performance of this Agreement. Upon the termination of this Agreement, confidential information furnished by the Commissioning Party to Developer shall be returned.

10. No Assignment

This Agreement and the rights granted hereunder may not be assigned by Developer without the Commissioning Party's prior written consent. Subject to the foregoing, this Agreement shall inure to the benefit of and be binding on the successors and assigns of the parties.

11.   Integration

This Agreement sets forth the entire agreement between the parties with respect to the subject matter hereof, and may not be modified or amended except by written agreement executed by the parties hereto.

12.   Severability

If any provision of this Agreement is declared to be invalid, void or unenforceable, (a) the remaining provisions of this Agreement shall continue in full force and effect, and (b) the invalid or unenforceable provision shall be replaced by a term or provision that is valid and enforceable and that comes closest to expressing the intention of such invalid or unenforceable term or provision.

13.   Governing Law

This Agreement shall be governed by the laws of the State of [*the Commissioning Party*] applicable to agreements made and to be wholly performed therein (without reference to conflict of laws). Any legal action, suit or proceeding arising out of or relating to this Agreement or the breach thereof shall be instituted in a court of competent jurisdiction, in the County of [*the Commissioning Party*] in the State of [*the Commissioning Party*] and the Commissioning Party and Developer hereby submit to the jurisdiction of such court and waive any right each might otherwise have to claim lack of personal jurisdiction or forum non conveniens.

14.   Independent Contractor

Developer shall be deemed to have the status of an independent contractor, and nothing in this Agreement shall be deemed to place the parties in the relationship of employer-employee, principal-agent, partners or joint venturers. Developer shall be responsible for any withholding taxes, payroll taxes, disability insurance payments, unemployment taxes and other taxes or charges on the payments received by Developer hereunder.

15.   Notice

The address of each party hereto as set forth above shall be the appropriate address for the mailing of notices and payments hereunder. Notices to Developer shall be addressed to the attention of _____. Notices to the Commissioning Party shall be addressed to the attention of the _____ _____. All notices which a party is required or may desire to serve upon the other party may be served personally or by certified or registered mail (postage prepaid), or by facsimile transmission confirmed by first class mail. Either party may change its mailing address by written notice to the other.

16.   Waiver

No waiver by either party, whether express or implied, of any provision of this Agreement shall constitute a continuing waiver of such provision or a waiver of any other provision of this Agreement. No waiver by either party, whether express or implied, of any breach or default by the other party, shall constitute a waiver of any breach or default of the same or any other provision of this Agreement.

17.   Paragraph Headings

Paragraph headings contained herein are for the convenience of the parties only. They shall not be used in any way to govern, limit, modify, or construe this Agreement and shall not be given any legal effect.

18.   Counterparts

This Agreement may be executed in two or more counterparts and all counter-parts so executed shall for all purposes constitute one agreement, binding on all parties hereto.

IN WITNESS WHEREOF, the parties have caused this Software Development Agreement to be executed by their duly authorized representatives on the date set forth above.

Commissioning Party   **Developer**

By: _____   By: _____

Name: _____   Name: _____

Title: _____   Title: _____

Date: _____   Date: _____

EXHIBIT A

[Final Product Specification]

EXHIBIT B

DELIVERABLE	DUE DATE	FEE (IF ANY) DUE FROM UPON ACCEPTANCE
Prototype: A stand-alone, fully executable program demonstrating all main screens of the final software in terms of look, feel and functionality. This deliverable should be detailed enough to judge the experience a user will have using the final product.		
Final Product Specification: A complete, final product specification including user and hosting hardware specifications, story boards, functional specifications, and full description.		
Alpha: A stand-alone, untested executable program demonstrating all screens of the final software in terms of look, feel, and functionality and one example of each type of content as it will appear in and be prepared for the final softwar e (i.e., one compressed video, one animation, one photo, one audio clip, etc.).		
Beta 1: Same as Alpha including 60% of final content.		
Final Beta: Same as Alpha except should be a standalone, fully functional executable program containing all content and suitable for testing.		
Formal Product: Same as final beta except should be fully tested and free of all known bugs.		

Moderator Agreement for Threaded Online Discussion as Part of Distance Learning Project

Distance learning is a revolution in process. Booksellers, for-profit universities, and globally recognized academic institutions are all using the Web in efforts to establish viable methods of teaching students from remote locations. These efforts require software, content, and individuals who are skilled in the relevant fields to provide assistance and instruction.

Form 3.2 is an agreement with an independent contractor to serve as a moderator for a threaded online discussion. The form is non-negotiated, and as such may be too strong for certain situations, such as the hiring of a top professor to serve as a moderator for his or her own textbook.

It is worth remembering that although the moderator may technically transfer all copyrights to the publisher, in the absence of a signature (digital or paper and ink) from the end-user posing the questions, the publisher's rights are at best nonexclusive.

Moderator Agreement

October 31, 20___

[name] [address]

Dear _____:

This letter when signed by you and returned to me shall constitute an Agreement between you and _____ (Publisher) for your services as the moderator for the threaded on line discussion on the subject of _____ at the Web site _____, which is part of Publisher's distance learning project.

  Beginning _____ through _____, you shall answer questions posed electronically by users at the Web site. You will choose which questions to answer based on your professional judgment as to which questions will be most helpful to the greatest number of users. The questions and answers must be posted within seventy-two hours of the initial posting/sending of the questions. All of your answers and other material you create as part of this assignment shall constitute a work-made-for-hire and shall be owned exclusively by Publisher. To the extent that the material you create under this Agreement is not a work for hire, you hereby assign to Publisher all rights, including copyright, in such material.

You may hire others to assist you in performing some portions of your obligations under this Agreement, but you shall be solely responsible to compensate any such third parties and to provide them with and file all necessary tax and other required forms. Further, each person you engage must sign a release providing (1) that he/she is providing services as a work-made-for-hire and that the rights in all of the materials created are exclusively the property of Publisher, and (2) that he/she shall look only to you for any compensation for the services.

You represent and warrant that you have the right to enter into this agreement, that none of the material you create and post will violate any copyrights, trademarks or other rights of third parties, that the content of the material shall be appropriate, current and accurate and shall not defame or offend any third party. You further represent and warrant that you will not include or post material created by others that you know or have reason to suspect would violate any of the foregoing. These representations and warranties shall survive termination of this Agreement. You agree that you will make timely corrections to your material if you and the Publisher reasonably believe that the material contains inaccuracies, and that the Publisher has the right to delete any material without notice in the event that the Publisher believes in its sole discretion that such material may give rise to legal liability.

In consideration of the foregoing, Publisher shall pay you, on execution of this Agreement, the sum of _____, as a one-time fee, paid in advance for the entire term of the Agreement. If for any reason you are unable or fail to complete your obligations, Publisher may terminate this Agreement on thirty days written notice and you shall be obligated to return this fee to Publisher, less an amount pro-rated to reflect the actual percentage of the time you did perform. You shall be solely responsible to acquire and maintain any and all hardware and software you require to perform your obligations hereunder, with the exception, of course, with the password(s) necessary to enable you access to the course site.

You recognize that you are an independent contractor and nothing herein or in connection herewith shall create or imply a relationship of agency, employment, co-venturers or the like. Neither party may enter into any agreement which will be binding upon the other.

Your engagement is personal and the rights hereunder granted to you are not assignable nor may the obligations imposed be delegated without our prior written consent, provided, however, that you may assign any sums due to you hereunder without Publisher's consent.

Except as provided in the preceding subparagraph, this Agreement shall inure to the benefit of the heirs, successors, subsidiaries, administrators, and permitted assigns of the parties.

This Agreement shall not be subject to change or modification in whole or in part, unless in writing signed by both parties.

No waiver of any term or condition of this Agreement or of any part thereof shall be deemed a waiver of any other term or condition of this Agreement or of any breach of this Agreement or any part thereof.

This Agreement shall be construed and interpreted pursuant to the laws of the State of New York applicable to contracts wholly entered into and performed in the State of New York. Any legal action, suit or proceeding arising out of or relating to this Agreement or the breach thereof shall be instituted in a court of competent jurisdiction in New York County in the State of New York and each party hereby consents and submits to the personal jurisdiction of such court, waives any objection to venue in such court and consents to service of process by registered or certified mail, return receipt requested, at the last known address of such party.

We look forward to working with you on what we believe will be an exciting project.

Sincerely,

AGREED AND ACCEPTED

By: _____

Name: _____

Address: _____

SS#: _____

FORM 3.3

Blogger Agreement

After several years of rapid growth, there are now an almost infinite number of blogs covering an equally large number of topics, ranging from personal online journals to highly sophisticated news-and-media operations.

Typically, a blogger performs a function somewhere between editor and author. Others may also serve as business managers and advertising sales representatives. There are many ways to structure blogging agreements, but the form below should highlight some options.

Agreement

October 31, 20__

[name] [address]

Dear _____ :

This letter when signed by you and returned to me shall constitute an Agreement between you and _____ (Publisher) for your services on behalf of Publisher.

Beginning _____ and lasting for a period of ___, you will write content for a daily blog on the topic of __ which will be hosted by Publisher at www. address.com. You will be responsible for researching [topic], editing, tagging, and posting all content. Additionally, you will review e-mail and post comments from readers of the blog so as to make the site editorially attractive for users interested in [topic]. All of the material you create as part of this assignment shall constitute a work-made-for-hire and shall be owned exclusively by Publisher. To the extent that the material you create under this Agreement is not a work for hire, you hereby assign to Publisher all rights, including copyright, in such material. For material written by readers and others, you will acquire permission to post it using a permission form provided Publisher. We shall have the right to use your name and likeness on and in connection with the blog.

You may hire others to assist you in performing some portions of your obligations under this Agreement, but you shall be solely responsible to compensate any such third parties and to provide them with and file all necessary tax and other required forms. Further, each person you engage must sign a release providing (1) that he/she is providing services as a work-made-for-hire and that the rights in all of the materials created are exclusively the property of Publisher, and (2) that he/she shall look only to you for any compensation for the services.

[You/Publisher] shall be solely responsible for securing advertisers whose advertisements will be placed on the blog.

You will meet periodically with Publisher's staff to discuss possible new features and section for the blog.

You represent and warrant that you have the right to enter into this agreement, that none of the material you create and post will violate any copyrights, trademarks or other rights of third parties, that the content of the material shall be appropriate, current and accurate and shall not defame or offend any third party. You further represent and warrant that you will not include or post material created by others that you know or have reason to suspect would violate any of the foregoing. These representations and warranties shall survive termination of this Agreement. You agree that you will make timely corrections to your material if you and the Publisher reasonably believe that the material contains inaccuracies and that the Publisher has the right to delete any material without notice in the event that the Publisher believes in its sole discretion that such material may give rise to legal liability.

In consideration of the foregoing, Publisher shall pay you, on execution of this Agreement, [the sum of _____, as a one-time fee, paid in advance for the entire term of the Agreement] [__% of all advertising revenues attributable to the blog][$__ for each 1,000 viewers per month who visit the blog]. If for any reason you are unable or fail to complete your obligations, Publisher may terminate this Agreement on thirty days written notice [and you shall be obligated to return any fees advanced by Publisher, pro-rated as of the date of termination.]

You recognize that you are an independent contractor and nothing herein or in connection herewith shall create or imply a relationship of agency, employment, co-venturers or the like. Neither party may enter into any agreement which will be binding upon the other.

Your engagement is personal and the rights hereunder granted to you are not assignable nor may the obligations imposed be delegated without our prior written consent, provided, however, that you may assign any sums due to you hereunder without Publisher's consent.

Except as provided in the preceding subparagraph, this Agreement shall inure to the benefit of the heirs, successors, subsidiaries, administrators, and permitted assigns of the parties.

This Agreement shall not be subject to change or modification in whole or in part, unless in writing signed by both parties.

No waiver of any term or condition of this Agreement or of any part thereof shall be deemed a waiver of any other term or condition of this Agreement or of any breach of this Agreement or any part thereof.

This Agreement shall be construed and interpreted pursuant to the laws of the State of New York applicable to contracts wholly entered into and performed in the State of New York. Any legal action, suit or proceeding arising out of or relating to this Agreement or the breach thereof shall be instituted in a court of competent jurisdiction in New York County in the State of New York and each party hereby consents and submits to the personal jurisdiction of such court, waives any objection to venue in such court and consents to service of process by registered or certified mail, return receipt requested, at the last known address of such party.

We look forward to working with you on what we believe will be an exciting project.

Sincerely,

AGREED AND ACCEPTED

By: _____

Name: _____

Address: _____

SS#: _____

All-Purpose Programmer Agreement (Short Form)

The following is a short form agreement with a programmer to provide services on an independent contractor "for hire" basis. In addition to standard language concerning ownership, independent contractor status, and "at will" termination, it contains an important clause (Clause 8) that the programmer's sole remedies in the event of a breach are in monetary damages. This should help avoid the argument that a material breach by the publisher gives rise to copyright infringement and the possibility of injunctive relief.

All-Purpose Programmer Agreement

Agreement made this ____ day of ___, 20__, between _____
("Programmer") and _____ ("Publisher").

Publisher and Programmer hereby agree as follows:

1. Publisher hereby engages Programmer, and Programmer agrees to be engaged, on the terms and conditions of this Agreement, to provide programming services and develop Software Products as requested by Publisher. Programmer shall be paid within days of submission of invoices at compensation to be set forth in writing and agreed upon by the parties prior to the commencement of any individual project.

2. Programmer hereby acknowledges that Programmer's work and services hereunder and all results and proceeds thereof, including without limitation, the Software Products, and the materials contained therein to the extent not copyrighted by or proprietary to third parties, are work done and services provided under Publisher's direction and control and have been specially commissioned by Publisher for use as a contribution to a product, service or work and that all such products, work, and services shall be considered as works made for hire. For purposes of copyright, Publisher shall own all rights in and to the copyright of the Software Products and Publisher shall have the right to register the copyright of all such Software Products in its name. To the extent such rights do not vest in Publisher as a work made for hire, Programmer hereby grants, assigns and transfers to Publisher all of Programmer's right, title and interest in and to the Software Products and all materials contained therein, including but not limited to the sole and exclusive right in perpetuity throughout the world in all languages to use and exploit all or any part of the Software Products and all or any part of any material contained therein or prepared therefor, whether or not used therein, by any means and in any and all media of expression now known or later developed. Any Publisher-owned or provided work or material constitutes the proprietary property of Publisher and Publisher retains all ownership and all other rights, title and interest in and to such work and materials. Programmer shall identify in writing any third-party material included in the Software Products.

3.   Programmer is an independent contractor and Publisher shall exercise no immediate control over Programmer or the manner in which Programmer performs its services or labor under this Agreement, except to the extent that Publisher provides instructions to Programmer or exercises the right to accept or reject any submission to it by Programmer. Programmer shall be solely responsible for any unemployment or disability insurance payments, or any social security, income tax or other withholdings, deductions or payments which may be required by federal, state or local law with respect to any sums paid Programmer hereunder. Programmer shall not be entitled to any employee benefits of any nature from Publisher.

4.   Programmer is not Publisher's agent or representative and has no authority to bind or commit Publisher to any agreements or other obligations.

5.   Programmer warrants and represents that Programmer has full power and authority to make this Agreement; that in performing hereunder Programmer will not violate the terms of any agreement Programmer may have with any third party; that the Software Products, and all material contained therein and elements and parts thereof, as finally determined by Publisher to be accept-able, will not infringe any statutory or common law copyright, will not violate any right of privacy or publicity, or otherwise violate any law or any person's personal or property rights. Programmer shall indemnify Publisher and hold it harmless against any liabilities, losses, damages, costs or expenses (including attorneys' fees), arising from any claim, action or proceeding based upon or in any way related to any breach or alleged breach of the foregoing warranties and representations. These warranties and representations and Programmer's indemnity shall survive termination or expiration of this Agreement for any reason. Programmer's warranties and representations shall not apply to any elements of the Software Products supplied to Programmer by Publisher.

6.   In performing its obligations under this Agreement, each party may receive confidential written information of the other. Both parties acknowledge and agree that all written information expressly marked as "proprietary" or "confidential," including marketing plans and business plans, and all written information that by the nature of the circumstances surrounding the disclosure, ought in good faith to be treated as confidential, constitute proprietary infor-mation and/or trade secrets; and to the extent that either party acquires any access to or knowledge of the other party's confidential written information, it shall be used solely to further the specific purposes provided for under this Agreement and for no other purpose whatsoever. Both parties shall protect the confidential written information supplied by the other from disclosure to other parties with the same degree of care as that which is accorded to its own proprietary information. This provision shall be interpreted so as to provide both parties the maximum protection afforded by law with the intent to preserve the rights in and the confidentiality of each party's confidential written information. Information will not be subject to this provision if it is or becomes a matter independently developed by the other party without reference to information disclosed by the other party, if it was or is received from a third person under circumstances permitting its disclosure, or such information becomes available to the public at no fault of either party or its disclosure is required by law.

7.   This Agreement shall commence on the date first written above and may be terminated by either priority, with or without cause, on fifteen days prior written notice.

8.   Programmer's remedy, if any, for any breach of this Agreement by Publisher shall be solely in money damages and Programmer shall look solely to Publisher for recovery of such damages.

9.   This Agreement sets forth the entire agreement between the parties, supersedes any prior agreements or understandings, oral or written, with respect to the specific subject matter hereof, and shall be binding on Publisher only when it is accepted by an authorized officer of Publisher. The engagement of the Programmer is personal and neither party may assign this Agreement without the other's prior written consent.

10.   This Agreement shall be construed and interpreted pursuant to the laws of the State of New York applicable to contracts wholly entered into and performed in the State of New York. Any legal action, suit or proceeding arising out of or relating to this Agreement or the breach thereof shall be instituted in a court of competent jurisdiction in New York County in the State of New York and each party hereby consents and submits to the personal jurisdiction of such court, waives any objection to venue in such court and consents to service or process by registered or certified mail, return receipt requested, at the last known address of such party.

ACCEPTED AND AGREED

PROGRAMMER   PUBLISHER

By: _____   By: _____

Name: _____   Name:_____

Title: _____   Title: _____

FORM 3.5

Shrink-Wrap License

This form is a standard "shrink-wrap" agreement, so named because it is often
delivered as part of a shrink-wrapped package with off-the-shelf software. If
delivered in other ways, these agreements are sometimes known as "click-
through" or "click-wrap" licenses (e.g., Forms 3.7 and 3.8), but "shrink-wrap"
seems to be the most commonly used generic nomenclature. Regardless of the
name, these are the types of agreements that are typically only read by attorneys trying to find good language for their own versions.

Although at one time these agreements were of questionable enforceability,
since *ProCD v. Zeidenberg*, 86 F.3d 1447 (7th Cir. 1996), courts have generally
enforced them, subject to certain limitations. As a practical matter, they should
not violate traditional notions of fair play and justice (exclusive forum clauses
are particularly suspect), and they should enable the user to repudiate the contract. For a product purchased online, the ability to read the agreement prior to
purchase should be adequate. The requirement that a purchaser click "agree"
before being allowed to make a purchase or access the content provides good
further evidence of manifestation of assent. *See, e.g.,* Form 3.8. For a product
shipped to a user after receipt of payment, a no-questions-asked money-back
guarantee for a reasonable limited time such as the one drafted below should
address the repudiation issue, and if the product is programmed to require the
user to click "agree" before it loads for the first time, that is even better.

Limited Use License Agreement

Carefully read the following Terms and Conditions before opening this package. By opening this package you indicate your acceptance of the terms
and conditions of this Agreement. If you do not agree to these Terms and
Conditions, you may return this unopened package with your proof of purchase to your retailer within 90 days for a full refund.

1. License

_____, Inc. ("Softco") hereby grants you, and you accept, a nonexclusive
and non-transferable license, to use _____ (the "System"), including
the right to access and use data from the current release of its Database (the
"Database").

2. Term

This License Agreement is effective until terminated. You may terminate it at
any time by destroying the Licensed Program with all copies made (with or
without authorization).

3.   Authorized Use of System

You shall have the right to load the System on a single computer and at a single location designated by you. You may not use the System on a network or multi-user basis without notifying Softco and obtaining and paying for an appropriate network license. You may selectively download, modify, merge and print limited content of the Database for your personal non-commercial use on a single machine; provided, however that any such portions of the Database downloaded or merged into another program or database will continue to be subject to the terms and conditions of this License, and you acknowledge that any copy, modification, or portion printed or merged into other programs is protected by U.S. copyright law. Upon termination of this License, you agree to destroy all copies, modifications, and merged content in any form. IF YOU TRANSFER POSSESSION OF ANY COPY, MODIFICATION, OR MERGED PORTION OF THE DATABASE TO ANOTHER PARTY, YOUR LICENSE IS AUTOMATICALLY TERMINATED.

4.   Use Restrictions

You may not (a) copy the System, except to load it into a computer in accordance with instructions set forth in the User's Manual; (b) distribute copies of the Database or System to any other person; (c) modify, adapt, translate, reverse engineer, decompile, disassemble, or create derivative works based on the System; (d) copy, download, store in a retrieval system, publish, transmit, or otherwise reproduce, transfer, store, disseminate, or use, in any form or by any means, any part of the data contained within the Database except as expressly provided for in this License; (e) transfer, resell, sublicense, lease, or grant any other rights of any kind to any individual copy of the Database or the System to any other person; or (f) remove any proprietary notices, labels or marks on the Database or System.

You shall take reasonable measures to maintain the security of the Database and the System.

5.   Proprietary Rights

You acknowledge and agree that the System is the sole and exclusive property of Softco, and the System and User Manual are licensed to you only for the term of this License and strictly under the terms hereof. Softco owns all right, titles, and interest in and to the content in the System and the Database. Except for the limited rights given to you herein, all rights are reserved by Softco.

6.   Termination

If you should fail to perform in the manner required in this License, this License shall terminate and Softco may exercise any rights it may have. Upon termination, Softco may require that you destroy all of these materials and that you so certify, in writing to Softco. All provisions of this License with regard to the protection of the proprietary rights of Softco shall continue in force after such termination.

7.   Warranties, Indemnities, and Limitation of Liability

THE SYSTEM IS PROVIDED "AS IS," WITHOUT WARRANTY OF ANY KIND, EXPRESS OR IMPLIED, INCLUDING BUT NOT LIMITED TO THE IMPLIED WARRANTIES OF MERCHANTABILITY OR FITNESS FOR A PARTICULAR PURPOSE. SOFTCO NEITHER GIVES NOR MAKES ANY OTHER WARRANTIES OR REPRESENTATIONS UNDER OR PURSUANT TO THIS LICENSE. Softco does not warrant, guarantee or make any representations that the functions contained in the System will meet your particular requirements or that the operation of the System will be uninterrupted or error free. The entire risk as to the results and performance of the System is assumed by you.

If the System disc is defective in workmanship or materials and Softco is given timely notice thereof, Softco's sole and exclusive liability and your sole and exclusive remedy, shall be the replacement of the defective disc. In the event of a defect in a disc covered by this warranty, Softco will replace the disc provided that you return the defective disc to Softco. The foregoing states your sole remedy and Softco's sole obligation in the event of the occurrence of a defect coming within the scope of the Limited Warranty.

IN NO EVENT SHALL SOFTCO, ITS SUPPLIERS, OR ANYONE ELSE WHO HAS BEEN INVOLVED IN THE CREATION, PRODUCTION OR DELIVERY OF THE DATABASE, SYSTEM OR DOCUMENTATION BE LIABLE FOR ANY LOSS OR INACCURACY OF DATA OF ANY KIND OR FOR LOST PROFITS, LOST SAVINGS, OR ANY DIRECT, INDIRECT, SPECIAL, CONSEQUENTIAL OR INCIDENTAL DAMAGES ARISING OUT OF OR RELATED IN ANY WAY TO THE USE OR INABILITY TO USE THE SYSTEM, EVEN IF SOFTCO OR ITS SUPPLIERS HAVE BEEN ADVISED OF THE POSSIBILITY OF SUCH DAMAGES. THIS LIMITATION OF LIABILITY SHALL APPLY TO ANY CLAIM OR CAUSE WHATSOEVER WHETHER SUCH CLAIM OR CAUSE IS IN CONTRACT, TORT OR OTHERWISE.

The limited warranty set forth above is in lieu of all other express warranties, whether oral or written. The agents, employees and distributors of Softco are not authorized to modify this warranty, nor to make additional warranties binding on Softco. Accordingly, additional statements such as distributor representations, whether written or oral, do not constitute warranties of Softco and should not be relied upon as a warranty of Softco. In no case shall Softco's liability exceed the cost of the System. You agree to indemnify and hold Softco, its suppliers, and all of their officers, directors, employees and agents, as well all those individuals or organizations providing information for the Database, harmless from any and all claims of third parties resulting from or incidental to your use or operation of the System, or arising from any breach by you of any provisions of this License. Softco may, at its option, institute or defend any action arising out of the aforesaid clauses with counsel of its own choice.

[Some states do not allow exclusions or limitations of implied warranties or liability in certain cases, so the above exclusions and limitations may not apply to you.]

8. General

(a) This License shall be governed by the laws of the State of New York in so far as they do not conflict with U.S. Federal regulations.

(b) If any provision of this License is deemed to be unlawful, invalid, or unenforceable, the remaining provisions shall remain in full force and effect as if the unlawful, invalid, or unenforceable provision had been omitted.

(c) Any legal action, suit, or proceeding arising out of or relating to this License or the breach thereof shall be instituted in a court of competent jurisdiction in New York County in the State of New York and each party hereby consents and submits to the personal jurisdiction of such court and consents to service of process by registered or certified mail, return receipt requested, at the last known address of such party.

(d) The above warranties and indemnities shall survive the termination of this License.

(e) Use, duplication, or disclosure by the Government is subject to restrictions as set forth in FAR 52.227-14 (June 1987) Alternate III (g)(3) (June 1987), FAR 52.227-19 (June 1987), or DFARS 52.227-701 (c)(1)(ii)(June 1988), as applicable. System licensor: Softco, Inc. [Address].

(f) If you are located in Canada, you agree as follows: The parties hereto confirm that it is their wish that this License, as well as all other documents relating hereto, including notices, have been and shall be drawn up in the English language only.

9. Acknowledgment

YOU ACKNOWLEDGE THAT YOU HAVE READ THIS LICENSE, UNDERSTAND IT, AND AGREE TO BE BOUND BY ITS TERMS AND CONDITIONS. YOU ALSO ACKNOWLEDGE THAT THIS LICENSE IS THE COMPLETE AND EXCLUSIVE STATEMENT OF THE AGREEMENT BETWEEN SOFTCO AND YOU, AND THAT IT SUPERSEDES ANY PROPOSAL, PRIOR AGREEMENT, OR OTHER COMMUNICATIONS, WHETHER ORAL OR WRITTEN, BETWEEN YOU AND SOFTCO RELATING TO THE SUBJECT MATTER OF THIS LICENSE. THIS LICENSE CANNOT BE MODIFIED OR AMENDED EXCEPT BY A FURTHER WRITTEN INSTRUMENT EXECUTED BY YOU AND SOFTCO.

Site License Agreement Incorporating User Terms of Service

Form 3.6 is a standard site license for use with a CD-ROM product. As drafted, it allows the use of the product at a single site, with no restrictions on the number of terminals from which it can be accessed and no restrictions on concurrency of use. It is therefore most appropriate to use this version with products that are either (1) priced on a per capita basis (e.g., $2,000 for licensees with up to 5,000 employees, $3,000 for licensees with more than 5,000 employees) or (2) unlikely to be bought in multiple copies. For other products, one should consider limiting the number of concurrent users (which, for most products, is a meaningless restriction above a low number such as three), the number of workstations from which it can be accessed, or both. From a marketing point of view, it may be easier to license ten workstations than to license two concurrent users, even though the ten-workstation limitation may in fact be more restrictive.

This agreement incorporates user terms of use and places the burden on the licensee to appoint a network administrator, who is supposed to require that users read and agree to the terms of use before being granted access, although there is no meaningful mechanism to ensure compliance. The publisher should always make the terms of use as available as it can to users, and the terms should ideally reside both in the product (usually in the "help about" section) and in the user manual. Also, if possible the terms should have a click-through component each time they are loaded on a new machine, but the failure to do so should not be fatal to enforceability.

Site License Agreement

This License sets forth the terms and conditions under which SoftPub, Inc., a Delaware Corporation with offices located at _____, will allow the Licensee to install _____, CD-ROM (the "Product") on a Site controlled by you. Carefully read the following Terms and Conditions before installing the Product. By installing the Product, you indicate acceptance of these Terms and Conditions. If you do not agree with these terms, you may return the Product along with all documentation and packaging, and your proof of purchase within thirty (30) days for a full refund.

Licensee hereby licenses the Product from SoftPub and agrees as follows:

1. Definitions

The following terms shall be deemed to have the meaning as stated below:

    (a) Licensee—The customer which has accepted this License and is responsible for payments for the Product and administration of this License.

(b) Site—A geographically contiguous office building, complex or campus location within Licensee's control.

(c) Users—Those persons within Licensee's Sites who are authorized by the Licensee to have access to the Product. Users must be bona fide faculty, students, researchers, librarians, executives or employees of the Licensee, and may also include users from the general public or business invitees who are permitted by the Licensee to access the Product from designated terminals within a Licensee-controlled Local Area Network (LAN). These designated terminals shall be physically located in premises such as libraries under the Licensee's direct control and administration.

(d) The Product—The network version of Product, which includes content from the most recent release of the Product and the accompanying search and retrieval software program ("Software") developed by ("Developer"), as well as the online or print user documentation ("User's Guide").

2.   License

(a)   SoftPub hereby grants to Licensee for the term hereof a nonexclusive, non-transferable and limited license to install and use, and arrange for authorized Users to have access to, the Product on a secure network located at one Site within Licensee's control, on the terms and conditions set forth herein.

(b)   Licensee shall use the Product only at one designated Site, and shall not connect the Product to a network which permits use anywhere other than that Site. The Product must be protected by a firewall or other secure means of protection from release on the Internet at large.

(c)   The rights and restrictions governing access to the Product by individual Users are outlined in the attached User Terms of Service Agreement.

(d)   Licensee shall not alter or change the Product in any way.

3.   Term

This License is effective from the date Licensee installs the Product and shall remain in force until terminated.

4.   Authorized Use of System

Licensee agrees to authorize a Network Administrator(s) to install and manage access to the Product. The Network Administrator hereby represents that the Product will only be used pursuant to the access restrictions contained herein.

Licensee and the Users may selectively download, modify, merge, and print limited content from the Product for their personal non-commercial use as specified in the User Terms of Service Agreement; provided, however, that any such portion of the Product will continue to be subject to the terms and conditions of this License.

This License grants access to the Product only to Users as defined herein. There is no restriction on the number of Users who may use the Product.

The User Terms of Service Agreement (including SoftPub's Rules of Use) must be read by each User before the User uses the Product. SoftPub reserves the right to modify the User Agreement as described therein.

The Licensee will:

(i) inform potential Users of the need to maintain password security or to comply with such other access controls as may be specified by SoftPub;

(ii) make access available to Users only at one Site, undertake reasonable measures within its control to prevent access to and improper use of the Product by unauthorized persons and take responsibility for terminating any unauthorized access of which it has actual notice or knowledge; and

(iii) promptly notify SoftPub of any copyright infringement or unauthorized usage of the Product which comes to the Licensee's attention and cooperate with SoftPub in the investigation of such infringement or unauthorized use, and in any action which SoftPub takes to enforce its copyright, at SoftPub's expense.

5. Proprietary Rights

Licensee acknowledges and agrees that the Product is the exclusive property of SoftPub and that the Product, Software and the User's Guide are licensed to Licensee only for the term of this License and strictly under the terms hereof. SoftPub owns all right, title, and interest in and to the content of the Product, and the Software contains copyrighted and confidential trade secret information that is the property of, or is licensed by, Developer. Except for the limited rights given to the Licensee herein, all rights are reserved by SoftPub and Developer.

Licensee shall not, and shall ensure that Users shall not, remove any copyright or proprietary notices, labels or marks on the Product, Software or User's Guide, nor disclose the Product or any of SoftPub's or Developer's confidential information to third parties.

6. Termination

If Licensee or its Users should fail to perform in the manner required in this License, SoftPub may terminate this License or exercise any other rights it may have. Upon termination, Licensee shall immediately uninstall the Product, and SoftPub may require that the Licensee destroy all of these materials and that it so certify in writing to SoftPub. All provisions of this License with regard to the protection of the proprietary rights of SoftPub shall continue in force after such termination.

7. Warranties and Limitation of Liability

Licensee recognizes that the Product is to be used only as a reference aid by research professionals. It is not intended to be a substitute for the exercise of professional judgment by the Users. THE PRODUCT IS PROVIDED "AS IS," WITHOUT WARRANTY OF ANY KIND, EXPRESS OR IMPLIED, INCLUDING BUT NOT LIMITED TO THE IMPLIED WARRANTIES OF MERCHANTABILITY OR FITNESS FOR A PARTICULAR PURPOSE. SOFTPUB NEITHER GIVES NOR MAKES ANY OTHER WARRANTIES OR REPRESENTATIONS UNDER OR PURSUANT TO THIS LICENSE. SoftPub does not warrant, guarantee or make any representations that the functions contained in the Product will meet the Licensee's particular requirements or that the operation of the Product will be uninterrupted or error free. The entire risk as to the results and performance of the Product is assumed by Licensee.

If the Product is found to be defective in workmanship or materials and SoftPub is given timely notice thereof, SoftPub's sole and exclusive liability and Licensee's sole and exclusive remedy, shall be replacement of the defective system. If SoftPub is unable to provide a system that is free from such defects, Licensee may terminate this License by returning the Product and all associated documentation to SoftPub for a full refund.

IN NO EVENT SHALL SOFTPUB, DEVELOPER, OR ANYONE ELSE WHO HAS BEEN INVOLVED IN THE CREATION, PRODUCTION OR DELIVERY OF THE PRODUCT, SOFTWARE OR USER'S GUIDE BE LIABLE OR RESPONSIBLE FOR ANY LOSS OR INACCURACY OF DATA OF ANY KIND NOR FOR ANY LOST PROFITS, LOST SAVINGS, OR ANY OTHER DIRECT OR INDIRECT, SPECIAL, INCIDENTAL OR CONSEQUENTIAL OR EXEMPLARY DAMAGES ARISING OUT OF OR RELATED IN ANY WAY TO THE USE OR INABILITY TO USE THE PRODUCT, EVEN IF SOFTPUB OR ITS SUPPLIERS HAVE BEEN ADVISED OF THE POSSIBILITY OF SUCH DAMAGES. THIS LIMITATION OF LIABILITY SHALL APPLY TO ANY CLAIM OR CAUSE WHATSOEVER WHETHER SUCH CLAIM OR CAUSE IS IN CONTRACT, TORT, OR OTHERWISE.

The limited warranty set forth above is in lieu of all other express warranties, whether oral or written. The agents, employees and distributors of SoftPub are not authorized to modify this warranty, nor to make additional warranties binding on SoftPub *or* Developer. Accordingly, additional statements such as distributor representations, whether written or oral, do not constitute warranties of SoftPub and should not be relied upon as a warranty of SoftPub. SoftPub's pricing of the Product reflects this allocation of the risk and limitations of liability contained in this clause; in no case shall SoftPub's liability exceed the amount of the license fee. No action, regardless of form, arising out of this License may be brought by Licensee more than one year after the cause of action has accrued.

[*Some states do not allow exclusions or limitations of implied warranties or liability in certain cases, so the above exclusions and limitations may not apply.*]

8.   General

(a)   SoftPub may assign this License to its successors, subsidiaries, or assigns. This License may not be assigned by the Licensee except upon the written consent of SoftPub.

(b)   This License shall be governed by the laws of the State of New York in so far as they do not conflict with U.S. Federal regulations, and each party submits to the personal jurisdiction of such court. If any provision of this License Agreement is deemed to be unlawful, invalid, or unenforceable, the remaining provisions shall remain in full force and effect as if the unlawful, invalid, or unenforceable provision has been omitted. Any legal action, suit, or proceeding arising out of or relating to this License or the breach thereof shall be instituted in a court of competent jurisdiction in New York County in the State of New York and each party hereby consents and submits to the personal jurisdiction of such court and consents to service of process by registered or certified mail, return receipt requested, at the last known address of such party.

(c)   The above warranties and limitations on liabilities shall survive the termination of this License.

(d)   Sales tax is applicable on a "destination" basis.

(e)   Use, duplication, or disclosure by the Government is subject to restrictions as set forth in FAR 52.227-14 (June 1987) Alternate III (g)(3) (June 1987), FAR 52.227-19 (June 1987), of DFARS 52.227-701 (c)(1)(ii)(June 1988), as applicable. Software licensor: John SoftPub & Sons, Inc., 605 Third Avenue, New York, N.Y. 10158.

(f)   If the Licensee is located in Canada, Licensee agrees to the following: The parties hereto confirm that it is their wish that this License, as well as all other documents relating hereto, including notices, have been and shall be drawn up in the English language only.

(g)   The User Terms of Service Agreement is incorporated herein by reference.

9.   Acknowledgment

LICENSEE ACKNOWLEDGES THAT ITS AUTHORIZED AGENT HAS READ THIS LICENSE, UNDERSTANDS IT, AND LICENSEE AGREES TO BE BOUND

BY ITS TERMS AND CONDITIONS. LICENSEE ALSO ACKNOWLEDGES THAT THIS LICENSE IS THE COMPLETE AND EXCLUSIVE STATEMENT OF THE AGREEMENT BETWEEN SOFTPUB AND THE LICENSEE, AND THAT IT SUPERSEDES ANY PROPOSAL, PRIOR AGREEMENT, OR OTHER COMMUNICATIONS, WHETHER ORAL OR WRITTEN, BETWEEN LICENSEE AND SOFTPUB RELATING TO THE SUBJECT MATTER OF THIS LICENSE. THIS LICENSE MAY BE MODIFIED BY SOFTPUB BY WRITTEN NOTICE OF NEW TERMS AND CONDITIONS. IN SUCH CASE, LICENSEE'S CONTINUED USE OF THE PRODUCT SHALL BE DEEMED ACCEPTANCE OF THE MODIFIED TERMS. EXCEPT AS SET FORTH IN THIS PARAGRAPH, THIS LICENSE CANNOT BE MODIFIED OR AMENDED EXCEPT BY A FURTHER WRITTEN INSTRUMENT EXECUTED BY LICENSEE AND SOFTPUB.

User Terms of Service Agreement

The following Terms of Service dated as of _____, govern use by Users of _____, CD-ROM (the "Product"). Please read them using the Product. By using the Product you agree to the terms hereof.

Your institution may have subscribed to a License which permits you additional uses; contact your institution's librarian/administrator for more information. The rights licensed to you under this Agreement by the publisher of the Product, SoftPub, Inc. ("SoftPub") cannot be transferred, loaned, sold or rented to anyone else.

Copyright

The entire contents of the Product are protected by copyright (unless otherwise indicated on the Product). As a User, you have certain rights set forth below; all other rights are reserved.

Rules of Use

A. To make the Product useful, the following rules apply to all Users. You may download, view, copy and save to hard disk or diskette and store or print out single copies of individual items for your own personal and non-commercial use, scholarly, educational or scientific research or study. You may transmit to a third party, in hard copy or electronically, a single item from the Product for that party's own personal and noncommercial use or scholarly, educational, or scientific research or study, or for corporate informational purposes. In addition, you have the right to use, with appropriate credit, figures, tables and brief excerpts from the Product in your own scientific, scholarly and educational works or similar work product.

B. Except as provided in Paragraph (A) above, you may not copy, distribute, transmit or otherwise reproduce material from the Product or systematically store such material in any form or media in a retrieval system; or download and/or store an entire alphabetical entry; or store content from the Product in electronic format in electronic reading rooms or print out multiple copies for inclusion in course packs; or transmit any material from the Product, directly or indirectly, for use in any paid service such as document delivery or listserv, or for use by any information brokerage or for systematic distribution of material, whether or not to another User and whether for commercial or non-profit use or for a fee or free of charge.

In order to protect the integrity and attribution of the materials in the Product, you agree not to remove or modify any copyright or proprietary notices, author attribution or disclaimer contained in the material or on any screen display, and not to integrate material from the Product with other material or otherwise create derivative works in any medium based on or including materials from the Product. This is not meant to prohibit quotations for purposes of comment, criticism or similar scholarly purposes.

Finally, you may not do anything to restrict or inhibit any other User's access to or use of the Product.

C. If you refuse or fail to abide by these rules or violate any other terms or conditions of this Agreement, SoftPub reserves the right in its sole discretion to suspend or terminate your access to the Product immediately without notice, in addition to any other available remedies.

Additional Terms

SoftPub is not responsible for any charges associated with accessing the Product, including any computer equipment, telephone lines, or access software.

SoftPub may modify any of the terms of this Agreement at any time by providing notice to your institution's network administrator. Your continued use of the Product shall be conclusively deemed acceptance of such modification.

Warranty Limitations

(i) THE PRODUCT AND ALL MATERIALS CONTAINED THEREIN ARE PROVIDED ON AN "AS IS" BASIS, WITHOUT WARRANTIES OF ANY KIND, EITHER EXPRESS OR IMPLIED, INCLUDING, BUT NOT LIMITED TO, WARRANTIES OF TITLE, OR IMPLIED WARRANTIES OF MERCHANTABILITY OR FITNESS FOR A PARTICULAR PURPOSE;

(ii) THE USE OF THE PRODUCT AND ALL MATERIALS CONTAINED THEREIN IS AT THE USER'S OWN RISK;

(iii) ACCESS TO THE PRODUCT AND THE ELECTRONIC TITLES MAY BE INTERRUPTED AND MAY NOT BE ERROR FREE; AND

(iv) NEITHER SOFTPUB NOR ANYONE ELSE INVOLVED IN CREATING, PRODUCING OR DELIVERING THE ELECTRONIC TITLES OR THE

MATERIALS CONTAINED IN THE PRODUCT, SHALL BE LIABLE FOR ANY DIRECT, INDIRECT, INCIDENTAL, SPECIAL, CONSEQUENTIAL OR PUNITIVE DAMAGES ARISING OUT OF THE USER'S USE OF OR INABILITY TO USE THE PRODUCT, AND ALL MATERIALS CONTAINED THEREIN.

(v) LICENSEE RECOGNIZES THAT THE PRODUCT IS TO BE USED ONLY AS A REFERENCE AID BY RESEARCH PROFESSIONALS. IT IS NOT INTENDED TO BE A SUBSTITUTE FOR THE EXERCISE OF PROFESSIONAL JUDGMENT BY THE USER.

[*Some states do not allow exclusions or limitations of implied warranties or liability in certain cases, so the above exclusions and limitations may not apply*]

This Agreement shall be construed and interpreted pursuant to the laws of the State of New York applicable to contracts wholly entered into and performed in the State of New York, excluding that body of law dealing with conflict of laws. Any legal action, suit or proceeding arising out of or relating to this Agreement or the breach thereof shall be instituted in a court of competent jurisdiction in New York County in the State of New York and each party hereby consents and submits to the personal jurisdiction of such court, waives any objection to venue in such court and consents to the service of process by registered or certified mail, return receipt requested, at the last known address of such party.

Click-On License for Electronic Access

This agreement is a basic license that allows libraries to subscribe for a limited period to access online content for their customers. Although the example is for online academic journals, the license works equally well for many types of published content, including magazines, books, handbooks, and major reference works (e.g., encyclopedias). In this agreement, an institution that buys a copy of a print work is licensed access rights to the electronic version of the journal from a single site. This limitation is enforced by limiting the range of IP addresses that will be authenticated by the publisher's system as users attempt to access the journals. As with a print work, access is limited to one concurrent user per purchased subscription. One interesting feature of this license is that it also allows the licensee certain special rights, such as the ability to make certain interlibrary loans, that are not afforded to individual users.

Basic Access License

This License, dated as of _____, sets forth the terms and conditions under which Online Publishers, Inc. ("Online"), a _____ corporation, will provide the Licensee as defined below, with access to the electronic edition of the Journal or Journals subscribed to by the Licensee via OnlineWebVentures, an online service, as follows, under the following terms and conditions:

A. Definitions

The following terms shall be deemed to have the meaning as stated below:

1.   OnlineWebVentures—The online service available from Online or its affiliates on the World Wide Web and all products, services and features offered through said service.

2.   Licensee—The customer named in the registration process, which has authorized the acceptance of this License and the completion of the online registration process, provides access, via its secure network, to OnlineWebVentures for its Authorized Users as defined below, and is responsible for payments and implementation of the License.

3.   Electronic Journal(s)—The electronic (online) editions of Online Journals licensed hereunder including tables of content, abstracts, full text and illustrations and any additional electronic journal content not included in the print versions of the Journal(s).

4.   Site—A single, geographically-contiguous office building or complex or campus location plus dial-in access by Authorized Users to the Licensee's secure

network, identified by the Licensee's relevant Internet Protocol (IP) addresses. The Licensee may not extend access to OnlineWebVentures, through the Licensee's network, to partners, joint ventures and affiliates. Online may refuse to grant a Basic Access License to an institution claiming a range of IP addresses that, in Online's opinion, represents more than one campus or office complex.

5.   Authorized Users—Those persons who are authorized by the Licensee to have access to OnlineWebVentures from within the Licensee's relevant IP addresses. Authorized Users must be bona fide faculty members, students, researchers, staff members, librarians, executives or employees of the Licensee. Walk-in Users from the general public or business invitees may also be permitted by the Licensee to access OnlineWebVentures from designated terminals with a Licensee-controlled IP address. These designated terminals shall be physically located on the Site in premises such as in libraries or similar premises under the Licensee's direct control and administration.

B.   Licensed Electronic Journals and Access Privileges

1.   Online grants to the Licensee and its Authorized Users, a one-year nonexclusive, non-transferable right and license to access, via Online-WebVentures, the full text of the Electronic Journals on the terms and conditions described herein.

2.   A subscription to calendar year print Journal content includes access for Authorized Users to the full text of the year _____ electronic editions of such Journals and may include full text of the electronic editions of such Journals from ____ where available.

3.   The number of the Licensee's Authorized Users who may log onto OnlineWebVentures is unlimited. However, access to full text will be limited to one concurrent Authorized User per Journal subscription.

4.   The Licensee acknowledges that the Electronic Journals and OnlineWebVentures are protected by copyright. All rights not specifically granted to the Licensee are expressly reserved. The contents of OnlineWebVentures and the Electronic Journals are intended for the personal, non-commercial use of the Authorized Users.

C. Terms and Conditions of Use

1.   The rights and restrictions governing access to OnlineWebVentures and the Electronic Journal(s) by the Licensee and its Authorized Users are outlined in the Terms and Conditions of Use below.

a. Authorized Users may download, view, copy and save to hard disk or diskette and store or print out single copies of individual articles or items for Authorized

Users' own personal use, scholarly, educational or scientific research or internal business use. Authorized Users may transmit to a third-party colleague in hard copy or electronically, a single article or item from OnlineWebVentures for personal use or scholarly, educational, or scientific research or professional use or for corporate information purposes but in no case for re-sale. In addition, Authorized Users have the right to use, with appropriate credit, figures, tables and brief excerpts from individual articles in the Electronic Journal(s) in the Authorized User's own scientific, scholarly and educational works.

b. The Licensee but not Authorized Users may print out and send single paper copies of articles from the Electronic Journal(s) for interlibrary loan.

2.   Except as provided in Paragraph C (1) above, Authorized Users may not copy, distribute, transmit or otherwise reproduce material from Electronic Journal(s); store such material in any form or medium in a retrieval system; download and/or store an entire issue of a Electronic Journal or its equivalent; or transmit such material, directly or indirectly, for use in any paid service such as document delivery or listserv, or for use by any information brokerage or for systematic distribution, whether or not for commercial or non-profit use or for a fee or free of charge.

3.   In order to protect the integrity and attribution of OnlineWebVentures and the Electronic Journal(s), the Licensee and its Authorized Users may not remove, obscure or modify any copyright or proprietary notices, author attribution or disclaimer contained therein or on any screen display. Authorized Users may not integrate material from the Electronic Journal(s) with other material or otherwise create derivative works in any medium. This is not meant to prohibit quotations for purposes of comment, criticism or similar scholarly purposes.

4.   Authorized Users may not do anything to restrict or inhibit any other Authorized User's access to or use of OnlineWebVentures and the Electronic Journal(s).

5.   If an Authorized User fails to abide by these Terms and Conditions of Use or other terms of this Agreement, Online reserves the right in its sole discretion to suspend or terminate such Authorized User's access to OnlineWebVentures and the Electronic Journal(s) immediately without notice, in addition to any other available remedies.

D.   Fees and Charges

1.   Payment of the full rate subscription price for a Journal for the calendar year _____ provides the Licensee with electronic access for one concurrent User to the full text of each Electronic Journal per subscription and other features of OnlineWebVentures as described herein.

2.   The Licensee is responsible for any charges associated with accessing OnlineWebVentures and the Electronic Journal(s), including any computer equipment, telephone or Internet connections and access software.

E.   Mutual Obligations

1.   Online will:

   a. make reasonable efforts to ensure uninterrupted online access to and continuous availability of the Electronic Journal(s) to Authorized Users at the Site in accordance with this License, and to restore access to the Electronic Journal(s) as promptly as possible in the event of an interruption or suspension of the OnlineWebVentures service;
   b. after termination of the License, provide the Licensee with access to the full text of the Electronic Journal(s) published during the Term of this License, either by continuing online access to the same material on Online's server or in an archival copy in the electronic medium selected by Online, at a cost-based fee to be mutually agreed;

2.   The Licensee will:

   a. take all reasonable measures to inform Authorized Users of the Terms and Conditions of Use governing access to OnlineWebVentures and emphasize to such Authorized Users the need to comply with whatever restrictions on access, use, reproduction and transmission are included therein;
   b. make access available to Authorized Users only through the Licensee's secure network and from valid IP addresses at the Site; undertake reasonable measures within its control to prevent access to and improper use of the Electronic Journal(s) and OnlineWebVentures by unauthorized persons; and take responsibility for terminating any unauthorized access of which it has actual notice or knowledge;
   c. provide Online with information about the Licensee's IP addresses, as updated from time to time, which can be used by Online to authenticate Authorized Users;
   d. promptly notify Online of any copyright infringement or unauthorized usage of the Electronic Journal(s) which comes to the Licensee's attention; and cooperate with Online in the investigation of such infringement or unauthorized use and in any action which Online takes to enforce its copyright, at Online's expense.

F.   Privacy and Data Protection Policy

Online recognizes the importance of protecting the information it collects in the operation of OnlineWebVentures and will take all reasonable steps to maintain the security, integrity and privacy of this information. Online will ensure that any information it collects will be adequate, relevant and not excessive for purposes of operating OnlineWebVentures; it will be kept accurate and up-to-date based on information provided and will be deleted when no longer needed. Except where necessary in connection with services provided by appropriate intermediaries, who will be required to comply with the confidentiality provisions of this policy, Online will not disclose any personal information identifying Authorized Users or the Licensee to any third party, unless required by law or to enforce OnlineWebVentures Terms and Conditions of Use.

Any private communications or information supplied to Online by an Authorized User may be used by Online for internal business and research purposes and to help enhance and develop OnlineWebVentures but will not be shared with third parties.

Online will only disclose to third parties navigational and transactional information in the form of anonymous, aggregate usage statistics (including "hits" on OnlineWebVentures and the Electronic Journal(s)) and demographics in forms that do not reveal an Authorized User's or the Licensee's identity or confidential information, except as required by law.

Links may be provided from OnlineWebVentures to other Web sites. In using such links, Authorized Users should be aware that each web site will vary in terms of its privacy and data protection policies, and Online does not take responsibility for the privacy policies of, and usage of personal information collected by, others.

Please note that Online's privacy and data protection policy is reviewed periodically. Any comments or questions concerning this policy should be addressed to: OnlineWebVentures Privacy Policy at _____.

G.   Term and Termination

1.   The Term of this License shall commence as of _____ and be automatically renewed on _____ on payment of the subscription renewal fee for the calendar year ___ at prices to be determined.

2.   Pursuant to Paragraph C(5) above, Online shall have the right to request the Licensee to terminate access to OnlineWebVentures by an Authorized User who breaches Online's Terms and Conditions of Use or infringes copyright in the Electronic Journal(s) or OnlineWebVentures. Notwithstanding the above, the Licensee shall not be responsible for such unauthorized use which is without the express or implied consent of the Licensee, provided that the Licensee has taken reasonable steps to prevent such misuse and, upon learning of it, notifies Online promptly of any such breach or infringement.

3.   Online may terminate this License if the Licensee materially breaches its obligations under this License and fails to cure such material breach, provided that Online shall give written notice of its intention to terminate and shall allow the Licensee 30 days after receipt of such notice to remedy the breach.

H. Warranty and Disclaimers

1.   Online represents and warrants that it has the right and authority to make OnlineWebVentures available to the Licensee and its Authorized Users pursuant to the terms and conditions of this License and that, to the best of Online's knowledge, OnlineWebVentures and the Electronic Journal(s) do not infringe upon any copyright, patent, trade secret or other proprietary right of any third party.

2.   OnlineWebVentures may provide Authorized Users with links to third-party Web sites. Where such links exist, Online disclaims all responsibility and liability for the content of such third-party Web sites. Authorized Users assume sole responsibility for the accessing of third-party Web sites and the use of any content on such Web sites.

3.   Except for the warranties in paragraph 1 above,

a. ONLINEWEBVENTURES AND THE ELECTRONIC JOURNALS AND ALL MATERIALS CONTAINED THEREIN ARE PROVIDED ON AN "AS IS" BASIS, WITHOUT WARRANTIES OF ANY KIND, EITHER EXPRESS OR IMPLIED, INCLUDING, BUT NOT LIMITED TO, WARRANTIES OF TITLE, OR IMPLIED WARRANTIES OF MERCHANTABILITY OR FITNESS FOR A PARTICULAR PURPOSE;

b. THE USE OF THE ELECTRONIC JOURNALS, ONLINEWEBVENTURES AND ALL MATERIALS IS AT THE AUTHORIZED USER'S OWN RISK;

c. ACCESS TO ONLINEWEBVENTURES AND THE ELECTRONIC JOURNALS MAY BE INTERRUPTED AND MAY NOT BE ERROR FREE; AND

d. NEITHER ONLINEWEBVENTURES, THE ELECTRONIC JOURNALS, ONLINE, OR ANYONE ELSE INVOLVED IN CREATING, PRODUCING OR DELIVERING THE ELECTRONIC JOURNALS OR THE MATERIALS CONTAINED IN ONLINEWEBVENTURES, SHALL BE LIABLE FOR ANY DIRECT, INDIRECT, INCIDENTAL, SPECIAL, CONSEQUENTIAL OR PUNITIVE DAMAGES ARISING OUT OF THE AUTHORIZED USER'S USE OF OR INABILITY TO USE ONLINEWEBVENTURES, THE ELECTRONIC JOURNALS AND ALL MATERIALS CONTAINED THEREIN.

I.   General Provisions

1.   Online may assign this License to its successors, subsidiaries or assigns. This License may not be assigned by the Licensee except with the prior written consent of Online.

2.   This License shall be construed and interpreted pursuant to the laws of the State of New York applicable to contracts wholly entered into and performed in the State of New York. Any legal action, suit or proceeding arising out of or relating to this License or the breach thereof shall be instituted in a court of competent jurisdiction in New York County in the State of New York and each party hereby consents and submits to the personal jurisdiction of such court, waives any objection to venue in such court and consents to the service of process by registered or certified mail, return receipt requested, at the last known address of such party.

If you have a legal problem with contracting under New York law, please contact our <u>Contract Inquiry Department</u>. For all other inquiries, contact <u>Customer Service</u>.

3.   In the event of a material breach of the terms and conditions of this License by either party, the non-breaching party shall be entitled, in addition to any other remedies available pursuant to this License or at law, to equitable, including injunctive, relief.

4.   This License constitutes the complete understanding of the parties and supersedes all prior understandings between the parties with respect to the subject matter of this License. No modification, amendment or waiver of any provisions shall be valid unless in writing and signed by both parties. Any waiver in one or more instances by either of the parties of any breach by the other of any terms or provisions contained in this License shall not be considered a waiver of any succeeding or preceding breach.

J.   Acceptance Procedure

If you have read and consent to all of the terms and conditions of this License, please click the button below marked "I ACCEPT." This will constitute a binding agreement, enforceable according to its terms. Upon acceptance you will be prompted to input your customer account information, and you and your Authorized Users will then have access to OnlineWebVentures and the Electronic Journals. If you do not consent, select "I DO NOT ACCEPT," in which case your registration will not be processed and you and your Authorized Users will not have access to OnlineWebVentures and the Electronic Journals.

| I ACCEPT | I DO NOT ACCEPT |

E-Newsletter Subscription Agreement (Click-On)

This form is a standard click-on (aka "click-through" or "click-wrap") agreement for subscribers to an e-newsletter or listserv. The subscriber is required to click "accept" prior to being given access to the content, thereby manifesting assent to be bound by the terms. For the publisher, the most important elements are:

- the license to use any material posted by the subscriber,
- disclaimers and limitations of liability, and
- indemnification with respect to any material posted by the subscriber.

In the electronic publishing world, this type of agreement can also be useful to set the tone and help establish "community" by setting forth the aims of the community with respect to content and conduct. It is worth remembering, however, that subscriber agreements will usually be read only once, if at all, and any community-building language should be included in other, additional places.

E-Newsletter Subscription Agreement

1. General Information

Art E-News is an e-mail service operated by ArtCo. Publishing, Inc. ("ArtCo.") in connection with its Web site located at http://www.___.org (the "ArtCo. Web site"), and is dedicated to fostering communication and community in the field of new media art. To this end, it is critical that all subscribers to Art E-News be sensitive to the rights of others. Accordingly, each subscriber must agree to comply with all the terms and conditions in this agreement. IF THE TERMS OF THIS AGREEMENT ARE UNACCEPTABLE TO YOU, DO NOT CLICK ACCEPT.

Your right to use and receive Art E-News is personal to you and is not transferable. You are responsible for all postings contributed from your e-mail address by any person.

ArtCo. may modify these terms and conditions from time to time, and such modifications will be effective upon notice posted to Art E-News.

2. Subscriber Submissions

By sending or posting material to Art E-News you agree to grant ArtCo. the nonexclusive, worldwide, perpetual, royalty-free right to reproduce, modify, edit, publish, sub-license, make derivative works from and distribute such material in any form or media, including posting such material on Art E-News or the ArtCo. Web site. ArtCo. reserves the right, in its sole discretion, to edit any subscriber posting, and to chose to include or not include such posting in Art E-News or the ArtCo. Web site.

You must own all rights to any material that you submit to Art E-News or, if you have the right to post works copyrighted by another, you must include with your posting a statement describing where you obtained the work. In no event may you post to Art E-News any material protected by copyright without the permission of the copyright owner.

Although we encourage thoughtful criticism, you may not post any material that defames any person, invades their privacy, infringes their right of publicity, infringes their trademark or other rights, or which is otherwise unlawful.

3. No Commercial Use

Postings to Art E-News may not include any advertising or commercial solicitation. You may not distribute any material posted to Art E-News for any commercial purposes.

4. Permitted Use

The contents of Art E-News are copyrighted under United States copyright laws. You may download any of the postings from Art E-News for your own personal, non-commercial use, provided that you agree to abide by any copyright notice or other restriction contained in any individual posting and include any author attribution, copyright or trademark notice or restriction in any materials that you download.

5. Third-Party Art Works

Art E-News is an unfiltered, unmoderated and unedited mailing list consisting of contributions from subscribers. ArtCo distributes subscriber postings automatically to all subscribers on the list, without any review or editing whatsoever. Certain content from Art E-News and other sources is compiled into a single weekly message. ArtCo. is not responsible for screening, monitoring or verifying the content of Art E-News, including with respect to such content's accuracy, reliability, or compliance with copyright and other laws. Without limiting the foregoing, ArtCo. reserves the right, but does not have the obligation, to monitor, edit and delete any material on Art E-News.

ArtCo. does not endorse any opinion, statement or other material posted on Art E-News. Any opinions, statements or other material expressed by third parties (including other subscribers) are those of the respective author(s) or distributor(s) and not of ArtCo.

6. Disclaimer of Warranty; Limitation of Liability

NEITHER ARTCO. NOR ITS EMPLOYEES, AGENTS, REPRESENTATIVES, INFORMATION PROVIDERS OR LICENSORS ("AFFILIATES") REPRESENT OR

WARRANT THE ACCURACY, RELIABILITY, TIMELINESS OR COMPLETENESS OF ANY OPINION, STATEMENT OR OTHER MATERIAL POSTED ON ART E-NEWS OR THAT THE SAME IS NON-DEFAMATORY, NON-INFRINGING OF COPYRIGHT OR OTHER RIGHTS, OR OTHERWISE LAWFUL. YOU ACKNOWLEDGE THAT ANY RELIANCE ON OR USE OF SUCH OPINION, STATEMENT OR MATERIAL SHALL BE AT YOUR SOLE RISK.

NEITHER ARTCO. NOR ITS AFFILIATES WARRANT THAT ART E-NEWS WILL BE AVAILABLE ON A TIMELY BASIS, OR WILL BE UNINTERRUPTED OR ERROR FREE. ART E-NEWS IS PROVIDED ON AN "AS IS" BASIS WITHOUT WARRANTIES OF ANY KIND, EITHER EXPRESS OR IMPLIED, INCLUDING BUT NOT LIMITED TO WARRANTIES OF TITLE OR IMPLIED WARRANTIES OF MERCHANTABILITY OR FITNESS FOR A PARTICULAR PURPOSE.

IN NO EVENT SHALL ARTCO. OR ITS AFFILIATES BE LIABLE FOR ANY DIRECT, INDIRECT, INCIDENTAL, SPECIAL OR CONSEQUENTIAL DAMAGES ARISING OUT OF THE USE OF OR INABILITY TO USE ART E-NEWS.

7.   Indemnification

You agree to defend, indemnify and hold harmless ArtCo. and its Affiliates from and against all claims and expenses (including attorneys' fees) arising out of any posting to Art E-News by you or anyone using your e-mail account or any breach by you of the terms of this agreement.

8.   Right to Terminate Subscription

ArtCo. reserves the right to terminate your subscription to Art E-News at any time in the event that it considers, in its sole discretion, any conduct by you to be in violation of the terms of this agreement or otherwise in violation of the spirit of Art E-News.

9.   Miscellaneous

This agreement constitutes the entire agreement of the parties with respect to such subject matter of this agreement. No waiver by either party of any breach or default hereunder shall be deemed to be a waiver of any preceding or subsequent breach or default. This agreement shall be construed in accordance with the laws of the State of New York, without regard to its conflict of laws rules. The courts located in the State of New York, County of New York, shall have exclusive jurisdiction of any dispute between you and ArtCo.

[   ] Click to Accept

Electronic Book Distribution and Resale Agreement

"Electronic books" come in many forms and are distributed pursuant to a variety of licensing and financial models. Form 3.9 is one of the simplest models for print publishers. It tracks closely with the traditional print book sales model of selling books to resellers at a discount off the list price and is thus compatible with many contracts signed before publishers imagined there would be technologies and markets that could support electronic books. The following form is particularly flexible because it anticipates a fluid relationship, with new works being added and old works being placed "out of print," just as one would expect with a brick and mortar bookstore.[1]

E-Book Resale Agreement

This E-Book Resale Agreement (this "Agreement") is entered into as of the ____ day of _____, 20___ by and between eSeller, a _____ corporation having an office at _____ ("eSeller"), and _____, a ____ corporation located at _____ ("Publisher").

WITNESSETH

Whereas Publisher desires to have eSeller market, resell and distribute certain books that are available in an electronic format; and

Whereas eSeller desires to market, resell and distribute such books on the terms and conditions set forth herein.

Now therefore, for good and valuable consideration, the Parties agree as follows:

1.   Rights of Use; Ownership

1.1. Right of Use. Publisher hereby grants to eSeller the nonexclusive right during the Term (as defined below) to market, resell and distribute, certain electronically formatted books as determined by Publisher (each an "E-Book Title") [in the _____ format, for use in the _____ device.]

1.2. Publisher as Owner. eSeller acknowledges that Publisher owns or is licensor to all rights, title and interests in and to the E-book Titles.

---

1 For discussion of electronic books and issues relating thereto, *see* Mark A. Fischer, E. Gabriel Perle and John Taylor Williams, *Perle and Williams on Publishing Law*, § 4.02[A] (3d ed., Aspen L. & Bus. 2001).

2.   Delivery of E-Book Titles

2.1. <u>E-book Titles</u>. From time to time during the term of this Agreement, Publisher will make available to eSeller certain E-book Titles for resale. Subject to the terms hereof, eSeller may market, resell and distribute digital reproductions of the E-book Titles. Publisher may revoke eSeller's rights to market, resell, and distribute any E-book Title with thirty (30) days notice to eSeller, except that if there is a legal claim in connection to any title, eSeller shall immediately discontinue selling and distributing such title upon written notice from Publisher. Publisher shall have the right to embed user terms and conditions in each E-book Title.

2.2. <u>Delivery</u>. Publisher or Publisher's designated conversion house shall deliver to eSeller each E-book Title in the _____ format, as soon as reasonably possible after the conversion process is completed.

2.3. <u>Security</u>. eSeller acknowledges that all E-book titles will require a level of security which shall be designated by Publisher. eSeller warrants the ability to support the level of security required for each title. If eSeller cannot support the level of security required for any title, it shall notify Publisher, in writing, and shall discontinue posting, reselling and distributing the title, until Publisher is satisfied with the security system in place.

2.4. <u>ISBN Number</u>. Publisher shall assign a separate format identifier or ISBN to each e-book offered for sale by eSeller hereunder, to facilitate the ordering and processing thereof.

2.5. <u>Additional Information</u>. Publisher shall provide eSeller with the following information (metadata) if available with respect to each E-book Title: (i) title; (ii) author(s)/editor(s); (iii) E-book List Price; (iv) unique ISBN for each Format; (v) referring ISBN and original publication date (if any); (vi) page count of E-book and print version (if any); (vii) rights restrictions, if any; (viii) short description; (ix) cover image; and (x) such other information as is reasonably requested by eSeller.

3.   Financial Terms

"E-book List Price" means the suggested retail price for an E-book Title determined by Publisher.

   "E-book Discount" means for each E-Book Title an amount equal to the trade discount of ___% off the E-book List Price for trade discounted titles and ___% off list price for professional discounted titles.

   "Retail Cost" means, with respect to an E-book Title, an amount equal to the E-book List Price of such E-book Title less the related E-book Discount.

   eSeller shall pay Publisher the amount equal to the Retail Cost of all sales of all E-book Titles by eSeller during such calendar month. Such amounts shall be payable to Publisher no later than thirty 30 days after the end of each calendar month during the Term, if no payment terms are established.

4. Reporting

eSeller shall provide Publisher with a report, which shall include, for each E-book Title, related sales information for each format during such calendar month and the calculation of the amounts payable to Publisher hereunder.

5. Term and Termination

5.1. <u>Term</u>. The initial term (the "Initial Term") of this Agreement shall commence as of the Effective Date and shall continue until the first anniversary of the Effective Date unless sooner terminated as provided herein, and shall continue for successive renewal periods each for a term of one year until terminated in accordance with the terms hereof (each a "Renewal Period"; the Initial Term together with any Renewal Period hereof is deemed the "Term."). Either party may terminate this Agreement at the end of the then current Term by providing the other party written notice at least sixty (60) days prior to the expiration of such Term. Publisher party may terminate this Agreement with at least sixty (60) days prior written notice to eSeller if Publisher discontinues the offering of E-book Titles for sale and distribution.

5.2. <u>Termination or Suspension Due to Breach</u>. Any Party may suspend performance and/or terminate this Agreement immediately upon written notice to the other Party if such other Party is in material breach of any representation, warranty, covenant, term or condition of this Agreement and fails to cure such breach within thirty (30) days after receiving written notice of such breach from the non-breaching Party.

5.3. <u>Force Majeure</u>. No Party shall be liable to any other Party under this Agreement for any delay or failure to perform its obligations under this Agreement if such delay or failure arises from any cause(s) beyond such Party's reasonable control, including labor disputes, strikes, acts of God, floods, fire, lightning, utility or communications failures, earthquakes, vandalism, war, acts of terrorism, riots, insurrections, embargoes, or laws, regulations or orders of any governmental entity.

6. Warranties

6.1. Each Party represents and warrants to the others that it has right and power to enter into and perform this Agreement according to its terms.

6.2. Publisher warrants to eSeller that: (i) the E-book Titles and eSeller's use of the same hereunder do not violate or infringe the rights of any third party or the laws or regulations of any governmental or judicial authority; (ii) each E-book Title shall not defame any third party; (iii) each E-book Title shall not contain any instructions to cause physical harm to any individuals or their property.

6.3. eSeller warrants that it will comply with all laws and regulations applicable to the distribution of the titles, [and further warrants that its proprietary platform(s) do not violate any third party rights.]

7.   Indemnification

Each Party ("Indemnifying Party") shall defend, indemnify and hold harmless the other Party and its affiliates, and their respective shareholders, partners, directors, officers, employees, contractors and agents, from and against any and all liabilities, claims, demands, causes of action, damages, losses and expenses, reasonable attorneys' fees, arising in whole or in part out of or in connection with the breach of any representation or warranty made by the Indemnifying Party herein or the default in performance of any term or covenant to be performed by the Indemnifying Party or its employees or agents hereunder.

8.   Limitation on Damages

Except as expressly provided herein, no party shall be liable to the other party hereto for any indirect, incidental, consequential, or special damages to such other party, even if such party has been advised of the possibility of such damages.

9.   Notices and Changes of Address

All notices shall be sent by overnight courier or registered or certified mail, return receipt requested, postage prepaid, to the Parties at the addresses given below. Each Party shall provide the others with notice of any change of address in accordance with this Section.

10.   Miscellaneous

10.1. Relationship of Parties. The Parties are independent contractors and nothing in this Agreement shall be construed as creating an employer-employee relationship, a partnership, franchise arrangement, agency relationship, or joint venture between or among them.

10.2. No Ongoing Waiver. A waiver of any breach of any of the provision of this Agreement shall not be construed as a continuing waiver of other breaches of the same or other provisions hereof.

10.3. Enforceability. This Agreement shall be binding upon the Parties and their respective heirs, successors, assigns and personal representatives.

10.4. Counterparts. This Agreement may be executed in counterparts, each of which shall be deemed an original, and as executed shall constitute one agreement, binding on all Parties even though all Parties do not sign the same counterpart.

10.5. Severability. If a court of competent jurisdiction finds any provision of this Agreement invalid or unenforceable, such provision shall be given the maximum effect permitted under applicable law, and the remainder of this Agreement shall remain valid and fully enforceable according to its terms.

10.6. <u>Headings</u>. The Section headings used in this Agreement are for ease of reference only, are not substantive, and shall not be used to interpret any provision of this Agreement.

10.7. <u>Governing Law</u>. The internal laws of the State of New York shall govern this Agreement, without regard to conflict of law principles, all claims to be brought in New York.

10.8. <u>Entire Agreement</u>. This Agreement constitutes the entire agreement between the Parties with respect to the subject matter hereof and supersedes all prior and contemporaneous agreements or communications with respect to the subject matter hereof.

IN WITNESS WHEREOF, the parties hereto, intending to be legally bound by the terms of this Agreement, have caused this Agreement to be executed by their duly authorized representatives as of the Effective Date.

eSELLER   PUBLISHER, INC.

By: _____   By: _____

Name: _____   Name: _____

Title: _____   Title: _____

OEM Form Software License

This form is an OEM license that allows a third-party equipment manufacturer to reformat the publisher's electronic content to sell to the manufacturer's customer base and to further sublicense the distribution right for the reformatted products to third parties who sell the manufacturer's equipment or compatible equipment. Although the look and feel differs from Form 3.9, it contains many of the same terms; they both allow the licensees to purchase electronic products at a discount for redistribution, both allow the publisher to change which products are licensed, and both allow reformatting of the material to render it compatible with the distributor's products while maintaining editorial integrity.

One important issue to remember, particularly if you are receiving a license of this sort, is to include the language of Clause 8.5, which provides that customer's rights survive termination of the OEM license. Otherwise, your customer's rights to use the purchased products could lapse when your distribution right terminates.

OEM Software License
This Software Distribution Agreement

Effective the ___ day of _____, _____is made between

_____

hereinafter called Publisher and

_____

hereinafter called Distributor.

_____

1. Definitions
1.1 The Products are the Publisher's products listed in Publisher's then-current price list set forth on Attachment A. The Publisher's price list current at the time of execution of this Agreement is appended hereto as Attachment A. Publisher reserves the right to exclude any Product from the license granted hereinafter.
1.2 For the purposes of this Agreement, the Products shall be deemed to include all relevant changes and upgrades thereto made by Publisher during the Term of this Agreement and any versions thereof created by Distributor pursuant to this Agreement.

2. Intellectual Property Rights

2.1 Publisher and its contracting partners retain all intellectual property rights in the Products, and except as explicitly provided herein, no license of intellectual property rights to Distributor is implied.

2.2 Subject to Publisher's prior written consent, Distributor may use Publisher's logos, trademarks and tradenames in conjunction with its marketing efforts for the Products. Distributor shall not remove, obscure or alter Publisher's or its contracting partners' logos, trademarks, tradenames, copyright notices or other intellectual property or indications thereof on any material that Distributor receives pursuant to this Agreement.

3. License

3.1 In consideration of the license fee specified hereunder Publisher will supply Distributor 1 master copy of the Products and grants Distributor the nonexclusive, non-transferrable, global right:

  (a) to reformat the Products for use with Distributor's products;
  (b) to use and reproduce the reformatted Products for the purposes of demonstration, training and support to its licensees; and
  (c) to grant licenses to use and reproduce the reformatted Products to its customers in exchange for a fee.

3.2 Distributor shall retain all copyright notices and other indications of intellectual property rights in the Products in each reformatted example thereof and ensure that such copyright notices and other indications of intellectual property rights are appropriately displayed when the reformatted Products are used with its products.

3.3 Distributor is not permitted:

  (a) to offer a service providing direct access by electronic or other means to the Products (e.g., Web-based or other online access) to third parties;
  (b) to make alterations to the Products other than those necessitated by the reformatting thereof for use with its own products;
  (c) except as explicitly provided under clauses 3.1 and 3.2, to use or distribute the Products in whole or in part in any derived form or to use them for the purpose of developing other products by way of reverse engineering, decompilation, transformation or like technique.

3.4 All copies of the Products distributed by Distributor shall be accompanied by end-user agreements substantially in the form of Attachment B hereto.

3.5 Distributor undertakes to implement a copy protection mechanism in each example of the Products licensed or otherwise made available by Distributor to its customers to hinder illegal use thereof and in particular:

(a) to hinder unauthorized reproduction and use of the Products as delivered by Distributor to its customers; and

(b) to hinder unauthorized abstraction of the Products and their use in forms or formats other than those supplied by him to its customers.

3.6 Publisher will have the right to review and approve the copy protection prior to its implementation.

4.   License Fee and Discounts

4.1 In consideration of the license granted herein, Distributor shall purchase the Products from Publisher at a discount off the list prices for license fees specified in Attachment A for the Products as set forth below:

(a)___% discount on sales or licenses by Distributor to end-users directly;

(b)___% discount on sales or licenses by Distributor through third-party OEM channels.

4.2 Distributor undertakes to keep the records necessary to document all its commercial transactions in respect of the Products and to make these records available on demand to a neutral auditor acting for Publisher provided that such audit shall take place not more than once in any 12-month period. The costs of the audit shall be borne by Publisher if it shows a discrepancy of 5% or less to Publisher's disadvantage, by Distributor otherwise.

4.3 Within 60 days of the end of each three-month quarterly period commencing with the effective date of this Agreement, Distributor shall provide Publisher with a list of all sales and licenses, specifying the Product in each case, made by Distributor within that quarter and shall remit to Publisher the monies due. Distributor shall retain a log of all copies made of the Products and their disposition.

5.   Business Plan

5.1 Distributor shall present its business plan for the forthcoming year in respect of the Products to Publisher annually on the anniversary of the effective date of this Agreement. The business plan shall not be binding on the parties to this Agreement.

6. Warranty

6.1 Publisher warrants that it and its contracting partners enjoy copyright and all other intellectual property rights in respect of the Products and that it is entitled to conclude this Agreement.

6.2 EXCEPT AS EXPRESSLY PROVIDED ABOVE PUBLISHER PROVIDES THE PRODUCTS PURSUANT TO THIS AGREEMENT "AS IS" WITH NO GUARANTEE, EXPRESS OR IMPLIED, THAT THEY ARE COMPLETE, CORRECT, ACCURATE OR FIT FOR ANY PARTICULAR PURPOSE.

6.3 Distributor warrants that it will comply with all relevant laws and regulations in distributing the Products, that it has all copyrights or other Intellectual Property rights necessary to reformat and distribute the reformatted Products to its customers.

7. Liability

7.1 In the event of any claim being made or action brought against Distributor alleging infringement of any third-party intellectual property rights in the Products, Publisher shall defend or settle such claim or action as it deems fit. Distributor undertakes to reasonably assist Publisher in the defense or settlement of such claim or action if requested.

7.2 In the event of any legally binding judgement being given against Distributor for infringement of third-party intellectual property rights in the Products pursuant to its exercise of its rights under this Agreement, Publisher shall indemnify Distributor for all actual costs incurred by it with respect thereto.

7.3 In the event of any claim being made or action brought against Publisher alleging infringement of any third-party intellectual property rights in the Products as reformatted, Distributor shall defend or settle such claim or action as it deems fit. Publisher undertakes to reasonably assist Distributor in the defense or settlement of such claim or action if requested.

7.4 In the event of any legally binding judgement being given against Publisher for infringement of third-party intellectual property rights in the Products pursuant to its exercise of its rights under this Agreement, Distributor shall indemnify Publisher for all actual costs incurred by it with respect thereto.

8. Duration and Termination

8.1 This Agreement shall become effective when signed by duly authorized representatives of both parties and shall remain in effect for a period of (5) years.

8.2 Distributor's rights to use and distribute the Products shall end on termination of this Agreement. On termination of this Agreement, Distributor shall turn over or destroy without cost to Publisher all copies of the Products in its possession. The fulfillment of contracts made before termination of this Agreement in accordance with usual commercial practice is excepted, subject to payment of the license fee.

8.3 Either party may terminate this Agreement early upon thirty (30) days prior written notice for a breach which is not cured in the thirty (30) day period.

8.4 Publisher may terminate this Agreement early in the event Distributor enters into voluntary or involuntary bankruptcy proceedings or otherwise becomes insolvent.

8.5 The rights of end-users to use the Products shall not be affected by termination of this Agreement so long as Publisher has received the appropriate license fee.

9. Concluding Provisions

9.1 This Agreement together with its attachments constitutes the entire agreement between the parties with respect to the subject matter and supersedes all previous agreements and statements.

9.2 No amendment to this Agreement shall be effective unless it is expressed in writing and signed by duly authorized representatives of both parties.

9.3 In the event that a provision of this Agreement shall be held to be invalid or unenforceable, or should this Agreement contain an omission, this shall not be deemed to invalidate the Agreement as a whole. In place of the invalid or unenforceable provision, or to cover the omission, a reasonable clause which reflects the intention of the parties and the spirit of the Agreement shall be included.

9.4 The rights licensed herein to Distributor are personal and may not be assigned without the prior written consent of Publisher.

9.5 The parties hereto are independent contractors, and neither shall have the right to bind the other to any third-party contracts.

9.6 This Agreement shall be governed by the laws of the State of Wyoming, U.S.A. Any claim, action or proceeding arising out of or relating to this Agreement shall be commenced in a court of competent jurisdiction in the State of Wyoming, County of_____, U.S.A, and each party hereby consents to the jurisdiction of that court and waives any objections to venue therein.

AGREED AND ACCEPTED

PUBLISHER   DISTRIBUTOR

By: _____   By: _____

Name: _____   Name: _____

Title: _____   Title: _____

Software Authorized Dealer Agreement

Forms 3.9 and 3.10 are simple agreements for what seems complex: the reformatting and redistribution of the publisher's content. Form 3.11 is a complex agreement for what is seemingly simple: the resale (technically, sublicensing) by an authorized dealer of software products created and manufactured by the publisher.

In this agreement, the parties have chosen to set forth many more terms of their relationship than did the parties in Forms 3.9 and 3.10. Some of the interesting provisions are:

- the grandfathering of price changes to accommodate sales made prior to the effective date of the change (Clause 1.2);
- the particularly strong independent contractor language (Clause 1.5);
- language concerning the passing of customer leads (Clause 2.2);
- details of the technical support offered to both the dealer (Clause 2.3) and the customers (Clause 3.3);
- discussions re: product seminars, meetings, and sales aids (Clauses 2.4 and 2.7); and
- the close parsing of acceptable and unacceptable promotional channels (Clause 3.2).

Accordingly, this form is a useful resource both for creating a comprehensive, all-encompassing agreement and for evaluating the sufficiency of other, simpler agreements.

Authorized Dealer Agreement

Agreement by and between _____, having its principal place of business at _____ ("Dealer") and _____, having its principal place of business at _____ ("Publisher").

Whereas Dealer wishes to obtain the benefits of having Publisher Authorized Dealer Status and has submitted an Authorized Dealer Application; and

Whereas Publisher has reviewed the Authorized Dealer Application and in reliance upon the information set forth therein would like to appoint Dealer as a Publisher Authorized Dealer on the following terms and conditions;

Now therefore, the Parties hereto agree as follows:

1. General Terms of Appointment

1.1 Products
Dealer shall enjoy the benefits of being a Publisher Authorized Dealer with respect to the products listed on Schedule A to this Agreement. Publisher may

from time to time add or delete products from Schedule A by giving written notice. Changes to the Publisher Price Guide constitute such notice.

1.2 Prices; Changes

Dealer will be given the opportunity to purchase the products at the price levels indicated on Schedule A to this Agreement.

Publisher will offer Dealer the same prices, discounts, margins, and terms that Publisher offers to other like dealers who order in like quantity. The prices shown in the Publisher Price Guide do not include freight, taxes, insurance, and similar charges which will be added to Dealer's cost where appropriate. Publisher may from time to time increase or decrease any of the prices shown in the Publisher Price Guide or the levels shown on Schedule A by giving notice of the increase or decreases and its effective date to Dealer. All products covered by this Agreement will be sold to Dealer at the applicable price in effect on the date of shipment (except that orders accepted prior to the effective date of a price increase and shipped within 30 days after the effective date will be sold to Dealer at the earlier or lower price).

1.3 Term of Sale

All sales of product to Dealer under this Agreement will be on Publisher's standard terms and conditions of sale in effect for sales to Publisher's Authorized Dealers at the time of sale. A copy of Publisher's current terms and conditions of sale is included in the Price Guide.

All shipments to Dealer will be FOB Publisher's point of shipment and will be shipped at Dealer's cost to its principal place of business unless otherwise agreed in writing by us. In case of a conflict between the terms of this Agreement and any purchase orders, acceptances or correspondence forming part of any order for products placed by Dealer, this Agreement shall govern and prevail unless otherwise agreed in writing by Publisher.

1.4 Nonexclusive Agreement

Dealer's appointment is nonexclusive. Publisher may appoint additional Publisher Authorized Dealers in the same geographical area or channel of trade or may otherwise sell, license or distribute any products either directly or through intermediaries.

1.5 Relationship

Publisher and Dealer are independent contractors each being in full control of its own business. Dealer and its employees are not entitled to any of the benefits, including workers' compensation, extended by Publisher to its own employees and Dealer disclaims any rights to such benefits. Under no circumstances shall either Publisher or Dealer have the right or authority to act or make any commitment on behalf of the other or represent the other as its agent in any way. Dealer agrees to hold Publisher harmless and indemnify it against any loss, expense, or damage arising out of or related to this Agreement or Dealer's actions or the action of its employees.

2.   Publisher's Obligations

2.1 General

Publisher shall use reasonable efforts to assist Dealer in the growth and conduct of Dealer's business as it relates to Publisher's products. Among other things, Publisher personnel with knowledge of the Authorized Dealer Program will be available to respond to questions from Dealer and to provide suggestions with respect to marketing, sales, customer development, and other business planning.

2.2 Customer Leads

Publisher may refer to Dealer, when Publisher deems appropriate, information identifying potential end-user customers in Dealer's geographical area. Publisher reserves the right to contact end-users directly.

2.3 Technical Support

Publisher shall provide reasonable telephone consultation to Dealer covering the use of the products and shall provide reasonable telephone consultation, assistance, and advise to Dealer covering technical questions raised by end-users which cannot be answered by Dealer's technical staff. Free consultation is limited to questions involving installation and operation of Publisher's products. Dealer's clients may also call Publisher directly at _____.

2.4 Meeting and Seminars

Publisher may, from time to time, sponsor meetings and seminars with respect to the products covered by this Agreement, new products, marketing opportunities, and such other subjects as Publisher believes may be of interest to the Publisher Authorized Dealers. When Publisher deems it appropriate, Dealer will be invited to attend and participate in such meeting and seminars. In certain instances, Dealer's customers or potential customers may also be invited to attend.

2.5 Advertising and Promotion

Publisher shall, consistent with its business needs, promote the sale and distribution of the products covered by this Agreement in such manner and at such prices as it deems appropriate. These promotional efforts shall take such form or forms as Publisher believes best suit its business needs and may include advertising in trade publications and appearances at trade shows.

2.6 Product Shipment

Publisher shall use reasonable efforts to ship Dealer's orders for product in the quantities and on the dates requested as long as the dates requested conform with Publisher's standard order processing times as stated in its current Publisher Price Guide. Publisher may, at its option, offer expedited service at an additional charge. The availability of this option will be determined by Publisher at the time each order is placed and will be applicable to that order only. All orders are subject to acceptance by Publisher. However, Publisher agrees that so long a Dealer is not in breach of this Agreement and its account is current, Publisher will promptly accept orders from Dealer for items in current inventory.

2.7 Sales Aids

Publisher shall offer to supply Dealer with Publisher standard sales aids, demonstration disks, product briefs, brochures, application notes, and similar literature made available by Publisher at the price stated in the Price Guide in effect on the date of Dealer's order for such literature is received.

2.8 Warranties

a. Publisher warrants the documentation and magnetic medium on which the products covered by this Agreement are recorded against defects in material or workmanship appearing with thirty (30) days of their delivery to Dealer. Any such defects, if located, must be communicated to Publisher in writing no later than thirty (30) days after delivery. Within a reasonable time after such notification, Publisher will either repair or replace the defective documentation or medium without charge to Dealer that is Dealer's sole and exclusive remedy.

b. Publisher does not warrant that the products will in any way meet Dealer's requirements or the customer's requirements that the operation of any computer program will be uninterrupted or errorfree. The warranty set forth in 2.8(a) does not cover any media or documentation which has been subjected to damage or abuse. The warranty does not cover any computer program that has been altered or changed in any way be anyone other than Publisher. Publisher is not responsible for problems caused by changes in the operating characteristics of computer hardware or computer operating systems which are made after publication of the product nor for problems in the interaction of the products with non-Publisher software.

c. THE EXPRESS WARRANTY SET FORTH ABOVE IS EXCLUSIVE AND IN LIEU OF, AND DEALER HEREBY EXPRESSLY WAIVES, ALL OTHER GUARANTEES AND WARRANTIES, EXPRESS OR IMPLIED, INCLUDING WITHOUT LIMITATION, ANY IMPLIED WARRANTY OF MERCHANTABILITY OR FITNESS FOR A PARTICULAR PURPOSE.

The agents and employees of Publisher are not authorized to make modifications to this warranty. Accordingly, additional statements, whether oral or written, do not constitute warranties and should not be relied upon.

2.9 Limitation of Liability

Publisher shall not in any case be liable for special, incidental, consequential, indirect, or other similar damages arising from breach of warranty, breach of contract, negligence, or any other legal theory. Such damages include but are not limited to, loss of profits or revenue, loss of use of the computer program, loss of data, costs or recreating lost data or any associated equipment, costs of capital, costs of substitute programs or equipment, facilities or services, down-time costs, losses caused by delays in delivery or claims of Dealer's customers for such damages.

3. Dealer's Rights and Obligations

3.1 General

Dealer shall promote the sale or license of products to end-user customers of the products covered by this Agreement.

3.2 Marketing

Dealer may market Publisher's products through the following channels:

1. Face to face contact with clients.
2. Retail outlets.
3. Direct mail.
4. Catalogs that are published by Dealer.

Without prior written approval, Dealer may NOT do the following:

1. Place ads with Publisher's name or product names in magazines or newspapers.
2. Market or show Publisher's software in conjunction with seminars and/or training of any kind.

If you have an interest in doing either of the above, contact us to discuss your specific situation.

3.3 Customer Support

Publisher will handle all of the support through its general support number: _____, and its Web site located at _____. Dealer will inform end-users that support from Publisher will be given only from the above number and Web site.

3.4 Payment

Dealer shall pay Publisher for all product shipments according to the terms established for Dealer's account. Dealer shall pay for all shipping charges unless other arrangements are made at the time Publisher accepts the order.

3.5 Licensing

a. Title and ownership of the products remain with Publisher. The products include proprietary information and trade secrets of Publisher, are copyrighted, and are distributed solely under license terms that Publisher determines and these terms may change in Publisher's sole discretion.

b. Dealer shall not attempt to reverse engineer, disassemble, copy, or reproduce any Licensed product provided by Publisher under this Agreement.

c. The end-user license agreement or product specification prepared by Publisher for each program shall specify the licensed program characteristics and under which operating system and/or microprocessors the licensed product will operate in. Dealer shall not make any representation as to any product other than as set forth in the end-user license agreement or product specification.

d. Dealer agrees to take all reasonable and necessary steps to protect the proprietary rights of Publisher.

4. Loss of Publisher Authorized Dealer Status; Consequences

4.1 Term and Termination

Dealer's appointment and initial term of this Agreement shall be for a period of one year from the date this Agreement is signed by both Publisher and Dealer. This Agreement shall thereafter be reviewed automatically additional one-year periods unless either party provides to other with written notice of termination at least 30 days prior to the end of the initial or any renewal term. Either party may cancel this agreement at any time and for any reason by giving the other at least 90 days prior written notice.

4.2 Loss of Status

Dealer may lose its status as a Publisher Authorized Dealer immediately upon written notice, at Publisher's option, if (1) it breaches any of its obligations to Publisher under this or any other agreement pertaining to its participation in Publisher Authorized Dealer program, (2) it becomes insolvent or enters into voluntary or involuntary bankruptcy proceedings, or (3) it fails to purchase any product within a six (6) month period. Dealer will also lose its status as a result of termination under Clause 4.1 above.

4.3 Consequences of Loss of Status

a. Upon the loss of Authorized Dealer status, Dealer shall forthwith cease holding itself out as a Publisher Authorized Dealer and shall have no further right to use Publisher's name, logo, trademarks, or documents, promotional material supplied to it by Publisher, material identifying it as a Publisher

Authorized Dealer, and all other assets or property in its possession belonging to Publisher.

b. Upon the loss of Dealer's status as a Publisher Authorized Dealer, Publisher shall have no further obligation to Dealer under this Agreement, but may at its sole option, may continue to honor orders submitted by Dealer. Under no circumstances shall Publisher have any obligation to purchase or accept for credit any of Dealer's unsold inventory or have any other liability in connection therewith. Further, Publisher shall not be liable to Dealer for any damage, expenditure, loss of profit, prospective profit, or consequential damages of any kind or nature alleged to have been sustained by Dealer or allegedly arising out of or related to this Agreement or the loss of Dealer's status as a Publisher Authorized Dealer. No loss of such status due to termination, however, shall excuse or release Dealer from making payments which may be or shall become due or owing to Publisher.

5.   Miscellaneous

5.1 Notices

All notices and other communications shall be deemed given when deposited in the United States mail as certified mail, postage prepaid, addressed to Publisher or to Dealers at their principal offices set forth on the first page of this Agreement. Either party may change the address by giving the other 30 days prior written notice of such change.

5.2 Entire Agreement; Amendment

This Agreement including the attachments and exhibits attached hereto and made a part hereof supersedes all prior communications or understanding between Publisher and Dealer (concerning the Publisher Authorized Dealer relationship) and constitute the entire agreement of writing as executed by both Publisher and Dealer (except that Publisher may, from time to time, unilaterally change the prices and products list in the Price Guide and on Schedule A).

5.3 Governing Law

This agreement is made under, governed by, and shall be construed solely in accordance with the internal laws of the State of California. All action or suits under this agreement shall be brought only in federal or state courts of California, County of _____. All causes of action by Dealer against Publisher must be instituted within one (1) year for the date of the event which gave rise to the cause of action.

5.4 Assignment

This Agreement is personal to and not transferable by Dealer. Dealer shall not assign, sell, or otherwise transfer this Agreement or any rights hereunder without prior written consent of Publisher. For these purposes, the term "assign" shall be interpreted broadly and shall include a merger, sale of assets or business, or other transfer of control, direct to indirect, or by operation of law or otherwise.

5.5 Authority

Dealer represents that it has the right and lawful authority to enter into and perform this Agreement, that the Agreement is a valid and binding obligation of Dealer, and that there are no other outstanding agreements or obligations inconsistent with the terms and provisions hereof.

This agreement contains _____ (__) pages and the following schedules:
A. Products, Pricing and Terms Agreed to this _____ day of _____, 20__

By: _____

Name: _____

Title: _____

Agreed to this _____ day of _____, 20__

By: _____

Name: _____

Title: _____

CHAPTER

4

Litigation and Litigation Avoidance

§ 4.01 Background

This chapter contains materials relating to common disputes in the publishing industry. It includes a cease and desist letter for trademark infringement (Form 4.1), followed by a trademark "coexistence agreement," which is typically entered into between parties as a settlement to a dispute.[1]

This chapter also contains a variety of copyright infringement cease and desist and anti-piracy materials letters (Forms 4.3, 4.6, 4.7, 4.8, and 4.9) and a settlement and release agreement for author dispute (Form 4.4). Lastly, I have included sample disclaimers (Form 4.5).

§ 4.02 Avoiding Libel, Invasion of Privacy, and Infringement Lawsuits

Most responsible publishers will conduct prepublication review of sensitive material and try to follow codes of practice for investigative reporting. The following material, adapted from a paper written by Michelle Worrall Tilton of First Media Insurance Specialists, Inc.,[2] provides useful guidance for (1) prepublication review, (2) the development of investigative reporting codes of practice, and (3) resolving disputes when they occur.

[A] Use of Criminal Justice Terminology

Be familiar with criminal justice terminology, for example, the difference between an arrest and a conviction. Just because a criminal defendant has

---

1 Related documents in other chapters are Form 5.13 (Trademark Assignment) and Form 5.10 (Trademark License).

2 (www.firstmediainc.com). Reprinted with permission.

been arrested or charged with a crime does not mean that he or she will ultimately be convicted of that same crime. The action may be dismissed or the defendant may plead to a lesser charge. Be very careful when relying on old newspaper reports or file footage to fill in the criminal background of a subject involved in a current news story. Always rely on court records as much as possible. Criminals have lots of time, and they are litigious.

[B] Private Property

Do not enter a private dwelling or trespass on private property without valid consent. The same is also true for "private" areas of businesses. Minors, relatives, and neighbors cannot consent to entry. Consent will be invalid if it is elicited through a misrepresentation or false pretenses.

[C] Doctors and Lawyers

Be careful when reporting on the wrongdoing of professionals. Doctors and lawyers have been very successful libel plaintiffs. They make very good witnesses on their own behalf and have the money—and ego—to vigorously litigate a defamation claim against the media.

[D] Names

Many different people may share the same name. When researching information about a person, make sure that you are not confusing your subject with another person of the same name.

[E] Financially Unstable Businesses

If you report on a business in financial difficulty, always make sure that the figures are correct, with public records to back them up. Business owners are quick to allege that the offending story was the cause of the financial instability. If the business goes bankrupt, its libel claim may be its sole "asset."

[F] Old File Footage

Be careful when using old file footage or photographs to illustrate a new and unrelated story.

[G] Advertisements

Just because an advertiser executes a hold harmless agreement with the publisher does not mean that the publisher will not be sued as a contributory infringer for publishing the infringing advertisement. Be wary of superheroes and the Oscar statuette. Their copyright owners vigorously protect their ownership interests.

[H] Children

Children are often careless in their words and actions. Be careful when interviewing and photographing a child without the guardian's consent—especially in an unflattering story. Parents are quick to sue on their child's behalf. Also, be careful when photographing accident scenes involving identifiable children, as parents may sue for emotional distress.

[I] Neighbors

When interviewing the neighbors of a story subject, use caution. Neighbors often have an axe to grind and frequently cannot resist the opportunity to backstab.

[J] Tipsters and Confidential Sources

Always try to corroborate tips with public records, or with speakers willing to go on the record.

[K] Diseases

Be cautious when reporting on and identifying people with diseases, especially where the diseases may carry social stigma, such as AIDS.

[L] Police Officers

Treat police officers in the same manner as confidential sources. "Unofficial" statements are easily recanted.

[M] Notes

Be consistent with notes and e-mail. Make sure you keep either everything or throw it away. It is best to document, and to follow, a policy.

[N] Dead People

Dead people cannot be libeled, but they may have post-mortem publicity rights.[3]

[O] Complaints

It is crucial to return calls, respond to e-mails, and be courteous to people who have been offended by statements made about them. Often, listening to people and offering fair solutions can make problems go away.

[P] Retraction

If a mistake has been made, correct it. A retraction or apology may help mitigate damages. In some jurisdictions, a libel plaintiff may be limited to actual damages if a retraction has been published. Remember to check all online versions of your publication when investigating a retraction demand. Check out *www.slipup.com* for information about online corrections.

[Q] Stalking

Some states have anti-stalking laws that could be used against investigative reporters. Check with counsel to make sure the proposed newsgathering activities do not constitute stalking or harassment.

[R] Promises

Try to use a linking agreement to minimize liability for online linking. Never deep-link and bypass the homepage of the site to which you are linking unless you have written permission.

[S] Food

Many food producers and distributors file trade disparagement suits when the integrity of their food products has been questioned. Likewise, restaurant owners are quick to sue if unappetizing words like hepatitis, roaches and E.coli bacteria are linked with their restaurants.

---

3 *See, Art Law Handbook,* App. 3-A (Roy Kaufman ed., Aspen L. & Bus. 2000).

[T] Medical Records

There are numerous laws protecting the confidentiality of medical records. Be careful when publishing or broadcasting x-rays, mammograms, early cancer detection breast examination footage or medical records without permission from the patient. If such records or clips are received from the hospital, treating physician or a health support group, assume that the requisite consent has not been procured and ensure that the patient cannot be identified.

[U] Internet Sources

Web surfing reporters must use caution with anything posted on the Internet. Treat all information as if it has been provided by an anonymous tipster and seek corroboration from a credible source.

[V] Web Site Errors

Many times Web sites are refreshed or updated by computer people and not editors or reporters. Sometimes a corrected error reappears as a result of posting a cached copy.

Cease and Desist Letter—Trademark Infringement[4]

Cease and Desist Letter

WITHOUT PREJUDICE

[*date*]

Ms. Camille B. DeMille
Owner
Junior Publishing, Inc.
1313 Mockingbird Lane
Springfield, Alaska

Dear Ms. DeMille:

I am writing to inform you about a trademark problem. Senior Publishing, Inc. ("SP") is publisher and owner of all rights in a proprietary print book series marketed through the use of the trademark "BOOKS ARE SUPER" (the "Trademark"). SP has been using the Trademark continuously since _____, and the Trademark is registered in International Class 16 (Paper Goods and Printed Matter) in the United States and abroad. A copy of the United States registration is attached hereto.

SP has recently learned that you are currently selling, distributing, marketing and publishing a series of books under the series name ''BOOKS ARE SOUPER". We believe that your use of the BOOKS ARE SOUPER name in the same categories as our use not only gives rise to a high likelihood of consumer confusion, but has actually caused market-place confusion. In fact, we learned of your company's use of the BOOKS ARE SOUPER name as a direct result of customers attempting to place orders for your series through our sales representatives. As such, your use violates both federal and state laws regarding trademark infringement and unfair competition.

In these circumstances, we require your written assurances that you will stop selling, distributing, publishing and promoting books under the name BOOKS ARE SOUPER. If you like, we are willing to work with you to find a new, mutually acceptable name. We hope that you share our sincere interest in avoiding consumer confusion and in resolving this matter amicably.

---

4 *See generally*, Mark A. Fischer, E. Gabriel Perle and John Taylor Williams, *Perle and Williams on Publishing Law*, Ch. 25 (3d ed., Aspen L. & Bus. 2001).

If you have any questions, feel free to call me, or to have your attorney call me, at _____. Please note that this letter is without prejudice to our rights including our rights to seek monetary damages, and that if we have not heard from you by _____, we reserve the right to take further action.

Sincerely,

Fred T. Lawyer

Trademark Coexistence Agreement

Form 4.1 is a draft letter complaining of the use by one publisher of a trademark that is deceptively similar to that of another. In situations where the parties legitimately determine that their trademarks can coexist, such as where the marks are similar but used in different fields, the parties may forego the vagaries of litigation and enter into a coexistence agreement like the one below. For such an agreement to be effective (and valid), the parties must differentiate between the permitted uses of each mark, and usually agree to work together if, notwithstanding their efforts, confusion occurs in the marketplace.

Coexistence Agreement

Agreement made as of this _____ day of _____, 20__ by and between Senior Publisher, Inc. a corporation organized under the laws of the State of _____ with offices at _____ (hereinafter called "Senior"), and Junior Publisher, Inc. a corporation organized under the laws of the State of _____ with offices at _____ (hereinafter called "Junior").

WHEREAS Senior is the owner of the trademark "Books are Super," Registration Number _____, for a series of trade books on the topics of literature, philosophy, and combustion engines, and also owns a unique trade dress used in conjunction with the Books are Super trademark consisting of, *inter alia*, a yellow border (see attached Exhibit A), and Senior has used said trademark and trade dress in interstate commerce since at least as early as March, 1995; and

WHEREAS Junior recently published a series of books under the series title "Books are Souper" for the culinary and hospitality markets with a unique trade dress consisting of, *inter alia*, a green border, similar to that attached as Exhibit B; and

WHEREAS Senior has objected to the use by Junior of the "Books are Souper" series title; and

WHEREAS the parties have exchanged information regarding their respective businesses and product lines, and have concluded that provided the terms of this Agreement are followed, there would be no likelihood of confusion as to the concurrent use of their marks for their respective products; and

WHEREAS the parties have pursuant to the foregoing agreed to enter in an agreement on the terms and conditions set forth hereunder;

NOW, THEREFORE, in consideration of the promises, and of the mutual covenants of the parties hereto, it is hereby agreed as follows:

1. Junior undertakes that it will confine all use of the Books are Souper series title to the culinary and hospitality markets. For the avoidance of doubt, Junior shall be the owner of the Books are Souper series title for culinary and hospitality markets.

2. Junior will avoid the use of any trade dress which is confusingly similar to Senior's trade dress as evidenced by Exhibit A. The parties agree that the use of a yellow border on the cover is part of Senior's distinctive trade dress, and Junior may not use a yellow border.

3. Senior will avoid the use of any trade dress which is confusingly similar to Junior's trade dress for its Books are Souper series as evidenced by Exhibit B.

4. Junior acknowledges that Senior has exclusive rights to the Books are Super trademark and trade dress in relation to the topics of literature, philosophy, and combustion engines. Senior acknowledges that Junior has exclusive rights to the Books are Souper series title and trade dress in relation to culinary and hospitality books.

5. Nothing herein shall be read so as to limit the rights of Junior to publish books on the topics of literature, philosophy, and combustion engines, or of Senior to publish culinary or hospitality books, if these publications do not use the trademarks, series titles, or distinctive trade dress of the other party.

6. Nothing herein shall be read to limit distribution channels for either party's products. Either party may advertise, promote and distribute their respective book series in any media, including without limitation on the Internet.

7. Neither party will materially alter the trade dress for those products discussed herein without the prior written consent of the other party.

8. If, notwithstanding the expectations of the parties that there will be no likelihood of confusion, and further considering the steps that will be taken by the parties to ensure this result, either party learns of actual confusion, the parties undertake to work together to avoid the recurrence of such event.

9. The parties each agree to sign any such further documents requested by the other to effectuate the intent of this Agreement.

10. This Agreement shall be governed by the laws of the State of New York without reference to its conflicts of laws provisions. The Courts the State of New York, County of New York shall have exclusive jurisdiction over any dispute or controversy relating to this Agreement.

11.   This Agreement sets forth the entire Agreement between the parties relating to the subject matter hereof and may not be varied except by a written instrument signed by the parties.

IN WITNESS WHEREOF, this Agreement has been executed by the parties hereto as of the day and year first above written.

SENIOR PUBLISHER

By: _____

Name: _____

Title: _____

JUNIOR PUBLISHER

By: _____

Name: _____

Title: _____

Cease and Desist Letter—Direct Copyright Infringement (Online Use)[5]

This form is to be used where the Web site posted the infringing material for its own direct use. For other forms related to more blatant piracy, see 4.6–4.9

Cease and Desist Letter

WITHOUT PREJUDICE

[*date*]
[*name*]
[*address*]

Dear Sir:

I am writing this letter on behalf of Publisher, Inc. ("Publisher"). As you may be aware, Publisher is a global publisher of, *inter alia*, magazines distributed to professionals working in the field of _____. Two such magazines are _____ and _____.

We have recently learned that _____ ("WebCo."), is posting articles owned and published by Publisher, its affiliates and subsidiaries, in electronic format on its portal site located at www.webco.com, with a WebCo. copyright notice, notwithstanding the fact that WebCo. has no license to do so. Attached hereto are copies of two of Publisher's articles, which were obtained from your site, and which were originally published in the above-referenced magazines.

The facts set forth above allege a pattern of willful copyright infringement. In order to prevail on a copyright infringement claim, Publisher need only show that Publisher owns its copyrights, and that WebCo. infringed them. Publisher's copyright registration certificates for the articles published on the WebCo. site (copies attached hereto) are presumptive evidence of ownership. Your company's violation of Publisher's rights, and its use of WebCo.'s copyright notice on Publisher's material, provide evidence of bad faith and willfulness, and, as such, may entitle Publisher to statutory damages of $150,000 per infringement, plus attorneys fees.

Publisher may also have claims against WebCo. for contributory infringement based on WebCo.'s enabling easy electronic redistribution of Publisher's material. Publisher will hold WebCo absolutely responsible if Publisher material is further distributed by third parties that acquire it from the WebCo. site as evidenced by the WebCo. copyright notice.

---

5 *See generally*, Mark A. Fischer, E. Gabriel Perle and John Taylor Williams, *Perle and Williams on Publishing Law*, Chs. 11–15 (3d ed., Aspen L. & Bus. 2001).

Publisher hereby demands that WebCo. immediately cease and desist from the display, sale, license, reformatting or distribution of electronic copies of any Publisher-owned material. Additionally, we demand that WebCo. provides, by _____: (1) written confirmation of compliance with the foregoing demand; (2) a complete list of any and all Publisher material displayed, sold, licensed, reformatted or distributed by WebCo.; and (3) written confirmation that all electronic and print copies of Publisher material in WebCo.'s possession, custody and control have been deleted or otherwise destroyed.

Your prompt and full cooperation will be appreciated, and will facilitate reasonable settlement. All correspondence should be addressed to my attention. This letter is without prejudice to the rights of Publisher, all of which are expressly reserved.

Sincerely,

[*name*]
[*title*]
[*address*]

Settlement and Release Agreement for Author Dispute

Disputes between authors and publishers do occur. From the publisher's side, it is usually because the author fails to provide manuscript "acceptable" to the publisher within a "reasonable" time period. For authors, the allegations usually involve marketing. After all, if a book is not successful, someone other than the author must be to blame.

The following is an agreement settling such a "marketing" dispute between a publisher and an author of subscription books, pursuant to which the publisher allows the author to buy the rights to, and inventory of, two books written by the author and published by the publisher to everyone's mutual dissatisfaction.

Settlement and Release Agreement

Agreement dated as of the _____ day of _____, 20__, by and between Publisher, Inc. ("Publisher"), a Massachusetts Corporation, and _____ (the "Author");

WHEREAS Publisher is the publisher of, and owner of all rights in, certain books entitled _____ and _____, which were written by the Author for Publisher (the "Works"); and

WHEREAS the Author has made certain claims against Publisher regarding Publisher's sales and promotional efforts with respect to the Works; and

WHEREAS the parties hereto wish to totally resolve, settle and compromise all such claims and any other claims by the Author against Publisher, its subsidiaries, affiliates, successors and assigns, or any claims that Publisher, its subsidiaries, affiliates, successors and assigns may have against the Author;

NOW, THEREFORE, in consideration of the foregoing and of the mutual covenants that follow, it is agreed that upon execution of this Settlement and Release Agreement:

1. Subject to the Author's right to receive royalties therefor, Publisher shall continue to market the Works until such time as the Author locates another publisher which agrees to Publisher's conditions for an assignment as set forth in Paragraph 3 below, or the Author agrees to the conditions for a reversion as set forth in Paragraph 3 below. The Author's right to receive royalties for Publisher's sales of the Works before and after the signing of this Agreement survive the execution of this Agreement.

2. The Author may immediately commence a search for a new publisher for Works.

3. Either the Author or the new publisher, at the time of reversion or assignment, will purchase the then current inventory of the Works, at half their inventory cost, plus half their composition cost, to be shipped to a location designated by the Author. Shipping costs are to be paid by the Author or the new publisher. The Author's certified public accountant may, at the Author's sole expense, inspect the books and records of Publisher relating to the Works to verify the inventory and composition costs. The maximum costs of inventory and composition are _____. Upon tendering payment pursuant to this paragraph, all of Publisher's right, title and interest in the Works shall revert to the Author or be assigned to the new publisher.

4. Upon payment as described in Paragraph 3, Publisher will supply the Author with one copy of the names and addresses of all subscribers to the Works to the extent maintained by Publisher, solely for use in connection with the Works. Publisher will also supply the Author or the new publisher with available production material for the Works at no additional charge.

5. Neither the Author, the new publisher, nor anyone acting on their authority or with their consent (other than Publisher) shall distribute the Works or any promotional material relating thereto with any trademark, name, colophon or other symbol which identifies Publisher, its subsidiaries or affiliates (collectively the "Trademarks"). The Author or the new publisher may dispose of the inventory purchased pursuant to Paragraph 3 by gift or in any commercially reasonable manner, provided that the Author or the new publisher rebinds the inventory or stickers over the Trademarks.

6. This Agreement and all of the terms and conditions hereof shall be kept confidential and shall not be revealed by the parties, other than under compulsion of proper judicial process, to any person or entity except the parties' accountants, attorneys, or the United States Internal Revenue Service and state revenue services; provided, however, that the parties may advise anyone making inquiry that the controversies between the parties have been settled. Neither party shall make disparaging statements about the other party to any third parties, including but not limited to disparaging statements by the Author concerning Publisher's promotional efforts concerning the Works or any other dealings between the parties hereto.

7. Except for the royalty rights preserved in Paragraph 1 above, the Author hereby releases Publisher, Publisher's subsidiaries, affiliates, successors and assigns from all actions, causes of action, suits, debts, dues, sums of money, accounts, reckonings, bonds, bills, specialties, covenants, contracts, controversies, agreements, promises, variances, trespasses, damages, judgments, extents, executions, claims, and demands whatsoever, in law or equity, against Publisher, its subsidiaries, affiliates, successors and assigns, which the Author, his executors, administrators, successors and assigns ever had, now have or hereafter can, shall or may, have for, upon, or by reason of any matter, cause or thing whatsoever, from the beginning of the world to the date of this Agreement.

8. Publisher hereby releases the Author, the Author's heirs, executors, administrators, successors and assigns from all actions, causes of action, suits, debts, dues, sums of money, accounts, reckonings, bonds, bills, specialties, covenants, contracts, controversies, agreements, promises, variances, trespasses, damages, judgments, extents, executions, claims, and demands whatsoever, in law or equity, against the Author, his heirs, executors, administrators, successors and assigns, which Publisher, its subsidiaries, affiliates, successors and assigns ever had, now have or hereafter can, shall or may, have for, upon, or by reason of any matter, cause or thing whatsoever, from the beginning of the world to the date of this Agreement.

9. Publisher agrees to provide whatever further documentation is necessary to confirm the assignment and transfer of copyright in and to the Works to the Author or to the new publisher.

10. This Agreement constitutes the entire agreement between the parties. There are no other terms, conditions or provisions, express or implied, and any amendment or waiver of the terms, conditions or provisions of this Agreement shall be made only in writing signed by the parties.

11. Neither of the parties concedes any liability or the commission of any wrongful act, nor the propriety of any of the claims referenced herein.

12. This Agreement shall be construed and interpreted pursuant to the laws of the Commonwealth of Massachusetts applicable to contracts wholly entered into and performed in the Commonwealth of Massachusetts. Any legal action, suit or proceeding arising out of or relating to this Agreement or the breach thereof shall be instituted in a court of competent jurisdiction in the county in which the defendant resides if the defendant is an individual, or the county in which the defendant maintains its principal place of business if the defendant is a corporation, and each party hereby consents and submits to personal jurisdiction of such court, waives any objection to venue in such court and consents to service of process by first class mail at the last known address of such party.

IN WITNESS WHEREOF, the parties have executed this Agreement as of the day and year first written above.

FOR THE AUTHOR   **FOR PUBLISHER, INC.**

By: _____   By: _____

Name: _____   Name: _____

Title: _____   Title: _____

Sample Disclaimers

The strong First Amendment protection afforded publications makes disclaimers largely unnecessary from a legal point of view. However, a responsible publisher will never be punished for warning readers of risks, and the effects of a disclaimer on a potential plaintiff should not be overlooked.

Disclaimers

Long Form General Disclaimer

The publisher and the author make no representations or warranties with respect to the accuracy or completeness of the contents of this work and specifically disclaim all warranties, including without limitation warranties of fitness for a particular purpose. No warranty may be created or extended by sales or promotional materials. The advice and strategies contained herein may not be suitable for every situation. This work is sold with the understanding that the publisher is not engaged in rendering legal, accounting, or other professional services. If professional assistance is required, the services of a competent professional person should be sought. Neither the publisher nor the author shall be liable for damages arising herefrom. The fact that an organization or Web site is referred to in this work as a citation and/or a potential source of further information does not mean that the author or the publisher endorses the information the organization or Web site may provide or recommendations it may make. Further, readers should be aware that Internet Web sites listed in this work may have changed or disappeared between the time when this work was written and the time when it is read.

Travel Rider to Long Form General Disclaimer

Please be advised that travel information is subject to change at any time and this is especially true of prices. We therefore suggest that readers write or call ahead for confirmation when making travel plans. The author and the publisher cannot be held responsible for the experiences of readers while traveling.

Sports/Diet Rider to Long Form General Disclaimer

Some of the exercises and dietary suggestions contained in this work may not be appropriate for all individuals, and readers should consult with a physician before commencing any exercise or dietary program.

Legal and Professional Publications

This publication is designed to provide accurate and authoritative information in regard to the subject matter covered. It is sold with the understanding that the publisher is not engaged in rendering legal, accounting, or other professional services. If legal advice or other expert assistance is required, the services of a competent professional person should be sought. [*From a Declaration of Principles jointly adopted by a Committee of the American Bar Association and a Committee of Publishers.*] The author and publisher specifically disclaim any and all liability arising directly or indirectly from the use or application of any information contained in this publication.

Modified Form of Above—Includes Medical or Other Professional Advice

This publication is designed to provide accurate and authoritative information in regard to the subject matter covered. It is sold with the understanding that the publisher is not engaged in rendering professional services. If legal, accounting, medical, psychological, or any other expert assistance is required, the services of a competent professional person should be sought. The author and publisher specifically disclaim any and all liability arising directly or indirectly from the use or application of any information contained in this publication.

Legal Form Book With Software

This book and the accompanying software are designed to provide information about the subject matter covered. While every effort has been made to make this book and the accompanying software as complete and accurate as possible, any use of the information and forms is at the reader's discretion, and the authors and the publisher specifically disclaim any and all liability arising directly or indirectly from the use or application of the contents of this book and the accompanying software. This book and the accompanying software are not intended to serve as a replacement for professional legal, accounting, or financial advice. If legal advice or other expert assistance is required, the services of a competent professional person should be sought. THIS PRODUCT IS SOLD "AS IS" WITHOUT WARRANTIES OF ANY KIND, EITHER EXPRESS OR IMPLIED, INCLUDING BUT NOT LIMITED TO THE IMPLIED WARRANTY OF MERCHANTABILITY OR FITNESS FOR A PARTICULAR PURPOSE. (Some states do not allow the exclusion of implied warranties, so the exclusion may not apply to you.)

Travel Publications—Short Form

Although the author has made every effort to provide the most up-to-date and accurate information possible, the author and publisher specifically disclaim any and all liability arising directly or indirectly from the use or application of any information contained in this publication. Please call ahead before relying on any information. [We also appreciate feedback from our readers. Please direct comments and suggestions to: _____]

Medical Publications—Short Form

The information contained in this publication is not intended to serve as a replacement for professional medical advice. Any use of the information in this publication is at the reader's discretion. The author and publisher specifically disclaim any and all liability arising directly or indirectly from the use or application of any information contained herein. A competent health care professional should be consulted regarding your specific situation.

Medical Publications—Diet—Short Form

The information contained in this publication is not intended to serve as a replacement for the advice of a professional nutritionist. Any use of the information in this publication is at the reader's discretion. The author and publisher specifically disclaim any and all liability arising directly or indirectly from the use or application of any information contained in this publication. A competent health care professional should be consulted regarding your specific situation.

Medical—Long Form

The contents of this work are intended to further general scientific research, understanding, and discussion only and are not intended and should not be relied upon as recommending or promoting a specific method, diagnosis, dosage, or treatment by physicians for any particular patient. The publisher and the author make no representations or warranties with respect to the accuracy or completeness of the contents of this work and specifically disclaim all warranties, including without limitation any implied warranties of fitness for a particular purpose. In view of ongoing research, equipment modifications, changes in governmental regulations, and the constant flow of information relating to the use of medicines, equipment, and devices, the reader is urged to review and evaluate the information provided in the package insert or instructions for each medicine, equipment, or device for, among other things, any changes in the instructions or indication of usage and for added warnings and precautions. Readers should consult with a specialist where appropriate. The fact that an organization or Web site is referred to in this work as a citation and/or a potential source of further information does not mean that the author or the publisher endorses the information the organization or Web site may provide or recommendations it may make. Further, readers should be aware that Internet Web sites listed in this work may have changed or disappeared between when this work was written and when it is read. No warranty may be created or extended by any promotional statements for this work. Neither the publisher nor the author shall be liable for any damages arising herefrom.

Medical Self-help—Long Form

Attention: Important Note to Readers

This publication should not be used as a substitute for professional medical advice or care. The reader should consult a physician in matters relating to his or her health. In particular, the reader should consult with a competent professional before acting on any of the information or advice contained in this publication or undertaking any form of self-treatment.

Modifying a medical regimen can be very dangerous. Any side effects should be reported promptly to the physician. A reader concerned about adverse effects of medication should discuss with his or her doctor the benefits as well as the risks of taking the medication.

The information contained in this publication regarding health and mediations is the result of review by the authors of relevant medical and scientific literature. That literature at times reflects conflicting conclusions and opinion. In addition, information about drug effects remains incomplete, as new dangers are discovered all the time and, the effects drugs can have vary from person to person. As a result, the reader should not assume that because an adverse reaction or interaction is not mentioned in connection with a drug listed in this publication, that drug could not cause it. The authors have expressed their view on many of those issues; the reader should understand that other experts might disagree. The author and publisher specifically disclaim any and all liability arising directly or indirectly from the use or application of any information contained in this publication.

Character Composites—Trade Books

The individuals and situations described in this book are composites based in part on the author's experiences [and in part on his imagination]. Names and other information have been changed to protect the privacy of the people involved. No resemblance to specific individuals is intended or should be inferred [, unless specifically stated otherwise].

Scientific Experiments and Protocols

The procedures in this text are intended for use only by persons with prior training in the field of _____. In the checking and editing of these procedures, every effort has been made to identify potentially hazardous steps and to eliminate as much as possible the handling of potentially dangerous materials, and safety precautions have been inserted where appropriate. If performed with the materials and equipment specified, in careful accordance with the instructions and methods in this text, the author and publisher believe the procedures to be very useful tools. However, these procedures must be conducted at one's own risk. The author and publisher do not warrant or guarantee the safety of individuals using these procedures and specifically disclaim any and all liability arising directly or indirectly from the use or application of any information contained in this publication.

Scientific Experiments—Alternative View

The publisher and the author make no representations or warranties with respect to the accuracy or completeness of the contents of this work and specifically disclaim all warranties, including without limitation any implied warranties of fitness for a particular purpose. This work is sold with the understanding that the publisher is not engaged in rendering professional services. The advice and strategies contained herein may not be suitable for every situation. In view of ongoing research, equipment modifications, changes in governmental regulations, and the constant flow of information relating to the use of experimental reagents, equipment, and devices, the reader is urged to review and evaluate the information provided in the package insert or instructions for each chemical, piece of equipment, reagent, or device for, among other things, any changes in the instructions or indication of usage and for added warnings and precautions. The fact that an organization or Web site is referred to in this work as a citation and/or a potential source of further information does not mean that the author or the publisher endorses the information the organization or Web site may provide or recommendations it may make. Further, readers should be aware that Internet Web sites listed in this work may have changed or disappeared between when this work was written and when it is read. No warranty may be created or extended by any promotional statements for this work. Neither the publisher nor the author shall be liable for any damages arising herefrom.

Directories

While every effort has been made to ensure the reliability of the information presented in this publication, the author and publisher do not guarantee the accuracy of the data contained herein and specifically disclaim any and all liability arising directly or indirectly from the use or application of any information contained in this publication. The publisher accepts no payment for listing; and inclusion in the publication of any organization, agency, institution, publication, service, product, or individual does not imply endorsement by the author or publisher.

Errors brought to the attention of the publisher and verified to the satisfaction of the publisher will be corrected in future editions.

Catalogues Raisonneé

While the Publisher and cataloguers of this *Catalogue Raisonneé* have made their best professional efforts to identify all genuine artworks by [artist] for inclusion herein, authentication of artwork is necessarily a subjective enterprise, and the information contained herein is not meant as a guarantee of authenticity, nor should it be relied upon as the sole basis of a determination of authenticity when contemplating the purchase of an artwork by [artist]. Similarly, the exclusion of an artwork from this *Catalogue Raisonneé* does not necessarily indicate that the excluded artwork is not authentic. Scholarship about artists often changes, and any decision with respect to the authenticity of an artwork should be made by specifically retained, qualified experts. The publisher and catalogers hereby expressly disclaim any liability arising from any use of the information contained in this book.

FORM 4.6

ISP Cease and Desist Letter

The Digital Millennium Copyright Act has given many Internet service providers (aka "online service providers") a degree of safe harbor protection with which to build businesses powered by infringements. Nonetheless, only the most piratical ISPs located in offshore jurisdictions ignore DMCA compliant takedown notices like the one below. Note that this template has a paragraph requesting the ISP to take active steps to police its site in the future. This is usually ignored, but the degree to which the law requires ISPs to actively police their sites is likely to be highly litigated, so one should do what is necessary to preserve these claims. Parties who actually sell and post the content are not entitled to safe harbor, and Form 4.7 is therefore recommended. See also, Forms 4.8 and 4.9.

Web Site Letter (Sent by E-Mail)

To Whom it May Concern:

I, the undersigned, CERTIFY UNDER PENALTY OF PERJURY that I am an agent authorized to act on behalf of the owner of certain intellectual property rights, said owner being named _____, or one of its related companies ("Publisher").

We recently learned that an unauthorized copy of the material listed below is available for download on a website hosted by your company at the following URL address: **[insert URL]**. The material is as follows:

1. TITLE, (ISBN #) by AUTHOR
2. TITLE, (ISBN #) by AUTHOR
3. (and any additional titles, as appropriate)

I have a good faith belief that the use of the title(s) identified above is (are) not authorized by Publisher, its agent, or the law and therefore constitute a serious infringement of, *inter alia*, Publisher's copyrights.

We understand that many responsible ISPs inadvertently infringe the copyrights of others, and that this may be one such case. Accordingly, we will forbear legal action against your company provided that you comply with the following:

1. You remove or block access to the infringing matter within 48 hours of the time and date of this e-mail; and

2. You provide reasonably requested assistance in helping Publisher to find and prosecute the responsible party/parties. This includes sending me any information you have on file regarding the owner of the offending Web site.

Please be advised that each time this item is posted in this format (i.e., PDF, ZIP, RAR, HTML, etc.), it is, per se, an infringing copy. We request that any such item posted by a user after this date be removed without the necessity of Publisher providing a DMCA Notice. All rights reserved.

Thank you in advance for your cooperation.

Sincerely,
[Name]
[Title]
[Address]

My name, typed above, constitutes an electronic signature under Federal law, and is intended to be binding.

Cease and Desist Letter for Posting Party

There is no shortage of people around the world who post copyrighted content on the Internet. While many of these are anonymous and not likely to respond to letters, a short e-mail to the posting party will sometimes get the material removed. See also, Forms 4.6, 4.8, and 4.9.

Posting Party Letter

To: Whom It May Concern:

I am an employee of _____., a global publisher of books, journals, and other products. One of the books we publish is <u>TITLE</u>, by AUTHOR.

We recently learned that an unauthorized copy of that book is available for download on a peer-to-peer site, posted by you at **[insert URL]**. The text is as follows:

> [copy description of text from Web site]

Needless to say, this constitutes a serious violation of our rights, and we demand that this material be deleted immediately. Under the U.S. Copyright Act, a copyright holder may seek, in addition to other relief, up to $150,000 per work infringed, plus a recovery of its attorney's fees. While we reserve all rights to subpoena recor
ds of your identity, and to bring a lawsuit, your promptness in removing the material will be factored into our decision.

I look forward to a prompt reply.

Sincerely,

[Name]
[Address]
[E-mail address]

Piracy Demand Letter

Each publisher needs to determine its tolerance for online piracy. While no one likes being pirated, very few publishers aggressively combat piracy by demanding damages from individuals selling pirated works. Some publishers have discovered that they could cost effectively pursue infringers who use sites such as eBay. Before sending these types of letters, the publishers sent cease and desist notices which, while ending the specific auctions, did not always stop infringers from reposting. This letter, with negotiated settlements, follow up, and occasional lawsuits, was more successful.

Although drafted for the eBay auction site, this template is readily adaptable to infringements found elsewhere. This letter is used in connection with the resolution letter which follows as Form 4.9.

———————————

[DATE]

[NAME / ADDRESS]

Dear [NAME]:

I am the [President of/attorney for, etc.] Infringed Publishers, Inc. ("Publisher").

I am responsible, along with others, for protecting the copyright interests of Publisher. Publisher has discovered that you are engaged in selling material which infringes Publisher's copyright, as well as the interests of our authors, through the eBay auction site. Section 6.2 of the eBay User Agreement, to which you have agreed, states that you, as a Seller, may not "infringe any third party's copyright …". Moreover, under the Copyright Act, the owner of the copyright in a work has the exclusive rights to reproduce and distribute the copyrighted work to the public by sale or other transfer. 17 U.S.C. §§106(1) and (3).

Notwithstanding the law, and your eBay User Agreement, on [DATE], you offered for sale a pirated copy of [TITLE], auction # (#).

Key Legal Principles

We encourage you to take legal advice at this stage. However, it may be useful to explain certain aspects of copyright law here.

1. What damages can a court award in a copyright infringement case?

Publisher regularly registers copyrights in the works it publishes, including [TITLE]. Accordingly, it may elect to recover in litigation, for each work infringed, either actual damages, or statutory damages of "not less

than $750.00 or more than $30,000.00 as the court considers just."
17 U.S.C.§504(c)(1). This amount may be increased to $150,000.00 per work
if the infringement is willful. 17 U.S.C.§504(c)(2). Blatant piracy will almost
always be deemed "willful."

2. What if I am sued and choose to ignore it?

If you are sued by Publisher, you will need to hire a lawyer to defend the case,
or defend the case yourself. If you do neither, Publisher will ask the court to
enter a "default judgment" in the maximum amount of damages allowed by
law. Such a judgment would then be enforced against you by, e.g., attaching
your bank accounts and other assets.

3. Who pays attorneys' fees?

Under the Copyright Act, the court may, in its discretion, award Publisher its
costs and attorney's fees in bringing this action. 17 U.S.C. §505. See Basic
Books, Inc. v Kinko's Graphics Corp., 758 F. Supp. 1522 (S.D.N.Y. 1991). In
all events, you will be liable for your own costs and fees, which conservatively
could exceed $40,000.00 through trial, for a case that you will lose.

4. What if I declare bankruptcy?

Copyright infringement is a "willful tort," and as such, it is not dischargeable
in bankruptcy. Broadcast Music. Inc. v. Leisure Properties, Inc., 1978 US Dist.
Lexis 14312 (N.D. Ohio 1978). Thus, even if you declare bankruptcy, the debt
will remain. Moreover, interest will accrue until all monies are paid.

Acceptable Resolutions

However, we are also willing to settle this claim early if we can avoid the
inconvenience of a lawsuit. This can be done only if you respond promptly to
this letter and we enter into a constructive dialogue. You should be aware that
we generally insist upon the following:

1. That infringers immediately cease making, distributing, and offering for
    sale, unauthorized copies of our books.

2. That infringers provide us with all information you have on others who
    may be participating in the sale or distribution of infringing copies of
    Publisher's works.

3. If they purchased and/or sold infringing copies of Publisher's works from other parties, that infringers will provide us with complete records with respect to these transactions.

4. That infringers agree that if they infringe upon Publisher's copyrights in the future, they consent to the entry of damages against you in the amount of $5,000 per copy.

We also require a payment to Publisher as compensation for the infringement.

I strongly recommend that you discuss this letter with a copyright attorney. You should know that if you do not respond to this letter, we will consider you to be acting in bad faith. That may affect our willingness ever to amicably resolve this matter.

My contact details are set forth above. If I do not hear from you within ten (10) business days, please understand that I will assume that you have chosen not to respond and that your past activity is likely to continue.

Respectfully,

[Name]

FORM 4.9
Piracy Resolution Letter

See comments to Form 4.8.

_____

[DATE]

[NAME / ADDRESS]

Dear [NAME]:

RE: Publisher's letter of [DATE], in response to your selling pirated Publisher works on the eBay auction site.

After reviewing the additional information you provided in your e-mail and phone call of [DATE] with legal counsel here at Publisher, we will consider this matter settled upon receipt of payment of [AMOUNT], in the form of a certified check, payable to **Infringed Publisher, Inc**. within ten (10) business days of this letter.

Per our [DATE] letter, you also agree to the following:

1. You immediately cease making, distributing, and offering for sale, unauthorized copies of our books.

2. If you purchased infringing copies of Publisher's works from other parties, you will provide us with complete records with respect to these transactions.

3. You agree that if you infringe upon Publisher's copyrights in the future, you consent to the entry of damages against you in the amount of $5,000.00 per copy.

Please sign and return one (1) copy of this letter, within ten (10) business days of your receipt thereof, along with the specified payment of [AMOUNT], as evidence of your agreement to the above.

Thank you for your prompt attention to this matter.

Respectfully,

[NAME]

ACCEPTED AND AGREED

_____   _____
[NAME]   Date

CHAPTER

5

Miscellaneous Forms

§ 5.01 Background

Chapter 5 contains forms that do not neatly fit within any of the chapters or that belong in more than one chapter. The first form, a short form letter to author regarding confidentiality is designed to protect publishers from idea appropriation lawsuits.

The next four forms, a long form freelance ("ghost writer") agreement (Form 5.2), a short form editorial services ("ghost writer") agreement (Form 5.3), an agreement for foreword (Form 5.4), and a translation agreement (Form 5.5), are all related to various editorial services performed on works authored by others.

These forms are followed by two others used by publishers to sell books in territories where they have insubstantial marketing presences: a book distribution agreement (Form 5.6) and a nonexclusive sales representative agreement (Form 5.7).

There is a literary agent agreement (Form 5.8), an independent contractor application/status form (5.9), a trademark license agreement (Form 5.10), and a mutual non-disclosure agreement for general use when discussing business opportunities with competitors or potential competitors (Form 5.11). Lastly, I have included quitclaim assignments of copyrights and trademarks (Forms 5.12 and 5.13).

Letter to Author Regarding Confidentiality (Short Form)

Inexperienced and paranoid authors will occasionally ask publishers to sign confidentiality agreements prior to submitting book proposals for review. Few publishers will enter into such agreements.[1] Copyright laws do not protect ideas, and few ideas are so "original" that no one else has thought of them. Signing a confidentiality agreement becomes an invitation to litigation, and the fear of idea-appropriation litigation is one factor in the decision of some publishers to not review unsolicited manuscripts from unknown third parties.

If an author wants such an agreement, it is best to explain that no editor wants to "steal" a great idea where there is a ready, willing, and able author, but that for reasons set forth above, it violates policy to sign such an agreement. For material submitted by mail, the following letter is recommended.

Letter to Author Regarding Confidentiality
[date]

Re: Proposal for Book on _____
Dear Author:

This letter will confirm our understanding with respect to materials which you may submit to us in connection with _____. These materials contain certain information that you have asked us to keep confidential. The purpose of letter is to indicate that we do not, as a matter of policy, enter into "non-disclosure" or "confidentiality" agreements to keep ideas, or other non-copyrightable subject matter, in confidence, since to do so would present an unacceptable barrier to our ability to publish materials on a worldwide basis. We would, however, like to give you our written assurance that we will respect your rights in the copyright in the materials you submit to us as provided by the United States Copyright Law.

We would also like to confirm, without obligation of confidentiality, that it is not our practice to make copies of any proposals except on an as needed basis in order to evaluate your materials. [Include a provision as to whether or not materials will be returned.]

Sincerely,

ACCEPTED AND AGREED

By: _____

Name: _____

Title: _____

Date: _____

---

1 The major exception to this rule is that some publishers will sign narrowly tailored agreements when reviewing highly sensitive material relating to potential exposé or similar books.

Freelance ("Ghost Writer") Agreement (Long Form)

Freelance writers will often provide services on an anonymous basis to clients, who will then publish books without identifying the writers. The following form, adapted from a agreement prepared by William M. Hart of the New York office of Proskauer Rose, LLP,[2] sets forth in detail the rights and obligations of the parties, who in this case are a freelance writer and a corporation that wants the writer to help its chief executive prepare a book that does not yet have a publisher. For a simpler form, see Form 5.3.

Literary Rights Agreement

This Agreement ("Agreement"), is made as of _____, 20__, by and between _____ corporation located at _____ ("Corp"), and _____ an individual located at _____ ("Writer").

Recitals

WHEREAS _____, Chief Executive Officer and President of Corp, has conceived, developed and authored a program which consists of, *inter alia*, a series of writings concerning _____; and

WHEREAS Corp wishes to engage Writer to make certain contributions to, including editing of, a book by _____ tentatively entitled "_____" (the "Work"), for possible publication; and

WHEREAS the parties desire to memorialize their respective rights and obligations in connection with the development of the Work and its possible publication;

NOW, THEREFORE, the parties agree as follows:

Terms of Agreement

In consideration of the mutual promises contained herein, the parties hereby agree:

1.   General Obligations of Writer

Writer shall make herself available, on a nonexclusive basis, to provide the contributions to the Work specified in the attached Schedule A. All expenses necessary to fulfill Writer's obligations under this Agreement are the sole responsibility of Writer.

---

2 Reprinted with permission.

2. General Obligations of Corp

Corp shall use its reasonable efforts to make available to Writer persons, including _____, necessary to fulfill Writer's obligations under the terms and conditions of this agreement.

3. Materials Prepared by Writer

All materials prepared by Writer shall:

3.1 fully comply with all of Writer's representations and warranties set forth in paragraph 12 of this Agreement.

3.2 consist entirely of Writer's own authorship and shall not contain any matter prepared or authored by any other person, except for materials furnished or created by Corp. No other person shall contribute to the Work, or any derivatives thereof, without Corp's prior written approval. Writer shall not include in any matter delivered to Corp any matter which is subject to the rights (including, but not limited to, copyright) of any other person, unless it is first identified in writing to, and approved in writing by, Corp along with the proposed terms of any clearance or permission relating thereto.

4. Deadlines

Writer shall comply with the deadlines for delivery of Writer's contributions as set forth in Schedule A, including any deadlines specified by Corp for revisions or rewrites. Corp shall have the sole right to, upon reasonable written notice to Writer, change the deadlines set forth in Schedule A.

5. Revisions

Corp shall have the absolute right, at any time, with respect to any aspect of the Work, to revise or adapt the Work, including Writer's contributions thereto, and/or to hire other writers to do so, an/or to couple Writer's contributions with any other material of Corp's own choosing, all in Corp's sole discretion and without and right of approval by, or additional remuneration (other than that payable under paragraph 9 of this Agreement) payable to, Writer. Corp shall have no obligation to permit Writer to undertake any revisions or adaptations of the Work, or any derivatives thereof, and shall have the sole right, in its discretion, to complete and publish the Work, or any derivatives thereof, without further obligation to Writer of any manner whatsoever.

6. Writer's Failure to Deliver

Without limiting any other provision of this Agreement, or any of Corp's rights or remedies under this Agreement or otherwise, if Writer fails to fulfill Writer's obligations under this Agreement (including, but not limited to, compliance with the deadlines for delivery of Writer's contributions specified in Schedule A), for any reason (including Writer's death or incapacity), Corp shall have the absolute right to engage any other writer, and to complete the Work as it sees fit without further obligation to Writer and/ or Writer's estate.

7.   Ownership of Rights

Writer expressly acknowledges that all of the results and proceeds of every kind rendered by Writer in connection with the Work, whether or not delivered to Corp hereunder, shall be deemed works "made-for-hire" for Corp and Corp shall be deemed the author and exclusive owner of all rights (including, but not limited to, copyright) in the Work, and any derivatives thereof, for all purposes throughout the universe. If, for any reason, any contribution by writer does not constitute a work "made-for-hire," Writer hereby assigns to Corp all rights (including, but not limited to, copyright) now known or hereafter recognized, throughout the universe, in and to all of Writer's contributions in any and all media now known or hereafter devised, in perpetuity, in all configurations as Corp determines. Writer shall take such additional steps and execute such further documents as Corp reasonably requests to confirm, enforce or implement the provisions of this Agreement or to satisfy the requirements of any third party with whom Corp may deal. Without limiting any of the foregoing, Writer shall execute the short form assignment attached as Schedule B.

7.1 Writer has no rights in the Work, or any derivatives thereof, and has no right to any remuneration, in the form of royalties or otherwise, resulting from the exploitation thereof, except for the payment provided for in paragraph 9 of this Agreement. Without limiting the foregoing:

> 7.1.1 Writer waives any so-called moral rights (including rights of attribution and integrity) and any analogous rights with respect to the uses of the Work, or any derivatives thereof, contemplated by this Agreement or any agreement Corp may make with a third party with respect to exploitation of the Work or any derivatives.

> 7.1.2 Writer shall have no rights to exploit, or authorize any other person to exploit, the Work, or any derivatives thereof, in any form or media.

8.   Publication

Corp, in its sole discretion, shall have the exclusive right to determine if, when, and in which media the Work, or any derivatives thereof, are published. Notwithstanding the foregoing, Writer expressly acknowledges that Corp shall have no obligation to publish the Work, nor any derivatives thereof, or to maintain the commercial availability of the Work, or any derivatives thereof, in any media now known or hereafter developed, at any time, and that failure to publish or maintain the commercial availability of the Work shall not trigger a reversion of any rights in the Work, or any derivatives thereof.

9.   Payment

In consideration of all contributions made and to be made by Writer, and for all rights granted to Corp hereunder, Corp shall pay Writer as follows:

> [$_____ *upon execution of this Agreement*]; and
> [$_____ *upon delivery by writer of all the materials specified in Schedule A*].

All payments to Writer shall be payable to and in the name of _____. Writer acknowledges that the amounts specified in this paragraph shall be the sole remuneration payable to Writer for her contributions in connection with the work, and any derivatives thereof, and that Corp shall have no obligation to make any other payments to Writer, in any form or amount, at any time, in connection with this Agreement, or Corp exercise of any rights with respect to the work, or any derivatives thereof, whether or not consisting of Writer's contributions.

10.   Attribution of Authorship

Writer shall be entitled to no credit, in any form, whether as an author, co-author or otherwise, in connection with the Work, or any derivatives thereof, or any advertising or promotion relating thereto. Corp shall be entitled to determine, in its sole and absolute discretion, all credits that may be afforded to persons in relation to any of the foregoing, at any time. Without limiting any of the foregoing, such credits may be provided only in _____'s name and/or the name of any other writer engaged by Corp now or in the future.

11.   Prosecution of Claims

Corp has the sole right to prosecute, or decline to prosecute, any claims, including claims for copyright or trademark infringement, with respect to the Work, or any derivatives thereof. Writer expressly authorizes and empowers Corp to prosecute any such claim in her name at Corp's expense. Corp shall be solely responsible for the payment of all legal fees and expenses incurred in connection with the prosecution of any such claims, and shall have complete and exclusive right and title to any award, judgment or settlement resulting therefrom.

12.   Representations and Warranties by Writer; Indemnity

Writer hereby represents and warrants that:

12.1 Writer has the absolute right and authority to enter into this Agreement, and has no other contractual or other commitment of any kind which will or might conflict or interfere with the performance of Writer's obligations under this Agreement.

12.2 Writer shall use best efforts to make the contributions contemplated by this Agreement, including all revisions requested by Corp in a timely fashion in accordance with the terms of this Agreement.

12.3 Writer is not affiliated with or obligated to any agents or other persons to whom Writer may owe fees arising from this Agreement, or Writer's performance thereunder, including, but not limited to, any agency commissions.

12.4 All material furnished or submitted by Writer shall be Writer's own original work (except for those materials furnished by Corp), and shall not infringe upon or violate the rights of any person, firm, or corporation.

12.5 Writer shall be responsible for all unemployment and disability insurance, social security, income tax and other withholdings, deductions and payments required by Federal or state laws to be paid by Writer.

12.6 Writer indemnifies and holds Corp, it successors, permitted assigns and licensees harmless from any and all claims, demands, suits, losses, costs and expenses (including reasonable attorneys' fees and including any amount paid in settlement, but only if consented thereto in writing by Writer) which may be obtained against, imposed upon or suffered by Corp, its successors, assigns and licensees by reason of any breach of this Agreement, [or any other agreement], or the representations, warranties or covenants made by Writer in this Agreement [or any other agreement].

12.7 Defense of Claims and Proceedings. Corp shall control the defense of any claims or proceedings against any of the parties to this Agreement (without limitation the representations, warranties or indemnity obligations of Writer). The parties shall cooperate with each other in connection with all such proceedings and shall notify each other in writing promptly upon the receipt of any claim or other action which relates to their respective representations and warranties or indemnification obligations under this Agreement [or any other agreement].

13.   Representations and Warranties by Corp; Indemnity

Corp hereby represents and warrants that:

13.1 It has the bona fide intent to assist Writer in the preparation of Writer's contributions to the Work in accordance with the terms of the Agreement.

13.2 It has no other contractual or other commitments of any kind which will or might conflict or interfere with its obligations under this Agreement.

13.3 [All material furnished by it for inclusion in the Work, or other material submitted to a Publisher, shall be original and shall not infringe upon or violate the rights of any person, firm or corporation.]

13.4 It indemnifies and holds Writer harmless from any and all claims, demands, suits, losses, costs and expenses (including reasonable attorneys' fees and including any amount paid in settlement, but only if consented thereto in writing in Corp) which may be obtained against, imposed upon or suffered by Writer by reason of any breach of this [or any other agreement], or the representations, warranties or covenants made by Corp in this Agreement.

14.   Survival of Representations, Warranties and Indemnification Obligations

All representations, warranties, and indemnification obligations of Writer or Corp hereunder shall survive the termination of this Agreement or any other agreement to which such warranties, representations, or indemnification obligations pertain.

15.   Independent Contractor

Writer's relationship to Corp is that of an independent contractor. In no instance shall the parties' relationship under this Agreement be interpreted to create or constitute a joint venture.

16.   Governing Law

This Agreement shall be governed and interpreted in accordance with the laws of the State of _____ (irrespective of its choice of law principles) as an agreement made and to be performed wholly within the State of _____.

17.   Disputes; Arbitration

Except as otherwise provided in any agreement with a Publisher, any and all disputes arising by and among any or all of the parties to this Agreement shall be settled by arbitration in _____ under the rules of the American Arbitration Association in accordance with the provision of Schedule C.

18.   Parties Bound; Execution in Counterparts; Assignment

This Agreement, once executed by the parties (and such execution may be in counterparts), shall immediately become binding on the parties hereto, and shall constitute an enforceable agreement in accordance with its terms. This Agreement shall be binding upon and inure to the parties hereto, their respective heirs, successors, administrators, and permitted assigns. All rights, duties and obligations of writer hereunder are personal and non-assignable, and any purported assignment (other than an assignment of proceeds payable here-under) shall be deemed void *ab initio*. Corp shall be permitted to assign this Agreement or any of its rights, duties or obligations hereunder.

19.   Notices

Notices shall be sent by hand delivery or by facsimile and overnight courier to the parties as follows and shall be deemed given when sent:

   If to Corp:
   If to Writer:

20.   Entire Agreement

This Agreement constitutes the entire understanding of the parties and may not be changed except by written agreement by all of them.

21.   Confidentiality

The terms of this Agreement and any information learned by Writer in the performance of this Agreement is deemed confidential unless it is or becomes public other than by act or omission of writer.

IN WITNESS WHEREOF, the parties hereto have caused this agreement to be duly executed as of the day and year first above written:

WRITER:

By: _____

Name: _____

Address: _____

Social Security or Tax ID Number: _____

CORP:

By: _____

Name: _____

Title: _____

Editorial Services ("Ghost Writer") Agreement (Short Form)

Form 5.3 is a short version of Form 5.2. It contains the critical language regarding ownership and warranties (*see* Clauses 6 and 7, respectively) but lacks the formality and belt-and-suspenders coverage of the other agreement. It is particularly appropriate where the author and the freelance writer will work closely together on the project, and a "friendlier" agreement is required.

Agreement

Agreement dated this ___ day of _____ between _____ (the "Writer") and _____ (the "Author") for the purpose of assisting as Writer, the Author in preparing the work tentatively entitled _____ (the "Work"), to be published by _____ (the "Publisher").

1. Performance of Services

The Author shall retain the services of _____ as Writer. The Writer shall perform such services at such place or places as he may reasonably determine, subject to the approval of the Author. Unless otherwise agreed to in writing by the Author, the Author shall not be required to provide the Writer with office space, supplies, clerical or stenographic assistance.

2. Writer's Duties

The Writer agrees to:

[*Insert description of work to be performed by the writer, and all due dates*]

3. Compensation

In full consideration of the Writer's services under this Agreement (or other rights granted herein to the Author), the Writer shall be paid by the Author the sum of $_____, as follows:

[*Insert description of compensation payout, usually ties to deliverables*]
The Writer acknowledges that the Writer shall not be entitled to any compensation of any kind from the Publisher and the Writer shall look solely to the Author for any compensation.

4. Credit

Neither the Author nor the Publisher shall be required to give any credit to the Writer within the Work, but the Author may, in the Author's sole discretion, give credit to the Writer for assisting in connection with the Work, in an appropriate acknowledgment in the Work.

5. Term and Termination

Except for the provisions of Paragraphs 6 and 7 which shall survive the termination of this Agreement, this Agreement shall be in effect from the date of the Agreement until the Writer has completed the services. Notwithstanding the foregoing, if the Author determines, in the Author's sole judgment, that the Writer's services are not satisfactory or that the Writer's writing of the Work is not acceptable, the Author may, in addition to any other rights it may have, (i) request the Writer to rewrite, complete, or further correct, revise, or otherwise modify the Work within the time specified by the Author (the revision due date); or (ii) make other arrangements with respect to the Work as the Author deems appropriate, including but not limited to arranging with others to rewrite, complete, correct, revise or otherwise modify the Work. If the Author elects option (i), and the revision is not delivered to the Author by the revision due date, or the revision is not acceptable to the Author in organization, form, content, style and performance, the Author may, in addition to any other rights it may have, exercise option (ii) contained in this Article or to request the Writer to make further changes to the Work under option (i).

6. Ownership of the Work

Any copyrightable material prepared by the Writer pursuant to the terms of this Agreement shall be considered a work made for hire to the Author and the Author shall own the copyright in such material and all rights vested therein. To the extent, if any, that any such material does not qualify as a work made for hire, the Writer hereby transfers to the Author during the full term of copyright and all extensions thereof the full and exclusive rights comprised in the copyright in any such material in any media now known or hereafter devised throughout the world. The writer hereby waives any so-called "moral rights." The provisions of this paragraph shall survive termination of this Agreement.

7. Warranty

The Writer represents and warrants to the Author that any original material contributed by the Writer to the Work is original on the Writer's part except for such excerpts and illustrations from copyrighted works as may be included with the written permission of the copyright owners and except for any material provided by the Author. The Writer further warrants that such contributed material has not been previously published and contains no libelous or unlawful statements, contains no instructions that may cause harm or injury and does not infringe upon or violate any copyright, trademark, or other right or the privacy of others. The Writer agrees to indemnify the Author, the Publisher, and any licensee, successors and assigns of the Author and Publisher against all liability and expense, including reasonable counsel fees, arising from or out of any breach or alleged breach of these warranties. The provisions of this paragraph shall survive termination of this Agreement.

8.   Entire Agreement

This Agreement constitutes the entire agreement of the parties with respect to the subject matter hereof, and may only be modified in a written document signed by both parties hereto.

9.   Governing Law/Forum

This Agreement shall be governed and construed pursuant to the internal laws of the State of _____. Any dispute arising out of or relating to this Agreement shall be commenced in a court of competent jurisdiction in the State of _____, County of _____, and the parties hereby consent to the jurisdiction and waive any objections to venue therein.

AGREED AND ACCEPTED

_____   _____

[*writer*]   [*author*]

Agreement for Foreword (Short Form)

Agreement

AGREEMENT, dated this _____ day of _____, by and between _____, of _____ (the "Writer") and _____, of _____ (the "Publisher").

<u>Witnesseth</u>

This will confirm that the Publisher has commissioned the Writer to prepare an original and previously unpublished foreword (the "Foreword") for inclusion in the forthcoming work tentatively entitled _____ (the "Work"), by _____ (the "Author(s)"), to be published by the Publisher. The terms are as follows:

1.   The Foreword

The Foreword shall consist of approximately _____ printed pages (a printed page of text consists of approximately _____ words) including and shall be submitted not later than _____. The manuscript of the Foreword shall be submitted in an agreed electronic format, complete and satisfactory to the Publisher. The Publisher shall have the right to make such revisions, deletions or additions to the Foreword that the Publisher may deem advisable in the interest of space and uniformity of style and presentation, provided that the accuracy of the text is not impaired. Time is of the essence.

2.   Rights

The Writer hereby grants to the Publisher during the full term of copyright and all extensions thereof the full and exclusive rights comprised in the copyright in the Foreword, including any materials (if any) submitted with the Foreword, including but not limited to, the right, by itself or with others, throughout the world, to print, publish, republish, transmit and distribute the Foreword and to prepare, publish, transmit and distribute derivative works based thereon, in all languages and in all media of expression now known or later developed, and to license and permit others to do so.

3.   Warranty

The Writer represents and warrants that: the Foreword is original except for excerpts and illustrations from copyrighted works for which the Writer has obtained written permission from the copyright owners at the Writer's expense; the Foreword has not been previously published and is not in the public domain; the Writer owns and has the right to convey all the rights herein conveyed to the Publisher; and the Foreword contains no libelous or unlawful material, contains no instructions that may cause harm or injury and does not infringe upon or violate any copyright, trademark, trade secret or other right or the privacy of others.

4.   Use of Name

The Publisher shall have the right to use the Writer's name, likeness, biographical data or professional credits on any edition of the Work or in any derivative work thereof in which the Foreword is included, and in advertising, publicity or promotion related thereto and may grant such rights in connection with the license of any subsidiary rights in the Work in which the Foreword will be included.

5.   Compensation/Copies

In full compensation for the services to be performed and rights transfers set forth herein, the Publisher will pay the Writer upon acceptance of the Foreword. The Writer shall also receive without charge one free copy of the published Work in which the Foreword appears.

6.   Termination

The Publisher may terminate this Agreement in the event: (i) the Writer does not deliver the final manuscript on or before the Due Date pursuant to Paragraph I above, or fails or refuses to make reasonable changes requested by the Publisher; or (ii) the Publisher, in its sole judgment, chooses not to publish the Foreword. In such event this Agreement shall terminate, the Publisher shall return the Foreword to the Writer as soon as practicable and shall simultaneously revert all rights in the Foreword to the Writer, and thereafter neither party shall have any further obligation or liability to the other hereunder.

7.   General

This Agreement shall be construed and interpreted pursuant to the laws of the State of New York applicable to contracts wholly entered into and performed in the State of New York.

ACCEPTED AND AGREED

Publisher

By: _____

Name: _____

Title: _____

Writer

By: _____

Translation Agreement

Translation agreements resemble traditional author agreements (*see* Chapter 1, *supra*), except that the translators are usually paid a flat fee as opposed to a royalty. In drafting translation agreements from other languages, it is important to specify whether the work is to be translated into British, American, Canadian, or other forms of "English."

Translation Agreement

AGREEMENT made this _____ day of _____ between _____, of (the "Translator") and _____, of _____ (the "Publisher"), for the purpose of preparing an English language translation (the "Translation") of the work tentatively entitled _____ (the "Work") by _____ (the "Author").

1. Ownership of the Translation

The Translation shall be considered a work made for hire to the Publisher, and the Publisher shall own the copyright and all of the rights comprised in the copyright in the Translation. To the extent the Translation or any material contained therein or attached thereto does not qualify as a work made for hire, the Translator hereby transfers to the Publisher during the full term of copyright and all extensions thereof the full and exclusive rights comprised in the copyright in the Translation and any revisions thereof, including but not limited to, the right by itself or with others throughout the world to print, publish, republish, transmit and distribute the Translation and to prepare, publish, transmit and distribute derivative works based thereon in all languages and in all media of expression now known or later developed, and to license or permit others to do so.

2. Manuscript

(a) The Translator agrees to prepare and submit the final manuscript of the Translation, not later than _____, unless the Publisher has agreed to extend the time in writing (the "Due Date"). The final manuscript shall be submitted in an agreed electronic format together with two print-outs double-spaced on $8^1/_2''$ by 11" white paper printed on one side only with pages numbered consecutively, complete and satisfactory to the Publisher and to the Author in organization, form, content, and style, accompanied by a table of contents and any additional materials reasonably requested by the Publisher. If the Translator fails to supply any material on or before the Due Date, the Publisher shall have the right, but not the obligation, to obtain them and charge the reasonable cost against any sums due to the Translator.

(b)   The Translation will be a faithful rendition into idiomatic American English, and will neither omit anything from the Work nor add anything to it, other than slight verbal changes as are necessary for the translation into American English.

3.   Proofs

The Translator shall promptly correct and return proofs delivered to the Translator for that purpose and shall prepare indexes for the Translation from such proofs. If "translator's alterations" are made to the proofs, the costs incurred as a result thereof shall be borne by the Publisher to the extent of 15% of the cost of composition for the proofs originally submitted to the Translator, and the excess, if any, shall be charged against any sums due to the Translator. "Translator's alterations" are defined as deletions, additions, and other revisions made by the Translator to the proofs, including any revisions made in the illustrations, other than to correct compositor's and/ or proofreader's errors.

4.   Publication

The Publisher shall determine, in its sole judgment and discretion, whether or not to proceed with publication of the Translation. If the Publisher does so, it shall promote and sell the Translation in such manner and at such prices as it deems appropriate, and make any and all other arrangements it deems appropriate with respect to the Translation and the rights thereto granted to it herein.

5.   Copyright Notice and Registration

The Publisher shall print in each copy of the Translation published by it a notice of copyright in conformity with the United States Copyright Act and the Universal Copyright Convention and shall require its licensees to do the same. The Publisher shall have the right to register the copyright in the Translation with the United States Copyright Office.

6.   Credit

The Publisher shall credit the Translator on the copyright page of the Work as follows:

———————————————————

7.   Name and Likeness

The Publisher shall have the right (but not the obligation) to use the name, likeness and biographical data of the Translator on any edition of the Translation or in any derivative work thereof, and in advertising, publicity or promotion related thereto and may grant such rights in connection with the license of any subsidiary rights in the Translation. The Translator shall provide in a timely manner any information reasonably requested by the Publisher for use in promoting and advertising the Translation.

8.   Compensation

In full consideration for all services rendered by the Translator and for all rights granted or relinquished by the Translator under this Agreement, the Publisher shall pay the Translator a flat fee of $_____, payable as follows: $_____ upon signing of this Agreement; and $_____ upon acceptance of the final manuscript of the Translation, complete and satisfactory to the Publisher.

9.   Copies

If the Translation is published, the Publisher shall furnish to the Translator without charge _____ copies of the Translation. The Translator may purchase, for personal use only, additional copies of the Translation at a discount of 25% from the then current United States catalog list.

10.   Related and Competing Works

The Translator shall not, without the Publisher's prior written consent, prepare or assist in the preparation of any other work on the same subject as the Translation that might, in the Publisher's reasonable judgment, be directly competitive with the Translation.

11.   Remainder Sales

When the Publisher determines that the demand for the Translation is not sufficient to warrant its continued manufacture and sale, the Publisher may discontinue maintaining an inventory of the Translation and may remainder all bound copies and sheet stock.

12.   Revised Editions

If the Publisher determines that a revision of the Translation is desirable, the Publisher may request the Translator to prepare the revised edition and the Translator shall advise the Publisher within 60 days whether the Translator will do so in accordance with the schedule set forth by the Publisher. If the Translator advises the publisher that the Translator will prepare the revised edition, the Translator shall diligently proceed with the revision, keep the Publisher advised of the Translator's progress, and deliver the complete manuscript to the Publisher on the scheduled due date.

If the Translator does not participate in the revision, or if the Translator does not diligently proceed with the revision, or if the Publisher elects not to request the Translator to prepare the revision, the Publisher shall have the right to arrange with other for the preparation of the revised edition, in which event no additional money shall be paid to the Translator. The revised edition may be published under the same title and may refer to the Translator by name, but credit may be given to the reviser or revisers in the revised edition(s) and in advertising and promotional material with respect thereto.

Except as otherwise provided herein, the provisions of this Agreement (except for Paragraph 8 which shall be renegotiated if the Translator prepares the revision) shall apply to each successive revised edition as though it were the first edition.

13. Warranty

The Translator represents and warrants that: (i) the Translation is original on the Translator's part except for the underlying Work and is a faithful rendition into idiomatic American English of the underlying Work, neither omitting anything from the Work nor adding anything to it, other than slight verbal changes as are necessary for the translation into English; (ii) the Translation has not been previously published and is not in the public domain; (iii) the Translator has the right to enter into this Agreement; (iv) any material introduced into the Translation by the Translator contains no libelous or unlawful material, contains no instructions that may cause harm or injury and does not infringe upon or violate any copyright, trademark, trade secret, or other right or the privacy of others, and does not in any way misrepresent the underlying Work; and (v) any material introduced into the Translation by the Translator and asserted as fact in the Translation are either true or based upon generally accepted research practices. The Translator agrees to indemnify the Publisher and any licensee of any subsidiary right granted by the Publisher, against liability and expense, including counsel fees, arising from or out of any breach or alleged breach of these warranties.

14. Termination

The Publisher may terminate this Agreement in the event (i) the Translator fails to deliver a complete and satisfactory final manuscript pursuant to Paragraph 2 above; or (ii) the Publisher does not reach a satisfactory agreement with the Author or publisher of the underlying Work; or (iii) the Publisher, in its sole judgment and discretion, elects not to publish the Translation. Upon termination pursuant to section (i) above, the Translator shall promptly repay to the Publisher all payments made to the Translator under this Agreement and upon the Publisher's receipt of such repayment, the parties shall have no further obligation or liability to each other under this Agreement. Upon termination pursuant to sections (ii) or (iii) below, the Translator shall retain as liquidated damages in lieu of any other damages or remedies any payments received by the Translator from the Publisher hereunder.

15. General

(a) The engagement of the Translator is personal and the rights hereunder granted to the Translator are not assignable nor may the obligations imposed be delegated without the prior written consent of the Publisher; provided however, that the Translator may assign any sums due to the Translator hereunder without the Publisher's consent.

(b) Except as provided in the preceding subparagraph, this Agreement shall inure to the benefit of the heirs, executors, administrators, and permitted assigns of the Translator and the subsidiaries, successors, and assigns of the Publisher.

(c) All notices to be given by either party hereunder shall be in writing and shall be sent to the Translator at the Translator's address as it is set forth in this Agreement unless such address has been changed by proper written notice, or to the Publisher, addressed to the attention of the Vice President & General Manager.

(d) This Agreement shall not be subject to change or modification in whole or in part unless in writing signed by both parties.

(e) This Agreement shall be construed and interpreted pursuant to the laws of the State of New York applicable to contracts wholly entered into and performed in the State of New York. Any legal action, suit or proceeding arising out of or relating to this Agreement or the breach thereof shall be instituted in a court of competent jurisdiction in New York County in the State of New York and each party hereby consents and submits to the personal jurisdiction of such court, waives any objection to venue in such court and consents to service or process by registered or certified mail return receipt requested.

(f) The provisions of Paragraph 13 above and this Paragraph shall survive the termination of this Agreement.

ACCEPTED AND AGREED

PUBLISHER

By: _____

Name: _____

Title: _____

TRANSLATOR

By: _____

Name: _____

Title: _____

_____

Social Security or Tax ID #: _____

Book Distribution Agreement—Exclusive Rights (Dual ISBN)

The following distribution agreement is for use by publishers for markets in which they have insufficient marketing presence. In it, the U.S. distributor receives exclusive rights in the territory, and the original publisher creates a dual ISBN so that sales can be tracked according to the distributor's systems. The distributor then purchases works from the original publisher at a discount commensurate with the number of books ordered.

Book Distribution Agreement

AGREEMENT made this _____ day of _____, _____ between American Publishing, Ltd. (hereinafter termed the "Distributor") of the One Part, and British Publishing, Inc. (hereinafter termed the "Proprietor") of the other part, whereby it is mutually agreed as follows:

1.   Grant of Rights/Scope of Agreement

a)   The Proprietor hereby grants to the Distributor the exclusive right to market and distribute in the Americas (North, Central and South America), those works in field of _____ produced by the Proprietor under the _____ imprint (hereinafter termed the "Work(s)") which Works shall be detailed on Schedule A to this Agreement. The said Schedule may be added to or deleted from, by mutual written agreement, approximately every six (6) months. The Works shall not include any titles which the Proprietor is unable to sell in the Americas due to contractual restrictions or existing contractual obligations.

b)   The Distributor will stock, market and distribute all Works, as provided in Clause 2(b) below, unless it is mutually agreed not to do so.

c)   The Proprietor acknowledges that the Distributor cannot restrict the resale by the Distributor's wholesale and retail customers of copies of the Works sold to them by the Distributor in the ordinary course of business.

2.   Purchases: Initial Orders, Reorders, Free Copies, Returns

a)   The Proprietor will supply the Distributor with copies of the Works on a royalty inclusive basis subject to the following discount scale from the pound sterling price for the initial stock order for each of the Works:

   i)   For initial order of 500 copies or less; __% discount.
   ii)   For initial order between 501 and 700 copies; __% discount.
   iii) For initial order between 701 and 900 copies or more; __% discount.
   iv)   For initial order of 901 copies or more; by mutual agreement.

b)   The Distributor undertakes to make an initial purchase of each of the Works, and will keep each of the Works in stock so long as the demand foreseen by the Distributor shall be no fewer than 25 copies per Work per annum. In the event that the Distributor foresees the annual demand will fall below this number for any Work, the Distributor may declare such Work out-of-stock and will refer all subsequent orders for the Work to the Proprietor. The Proprietor shall, in such event, be free to service those orders and/or to re-promote the Work within the Distributor's territory, provided that if any new editions of such Works are published the Proprietor agrees to offer such new editions to the Distributor under the terms of this Agreement.

c)   Reorders for any of the Works will be supplied by the Proprietor at the same discount as for the initial stock order.

d)   The Proprietor will make available to the Distributor for review or other promotional purchases, but not for resale, additional free copies equal to 5% of the initial order for each Work to be sent with the Distributor's initial stock order. For college textbooks, additional free copies equal to 10% of the initial order for each Work will be sent with the Distributor's initial stock order. No free copies will be supplied with reorders. For the extensive mailing of free copies in order to solicit adoptions, the Distributor may, with the agreement of the Proprietor, purchase further copies at cost to be sent with the initial stock order, provided the initial stock order is for 500 or more copies, and provided such additional copies are not resold.

e)   The Proprietor shall provide the Distributor, by air courier, with two (2) advance copies of the Work as soon as it is off press.

f)   After two and one-half ($2^1/_2$) full years of sales of any individual Work covered by this Agreement, the Distributor will have the option to return Works (for cash reimbursement or credit toward future purchases at Distributor's option at the original invoice price, up to 20% of the value of the original purchase order for that Work).

3.   Imprint
a)   The Proprietor will arrange to print the Distributor's name, address and ISBN on each copy of the Work as follows:

[*insert*]

4.   Shipping/Payment Terms
a)   The Proprietor will normally deliver stock to the Distributor's shipping agent and pay freight and insurance costs for the Works to that point.

The Distributor will pay freight and insurance costs from the delivery of stock to the Distributor's designated agent at a U.K. container port or collection point.

b)   Payment by the Distributor to the Proprietor for the Works will be made in pounds sterling within sixty (60) days from the date of bill of lading. If a strike, embargo or other cause beyond the control of the Distributor occurs, which results in the delay of the arrival of the Proprietor's stock from the Distributor's shipping agent to the Distributor's warehouse (currently in Alaska), the Distributor shall pay the Proprietor for stock accepted by the shipping agent before the beginning of the strike, embargo or other cause beyond the parties' control and payment shall be due ninety (90) days after acceptance of stock by the shipping agent. In the event of such a strike, embargo or other cause beyond the parties' control occurring, the Distributor and the shipping agent shall have the right to refuse to accept any stock from the Proprietor until such strike, embargo or other cause beyond the parties' control no longer prevents delivery of stock to the Distributor's designated warehouse.

c)   If copies of any Works received by the Distributor are damaged or otherwise in an unsaleable condition, the Distributor may return such copies to the Proprietor and the Proprietor will replace such copies to the Distributor within thirty (30) days and reimburse the Distributor for cost of shipping.

5.   Other Distribution Rights

Unless otherwise agreed, the Distributor will refer to the Proprietor any customers from within the Distributor's exclusive territories who wish to purchase titles which fall within the scope of this Agreement and which are not stocked by the Distributor. The Proprietor will be entitled to fulfill such orders without payment of any commission to the Distributor. The Distributor will also refer to the Proprietor any customers from outside the Distributor's exclusive territories who wish to purchase titles which fall within the scope of this Agreement. The Proprietor agrees to refer to the Distributor any customers or orders within the Distributor's exclusive territories for any titles which fall within the scope of this Agreement. The Distributor shall be entitled to fulfill such orders without payment of any commission to the Proprietor.

6.   Sales Report

The Distributor will supply to the Proprietor a report on a monthly basis of the stock and sales levels of the Work.

7.   Royalty for Subsidiary Rights

All subsidiary rights in the Works are reserved by the Proprietor except that the Distributor shall act as agent for the Proprietor for the sale of the Works to book clubs in the United States of America subject to the Proprietor's prior written approval in respect of each book club edition; and the Distributor will be entitled to retain 50% of the royalties or proceeds received by the Distributor from the sale of such rights. The Proprietor agrees that it will not exercise any Subsidiary Rights in the Works within the Distributor's market territory which, in the Distributor's judgment, may interfere with or injure the sales by the Distributor of the Works, without the Distributor's prior written consent. The Distributor will pay the Proprietor its share of the royalties or proceeds within 30 days of receipt by the Distributor.

8.   Marketing

a)   The Distributor shall at all times during the period of this Agreement use its best efforts to promote, extend and maximize the sales of the Works in the Distributor's exclusive market as detailed in Clause 1 hereof. All copies of the Works will bear the imprint and the Proprietor hereby authorizes the Distributor to use the imprint and tradename in its marketing and promotional materials for the Works.

b)   The Proprietor will endeavor to provide the Distributor with accurate advance information about the Works, in a mutually agreed format, at the least nine (9) months before the expected date of publication. The Distributor will endeavor to place an initial stock order for a Work at least three (3) months before the expected date of publication.

c)   The Proprietor will cause to be printed on the Works the following:

On the title page:
Co-published in North, Central and South America by American Publishing, Inc., Peoria, Montego Bay.

On the imprint page:
Co-published in North, Central and South America by American Publishing, Inc., 13 Main Street, Peoria, Illinois, USA

with the American Publishing ISBN printed beneath Proprietor's ISBN and marked (American Publishing)

On the back cover:
Co-published in North, Central and South America by American Publishing, Inc., Peoria, Montego Bay.

American Publishing ISBN

In the case of the imprint page, the Distributor's ISBN will be followed by the words "in the Americas only." The Proprietor will apply directly for Library of Congress Cataloging-in-Publication Data for each title, but the Distributor will provide any assistance necessary to obtaining such data.

9.   Copyright/Warranties and Indemnities

a)   The Proprietor warrants and undertakes that it has the right to convey all the rights herein conveyed, that each of the Works is protected by copyright under the laws of the United States and the Berne Convention, that the Works are not in any way whatever a violation of any existing copyright, that they contain nothing defamatory or libelous, that all statements contained therein purporting to be facts are true, that they do not infringe the rights of any person or organization, that they do not contain any unlawful statements or instructions that may cause harm or injury to others, that the Proprietor has complied with and obtained all consent licenses and authorities necessary to distribute the Works in the territories covered by this Agreement. The Proprietor agrees to indemnify and hold the Distributor harmless from all costs and claims, demands, damages and expenses, whether or not finally sustained, arising out of or in connection with the foregoing representations and warranties.

b)   Neither party shall incur any liability on behalf of the other party or in any way to pledge the other party's credit to make any contract binding upon each other or to give or make or purport to give or make any warranty or representation on behalf of the other.

10.   Term; Termination

a)   This Agreement shall commence on the _____ day of _____ and shall endure in the first instance until the _____ day of _____, and thereafter shall continue in effect unless either party terminates the Agreement by giving six (6) months prior notice in writing to the other party. It is understood that neither party shall send such notice of termination prior to the _____ day of ____, _____, except by mutual consent.

b)   If the Proprietor gives notice of termination under Clause 10(a) hereof, then the Proprietor shall upon expiration of the Agreement repurchase at invoice cost all unsold stock in a saleable condition supplied to the Distributor. The Distributor agrees to transfer all such stock at the expense of the Proprietor to a U.S. or U.K. destination designated by the Proprietor. If the Distributor gives notice of termination under Clause 10 (a) hereof, then the Proprietor will be offered the option to repurchase, at invoice cost, either (i) all unsold stock supplied to the Distributor hereunder of (ii) individual titles; provided all such stock is in a saleable condition and is purchased at invoice cost. For all stock not repurchased by the Proprietor, the Distributor shall have the right to sell off its inventory for a period of six months following termination.

c)   The Proprietor will delete all reference to Distributor on the Works upon the next occasion it reprints following the termination of this Agreement. For all orders placed after notice of termination has been received the

Proprietor and the Distributor will agree on the quantity and unit cost of each of the Works to be supplied.

d)   Unless otherwise agreed, this Agreement shall be terminated if either party goes into liquidation other than for purposes of reconstruction. If the Proprietor goes into liquidation, the Distributor shall have the option to deplete its inventory or offer such inventory to the Proprietor under Clause 9(b) hereof. If the Distributor goes into liquidation, arrangements for the purchase of stock shall be provided for under Clause 9(b) hereof in respect of the Distributor giving notice of termination. Arrangements for the purchase of stock shall be as provided for under Clause 9(b) hereof, in respect of the Proprietor giving notice of termination.

e)   No act or failure to act by either party shall be deemed a material breach of any of the provisions of this Agreement, unless the respective party fails to remedy the same within 30 days after receipt of written notice from the other party giving full particuany breach is not remedied within such 30-day period after receipt of written notice by the breaching party (except for breach due to *force majeure* not capable of being remedied within such 30-day period), the party not in breach shall have the right to terminate this Agreement at the end of the 30-day period by further written notice to the party in breach.

f)   This Agreement shall be construed and interpreted pursuant to the laws of the State of New York applicable to contracts wholly entered into and performed in the State of New York. Any legal action, suit or proceeding arising out of or relating to this Agreement or the breach thereof shall be instituted in a court of competent jurisdiction in New York County in the State of New York and each party hereby consents and submits to the personal jurisdiction of such court, waives any objection to venue in such court and consents to service of process by first class mail at the last known address of such party.

11.   Notices

Any notice to be given hereunder shall be in writing and shall be mailed, certified or registered, return receipt requested, or delivered by hand or courier service addressed to the other party as follows:

For the Distributor: [*address*]

For the Proprietor: [*address*]

12.   General

This Agreement constitutes the entire understanding and agreement between the parties hereto. All prior negotiations and agreements between the parties hereto are superseded by this Agreement, and there are no representations, warranties, understandings or agreements other than those expressly set forth herein. This Agreement may not be modified or amended, in whole or in part, except by a written agreement hereafter signed by both of the parties.

AGREED AND ACCEPTED

DISTRIBUTOR   **PROPRIETOR**

By: _____   By: _____

Title: _____   Title: _____

Date: _____   Date: _____

Nonexclusive Sales Representative Agreement

In contrast to Form 5.6, pursuant to which a publisher enters into a distribution agreement for territories in which it has no presence, Form 5.7 offers the publisher a less drastic alternative: the appointment of a sales representative for the territory. For the publisher, the sales representative relationship is less involved. There is no dual imprint or co-publishing, and thus the relationship is more simple. Please note that local laws regarding termination of agents varies significantly depending on the jurisdiction. For example, under European Union rules, agents are often eligible for a payout in the event of contractual termination.

Sales Representative Agreement

AGREEMENT made this 1st day of _____, 20__, by and between Original Publishing, Inc., a corporation organized pursuant to the laws of the State of _____, U.S.A. and having offices at _____ ("Publisher") and _____, a corporation organized pursuant to the laws of the _____ and having its principal place of business at _____ (the "Sales Representative").

1.   Best Efforts

Publisher hereby appoints as its nonexclusive Sales Representative in the Territories listed on Schedule 1 (the "Territory"). Sales Representative agrees to use its best efforts to promote the sale of Publisher's publications (including Reports, Books, Journals, Newsletters, and Alert Services, etc.) as set forth on Schedule 2 hereto in the Territory during the term of this Agreement at its own expense. To this end, Sales Representative will (a) make regular visits to librarians, bookstores, educational institutions, corporations, governmental agencies, and other potential customers in the Territory; (b) advise Publisher on promotional activities and other endeavors which may improve distribution in the Territory; (c) advise Publisher regarding commercial aspects of tendering for and performing contacts for its businesses in the Territory; (d) assist in the organization of displays, exhibitions and participation at Book Fairs in the Territory; (e) assist Publisher in the collection of outstanding debts in the Territory; (f) provide oral and written translation services to assist Publisher in its communications with the customer(s) and others concerning its publications; (g) comply with all reasonable orders and requests of Publisher and instructions received from Publisher regarding the execution and management of the relationship set forth herein; (h) introduce Publisher to professional, legal and financial advisers competent in such matters where necessary; (i) provide planning and forecasting data as may be required to comply with Publisher's planning procedures; (j) communicate regularly with Publisher and submit written reports on Sales Representative's efforts and sales results from time to time but in any event at least once per month; (k) promptly forward orders for Publisher's publications; (l) acquire signed license agreements from subscribers to electronic products; and (m) provide support to and comply with all reasonable requests from Publisher's customers concerning Publisher's policies with respect to commercial aspects of its publications.

In accordance with the above responsibilities, Sales Representative will fulfill the SALES AND MARKETING PLAN FOR _____ attached hereto as Schedule 3.

Sales Representatives will not promote or sell Publisher's publications outside the Territory nor will it permit such sales by its customers. In the event Sales Representative becomes aware that a customer is selling Publisher's publications outside the Territory, Sales Representative will promptly notify Publisher of the pertinent facts.

2. Publisher's Payment

In consideration of the services to be performed by Sales Representative hereunder, Publisher agrees to extend to Sales Representative (a) a discount of ____% off the list prices set by Publisher for initial subscriptions to subscription-based products sold or licensed by Sales Representative, (b) a discount of ____% off the list prices set by Publisher for Books and Reports sold by Sales Representative, and (c) a discount of ____% off the list prices set by Publisher for renewals of subscriptions of any subscription-based products sold or licensed by Sales Representative. [Sales Representative will collect all subscription and renewal revenues from its clients and will submit them, less the discount, to Publisher no less frequently than monthly, along with the names, addresses, and other information requested by Publisher. Sales Representative will also collect revenues from the sale of Books and Reports and submit the revenue to Publisher, less the discount, on the same schedule.]

3. Fulfillment

Publisher will, at its option, drop ship [*books, reports, etc.*] sold by Sales Representative either to the customers directly or to Sales Representative. Publisher will fulfill all [Newsletter, Journal and Alert Service] subscriptions and renewals directly to subscribers. Publisher will have no obligation to fulfill subscriptions or ship orders if Publisher has not received the full revenue related to the subscriptions or orders. Publisher will have no obligation to fulfill subscriptions to electronic products if it has not received from Sales Representative an unaltered copy of the then-current license agreement signed by the subscriber. Sales Representative agrees to hold Publisher harmless from any and all claims concerning fulfillment of orders or subscriptions if Publisher has not received payments relating thereto.

4.   Promotional Material

Publisher will provide Sales Representative with promotional material and copies of products in reasonable quantities to be determined by the parties.

5.   Copyright Infringement

Sales Representative will advise Publisher of any copyright or trademark infringement or piracy which comes to its attention and Publisher shall have the right, but not the obligation, to pursue any claims which it may have with respect to such copyright infringement. Sales Representative agrees to cooperate fully with Publisher in any such enforcement proceedings, at Publisher's expense. All damages recovered in the course of such actions belong wholly to Publisher unless otherwise agreed in writing by both parties.

6.   Trademarks

Sales Representative may not use Publisher's name and logo except in connection with promotional activities for the publications set forth on Schedule 2 which have been approved in advance by Publisher. In no event shall Sales Representative use Publisher's name, trademarks, logo or service marks in any manner which might disparage Publisher or which Publisher may otherwise deem objectionable.

7.   Confidentiality

In performing its obligations under this Agreement, Sales Representative may receive confidential information from Publisher and its customers, which may be oral or written. Such information includes, but it is not limited to, the terms and conditions of this Agreement and information pertaining to unpublished titles, customers, subscribers, marketing plans and business plans, and all information that by the nature of the circumstances surrounding the disclosure, ought in good faith to be treated as confidential. Sales Representative shall use such confidential information solely to perform its obligations pursuant to this Agreement and for no other purpose whatsoever. Sales Representative shall protect all such information from disclosure to other parties with the same degree of care as that which is accorded to its own proprietary information. Sales Representative shall limit access to subcontractors who have need of such access for performance of this Agreement. Upon the termination of this Agreement, Sales Representative shall return to Publisher any confidential information previously furnished to it, and such confidential information shall belong solely to Publisher.

8.   Term and Termination

This Agreement shall commence upon the date first written above and shall extend until either party terminates this Agreement, such termination to take effect four (4) months following delivery of written notice to the non-terminatory party unless sooner terminated as provided below.

Either party may terminate this Agreement immediately upon written notice to the other in the event (a) the other party becomes bankrupt, insolvent or enters into voluntary or involuntary bankruptcy proceedings; (b) the other party breaches any provision of this Agreement; (c) the party becomes aware of any law or regulation which adversely affects its ability to honor its obligations hereunder. Publisher may terminate the Agreement immediately on written notice if Sales Representative infringes any copyright, trademark or other intellectual property right of Publisher, or its affiliates.

For the avoidance of doubt, Publisher's sole liability to Sales Representative is for the discounts set forth in Paragraph 2 above for sales or licenses actually made by Sales Representative prior to termination of this Agreement, and Publisher shall have no liability to Sales Representative for any sales or licenses made post-termination or on account of the business generally, except that Sales Representative shall be entitled to a twenty (20) percent commission on subscription renewals from existing customers procured by Sales Representative received by Publisher within four (4) months of termination.

9. Independent Contractors

This Agreement creates neither an employment relationship between the parties (or between any party or the other party's employees) nor a joint venture. At no time may either party represent itself as an agent or representative of the other without the express written consent of the other. Sales Representative may not bind Publisher to any agreement without Publisher's express written approval.

10. Indemnity

Sales Representative covenants and agrees to indemnify and hold Publisher free and harmless from and on account of any claim, demand or judgment arising out of or relating to its performance under this Agreement or of any unauthorized warranty or representation of its staff or agents. Sales Representative shall not pledge the credit of Publisher in any way.

Publisher covenants and agrees to indemnify and hold Sales Representative free and harmless from and on account of any claim, demand or judgment arising out of any alleged infringement of trademarks, copyright or any similar rights arising from its Publications.

11. Assignment

This Agreement and the rights hereunder granted to Sales Representative are not assignable nor may the obligations imposed be delegated without the prior written consent of the Publisher. Subject to the foregoing, this Agreement shall be binding upon and inure to the benefit of the parties, their successors and assigns.

12. Force Majeure

Neither party shall be liable to the other for a failure to perform any of its obligations under this Agreement where such failure is due to any event of *force majeure*. An event of *force majeure* shall be defined as any event reasonably outside the control of either Publisher or Sales Representative which, without prejudice to the generality of this Agreement, shall include any accident, fire, explosion, casualty, epidemic, Act of God, official labor dispute, lock-out, labor condition, unavailability of materials, transportation, riot, war or armed conflict or enactment of the law. Where such event of *force majeure* delays performance for more than one month, either party shall have the right to terminate this Agreement by notice in writing to the other party.

13. Notices

All notices to be given by either party hereunder shall be in writing and shall be sent be certified mail, postage prepaid, or by courier service to the parties at the addresses set forth above.

14. Complete Agreement

This Agreement sets forth the complete understanding of the party and supersedes all prior agreements or negotiations between the parties with respect to the subject matter of this Agreement. This Agreement shall not be subject to change or modification, in whole or in part, unless in writing, signed by both thereof shall not be deemed a waiver of any other term or condition of this Agreement or of any breach of this Agreement or any part thereof.

15. Governing Law

This Agreement shall be construed and interpreted pursuant to the laws of the State of New York, U.S.A. Any legal action, suit or proceeding arising out of or relating to this Agreement or the breach thereof shall be instituted in a court of competent jurisdiction in the State of New York, County of New York, and each party hereby consents and submits to the personal jurisdiction of such court and waives any objection to venue in such court.

ACCEPTED AND AGREED

_____   ORIGINAL PUBLISHING, INC.

By: _____   By: _____

Name: _____   Name: _____

Title: _____   Title: _____

Date: _____   Date: _____

Literary Agent Agreement

Publishing houses increasingly rely on literary agents in lieu of dealing with the potential authors themselves. Many require that the author first secure an agent and will not deal with authors directly or accept unsolicited material. Thus the literary agent has displaced the "slush pile" of unsolicited manuscripts through which publishers used to comb in search of publishable material.[3]

As agents have become the filter between authors and major publishers, manuscripts delivered "over the transom" have started to become history, as have transoms themselves. The substantive change is that authors, not publishers, bear the costs (in agent commissions) associated with separating the wheat from the chaff. The following sample agreement is favorable to the agents, who generally draft the agreements.

Agency Agreement (Single Work)

1. Appointment

I, _____, hereby appoint _____ ("Agency") as my sole and exclusive literary agent to advise me and negotiate the sale and disposition ("sale") of publication rights to my book-length literary material ("Work") currently entitled _____ and of subsidiary rights arising therefrom (including, but not limited to, publishing, motion picture, television, stage, radio, audio, video, electronic and merchandising rights) in all forms and media and for all future purposes, throughout the world.

2. Sub-Agents

Agency may appoint sub-agents to assist with such sales according to the terms outlined in Paragraphs 7(c) and 7(d).

3. No Agreement Without Consent

Agency agrees to make no agreements on my behalf without my approval, and no agreement shall bind me without my consent and signature.

---

3 *See generally*, Mark A. Fischer, E. Gabriel Perle and John Taylor Williams, *Perle and Williams on Publishing Law*, § 2.18 (3d ed., Aspen L. & Bus. 2001).

4.   Expenses

Agency shall pay expenses of selling the Work, except: photographic reproductions; photocopying of proposals and partial or complete manuscripts;
purchase of galleys and books; and legal advice and representation regarding
the Work, solicitation of such to have been agreed upon by me in advance.

5.   Best Efforts; First Refusal

Agency shall use its best efforts to sell the Work as long as it believes it feasible to do so. Agency will notify me in writing when the Work is in Agency's
opinion no longer salable, at which point I may do with the Work as I wish
without obligation to Agency. Subsequent to Agency's notification to me that
in Agency's opinion the Work is no longer salable, Agency shall have the right
of first refusal on all other book-length literary properties of mine both created
and uncommitted as of the date of this Agreement.

6.   Receipt of Payments

I authorize Agency to receive all payments accruing to me from sales of rights
(including subsidiary rights) to the Work, and I hereby agree that all contracts and
agreements regarding such sales entered into by me or on my behalf at any time
shall require all payments due me to be made to Agency. Agency agrees to remit
such payments to me, after deduction of Agency's commissions and expenses
as agreed to herein, within ten (10) business days after Agency's receipt thereof,
except in cases of reasonable extenuation and only when agreed to by me.

7.   Commission

In consideration of Agency's services, Agency is irrevocably entitled to deduct
as nonrefundable commission:

(a)   fifteen (15%) percent of all income from sales of United States print rights
to the Work, including any income accruing to me from the sale of such
print or non-print subsidiary rights as are retained by the United States
print publisher of the Work;

(b)   when those rights have been retained by me via publisher contract,
fifteen (15%) percent of all income from sales of United States print or
non-print
subsidiary rights arising from the Work, excluding dramatic rights;

(c)   when those rights have been retained by me via publisher contract,
twenty (20%) percent of all income from sales of United States
dramatic rights arising from the Work, and Agency shall pay any sub-
agent's commission; and

(d) when those rights have been retained by me via publisher contract, twenty (20%) percent of all foreign print and non-print subsidiary rights arising from the Work, or thirty (30%) percent of all foreign print and non-print subsidiary rights arising from the Work when one or more sub-agents are used, and Agency shall pay any sub-agent's commission.

8. Contracts and Agreements Covered

Agency's commission shall be payable as this Agreement provides for above with respect to:

(a) all contracts and agreements (and any extensions or renewals thereof and substitutions therefor) for the sale of any rights arising from the Work entered into by me during the term of this Agreement;

(b) all contracts and agreements referenced in Paragraph 9 hereof, which are hereby deemed to be covered by the terms of this Agreement; and

(c) any resumptions of any contracts and agreements covered by the terms of this Agreement which may have been discontinued during the term of this Agreement and resumed within one (1) year thereafter.

If, within six (6) months after termination of this Agreement, I enter into any contract or agreement concerning the Work with a person or firm with whom Agency has been substantially negotiating on my behalf prior to termination, that contract or agreement shall be deemed to have been entered into during the term of this Agreement. Agency shall supply a list of such persons and firms upon my request.

9. Termination

This Agreement shall continue in full force and effect until terminated as follows: Agency or I may terminate this Agreement with thirty (30) days' written notice to the other party by registered mail, certified mail, or overnight delivery with signature of recipient. It is understood, however, that if rights to the Work have been sold during the term of this Agreement, Agency's interest in the Work is irrevocable, and such irrevocable interest thereby and thereafter extends to any and all subsidiary rights arising from the Work. In recognition thereof, and in such case, I hereby:
(a) acknowledge and agree that, regardless of when made or by whom, any and all contracts or agreements (and any extensions or renewals thereof and substitutions therefor) regarding the Work are covered by the terms of this Agreement; (b) agree to arrange for all such contracts and agreements,

regardless of when made or by whom, to name Agency as my agent of record; and (c) agree to arrange for any monies due to me from agreements or contracts covered by the terms of this Agreement (regardless of when made or by whom), and accruing after termination of this Agreement, to be paid to Agency, which will then deduct commissions and unreimbursed expenses and remit to me as outlined above.

10.   Dissolution of Agency; Death or Incapacitation of Principals of Agency

In the event of the death or incapacitation of all principals of Agency or the dissolution of Agency, Agency's rights hereunder and interest in the Work shall survive and inure to the benefit of the designated heirs and assigns of Agency and/or the designated heirs and assigns of principals of Agency, as the case may be. Any purchasers, licensees or sublicensees of rights in and to the Work will be deemed hereunder to have the consent of the parties hereto to issue separate checks to such designated heirs and assigns according to the terms of Paragraph 7 hereof; provided, however, that the heirs or assigns of Agency, or the heirs or assigns of the individual principals of Agency, as the case may be, shall be fully responsible for notifying such purchasers, licensees and sublicensees as to the proper means of disbursement of monies accruing to Agency hereunder, and I am specifically released hereby from any obligation to Agency that might prejudice my ability to receive timely payment of monies accruing to me under the combined action of this and any other agreement.

11.   Assignment; Heirs and Assigns

None of the rights granted herein may be assigned by either party without the other party's prior written consent, such consent not to be unreasonably withheld or delayed. This Agreement is binding on our respective personal and business heirs and assigns.

12.   Construction

This Agreement shall be construed under and governed in accordance with the laws of the State of New York.

13.   Captions

Captions are for convenience only and are not deemed to be a part of this Agreement.

14.   Entire Agreement

This Agreement represents the sole and entire understanding between Agency and myself with respect to the subject matter hereof. This Agreement may not be altered, modified or amended except in a writing signed by myself and an authorized representative of Agency.

AGREED AND ACCEPTED

AUTHOR

By: _____

Name: _____

Title: _____

Address: _____

SSN or Tax ID: _____

AGENCY

By: _____

Name: _____

Title: _____

Independent Contractor Application/Status Form

A publisher using independent contractors should have a standard form listing the documentation required from the contractor and setting forth the parties' relationship. The following form lists documentation required from the contractor on the first page, and the second page provides, *inter alia*, (1) there is no reimbursement of expenses unless otherwise agreed (Clause 2), no taxes being withheld (Clause 4), the relationship is terminable "at will" (Clauses 5 and 7), and the contractor has no authority to bind the publisher.

Independent Contractor Application/Status Form

APPLICATION (to be completed by individual applying for freelance or independent contractor work)

Name:	Soc. Sec. No.	Taxpayer ID No.
Home Address:	Business Address:	
Home Phone:	Business Phone:	

CAPABILITIES

☐Copyediting	☐Proofreading	☐Typesetting	☐Illustration
☐Indexing	☐Copywriting	☐Typing	☐Design
Other (please describe)			

WORK BEING PERFORMED FOR:

Division:	Department:
Contact:	Extension:

If _____ employee, the following approval is required:

Department Manager	Next Level of Management	*Division or Senior VP
Dept. Name	Dept. No	Date

Only required when Freelance work is performed in employee's home department. If a project is less than $500, Division Vice President approval is required. If $500 or greater. Senior Vice President approval is necessary.

DETERMINATION OF STATUS (to be completed by individual applying for Freelance or Independent Contractor work)

The Taxing Authorities require companies to provide proof from outside vendors that they are independent contractors rather than employees working off-site. The main requirement is that contractors perform work for other businesses, in addition to _____, are actively soliciting work from other sources.

To be classified as an Independent Contractor, you must supply _____ proof that you provide services and are paid by others, or that you are soliciting work from others. You can prove your status by providing copies of several of the items indicated below. You should provide as much documentation as possible. *Information will be used only for Independent Contractor classification purposes, and will be kept strictly confidential.*

Check off which items you are enclosing with your form:

Preferred:	**Alternatively (supply several):**
☐A copy of Schedule C filed with the IRS	☐If employed by another company, company name and
☐Copies of forms 1099 you received for the previous year	Tax Identification Number_____: Name:_____ Tax ID:_____
☐Business License	☐Purchase order, invoices from other companies
☐Sales Tax Registration Number	☐Copies of advertising you have done notifying the general public of your services, listing in Yellow Pages, etc. ☐Proof of business rental/lease apart from residence ☐Business cards. ☐Proof of your employer identification number ☐A copy of your business insurance policy ☐A list of equipment owned and used in your business ☐Other:_____

Please read carefully the agreement set forth on the reverse of this form. By signing below, you agree to be bound by the terms and conditions set forth on the reverse. Further, you acknowledge that all information provided is truthful and accurate to be the best of your knowledge.

_____	_____
Contractor	Date

Send original and one copy of this form, the entire New Vendor form, and supporting documentation to:

If you have any questions regarding your Independent Contractor Status, please contact the Accounts Payable Coordinator at extension

DO NOT SEND ANY INVOICES WITH THIS FORM. ALL INVOICES MUST BE SENT TO YOUR HIRING DEPARTMENT.

For Financial Services Use:	☐ Independent Contractor	☐ Temporary/Freelance Employee	
Determination Status, Approved By:		Employ #:	Date:

Agreement

Terms and Conditions

This agreement, made between _____ Inc. ("_____" or the "company") and the individual entity referred to on the reverse of this page ("contractor"), sets forth the terms and conditions of the Contractor's engagement by

1.   Services to be Provided, Schedule and Terms of Payment

Services to be provided, the schedule of performance, and payment terms shall be determined by _____ and confirmed on a Purchase Order or other comparable document provided by _____.

2.   Reimbursement of Expenses

_____ shall not be liable to Contractor for any expenses paid or incurred by Contractor unless otherwise agreed to in writing.

3.   Equipment, Tools, Materials, or Supplies

Contractor shall supply, at Contractor's sole expense, all equipment, tools, materials, and/or supplies to accomplish the services to be performed.

4.   Federal, State, and Local Payroll Taxes for Independent Contractors: Benefits

A. For Contractors determined by _____ to be "Independent Contractors," _____ shall not withhold federal, state, local income or payroll taxes from payments made to Contractors, and Contractor shall be solely responsible for the payment of all such taxes arising out of all payments made to it under this Agreement. Contractor represents and warrants that it will pay all such taxes and shall hold _____ harmless from any liability resulting to _____ in the event Contractor fails to do so.

B. Contractors classified as Independent Contractors shall not be eligible to receive and shall not receive or participate in any employee pension benefit plans of any kind whatsoever.

5.   Temporary Freelance Employees

Contractors who are classified as a Temporary Freelance Employee acknowledge that their employment is for the term of the project only and that their employment shall terminate no later than upon completion of the project. Such Contractors further acknowledge that their employment is "At-Will" and may be terminated at any time by the Contractor or _____ with or without cause or notice. Benefits, if any, shall be in accordance with and subject to the terms and conditions of _____'s benefit plans.

6.   Not Responsible for Worker's Compensation

No workers' compensation insurance shall be obtained by _____ concerning Contractors classified as Independent Contractors. Contractor shall comply with the workers' compensation law and shall provide to _____ a certificate of workers' compensation insurance upon request.

7.   Term and Termination

Either party may terminate this Agreement with or without cause at any time without notice or penalty. If not terminated sooner, this agreement shall terminate on completion of the project.

8.   Non-Waiver

The failure of either party to exercise any of its rights under this Agreement for a breach thereof shall not be deemed to be a waiver of such rights or a waiver of any subsequent breach.

9.   No Authority to Bind

Contractor has no authority to enter into contracts or agreements on behalf of _____. This agreement does not create a partnership between the parties.

10.   Certification

Contractor certifies that Contractor has complied with all federal, state and local laws regarding business permits, certificates, and licenses that may be required to carry out the work to be performed under this Agreement.

11.   Notices

Any notice given in connection to this Agreement shall be given in writing and shall be delivered either by hand to the party or by certified mail, return receipt requested, to the party at the party's address stated herein. Any party may change its address stated herein by giving notice of the change in accordance with this paragraph.

12.   General

This Agreement represents the entire agreement between the parties and may not be changed or modified except in writing and signed by the party against whom enforcement is sought. This Agreement may not be assigned in whole or in part, by Contractor. This Agreement shall be governed by and contained as if wholly entered into and performed within the State of New York.

Trademark License Agreement[4]

Trademark licenses are used for many different purposes, including co-publishing ventures, acquisitions, and distribution relationships. Although they can be written in many ways, the two most important issues are to define the scope of the license (Clauses 2 and 3) and to ensure that the licensor is able to exercise adequate quality control (Clause 4). If the licensor does not both have the right to exercise quality control, and in fact exercise such control, the trademark may be lost.[5] Other standard pro-licensor clauses include confirmation of licensor's ownership (Clause 1), confirmation that there will be no registration of the trademarks by the licensee (Clause 5), and consent to injunction for breach by licensee of licensor's rights.

Trademark License Agreement

This Agreement is made this ___, day of _____, 20__, between _____, ("Licensor") and _____ ("Licensee").

WHEREAS, Licensor is the owner of certain trademarks; and

WHEREAS, Licensee wishes to obtain a nonexclusive license to use certain specified trademarks of Licensor under the terms and conditions of this Agreement;

NOW THEREFORE, for mutual considerations, the receipt and sufficiency of which are severally acknowledged, Licensor and Licensee agree as follows:

1. Trademark Ownership

(a) Licensee acknowledges and agrees that Licensor is the sole and exclusive owner of the entire right, title, and interest (including any and all accompanying goodwill) in and to the trademarks described in Exhibit A, collectively referred to as the "Licensed Marks."

(b) Licensee agrees that this Agreement gives it no rights whatsoever to the Licensed Marks except as specifically provided hereunder.

2. Territory

The Territory for this Agreement is the United States.

---

4 This form was prepared by William M. Hart, Esq. of the New York Office of Proskauer Rose, LLP and is used herein with his permission.

5 *See*, J. Thomas McCarthy, *McCarthy on Trademarks and Unfair Competition*, 18:42, 4th Ed. (West Group 2001).

3. Trademark License

Licensor grants to Licensee a nonexclusive limited license to (a) use the Licensed Marks as trademarks in the applicable Territory only in connection with the following goods and services: _____, subject to the following conditions:

(a) Licensee is not in default of any term or condition of this Agreement;

(b) Licensee will acknowledge in all usages of a Licensed Mark that each Licensed Mark (if registered in the Territory) is "a registered trademark of _____" and that each Licensed Mark is "licensed by _____" to Licensee. Licensee will include the above acknowledgment in conjunction with all usages of the Licensed Marks. Licensee will also cause the ® symbol to appear next to each of the Licensed Marks registered in the applicable Territory (or in any country of usage within the Territory) at least once in all published usages of such Licensed Marks; and to use the TM or SM (whichever is applicable) next to each of the Licensed Marks unregistered in the applicable Territory (or in any country of usage within the Territory) at least once in all published usages of such Licensed Marks;

(c) Except for its licensed use of the Licensed Marks hereunder, Licensee will not adopt or use any mark, logo, insignia, or design that is or is likely to be confusingly similar to or cause deception or mistake with respect to any of the Licensed Marks;

(d) Licensee may use the Licensed Marks only in connection with; and

(e) Licensee may not ship goods or provide services under any of the Licensed Marks without the prior written consent of Licensor.

4. Quality Control

(a) Licensee agrees that it will not use the Licensed Marks in a manner that would be offensive to good taste or would injure the reputation of Licensor and/or the Licensed Marks.

(b) Licensee agrees to permit Licensor and its designated representatives, at any time, to inspect the operations of Licensee at Licensee's place of business during normal working hours to ensure that the products and services provided under the Licensed Marks are up to Licensor's quality standards. If, in the judgment of Licensor, an inspection reveals deficiencies in quality of services, products, or materials bearing the Licensed Marks, Licensee agrees promptly to rectify all such deficiencies in quality to the satisfaction of Licensor.

5.   No Trademark Registration by Licensee

Licensee agrees that it will not, during the term hereof or at any time thereafter, make application for or aid or abet others to seek trademark registrations or recordings of trade names or company names in any state of the United States, in the United States Patent Office or other United States governmental agencies or in any foreign country of any mark or design which includes the Licensed Marks, or variations thereof, or limitations thereof, alone or in combination, except with the express prior written permission of Licensor, nor to contest Licensor's rights thereto. All goodwill and uses by Licensee of the Licensed Marks will inure to the benefit of Licensor. If Licensor deems it advisable to obtain design or trademark protection in connection with this Agreement, Licensee agrees to supply Licensor with all material it may request for such purposes and to give Licensor its full cooperation in connection therewith.

6.   Infringement

Licensee agrees to notify Licensor promptly of any adverse claim and will fully cooperate in any proceeding or settlement Licensor deems advisable. Licensee will have no right or obligation to proceed against or make any settlement with infringers and Licensor will have sole control thereof: unless Licensor agrees otherwise in writing. Further, Licensee will notify Licensor of any suspected or actual infringements of Licensor's trademarks, unfair competition, "palming off," or other intellectual property rights violations.

7.   Remedies

All remedies under this Agreement and under law are intended to be cumulative and not exclusive. Licensee acknowledges that Licensor has no adequate remedy hereunder or at law for Licensee's use of the Licensed Marks in violation of this Agreement and Licensor will be entitled to injunctive relief or other equitable remedies therefor.

8.   No Assignment

This Agreement will bind and benefit the parties hereto and their respective successors and permitted assigns. The rights granted herein are personal to Licensee and may not be assigned, sublicensed, or transferred, in whole or in part, by Licensee in any manner whatsoever, except with the prior written consent of Licensor. Any attempted assignment, transfer or sublicense of this Agreement, in whole or in part, in violation of the foregoing prohibition will be null and void, unless specifically ratified by Licensor. This license may be assigned by Licensor.

9.   Warranty and Indemnity

(a)   Licensee warrants and represents that it will respect all the Licensed Marks; that it will not claim or apply for registration of any Licensed Mark or a mark similar thereto; and that it will not violate the trademark, unfair competition, or the intellectual property right of Licensor or any third party.

(b)   Licensee agrees at its own cost and expense to defend, indemnify and hold harmless Licensor (including, without limitation, Licensor's subsidiaries, affiliates, stockholders, directors, officers, employees, and agents), harmless from and against any and all loss, liability, claims, suits, actions, proceedings, judgments, awards, damages, and expense (including, without limitation, attorneys' fees) that they, or any of them, may incur or suffer which arise out of or is claimed by the claimant to arise out of any state of facts which would constitute a breach by Licensee of any representation, warranty, covenant, or term of this Agreement or by reason of the operation of Licensee's business. Licensor agrees to notify Licensee promptly of any claim hereunder. Licensor may, at its own expense, have counsel of its own choice represent Licensor or its affiliates in such matters. However, if Licensee fails promptly and diligently to defend, Licensor may, but will have no obligation to, defend, or settle the same without Licensee's consent and Licensee agrees to pay the costs of defense and/or settlement, including, without limitation, counsel fees, and any judgments, awards and settlements incurred by Licensor and its affiliates related thereto. Notwithstanding the foregoing, Licensor will have sole control of such proceedings and settlements at Licensee's expense if (i) the same would adversely affect the Licensed Marks, or (ii) an adverse result would irreparably damage Licensor's goodwill, or (iii) Licensee fails to provide Licensor, at its request, with proof satisfactory to Licensor of the financial responsibility of Licensee or its insurers for any judgments which may be entered or, absent such proof, with a satisfactory surety bond to assure such payment.

10.   Insurance

Licensee will maintain liability insurance covering claims of trademark infringement, unfair competition, copyright infringement, and "palming off" in an amount determined by Licensor in its discretion.

11.   Applicable Law

This Agreement will be construed under the laws and in the state and federal courts of the State of New York. Licensor and Licensee waive any objection to the personal jurisdiction and venue of such courts.

12.   Notices

The written communications permitted or required by this Agreement are sufficiently conveyed to the other party if mailed first class by certified or registered mail, return receipt requested, postage prepaid, to the other party at the last known mailing address of the other party or to such other address as such other party may designate by written notice hereunder. All written communications given in compliance herewith will be effective on the date of mailing.

13.   Severability

Any provision of this Agreement found to be invalid, unenforceable, or prohibited by law will be ineffective only to the extent of such invalidity, unenforceability, or prohibition without invalidating the rest of this Agreement.

14.   Modifications

This Agreement may not be modified, except by written instrument signed by an authorized officer or partner of the party to be charged. This Agreement constitutes the complete understanding of the parties with respect to the subject matter hereof and supersedes all prior agreements and understandings.

15.   Captions

The headings and captions in this Agreement are for the convenience of the parties and will have no effect on the interpretation of this Agreement.

16.   Termination

(a)   Licensor may terminate this Agreement and all of the rights licensed to Licensee hereunder, upon written notice to Licensee.

(b)   Paragraphs 1(a), 5, 6, 7, 9, 11, 12, 13, 15, and this Paragraph 16(b) will survive termination of this Agreement for any reason.

IN WITNESS WHEREOF, the parties hereto have set their hands and seals to this Agreement as of the day and year above written.

_____

By: _____

Title: _____

Date Signed: _____

By: _____

Title: _____

Date Signed: _____

EXHIBIT A

The Licensed Marks

FORM 5.11

Non-Specific Mutual Non-Disclosure Agreement

When two parties who are competitors (or potential competitors) wish to discuss a collaborative business venture, they will often first enter into a mutual non-disclosure agreement. Many parties enter into these agreements blindly and assume that they are just a way of doing business. While they may be largely ignored, they are ignored at the peril of the signatory. Although during the 1990s "dot-com" boom non-disclosure agreements were overused to the point of absurdity, non-disclosure agreements can be an inducement to litigation, particularly for deals that do not close. Accordingly, before entering into an agreement, a party should focus on whether confidential information is truly to be exchanged.

Agreement

This Mutual Non-Disclosure Agreement is made and entered into as of _____, 20__ between _____, a _____ corporation with offices at _____ and _____, a _____ corporation with offices at _____ (hereinafter collectively referred to as the "Parties," or individually as a "Party").

1. Purpose

The Parties wish to explore a business opportunity of mutual interest. In connection with this opportunity, each Party may disclose to the other certain confidential scientific, technical and/or business information that the disclosing Party desires the receiving Party to treat as confidential.

2. Confidential Information

"Confidential Information" means any information disclosed by either Party to the other Party, either directly or indirectly, in writing, orally, electronically or by inspection of tangible objects (including without limitation documents, prototypes, samples, and equipment), which (i) is marked as "Confidential," "Proprietary," or some similar designation; (ii) is otherwise represented by the disclosing party as Confidential either before or within a reasonable time after its disclosure; or (iii) otherwise represents information which would be understood to be Confidential by a reasonable party. Confidential Information also may include information disclosed to a disclosing Party by third parties. Confidential Information shall not, however include any information which (i) was publicly known and made generally available in the public domain prior to the time of disclosure by the disclosing Party; (ii) becomes publicly known and made generally available after disclosure by the disclosing Party to the

receiving Party through no action or inaction of the receiving Party;
(iii) is already in the possession of the receiving Party at the time of disclosure
by the disclosing Party as shown by the receiving Party's files and records;
(iv) is knowingly obtained by the receiving Party from a third party without a
breach of such third party's obligations of confidentiality; (v) is independently
developed by the receiving Party without use of or reference to the disclosing
Party's Confidential Information, as shown by documents and other competent
evidence in the receiving Party's possession; or (vi) is required by law to be
disclosed by the receiving Party, provided that the receiving Party gives the
disclosing Party prompt written notice of such requirement prior to such
disclosure and assistance in obtaining an order protecting the information
from public disclosure.

3. Non-Use and Non-Disclosure

Each Party agrees not to use any Confidential Information of the other Party for
any purpose except to evaluate and engage in discussions concerning a potential business relationship between the Parties. Each Party agrees not to disclose
any Confidential Information of the other Party to third parties or to such Party's
employees except to those employees and/or authorized representatives of the
receiving Party who are required to have the information in order to evaluate
or engage in discussions concerning the contemplated business relationship.
Neither Party shall reverse engineer, disassemble, or decompile any prototypes,
software or other tangible objects which embody the other Party's Confidential
Information and which are provided to the Party hereunder.

4. Maintenance of Confidentiality

Each Party agrees that it shall take reasonable and customary measures to
protect the secrecy of, and avoid disclosure and unauthorized use of, the
Confidential Information of the other Party. Without limiting the foregoing,
each Party shall take at least those measures that it takes to protect its own confidential information and shall ensure that its employees who have access to
Confidential Information of the other Party are aware of and bound to comply
with the obligations set forth herein, prior to any disclosure of Confidential
Information to such employees. Neither Party shall make any copies of the
Confidential Information of the other Party unless the same are previously
approved in writing by the other Party. Each Party shall reproduce the other
Party's proprietary rights notices on any such approved copies, in the same
manner in which such notices were set forth in or on the original.

5. No Obligation

Nothing herein shall obligate either Party to proceed with any transaction
between them, and each Party reserves the right, in its sole discretion, to

terminate the discussions contemplated by this Agreement concerning the business opportunity.

6.   No Warranty

ALL CONFIDENTIAL INFORMATION IS PROVIDED "AS IS." EACH PARTY MAKES NO WARRANTIES, EXPRESS, IMPLIED OR OTHERWISE, REGARDING ITS ACCURACY, COMPLETENESS OR PERFORMANCE.

7.   Return of Materials

All documents and other tangible objects containing or representing Confidential Information which have been disclosed by either Party to the other Party, and all copies thereof which are in the possession of the other Party, shall be and remain the property of the disclosing Party and shall be promptly returned to the disclosing Party upon the disclosing Party's written request with the exception of one copy that may be retained by the receiving Party to confirm compliance with the non-use and non-disclosure provisions of this Agreement. Notwithstanding the foregoing, documents prepared by the receiving Party that include Confidential Information with such Party's analysis shall be destroyed upon the disclosing Party's written request for destruction and such destruction shall be certified by the receiving Party to the disclosing Party.

8.   No License/Trademark

Nothing in this Agreement is intended to grant any rights to either Party under any patent, mask work right or copyright of the other Party, nor shall this Agreement grant any Party any rights in or to the Confidential Information of the other Party except as expressly set forth herein. Further, except as agreed to in advance in writing, no right, express or implied, is granted by this Agreement to use in any manner the names _____, _____, _____, or any other trade name or trademark of a Party or the names of any employees thereof, for any purpose.

9.   Term

The obligations of each receiving Party hereunder shall survive for a period of five (5) years.

10.   Remedies

Each Party agrees that any violation or threatened violation of this Agreement may cause irreparable injury to the other Party, entitling the other Party to [seek] injunctive relief in addition to all legal remedies.

11. Competitive Works

The Parties acknowledge that other publishes or may publish programs and products that may be competitive with programs and products published or to be published by the disclosing Party. Nothing herein contained shall be construed to limit or restrict the right of each Party to publish its own programs and products, and the publication of such materials whether before or after the date of this Agreement shall not constitute a breach of this Agreement, notwithstanding any disclosure relating to any programs and products, so long as no Confidential Information is printed, referenced, or relied upon in connection with any publication.

12. Brokerage Fee

It is agreed that the Parties have no obligation under this Agreement to pay a brokerage fee in the event of a completion of a transaction between them.

13. Miscellaneous

This Agreement shall bind and inure to the benefit of the Parties hereto and their successors and assigns. This Agreement shall be governed by the laws of the State of New York without reference to conflict of laws principles. Any legal action, suit or proceeding arising out of, concerning, or relating to this Agreement shall be commenced in a court of competent jurisdiction in the State of New York, County of New York and the parties hereby consent to the jurisdiction thereof and waive any objections to venue therein. This document contains the entire agreement between the Parties with respect to subject matter hereof, and neither Party shall have any obligation, express or implied by law, with respect to trade secret or proprietary information of the other Party except as set forth herein. Any failure to enforce any provision of this Agreement shall not constitute a waiver thereof or of any other provision. This Agreement may not be amended, nor any obligation waived, except by a writing signed by both Parties hereto.

IN WITNESS WHEREOF, the parties hereto have caused this Agreement to be executed as of the date first written above by their respective authorized representatives. The parties hereby affirm that this Agreement accurately and completely reflects their understanding and agreements.

PARTY 1   PARTY 2

By:_____   By:_____

Name:_____   Name:_____

Title:_____   Title:_____

Quitclaim Assignment of Copyrights[6]

This basic Quitclaim Assignment of Copyrights transfers all of the assignor's interests in the copyrights identified on an attached schedule. If the assignee desires to record the assignments of registered copyrights in the U.S. Copyright Office, it may request two separate assignments of registered and unregistered copyrights.

Quitclaim Assignment of Copyrights

QUITCLAIM ASSIGNMENT made as of the _____ day of _____, 20__, by _____ (the "Assignor") to _____ (the "Assignee").

WITNESSETH

WHEREAS, the Assignor is the owner of various copyrights in and to various published and unpublished works (collectively, the "Publications") listed on Schedule 1 hereto; and

WHEREAS, the Assignee desires to acquire all Assignor's right, title and interest in and to all such copyrights;

NOW, THEREFORE, in consideration of One Dollar ($1.00), and for other good and valuable consideration, the receipt and sufficiency of which are hereby acknowledged, the Assignor hereby sells, transfers, conveys and assigns to the Assignee, its legal representatives, successors and assigns, all of Assignor's right, title and interest in and to those registered and unregistered copyrights (including any and all listed pending applications for registration) relating to the Publications, the copyright registrations pertaining thereto, if any, and the right to pursue past, present and future infringements thereof all rights, if any, of Assignor to obtain renewals and extensions of such copyrights that may be secured under the laws now or hereafter in force and effect in the United States of America, or in any other country or countries. Copies of certain copyright registrations and applications transferred hereunder are attached hereto.

The Assignor shall, upon the request of the Assignee, execute such other instruments of conveyance as may be necessary to permit Assignee to record the assignment made by this instrument.

---

6 For recordal of transfers in the United States Copyright Office, *see* Mark A. Fischer, E. Gabriel Perle and John Taylor Willliams, *Perle and Williams on Publishing Law,*§ 16.02 (3d ed., Aspen L. & Bus. 2001).

IN WITNESS WHEREOF, the undersigned has caused this Assignment to be duly executed and delivered as of the _____ day of _____, 20__.

Assignor, Inc.

By: _____

Name: _____

Title: _____

ACKNOWLEDGMENT

STATE OF NEW YORK   )

                                                    ss.:

CITY AND COUNTY OF NEW YORK   )

On _____, before me, _____, a Notary Public in and for the State of New York, personally appeared _____, the _____ of [*assignor*], personally known to me (or proved to me on the basis of satisfactory evidence) to be the person whose name is subscribed to the within instrument, and acknowledged to me that he executed the within instrument with authority of the Board of Directors in his capacity to act on behalf of said Corporation, and that, by his signature on the within instrument, the person or entity upon behalf of which he acted executed the within instrument.

WITNESS my hand and official seal.

Signature _____ (Seal)

Quitclaim Trademark Assignment

This basic Quitclaim Trademark Assignment transfers all of the assignor's rights in trademarks identified on an attached schedule. If the assignee desires to record the assignment of registered trademarks in the United States Patent and Trademark Office, it may request separate assignments for registered and unregistered trademarks.

Quitclaim Trademark Assignment

QUITCLAIM ASSIGNMENT made as of the day of _____, 20__, by (the "Assignor") to _____ (the "Assignee").

WHEREAS, the Assignor is the owner of various registered and unregistered trademarks (the "Trademarks") listed on Schedule 1 hereto; and

WHEREAS, the Assignee desires to acquire all Assignor's right, title and interest in and to such Trademarks;

NOW, THEREFORE, in consideration of One Dollar ($1.00) and other good and valuable consideration, receipt and sufficiency of which is hereby acknowledged, the Assignor does hereby sell, assign and transfer to the Assignee, its successors and assigns, all of Assignor's right, title and interest in the Trademarks, its rights, if any, together with the goodwill of the business symbolized by the Trademarks, all registrations thereof and the right to apply for registrations, and the right, if any, to sue and collect damages and/or profits for past infringements of the Trademarks, the intent being to substitute Assignee in the place of Assignor.

IN WITNESS WHEREOF, the Assignor has caused this instrument to be signed by a duly authorized officer as of the ___ day of _____, 20__.

ASSIGNOR

By: _____

ACKNOWLEDGMENT

STATE OF NEW YORK   )
                                                          ss.:
CITY AND COUNTY OF NEW YORK   )

On _____, before me, _____, a Notary Public in and for the State of New York, personally appeared _____, the _____ of [assignor], personally known to me (or proved to me on the basis of satisfactory evidence) to be the person whose name is subscribed to the within instrument, and acknowledged to me that he executed the within instrument with authority of the Board of Directors in his capacity to act on behalf of said Corporation, and that, by his signature on the within instrument, the person or entity upon behalf of which he acted executed the within instrument.

WITNESS my hand and official seal.

Signature _____ (Seal)

CHAPTER
6

Permissions and Subsidiary Rights

§ 6.01 Background

[A] Permissions and Subsidiary Rights (Not) Distinguished

Depending on the size and organizational structure of the publisher, permissions and subsidiary rights may be handled by the same or separate departments.

Regardless of the publisher's structure, these two areas are sufficiently related so as to have blurred distinctions. Generally, "permissions" relates to the use of small amounts of material published by another pursuant to a license, sometimes managed by a collecting society such as Copyright Clearance Center, whereas "subsidiary rights" relates to the use of larger portions of material published by another pursuant to a license. Both have historically been considered "found money," to which authors often receive a 50 percent share.[1]

[B] Permissions

Clearing permission for reuse is often seen as a nuisance and burden for authors and publishers, but it is a burden of their own making. To fully exploit rights in a work internationally, in all media and in all languages as publishers desire, publishers must acquire sufficiently broad licenses in (i.e., "clear") the rights of all material incorporated in their works published by others. Unfortunately, the same publishers who seek such broad licenses generally refuse to grant such licenses themselves. The result is confusion and frustration.

The permissions forms in this chapter are variously denominated as "requests" and "grants." This distinction is artificial. The real difference among the forms is whether they are drafted by the licensor or by the licensee (some licensors will require licensees to use a standard "request" form, and some licensees draft their requests as "grants"). Thus, Forms 6.1, 6.2, 6.3, and 6.12, which have been drafted by potential licensees, all grant broad rights; most of the remainder of the forms up to Form 6.13, which are used by licensors, have narrower grants.

In addition to the various permission grant/request forms, this chapter contains a form letter for use where the author has a consent right for permissions grants, and a two-year photocopying license (photocopy requests are standard "permissions" matters, although multiyear licenses to photocopy may be considered either "permissions" or "subsidiary rights"). This chapter also contains author permissions guidelines[2] and information regarding one of many industry initiatives trying to simplify the permissions process, the *STM Guidelines*.[3] Readers are encouraged to visit *www.copyright.com*, the Web site for Copyright Clearance Center ("CCC"). Many publishers outsource permission granting to CCC.

Permissions forms relating specifically to artwork can be found at the end of the chapter, with Forms 6.19–6.22.

---

1 *See, e.g.,* Form 1.1, Clause 4(a)(v), and Form 1.2, Clause 5(a)(10), *supra.*

2 See § 6.02, *infra.*

3 *See* § 6.03, *infra.*

[C] Subsidiary Rights

In contrast to permissions agreements which, owing to the small amount of material copied and money involved, are usually only one or two pages long, subsidiary rights agreements may be extremely complex. For example, Form 6.17, the academic journal translation license agreement, addresses editorial boards, complicated trademark ownership issues, and the scope of permitted advertising.

This chapter contains one generic license agreement that can be adapted for most uses (Form 6.16) and two specific subsidiary rights agreements: the academic journal translation license agreement mentioned above (Form 6.17), and a foreign-language translation agreement for books (Form 6.18).

§ 6.02 Sample Author Permissions Policy

Most author agreements place the initial burden of clearing permissions on the authors.[4] Although publishers may check permission grants in the production process, it is generally impractical for the publisher to perform all of the clearance functions for all of its authors. This is particularly true because it is not always apparent from a manuscript which material requires permission.

The text that follows outlines a permissions policy that can be given to authors, either in an official style guide or on a publisher's Web site. The purposes are to explain the permissions process, emphasize its importance, and provide some useful guidance. It necessarily reflects the (fairly conservative) prejudices and risk tolerance of the publisher for whom it was originally drafted and should be carefully reviewed before use.

[A] Definition of a Copyright

As an author, you have two concerns with copyright law: as the copyright proprietor of your own work and as the user of copyrighted works by other authors.

Your manuscript is protected by copyright from the time of its creation. Copyright protection means that the copyright owner has the exclusive right to reproduce, distribute, or adapt a work for any purpose, with certain limitations as specified by U.S. copyright law. Currently, the term of a copyright (with a few exceptions) is the life of the author plus 70 years. When you sign an agreement to publish with a publisher, in addition to publishing the work,

---

4 One major exception to this rule is the clearance of image rights for fine arts publishing, which is often performed by the publisher.

the publisher will seek to maximize income for the work by licensing rights to other publishers and granting appropriate permissions to others to use excerpts from your work. Also, in consultation with you, the publisher may pursue infringements that come to our attention.

The second main concern with respect to copyright relates to use in your manuscript of material copyrighted by others. It is your responsibility to obtain permission to use others' material in your work. This document will assist you in meeting your obligations.

[B] Permission Requirements

Although the copyright statute and court cases call for a fact-based, case-by-case analysis to determine whether use of third-party copyrighted material requires permission, it is not realistic or practical to assume that all authors are aware of the legal parameters. Hence, industry practice has resulted in a consensus on guidelines reflected in this advice. These guidelines apply whether the source material is old or recent, as long as it is in copyright. They apply whether the source material or your work is in print or in electronic form, and whether you change from one format or medium to another. However, there are special issues that relate to new media, noted below.

[1] Material That Requires Permission

[a] Copyright

As a general guide, permission is more likely to be needed if the source material from which you copy is short or the excerpt you wish to use represents a significant portion of either the work in which you found it or the one in which you intend to use it. Also, any material that constitutes or represents the heart or key elements of the source material, such that your use could possibly serve as a substitute for the original, will also require permission. More specifically, you should always secure permission for:

- A single quotation or several shorter quotes from a full-length book, more than 300 words in toto.
- A single quotation of more than 50 words from a newspaper, magazine, or journal.
- Artwork, photographs, or forms, whether or not from a published source. Sometimes more than one permission is required for a photograph, for example, from the photographer and also from the creator of the underlying work shown in the photograph.

- Charts, tables, graphs, and other representations where, inevitably, you are using the entire representation, since the copyrighted features are complete in themselves and inherent in the whole work.
- Material that includes all or part of a poem or song lyric (even as little as one line), or the title of song.
- Computer representations, such as the depiction of results of research on computerized databases, the on-screen output of software, reproduction of Web pages, and Internet or other online screen shots may require permission, and we invite you to discuss these with your editor. (For small and insignificant portions, "fair use" may apply; see description below.) Please note, however, that if a Web site invites or authorizes copying and there is nothing to indicate it contains material that is original to others and therefore would require permission from the original source, then you do not need to get permission from the site.
- Any third-party software to be distributed as an electronic component with your book. Please contact your editor if you plan to include third-party software.
- Use of materials from other of our publications, and from your own previously published works. Note that although we will not charge you a fee on our account to use materials we published, we may collect a fee on behalf of the author and/or the artist, and you still need to insert a credit line in the text of your work. Contact our permissions department if you need permission for use of material we published.

[b] Other Permissions

In addition to the above guidelines to obtain copyright permission, you are also responsible for securing all other required clearances, including releases from privacy claims. For example:

- You may need releases for photographs of people, especially private citizens as opposed to public officials and public figures. This is particularly necessary if such material will be used on the cover or in part of the promotion of the work and does not specifically illustrate material in the text. You should contact your editor for the approved release form.

[2] Material That Does Not Require Permission

The copyright law recognizes the value of the free flow of information in society and encourages authors to expand knowledge by building on the work of those who wrote before them. Copyright does not prevent the use of facts or ideas, but only the author's expression which, as discussed below, is more than just the words or pictures. In addition, even when material is protected by copyright, there are situations where permission to reproduce is not required.

[a] Fair Use

"Fair use" is a legal term, so you should not assume it will permit your use of copyrighted material from other authors just because such use seems "fair" to you. Generally, a use will constitute "fair use" if minimal, commercially insignificant portions of an existing work are copied, quoted, or paraphrased for purposes of comment, criticism, illustration, or scholarship. In a commercial context, the doctrine of "fair use" is quite limited. If you are in doubt about whether your use of copyrighted material is a fair use, go ahead and request permission.

Even if your use constitutes "fair use," and you do not have to obtain permission, you should give proper credit to the original source in the form described below.

[b] Interviews

Generally, you can use material from an interview you conduct, including direct quotes, without securing a signed release if the circumstances and your notes clearly reveal that the source knew you were conducting an interview for possible publication and did not indicate an intent to restrict your use of the material. Otherwise, you should ask the interviewee to sign a release. You should contact your editor for the approved release form.

[c] Facts, Information, and Ideas

You may use facts and information you obtain from another work. However, this does not permit you to use the author's original literary expression, which includes, for example, more than just the words or the specific lines of a drawing. Copyright encompasses the format, structure, organization, sequence, and style of presentation as well as the sense or feeling of the original. When paraphrasing from another work, even if you do not have to request permission because you are paraphrasing a very limited portion of the source, always give credit to the original source. You do not need to credit well-known concepts or theories or strictly factual information, however, as long as they are expressed in your own way.

[d] Public Domain

You do not need to obtain permission for materials that are in the "public domain." This includes all official U.S. government publications (except for a few databases) as well as materials for which the copyright has expired. The copyright expiration date is often difficult to determine. It is safest to assume that anything copyrighted in this or the 20th century is still protected. Modern translations of older works are also protected, as are certain photographs and other portrayals of public domain images. Other materials may be in the public domain because they were published without a notice of copyright at a time when such notice was required to preserve copyright. Once again, this is difficult to determine. Some material is intentionally and explicitly made available to copy or use, such as "clip art." Clip art includes standard line drawings that are available in books and on disks and are classified by subject area (sports, animals, etc.) specifically for free use in other publications.

[C] Responsibility for Obtaining Permissions

Obtaining written permission to use copyrighted material is the author's responsibility. The author should use the written permissions request form described below. In a multi-author volume, the chapter authors must obtain permission to use copyrighted material in their chapters, and the volume editor is responsible for making sure that they have done so.

[D] When to Apply

Request permission as early as possible. Response time of from four to six weeks is not uncommon, and it can take much longer. Follow-up calls after a few weeks can help to avoid further delay, but there are often additional snags, such as unexpected fees, rejections, or people who are difficult to reach. Under the terms of your publishing agreement, you should submit all permissions to us along with your final manuscript. If this is not possible, you should advise your editor of any permissions requests not yet granted and when you expect to receive them. Since publication of this material in your work is contingent upon receiving permission, it's important to follow up with your editor on any problems, to avoid jeopardizing the scheduled publication date.

[E] To Whom to Apply

Send your written request to the permissions department of the publisher whose material you wish to use, regardless of who holds the copyright. Always check credit lines on the sources you use to see if the material is actually original or from another book. If the material is credited to another book, then request permission from the original publisher. If the publisher does not control the rights, your request should be referred to the appropriate party, but you may have to call and follow up. You need to obtain the author's approval only if the publisher instructs you to do so. Rights might also belong to illustrators, photographers, agencies, or corporations. In addition, rights can be sold or willed to others, so it can be difficult to track down the actual copyright holder. Publishers usually respond to requests for permission within a reasonable time. The need to consult the author or refer your request to another copyright owner may, however, extend the time required for granting permission. If you are unable to identify or locate the copyright holder, please contact your editor.

[F] The Permission Request Form

Use the attached permissions request form (e.g., Forms 6.1 and 6.2) to request permission to use third-party copyrighted material. Prepare it in quadruplicate: Retain one copy in your file, send one copy to your editor, and mail the other two to the copyright owner. Enclose a photocopy of the requested material with your request and make sure that your publisher also has a copy. If you wish to delete or edit portions of a selection, say so in the request.

[G] Permission Fees

Under the terms of our publishing agreement, the author (or contributor in a multi-author volume) is responsible for the payment of permission fees. Fees charged for reprinting copyrighted material must be agreed on, in each case, by the seller and buyer of the rights. Most large publishers have standard rates for various classes of books, but there is no generally accepted set of rates for all publishers. Many publishers do not charge fees at all for small uses, and other publishers are willing to negotiate fees. If rates seem unusually high, require a pro rata share of your royalties, or if the rights holder makes any other demands (such as credit on the cover or a large number of free books), consult your editor before you sign an agreement with the copyright owner. If you decide not to use copyrighted material because of a high fee after permission has been granted, you should inform the copyright holder to avoid being inadvertently billed.

[H] What to Do with Permissions Granted

When you send your manuscript to us, include copies of the permission letters, all related correspondence, and a permissions summary as described below. Retain duplicates of all these documents for your records. These documents become part of our permanent record, which is used, for example, in determining market rights and in work on future editions. Signed permission forms should be sent to your editor along with the final manuscript. Failure to do this may delay the publication of your book. If you are still waiting to get signed forms back at this point, you may have to consider dropping the material in question from the book.

[I] How to Create a Permissions Summary

The permissions summary is an aid to help keep track of your requests and the permissions granted. A permissions summary should include the material used; the source (including title, author/artist, copyright owner, copyright date, and required credit line); the date of the grant; the fee paid; and any territorial, format, language, or temporal restrictions on use. Please note that the standard permission request form asks for all rights, but the copyright holders may note limitations when they sign and return the form. It is important that we know about any limitations. You must notify your editor if the permission granted to you is restricted in any way. If the restriction limits our rights in any medium or format, term, territory, or language, it may be necessary to delete this material from your manuscript.

If the grantor of the permission is to receive one or more copies of your book, state the number and attach the grantor's address.

When you have all your permissions finalized, send a copy of the summary with your permission letters to your editor.

[J] How to Give Credit

Be scrupulous in giving credit for material used from someone else's work. Whether or not permission was needed for its use, do acknowledge all material taken from another work and make clear which portions of your work come from another source. Acknowledgment, however, is not a substitute for permission to use material. It is your responsibility to include all necessary credit lines in your manuscript before sending it to us. Credit lines may be inserted on the page where the borrowed material appears, or they may all be grouped together in the frontmatter of the book. In granting the permission, the copyright owner may specify the form of the location of the credit line, or both. Note the line at the bottom of the permissions request form where a credit line cane be specified. Follow such instructions regardless of the style and method of acknowledgment used in the other credit lines in your book. If the form and location have not been specified, check the copyright page of your source material for the style to use. Indicate first that the quote is being used with permission, for example:

> From Brown, *The Best Book in the World*, 4th Edition. Copyright © 2000 Publisher, Inc. Reprinted by permission of Publisher, Inc.

It is not necessary to include any material beyond the copyright notice as given in the above example; for example, you do not need to include reference to the statutory provision of U.S. law, even if it is reproduced on the grantor's copyright page, unless the grantor makes that specific request.

Generally, a figure is credited in its legend/caption, a table in a source note, and a quotation in an endnote. If most of your reprinted material comes from a single source or only a few sources, you may wish to acknowledge it collectively in the front of the book unless it's specified in the permission letter that the credit lines must appear with reprinted material. You should supply a separate list of credits for this material with your manuscript. Note that even when full acknowledgment is given elsewhere, the source of each item should normally be indicated (author, date) wherever the item occurs.

[K] Reasons for Clearing Permissions

There are two reasons for clearing permissions. The first is your status as an author: You will want other authors to respect the copyright in your book by getting permission, crediting your book, and paying appropriate fees when they use material from your book.

Second, if your published book includes material copyrighted by third parties for which you do not obtain permission, you could face legal action for copyright infringement. The copyright holder has recourse to several remedies through the courts, including suing for fees and damages. It is even possible that all copies of your book would be taken off sale immediately, impounded, or destroyed. It is in everyone's best interest that you take the time to apply for permissions.

[L] Permissions Checklist

The following checklist may help you organize your effort. (If you have further questions, be sure to ask your editor.)

- Make a list of all items for which permission may be required.
- If you need to go over any questionable items with your editor, do it early. If you encounter any legal issues, your editor will take advice from the Permissions Department as appropriate.
- If you suspect it may take time to locate the copyright holder, start early and call first rather than writing immediately. When you find the copyright holder, apply for written confirmation. If you are unable to identify or locate the copyright holder, make a file with any efforts you have made.
- Make four copies of the permission requests and of the material for which you have requested permission. Send two copies to the copyright holder and one to the publisher. Keep one for yourself.
- Four to six weeks after sending the letters, follow up with a phone call on any that have not been returned to you.

- When you receive a signed permission form, make a note of it on the permissions summary. If there are restrictions, contact your editor because such restrictions may make the inclusion of the material unacceptable.
- If the grantor requests complimentary copies of the book, provide us with the grantor's address. (Note that we will not provide an unusually high number of complimentary copies without prior approval).
- Check the signed form for any specific directions concerning format or positioning of credit lines and follow them.
- Add credit lines either to the manuscript as footnotes or source notes or to a separate legend in the manuscript, or compile a list of all credit lines for the frontmatter and include it in the manuscript.
- Keep copies of signed permission forms and send the originals to us with your final permissions summary.

§ 6.03 STM Permissions Guidelines

Permissions clearance can be a nuisance, A request that generates a small amount of revenue can generate an enormous amount of paperwork. The industry response to this issue on the customer side was to start the Copyright Clearance Center,[5] which provides transactional, copy-shop, and blanket institutional licenses. On the publisher-to-publisher side, efforts have been more fragmented. The following guidelines, promulgated by the International Association of Scientific, Technical & Medical Publishers ("STM"), are the results of the collaborative efforts of one industry segment to try to reduce the mutual burden of permissions clearance. The *STM Guidelines* are also proof, however, that the publishing industry still needs to move forward on issues such as, *inter alia*, electronic permissions.

[A] Permissions Guidelines[6]

These Guidelines concern the granting of permission to re-use limited amounts of material from published works in subsequent print and electronic publications. The Guidelines set out general principles for working practice based upon historical practice, common decency and fairness. Adherence to the Guidelines is purely

---

5 *See* www.copyright.com. *See also* Mark A. Fischer, E. Gabriel Perle and John Taylor Williams, *Perle and Williams on Publishing Law*, § 2.07[A] (3d ed., Aspen L. & Bus. 2001). (*See* Forms 3.20–3.24).

6 Copyright © 2003 by the International Association of Scientific, Technical and Medical Publishers. Reprinted with permission.

Permission to Make Print or Electronic Library Archival Back-up Copy or to Lend Electronic Works to Library Patrons

[date]
[address]
We are in receipt of your letter dated _____ requesting permission to make one copy of the book titled _____.

We grant you permission to make one photocopy of this book based on the fact that the book is out of print and unavailable for purchase.

OR

We have no objection to your request dated [date] to make one back-up copy of the computer disk(s) accompanying [author/title], for the purpose of loaning to your patrons, provided that the back-up copy is labeled with an appropriate copyright notice (as shown below) and your patrons understand that they may not duplicate this material.

Credit must include the following components: Title, author(s) and/or editor(s), Copyright © (year and owner). Reprinted by permission of Publisher, Inc.

OR

We are in receipt of your letter dated _____ to loan to your patrons the work titled _____.

We have no objection to your lending the material requested in accordance with your library's policies, and under the terms of the end-user license that accompanies the work.

OR

We are in receipt of your letter dated [date], requesting permission to make one back-up copy of the software which accompanies the book titled [title].

We grant you permission to make one copy of this software, based on the fact that the book/software will be placed in the lending library of [institution].

OR

We have no objection to your request dated [date] to make a back up electronic copy of the work entitled [title] by [author] for access solely on terminals located within the library. No copyright notices may be modified or obscured in the making of that copy.

ALWAYS

The license set forth herein is personal to you.
Sincerely,
[name]
[title]
[phone number]
[fax number]

Two-Year Photocopy License with Instructions

Two-Year Photocopy License with Instructions

[*license date*]

Invoice #

[*first name*]
[*last name*]
[*company*]
[*street*]
[*city*], [*state*] [*zip code*]
VIA FACSIMILE TO: [*fax*]

Dear [*greeting*] [*last name*]:

In response to your [*request date*] letter, we grant permissions to [photocopy/post on electronic reserves] the material requested for educational use for 2 years beginning with the semester _____ at [*institution*] on the following terms:

Course	Professor	Ref. #	Material Requested	ISBN	Price per copy
[*course*]	[*professor*]	[*reference*]	[*author*]/ [*title*], pages [*pages*]	[*ISBN*]	$[*price per copy fee*]

1. You must credit our work on each photocopy as follows: Book/journal Title, author/editor, Copyright © (year and owner). Reprinted by permission of Publisher, Inc.

OR

Appropriate credit to our publication must appear be used as follows: Title, volume number, issue number, year (e.g., Vol. 1, No. 1, 20__), page numbers. Copyright © (year) Actual Copyright Owner. Reprinted by permission of Publisher, Inc.

2. Complete the applicable box below. Remit payment and a copy of this License to: Permissions Dept., Publisher, Inc., 16 Mill Road, Austerlitz, NY 12321 within 30 days of the end of each semester. Include our Invoice # on the check stub. (Our Tax ID number is: _____).

3.   Please sign and return a copy of the License within 30 days of the License Date, or, check off here to decline the License. We may terminate this License anytime if you fail to meet the conditions set forth above.

4.   This license is not transferable.

Sincerely,   **ACCEPTED:**

Permissions Department   _____

SPRING 20__	FALL 20__	SPRING 20__	FALL 20__
No. of students:	No. of students:	No. of students:	No. of students:
_____	_____	_____	_____
Enclosed Fee:	Enclosed Fee:	Enclosed Fee:	Enclosed Fee:
$_____	$_____	$_____	$_____

Additional boxes are provided below in case you wish to make copies for alternate semester/quarter during the period of this license.

Semester:	Semester:	Semester:	Semester:
No. of students:	No. of students:	No. of students:	No. of students:
_____	_____	_____	_____
Enclosed Fee:	Enclosed Fee:	Enclosed Fee:	Enclosed Fee:
$_____	$_____	$_____	$_____

Instructions for How to Use the Two-Year Photocopying License

In response to your recent request, the enclosed Two-Year Photocopying License is designed to simplify the permissions process. This license permits you to make as many copies as necessary of the requested material for the specified course each semester during a two-year period. To help you understand the terms and procedure for payment, please read the following instructions.

Instructions

1.   The license is also your invoice. The price per student of the material requested appears below the signature line on the license. To complete the invoice, multiply the price student by the number of students for the particular semester and write the total amount in the appropriate box.

2. Return a copy of the license with payment for each semester you use the material. You have 30 days from the end of the semester to make payment. **If no copies are made for a particular semester, return the license and indicate none were made.**

3. Send payments in U.S. Dollars to Permissions, Publisher, Inc., 1313 Mockingbird Lane, New York, NY 10027, or use the credit card payment information box. Include the invoice number on your check stub.

4. As most courses run on either a Fall/Spring or Winter/Summer cycle, the license is designed for such courses, as well as any for additional semesters during the two years.

5. If you are only using the material for one semester, please so indicate on the invoice. Most of our titles are licensed to the Copyright Clearance Center, Inc. (CCC) for use in their Academic Permissions Service. You may obtain permission from the CCC for a single semester use. The Customer Relations Department of the CCC can be reached at 222 Rosewood Dr., Danvers, MA 01923, phone: 978-750-8400, fax: (508) 750-4470.

Author Consent Letter Where Author Has Permissions Approval Right

Author Consent Letter

[*author name and address*]
RE: Title

Dear Author:

Please note the enclosed request from [*requestor's name*] to republish excerpts from your book, _____ in the forthcoming book entitled [*title of request-or's work*] to be published by [*requestor's publisher*] in [*requestor's projected publication date*].

Pursuant to our agreement, we are contacting you before we grant permission to use material from your book. So please, after reviewing the enclosed material, let us know if you have any objections to its use as outlined in the request. ***Please fax your reply to me at*** _____. If you have any questions and/or need further information please do not hesitate to call me at

_____.

As always, our permission license will require the licensee to include the following credit to the work: [*Title*], [*Edition*] by [*Author*], Copyright © [*Year*] [*Name*]. Reprinted by permission of the Publisher.

I thank you in advance for your consideration in this matter and look forward to your reply.

Sincerely,

FORM 6.16

Simple Nonexclusive Copyright License

All licenses have common elements. They identify (1) the work, (2) the licensed uses, (3) restrictions on use, (4) the territory, and (5) the duration. In addition, they often contain warranties of noninfringement, choice of law, and other boilerplate clauses. The following agreement, prepared by William M. Hart of the New York office of Proskauer Rose, LLP, provides the basics and is adaptable for most simple situations.

Simple Nonexclusive Copyright License

License

This license (the "License"), is granted by _____ (the "Licensor") to _____ (the "Licensee") as of the _____ day of _____ 20__, on the following terms:

1.   THE WORK. The work (the "Work") subject to this license is "___" performed by/written by _____.

2.   THE USE. Licensee's use (the "Use") covered by this License is _____.

3.   TERRITORY. The "Territory" covered hereby is _____.

4.   LICENSE TO _____. In consideration of the sum of _____ ($___.00), Licensor hereby grants to Licensee the nonexclusive right, license, privilege, and authority to [*copy, distribute, record, use, publicly perform, display, create a derivative work, etc.*] the Work in the Territory.

5.   LICENSE LIMITED TO EXPRESS PROVISIONS HEREIN STATED. This License does not authorize or permit any use of the Work not expressly set forth herein.

6.   DURATION OF LICENSE. This License in its entirety will be for _____ from the date hereof.

7.   WARRANTY. Licensor warrants and represents that it is the owner of and/or authorized agent for one hundred percent (100%) of the rights in the Work, that it has the full right and authority to enter into this License and grant the rights herein described; that the Work is original and does not and will not constitute an infringement of any copyright; that the use by Licensee of the Work is expressly authorized herein and will not infringe upon or violate the rights of any third party; no other rights, permission or consent are necessary for Licensee's use of the Work; and no fees, royalties, or reuse payments of any kind will be due in connection with the rights granted to Licensee hereunder, other than as provided in Paragraph 4 above. Licensor agrees to indemnify and hold harmless Licensee (and its employees, directors, officers, shareholders, and agents) from any claim, loss, liability, damage or expense (including reasonable attorneys' fees) arising out of any claim, lawsuit or demand which is inconsistent with the warranties, covenants, and representations herein.

8.   NONEXCLUSIVE LICENSE. All rights granted hereunder to Licensee are granted on a nonexclusive basis.

9.   TRANSFERS, ASSIGNMENTS, ETC. This License is binding upon and will inure to the benefit of the respective successors, licensees, heirs, administrators, and assigns of the parties hereto.

10. APPLICABLE LAW. This License is governed by the laws and in the state and federal courts of the State of New York and both parties waive any objections to the personal jurisdiction and venue of such courts.

IN WITNESS WHEREOF, the parties have set their hands and seals to the foregoing as of the day and year first set forth above.

LICENSOR   LICENSEE

By: _____   By: _____

Name: _____   Name: _____

Title: _____   Title: _____

Academic Journal Translation License Agreement

When a party is contemplating a license of translation rights for an academic journal, issues of content integrity, which are important in any translation agreement, are of paramount concern. For medical journals, mistakes can cause everything from embarrassment to death. Accordingly, many translation licenses for such publications, like the one below, require that the translations have their own editorial boards and a designated expert or editor to review the translation for accuracy (*see* Clause 2). Also, when a third party sponsors the translations, as is often the case for translated medical journals, the publisher needs to retain the right to approve any sponsor. Otherwise, the publication could be sponsored by a company that discredits the journal.

License Agreement

AGREEMENT dated as of _____, 20__ between Publisher, Inc., a _____ Corporation located at _____ ("Publisher") and _____, a _____ Corporation located at _____ ("Licensee").

WITNESSETH:

WHEREAS, Publisher is the publisher and owner of all rights in a proprietary journal entitled _____ (the "Journal"), which is currently published in the English language; and

WHEREAS, Licensee is the publisher of scientific journals in the language, including journals in translation, and is desirous of publishing a language translation of the Journal (the "Translation") under the title on a bi-monthly basis, which will contain full text _____ language translations of selected articles from the Journal, _____ language abstracts of articles published in the Journal, and limited original material in _____ on the terms set forth herein; and

WHEREAS, Publisher wants to license to Licensee the limited exclusive right to translate, publish and distribute up to _____ copies of each bimonthly issue of the Translation in _____;

NOW THEREFORE, the parties agree as follows:

1. Grant of Rights

Publisher hereby licenses to Licensee, for the Term as set forth in Paragraph 4 below, the exclusive right to translate into _____ selected articles from all issues of the Journal published in English during the Term (i.e., Volume ___ Issue ___ through Volume __ Issue __) and to publish and distribute up to _____ copies of each issue of the Translation in print only on a bi-monthly basis under the title _____. Licensee may not change the title without Publisher's prior written consent. The Translation shall include either full text _____ language translations or abstracts for each article originally appearing in the Journal, and limited original material as set forth below. Licensee shall chose which articles will be fully translated and which articles will be abstracted. Licensee may not publish, distribute or translate for the Translation abstracts of articles originally appearing in other journals.

2. Editorial Board

(a)   The translation of articles and abstracts, creation of original material in _____, and preparation of the Translation shall be supervised by Professor _____ and an editorial board comprising experts in the field of _____ (collectively, the "Editorial Board"). Licensee shall be responsible for any and all contractual relations relating to the Editorial Board, including Professor _____, and shall hold Publisher harmless for all costs and expenses, including reasonable attorneys' fees, incurred with respect to the Editorial Board. The Translation shall be of high quality and commensurate with the quality of the Journal, the material contained therein, and other high quality translation journals. In addition to translations and abstracts of material from the Journal, the Translation may include an editorial written by a member of the Editorial Board to introduce each issue, and may also include approximately three to four pages of text at the end of each issue which will be written by members of the Editorial Board who will comment on. In addition, there may be an advertisement for _____ on the fourth cover of each issue. No other material will be included in the Translation without prior written consent of Publisher.

(b)   Publisher shall have the right but not the obligation to appoint its own medical expert fluent in _____ to review the quality and technical accuracy of the Translation, and said expert's proposed changes, if any, must be incorporated into the Translation.

(c)   Publisher will send, when available, uncorrected page proofs of each issue of the Journal, with original art for halftones, without charge to Licensee.

3. Proprietary Rights

(a)   Publisher retains all right, title and interest in and to Journal and all material contained therein subject only to the rights specifically licensed herein by Publisher to Licensee (including without limitation all proprietary rights in the Journal). Licensee shall not use Journal except as contemplated in this Agreement. Licensee acknowledges that its translation of material from the Journal will not affect Publisher's continued and absolute ownership of Journal or its right to distribute Journal in any form or media of expression worldwide, or its right to sublicense the same. Nothing herein shall prevent Publisher from changing the frequency of the Journal. Nothing herein shall restrict Publisher from granting individual language permissions and translation rights for material appearing in the Journal on a case-by-case basis to third parties.

(b)The Translation shall bear a copyright notice in conformity with the United States Copyright Act and the Universal Copyright Convention and Licensee shall take all steps necessary or appropriate to protect the copyright in the Translation under _____ law and to secure the benefits of copyright protection under all international copyright conventions and agreements that are available for such protection.

(c)   For articles which are fully translated, as opposed to abstracted, the Translation will include adequate indices, halftones, tables and other illustrations if they are a part of the original text.

(d)   The Translation will be generally comparable in quality and appearance to the original, with such reasonable variations as are necessary for local printing requirements. The cover shall have a mutually agreed upon appearance. The current appearance of the cover of the Translation must be modified as shown on the attached Schedule A, or in such other manner as Publisher may designate. Licensee must acquire a new ISSN number for the Translation.

(e)   All ISSN numbers, trade names, trademarks, service marks and attendant goodwill related thereto now owned by Publisher shall remain its sole property and all benefits accruing from their use shall inure solely to the benefit of Publisher. Publisher shall also own the name of the Translation, the ISSN number, and all the goodwill related thereto. Licensee may not use the name of the Journal, or the trademarks or colophon of Publisher for any reason without the prior written approval of Publisher.

(f)   Publisher shall have the right to review and approve any and all advertising or promotional copy which uses its name, or the trademarks or colophon of Publisher or the Journal title. Publisher shall have ten (10) business days from receipt of any such material to approve or reject it. If Publisher does not reject any such material within the ten (10) day period, approval shall be deemed granted.

(g)   The Translation may not be sponsored by any party other than _____ without the prior written consent of Publisher.

4. Term and Termination

The Term of this Agreement shall be two (2) years. Thereafter, this Agreement may renew for additional Terms of one (1) year upon the prior written agreement of the parties. In the event either party fails to comply with any of the terms or conditions of this Agreement, and such failure is not cured within thirty (30) days of written notice by the non-breaching party, the non-breaching party shall have the right to terminate this Agreement. This Agreement may also be terminated early by either party in the event that the other party is declared bankrupt or enters into voluntary or involuntary bankruptcy or liquidation proceedings.

5. Fees

(a)   Licensee shall pay to Publisher a fee of $ _____ (_____ dollars) for the first two (2) year Term of this Agreement. Licensee shall pay to Publisher one-half ($^1/_2$) of this fee (i.e., $ _____) upon the signing of this Agreement, and the remainder shall be paid to Publisher by _____.

(b)   Licensee shall give to Publisher without charge up to five (5) complete subscriptions to the Translation, to be sent to the parties designated by Publisher.

6. Warranties

(a)   Licensee warrants and represents that: (i) Licensee has the right to enter into this Agreement; (ii) the Translation will be original except for excerpts and illustrations that are in the public domain or are published with the written permission of the copyright owner, and shall contain no libelous or unlawful material, no instructions that may cause harm or injury and will not infringe upon or violate any copyright, trademark, trade secret or other right or the privacy of others; (iii) in marketing the Translation, Licensee will obey all applicable laws and regulations; (iv) the Translation will contain no false, misleading, or illegal advertising; (v) the Translation will be complete and accurate, with such modifications of the original text as are necessary to achieve a competent and idiomatic translation without changing the meaning or otherwise materially altering the original text unless Publisher has given its prior written permission for such alterations; and (vi) all statements to be asserted as fact in the Translation will either be true or based upon generally accepted professional research practices. Licensee agrees to indemnify and hold Publisher harmless against all liability and expense, including reasonable attorneys' fees, arising out of any breach or alleged breach of these warranties. The foregoing shall not apply to material in the English-language version Journal, but shall only apply to the translation work itself or any work added to the Translation that did not originally appear in the English-language version of the Journal.

(b)   Each party shall promptly notify the other of any claim against either which, if sustained, would constitute a breach of Licensee's warranties.

Publisher shall have the right to defend such claim, action or proceeding with counsel of its own choice and to settle any such claim. Licensee shall fully cooperate with Publisher in such defense and may join in such defense with counsel of Licensee's selection, at Licensee's expense.

(c)   The provisions of this Paragraph 6 shall survive termination of this Agreement for any reason.

7. General

(a)   The parties to this Agreement shall be independent contractors and nothing in this Agreement shall be deemed to create an agency, joint venture, or partnership between Publisher and Licensee.

(b)   Licensee may not assign this Agreement without the prior written consent of Publisher. Notwithstanding the foregoing, consent is not required for an assignment to an affiliated entity. Subject to the foregoing, this Agreement shall inure to the benefit of the successors, administrators, and permitted assigns of the parties.

(c)   All notices to be given by either party hereunder shall be in writing in the English language and shall be sent to Licensee at the Licensee's address as it is set forth in this Agreement unless such address has been changed by proper written notice, or if to Publisher, addressed to the attention of _____.

(d)   This Agreement shall not be subject to change or modification in whole or in part, unless in writing signed by both parties.

(e)   No waiver of any term or condition of this Agreement or of any part thereof shall be deemed a waiver of any other term or condition of this Agreement or of any breach of this Agreement or any part thereof.

(f)   In the event any part or provision of this Agreement is deemed unenforceable, void or voidable, the remainder of this Agreement shall remain in effect.

(g)   This Agreement shall be construed and interpreted pursuant to the laws of the State of New York applicable to contracts wholly entered into and performed in the State of New York. Any legal action, suit or proceeding arising out of or relating to this Agreement or the breach thereof shall be instituted in a court of competent jurisdiction in New York County and each party hereby consents and submits to the personal jurisdiction of such court, waives any objection to venue in such court and consents to service of process by registered or certified mail, return receipt requested, at the last known address of such party.

IN WITNESS WHEREOF, the parties have executed this Agreement through their duly authorized representatives as of the day and year first above written.

Licensee   **Publisher, Inc.**

By: _____   By: _____
Name: _____   Name: _____
Title: _____   Title: _____

Foreign-Language Translation
Agreement—Print Only[7]

The following is a standard subsidiary rights agreement for a foreign-language version of a book. The language is tightly drafted, and each clause should be carefully read before use. It is worth noting the last paragraph of Clause 1(d), which states "[t]his grant of rights shall not apply to any text, illustrations or supplemental material from other sources that may be incorporated in the original Work." This sentence is illustrative of the difficulties presented with clearing permissions. As can be seen in this chapter, permissions to use quotations, excerpts, and artwork are often limited to single languages and editions. The publishers granting permissions only want to grant limited rights, and the publishers receiving permissions do not want to pay extra to clear rights for editions they might not use, even though ultimately, all publishers are faced with this issue from both sides. As a result, in this agreement, the rights holder places the burden of re-clearing the rights on the licensee, thereby absolving itself from responsibility. Unfortunately, this also complicates the license and, as a result, renders the publisher's works somewhat less salable.

Foreign-Language License Agreement

AGREEMENT made this _____ day of _____, 20 ____ between Rights, Inc., of ("Rights Holder"), and _____, of _____ (hereinafter called the "Publisher").

WITNESSETH

1. Rights Holder grants to Publisher the following *exclusive* rights, subject to the terms hereof and subject further to any compulsory license which may be granted pursuant to the laws of any nation:

(a) To prepare a _____ language translation (the "Translation") of the work entitled _____, ___ Edition, by _____ (the "Work");

(b) To print, publish, and sell the Translation in print form in the following territory: _____.

---

7 *See* Mark A. Fischer, E. Gabriel Perle and John Taylor Williams, *Perle and Williams on Publishing Law*, § 2.10[C] (3d ed., Aspen L. & Bus. 2001).

(c)   To license others to reprint the Translation for book club distribution, newspaper or magazine serialization or for use of portions thereof in an anthology or other collective work; provided however, that any such license shall be subject to Rights Holder's prior written approval in every case, which approval shall not be unreasonably withheld. All such licenses shall expressly provide that they are subject to any territorial restriction set forth above in Paragraph (1b). All payments received by Publisher for any such license shall be divided equally between Publisher and Rights Holder with the exception of first serial which shall be divided: 60% to Rights Holder; 40% to Publisher. Publisher shall account to Rights Holder for such payments according to the schedule set forth in Paragraph 5 below.

(d)   This grant of rights shall not apply to any text, illustrations or supplemental material from other sources that may be incorporated in the original Work; however, the Publisher may substitute therefor (with Rights Holder's prior written permission, which shall not be unreasonably withheld) other high-quality textual, illustrative or supplemental material for which Publisher has obtained the necessary rights, and which is relevant and in all other ways suitable for incorporation in the Translation. All rights now existing or which here after come into existence and which are not specifically granted to Publisher in this Agreement are hereby reserved by Rights Holder.

2.   Publisher shall prepare a Translation that is complete and accurate, with such modifications of the original text as are necessary to achieve a competent and idiomatic translation into _____ without changing the meaning or otherwise materially altering the original text (unless Rights Holder has given its prior written permission for such alteration). The Translation shall include adequate indices and tables if they are a part of the original Work.

3.   Publisher shall, at its own expense, prepare, print and publish the Translation within two years of the date of this Agreement. On or before the date of first publication of the Translation, Publisher shall forward to Rights Holder (i) _____ free copies of the Translation; and (ii) a statement in the English language showing the total number of copies printed and Publisher's catalog retail price. The foregoing statement and at least one free copy shall be sent to Rights Holder by registered airmail. If Publisher shall fail to comply with any of the provisions of Paragraph 3, the rights herein granted to Publisher shall revert to Rights Holder upon Rights Holder's written notice to Publisher, this Agreement shall terminate upon such notice, and Rights Holder shall be entitled to retain any payments theretofore made by Publisher.

4.   In consideration of the rights herein granted, Publisher shall make the following advance and royalty payments to Rights Holder in United States Dollars in New York, New York, U.S.A.:

_____

_____.

5.   Publisher shall render accounts of sales of the translation to Rights Holder as follows:

(a)   Each account shall be delivered to Rights Holder within six weeks following the termination of Publisher's standard accounting period (which shall be no less frequently than annually), together with payment of the amount shown to be due thereon. Each account shall be in the English language and shall include the total number of copies printed, Publisher's catalog retail price, the number of copies sold during accounting period, and the number of copies remaining on hand. Publisher shall also provide Rights Holder with all other relevant information and documentation which Rights Holder may reasonably require. Rights Holder shall have the right on reasonable notice to examine Publisher's relevant books and records in order to verify such accounts.

(b)   If any such inspection or audit amounts owed to Rights Holder are more than the amount actually paid, Publisher shall immediately pay any deficiency. In addition, if such deficiency is five (5) percent or more, Publisher shall immediately pay Rights Holder the costs Rights Holder incurs in connection with the inspection of audit including attorney and accountant fees.

(c)   Unless Publisher is hereafter otherwise notified in writing, all payments, statements, accounts, publications, documents and notices which Publisher is required to forward or deliver to Rights Holder pursuant to the terms of this Agreement shall be addressed to Rights Holder at the address herein above stated and marked to the attention of the Director, Subsidiary Rights.

6. The Publisher Undertakes:

(a)   To take all steps as may be necessary or appropriate to protect the copyright in the Translation under law and to secure the benefits of copyright protection under all international copyright conventions and agreements that are available for such protection;

(b)   To place notice of copyright the Translation in the name of
_____;

(c)   To print the following information on the title page, or on the reverse side thereof, in every copy of the Translation: (i) the English language title of the original Work; (ii) any acknowledgments appearing in the original Work; (iii) the copyright notice appearing in the original Work; and (iv) the following notice: "All Rights Reserved. Authorized translation from the English language edition published by Rights, Inc.";

(d)   To give due prominence to the name(s) of the author(s) on the title page and on the binding of every copy of the Translation and in all advertisements for the Translation, and shall require its permitted licensees to do the same; and

(e)   In addition to Publisher's own logo, Publisher shall print the Rights Holder's logo in the same typeface and design as it appears on the original Work, on the bottom left or right side of the front cover and on the spine of every copy of the Translation. In connection therewith, Publisher acknowledges that Rights, Inc., Rights Holder's logo and any book and series titles (collectively referred to as the "Marks") are the sole and exclusive property of Rights Holder. Rights Holder reserves all rights, including without limitation all worldwide trademark and service mark rights, in the Marks. Publisher shall take no action which shall be adverse to Rights Holder's exclusive rights in the Marks.

7.   Publisher shall absolve and hold Rights Holder and its successors and assigns free and harmless from any claim of whatsoever nature arising from the preparation, printing, publication and sale of the Translation or from the exercise of any other rights granted herein, except for any claim of copyright infringement by the original Work.

Publisher shall promptly notify Rights Holder in the event that Publisher becomes aware of any infringement of the proprietary rights in the Translation or the original Work, including but not limited to the existence of any pirated translation or other edition, any unauthorized copies or any other alleged or potential infringement. Rights Holder shall have the sole and exclusive right, but not the obligation, to pursue a claim for any such infringement in such manner as it deems appropriate, and Publisher agrees to reasonably cooperate with Rights Holder in connection therewith.

8.   The rights herein granted apply only to the edition of the Work referred to in Paragraph 1 above. Notwithstanding the foregoing, and provided that Publisher is in full compliance with all the terms and conditions of this Agreement, Publisher shall have the first option to negotiate with Rights Holder for the acquisition of translation rights to the next edition of the Work on mutually agreeable terms, provided Rights Holder controls such rights and provided further that Rights Holder wishes to license such rights. If Publisher and Rights Holder have not agreed upon such terms for such acquisition within sixty (60) days after notice from Rights Holder to the Publisher offering the translation rights, then Rights Holder shall be free to offer such rights to others.

9. The Agreement shall be valid for seven (7) years from the date of the Agreement and automatically extended for terms of one year each, unless one month before the expiration of the seven (7) year period, or of one of the subsequent one year terms, either party notifies the other in writing of its decision to terminate the Agreement.

(a)   Upon the effective date of termination, Publisher's right to manufacture additional copies of the Translation shall terminate and all rights shall revert subject to licenses previously granted; provided however, that Publisher shall have the right to continue to distribute, advertise and sell copies of the Translation then existing, subject to Publisher's royalty obligations in respect thereof, for a period of one (1) year.

(b)   Publisher shall notify Rights Holder in the event the Translation goes out of print. If Publisher fails to reprint within six months after the Translation goes out of print, or if Publisher should be declared bankrupt or become insolvent or if it should violate any of the terms of this Agreement and not rectify such violation within thirty (30) days following receipt of written notice from Rights Holder to do so, all rights herein granted to Publisher shall revert to Rights Holder and this Agreement shall forthwith terminate, without prejudice, however, to any claims which Rights Holder may have against Publisher.

10. Publisher shall not remainder copies of the Translation at or below cost within a period of four years from the date of Publisher's first publication of the Translation.

11. This Agreement shall not become effective unless an executed copy thereof and the advance payment herein above specified are received by Rights Holder not later than _____.

12. Publisher shall not assign, transfer or in any way encumber this Agreement or Publisher's rights and obligations here under without Rights Holder's prior written consent.

13. If the Publisher is acquired by another publishing company then this Agreement shall terminate in accordance with Paragraph 9(a) above. In such event, Rights Holder shall have the right to acquire the Publisher's (1) remaining inventory and printing plates at the Publisher's cost and (2) copyright in the Publisher's Translation for a mutually agreed upon price.

14. This Agreement may not be modified except by an instrument in writing signed by both Rights Holder and Publisher.

15. This Agreement shall be construed and interpreted under and in accordance with the laws of the State of New York in the United States of America. Any legal action, suit or proceeding arising out of or relating to this Agreement or the breach thereof shall be instituted in a court of competent jurisdiction in New York County in the State of New York in the United States of America and each party hereby consents and submits to the personal jurisdiction of such court, waives any objection to venue in such court and consents to service of process by registered or certified mail, return receipt requested, at the last known address of such party.

Rights, Inc.

By: _____

Name: _____

Title: _____

Publisher

By: _____

Name: _____

Title: _____

Form 6.19

Sample Permission Letter for the Use of Artwork in a Book

Republication of fine art requires special attention to issues such as integrity of the image. The following form, used with permission from the Visual Artists and Galleries Association, Inc. (VAGA),[8] is designed specifically for visual images.

Permission Letter

Dear:

One-time, nonexclusive [country and language] language rights are granted to reproduce [title and year image created] by [artist name] in the forthcoming [hard or soft cover] printed book titled [title of book], to be published in [year]. Reproduction will be in [color or black and white] and [¼, ½, ¾, full, chapter opener] page in size. **Print run is limited to** [number of copies] **copies**.

These rights are limited to the specific media and number of copies detailed above. This means that if additional copies or new editions are to be printed/ published in the media above, or new versions created in any other media whatsoever, including, but not limited to, electronic and multimedia, then VAGA's prior written authorization MUST be obtained. No rights are granted for distribution through databases. All reproductions must be full-toned black and white or full color and may not be reproduced on colored paper stock. There shall be no alteration of the image, including, but not limited to, cropping, overprinting and bleeding off the page.

Permission is given on condition that the following copyright credit line appear below or adjacent to the image along with the name of artist, title, year, size, media and owner (if applicable). The copyright credit line listed below must appear with the image and may not be placed solely on a separate credit page.

Failure to insert the proper copyright credit line and caption information as set forth herein shall result, at VAGA's option, in either a revocation of this license or a 100% surcharge on the invoiced amount.

Art © [name of artist] /Licensed by VAGA, New York, NY

Upon publication [number of] copy(ies) of the book shall be forwarded to VAGA.

An invoice (#) is enclosed for this use.

Sincerely,

encl.

---

8 Copyright © 2007 VAGA, Inc. Reprinted with permission.

Please sign below and return by fax or mail to VAGA to confirm your receipt and acceptance of the above terms and requirements. Failure to sign and return a copy of this agreement prior to the reproduction of the above-mentioned work(s) of art shall cause such reproduction(s) to be unauthorized and an infringement of the artists' rights. Notwithstanding the requirement to countersign this document, client's payment of the attached invoice shall constitute acknowledgement and acceptance of the terms herein.

By (Signature): _____ Print Name: _____

Form 6.20

Model Release with Optional Minor Language[9]

Release
For valuable consideration herein acknowledged as received, I hereby grant as follows:

1. I irrevocably grant to _____ ("Photographer") and its licensees, successors, agents and assigns the right to use, publish and copyright my name, voice, picture, portrait and likeness in any and all media and for any use whatsoever, including without limitation, art, stock, advertising, trade and promotion, in perpetuity. I agree that all photographs of me are owned by the Photographer and he/she may copyright material containing same. If I should receive any print, negative or other copy thereof, I shall not authorize its use by anyone else.

2. I agree that no advertisement, product or other material need be submitted to me for any further approval and the Photographer, its licensees, successors, agents and assigns shall be without liability to me for any distortion or illusionary effect or adverse result to me on account of the publication, distribution or broadcast of my picture, portrait or likeness. I consent to the use of my name or a fictitious name, and any print material in conjunction with the photograph.

3. I release, discharge and agree to save harmless the Photographer and his/her licensees, successors, agents and assigns from any liability arising out of or in connection with the use of the photographs, including any and all claims for libel and or and invasion of privacy or publicity.

4. I hereby warrant that I am of full age and have every right to contract in my own name in the above regard. I state further that I have read the above authorization, release and agreement, prior to its execution, and that I am fully familiar with the contents thereof.

9 Copyright © 2007 PACA, Inc. Reprinted with permission.

5. This release takes precedence over any release signed at the time of the job with exception of contracts and agency releases that contain the same information herein.

Dated:

_____(L.S.)

Signature

_____

Name

_____

(Address)

_____

(Phone)

_____

(Date of Birth)

_____

(Witness)

If model is not yet twenty-one (21) years old, complete the following form:

I, the undersigned, hereby warrant that I am the parent or guardian of the above named model, a minor, and have full authority to authorize the above Release which I have read and approved. I hereby release and agree to indemnify the licensed parties and their respective successors and assigns, from and against any and all liability arising out of the exercise of the rights granted by the above Release.

_____

Signature of Parent or Guardian

_____

Address

_____

Property Release[10]

Property releases are controversial. In general, property does not have "privacy rights," and a release is not needed to photograph and republish a building, at least not one visible from a public space.[11] This has not stopped an increasing number of spurious claims from parties who have registered trademarks comprising images of buildings,[12] or who have registered images of buildings for copyright, and some photographers and publishers will seek to clear the use of images of buildings to avoid such claims. Others will consciously not seek permission because they view the practice of clearing rights in buildings as the first step in limiting the rights of parties to make editorial use of such images.

For property that is not publicly visible, property releases are more appropriate. Such a use implicates the owner's rights of privacy. For example, if the photograph requires trespass on an individual's property or discloses the contents of an individual's home, then that person has a legitimate privacy interest. By having that person sign a property release, those claims are waived. Additionally, because the Copyright Act only exempts from infringement images of a building "located in or ordinarily visible from a public space,"[13] the architect's permission may also be required.[14] Note however that the form below assumes that the building owner has the right to authorize the taking of the photographs.

Property Release

For good and valuable consideration herein acknowledged as received, the undersigned being the legal owner of, or having the right to permit the taking and use of photographs of certain property designated as _____ does grant to _____, his agents or assigns, the full rights to use such photographs and copyright same, in advertising, trade or for any purpose.

I also consent to the use of any printed matter in conjunction therewith.

I hereby waive any right that I may have to inspect or approve the finished product or products or the advertising copy or printed matter that may be used in connection therewith or the use to which it may be applied.

I hereby release, discharge and agree to save harmless, _____, his legal representatives or assigns, and all persons acting under his permission

---

10 Copyright © 2007 PACA, Inc. Reprinted with permission.

11 17 U.S.C. Sec. 120(a).

12 *See, e.g.*, Rock and Roll Hall of Fame v. Gentile Prods., 134 F. 3d. 759 (6th Cir. 1998).

13 17 U.S.C. Sec. 120(a).

14 17 U.S.C. Sec. 102.

or authority or those for whom he is acting, from any liability by virtue of any blurring, distortion, alteration, optical illusion, or use in composite form, whether intentional or otherwise, that may occur or be produced by the taking of said picture or in any subsequent processing thereof, as well as any publication thereof even though it may subject me to ridicule, scandal, reproach, scorn and indignity.

I hereby warrant that I am of full age and have every right to contract in my own name in the above regard. I state further that I have read the above authorization, release and agreement, prior to its execution, and that I am fully familiar with the contents thereof.

Dated: _____

_____
(Signature)

_____
_____
(Address)

_____
(Witness)

FORM 6.22
Creative Services Purchase Order

This Purchase Order is designed as an all-purpose document for the purchase of artwork and design services, whether from a stock agency or from a freelance artist. Accordingly, the grant of rights language has two divergent alternatives: (1) the artwork is either a "work made for hire" or (2) the artwork is licensed for one version of one work. In either event, the publisher clears the right to use the artwork in the edition specified and in all "publicity, advertising, packaging, supplementary and promotional materials" related thereto. The publisher also clears the right to use it on other derivatives, subject at most to the payment of an additional fee of 50 percent of the original fee per additional use. With this language, the publisher tries to avoid the punitive threat of copyright infringement if it makes another use without first contacting the artist.

Creative Services Purchase Order

DATE_____   DUE DATE_____

For Artwork Only (due dates): Sketch: _____

Comp: _____

Final: _____

JOB TITLE/AUTHOR_____

ISBN_____ORDER #_____PL_____

JOB #_____CONTROL #_____

TO: (Vendor)

☐ WORK FOR HIRE

COVER WORK: AD & PROMO WORK:

☐ COVER ART [14]   ☐ ART PURCHASE

☐ FREELANCE DESIGNER [17]   ☐ FREELANCE DESIGNER

☐ FREELANCE MECHANCIAL [18]   ☐ FREELANCE MECHANCIAL

☐ PROOFREADING [19]   ☐ PROOFREADING

☐ COPYWRITING [20]   ☐ COPYWRITING

☐ DESIGN/MECH MATERIALS [23]   ☐ DESIGN/MECH MATERIALS

COMMENTS:

Originator_____Ext_____

[send white copy and invoice to originator]

459

Commission Artwork/Design Agreement

Grant of Rights

If "work for hire "has not been checked then,for the sum set forth on the reverse, you hereby grant to us the right to use the Artwork on the English-language work and in the media identified therein (the "Work") for distribution throughout the World. Such right includes the right to use the Artwork on all publicity, advertising, packaging, suppiementary and promotional materials for the Work,in all media now known or hereafter devised during the full term of copyright of the Artwork and any extensions thereof. Moreover, for the period of three (3) years following first publication of the Work,you may not license the Artwork for use on any product which would be competitive with the Work. In addition, you also grant us the right during the full term of the copyright and any extensions thereof to use the Artwork on any salable derivative or other version of the Work (such as paperback, CD-ROM, condensed versions, etc.) in any form, edition, or medium for a payment to you, per additional use, of one-half (1/2) of the price set forth on the reverse of this document, In such event, we will make reasonable efforts to locate you to make such payment. You shall retain all other rights in the Artwork.

If "work for hire" has been checked on the reverse, you hereby agree that for the sum set forth on the reverse, the artwork identified therein (the "Artwork") shall be considered a work made for hire, and copyright therein and all of the rights comprised in the copyright and all other rights shall vest initially in and shall thereafter belong to us. To the extent that the Artwork does not qualify as a work made for hire or copyright therein might otherwise vest in you, you hereby transfer and assign to us during the full term of copyright all extensions thereof, the full and exclusive rights comprised in the Artwork and all revisions thereof, in all media now known or hereafter developed, throughout the World.

Use of Name

We shall have the right, but not the obligation, to use your name and biographical data in connection with our publication of the Work.

Alterations

Because of manufacturing processes and our needs for supplementary/promotional materials, the Artwork in its final form may not appear identical to the Artwork as provided by you. We shall have no liability with respect to any such differences.

Delivery and Acceptance

You agree to provide a sketch, a comp, and a completed version of the Artwork on or before the dates specified on the reverse, which must meet the specifications supplied by us. We shall have the right in our sole discretion to accept or reject the Artwork. If the Artwork delivered at any stage is not accepted by us, then we may elect, at our option, to (1) terminate this Agreement in which case you may retain a sum equal to one-half (1/2) of the fee provided for on the reverse as full and complete payment, and we shall have no further liability or obligations to each other concerning the Artwork, or (2) require that you change the Artwork at no charge in the time specified by us according to our specifications. If you have made changes to the Artwork within the time specified by us but the Artwork is still not satisfactory, we may elect either of the two preceding options until such time as the Artwork is satisfactory or we terminate. If you fall to deliver the Artwork on time or fall to made the required changes, we shall have the right to terminate this Agreement and you must return any funds paid to you within ten (10) days. If we request changes to the Artwork that are not consistent with the original specifications, we will pay you a reasonable fee to be determined by mutual agreement for such changes.

Warranty

You warrant that the Artwork is original, does not and shall not infringe upon any copyright, right of publicity, trademark or any other right, is not libellous or otherwise contrary to law, and that the grant of rights in the Artwork as set forth in this Agreement does not confict with or violate any prior grant or license of rights. You agree to indemnify and hold us harmless from any loss, expense (including attorneys fees), or damage arising out of any breach of there warranties.

Return of Artwork

Unless this is a work for hire (in which case we shall own the Artwork), you shall retain ownership of the original Artwork. You may claim the original Artwork within six (6) months after publication of the Work. In adiition, we will make a reasonable effort to return it to you in the same (6) month period. Thereafter, the Artwork shall be deemed abandoned and may be disposed of at our discretion. In the event of loss or damage of the Artwork caused by us or the printer (other than for reasonable wear and tear) prior to the expiration of the six (6) month period, we will pay your actual damages up to a maximum of two (2) times the invoiced price. If the Artwork has been returned to you, you further agree to lend the original Artwork to us for use in later printings or editions of the Work within ten (10) days of our request.

General

This Agreement constitutes the entire understanding of the parties in relation to the subject matter hereof. No change or modification of this agreement shall be valid unless agreed to in writing and signed by the parties. This Agreement shall be construed and interpreted according to the laws of the State of New York applicable to contracts into and performed solely in the State of new York

The parties hereto are independent contractors and nothing herein shall be interpreted as creating an employment or agency relationship. Neither party shall have the right to contractually bind the other.

In the event of any conflict between this Agreement and any invoice or other document issued by you or your agent with respect to the Artwork, this Agreement shall control

Acceptance

Commencement of performance by you will constitute agreement to these terms.

voluntary and it is not intended that they should in any way affect the ability of STM publishers to make commercial judgements about the re-use of their material.

In the text below, the publisher is assumed to be the rightsholder. When the publisher is not the rightsholder, the principles may still provide useful guidance.

The International Association of Scientific, Technical & Medical Publishers (STM) believes it is in the interest of scholarly and professional publishers, their authors and the scholarly and professional community as a whole to facilitate the exchange of information by setting out common principles with respect to the granting of permissions for the use of limited amounts of material in other published works.

STM publishers support an approach based on common decency and fairness as well as mutual trust. We recognize that scholarly articles often require the direct reproduction of illustrative material (such as figures, tables, structures) for the purposes of discussion or comparison with other data, and that the electronic version of an article needs to contain the same illustrative material in order to maintain the authenticity of the record in both print and digital form. We therefore recommend the following Guidelines as the best working practice for dealing with permissions:

1. Permission should be granted free of charge for the following:

> a maximum of three figures (including tables) from a journal article or book chapter and a maximum of five figures (including tables) from a whole book single text extracts of less than 400 words or series of text extracts totalling less than 800 words.

It is recognized that these are broad Guidelines that will not necessarily apply to every situation. Some examples for which a charge might be appropriate would be:

- the re-use of amounts in excess of the above;
- material essential to the character of the previously published book or article, when re-use could compromise the sale of the publications (e.g., complex illustrations such as anatomical drawings; cartoons; maps; works of art; creative photographs).

This list is illustrative rather than exhaustive—the key point is that these Guidelines encourage free-of-charge granting for that which is likely to represent the vast majority of permissions requested for STM material, but it in no way gives carte blanche for inappropriate re-use, and always leaves the ultimate decision at the discretion of the publisher.

2. If permission is given for the re-use of material in print, it should also be granted for any electronic version of that work, provided that the material is

incidental to the work as a whole, the electronic version is essentially equivalent to or substitutes for the print version, and embedded material (or a specific link to it) remains in situ and is not separately exploited as, for example, part of a database or some other use which might conflict with or prejudice the exploitation of the material by the publisher.

3. When granting permission, STM publishers should agree in principle not to request a complimentary copy of the newly published work except in limited circumstances, for example where an author requests a copy because of the extent or character of the republished material.

4. STM publishers should not make the granting of permission contingent upon receipt of written permission from the author or artist, except when the author or artist holds the copyright or specifically requests this right, provided that full credit is given to the author or artist as described in section 5 below. Any re-use must maintain the integrity of the quoted material.

5. Full credit should be given to the author(s) and publisher(s) of the material(s) re-used. STM publishers should not require a specific credit line format provided the "quoting" publisher includes the following information clearly referenced to the republished material:

   a. For material republished from books: author, title, edition, publisher, city, Copyright © year;
   b. For material republished from journal articles: author, title of article, title of journal, volume number, issue number (if relevant), page range (or first page if this is the only information available), date, publisher.

6. STM publishers are encouraged to have any permission granted for a first edition apply also to a second and subsequent editions and for editions in other languages. It should be noted that permission to use a figure in a book does not constitute permission to use it as a cover or other promotional design. Such permission needs to be sought separately and explicitly.

7. STM publishers are encouraged to respond promptly to requests for permission even if they have to refer the request or do not control the rights themselves.

8. E-mail or Web requests and grants may be made, especially for free-of-charge permissions, as long as the granting publisher has a system and policy that accommodates this.

9. These Guidelines are intended to facilitate the exchange of scholarly and professional information. The Guidelines provide general principles to encourage publishers to permit the use of a reasonable amount of material in other published works, without charge, and with a minimum of administrative

difficulties. At the same time, the Guidelines leave the ultimate decision with respect to copyright protection and policy in the hands of the publisher.

Publishers may add their names to a list of signatories of the STM Guidelines. In so doing they would not be committed to follow any specific conduct with regard to permissions, but would be supporting the spirit of the Guidelines in facilitating the exchange of scholarly and professional information.

[B] List of Signatories

Signatories to the STM Permissions Guidelines in alphabetical order, as of May 2008.

American Chemical Society, Washington, D. C., USA

American Institute of Physics, New York, N.Y., USA

American Psychological Association, Washington, D. C., USA

Ardor Scribendi, New York, N.Y., USA

John Benjamins, Amsterdam, the Netherlands

Birkhäuser Verlag, Basel, Switzerland

Blackwell Publishing, Oxford, England

BMJ Publishing Group, London, England

CABI, UK

Cambridge University Press, Cambridge, England

Carl Hanser Verlag, Munich, Germany

Co-Action Publishing, Denmark, Norway, and Sweden

Deutsher Ärzte-Verlag, Köln, Germany

El Manual Moderno, Mexico City, Mexico

Electronic Publishing Services, London, England

Elsevier, Amsterdam, the Netherlands

Elsevier, Japan KK

Hans Huber Verlag, Bern, Switzerland

Henry Stewart Talks, London, England

S. Hirzel Verlag, GMBH, Stuttgart, Germany

Igaku-Shoin, Tokyo, Japan

Institution of Electrical Engineers (IEE), Stevenage, England

Institute of Physics (IOP), Bristol, England

John Wiley & Sons, Chichester, England

Koninklijke Van Gorcum, Assen, the Netherlands

Lucius & Lucius Verlagsgesellschaft, Stuttgart, Germany

The Mainichi Newspapers, Tokyo, Japan

Marcel Dekker, New York, N.Y., USA

Multi Science Publishing, Essex, England

Nankodo Co., Ltd, Tokyo, Japan

Nature Publishing Group, England

Oxford University Press/Journals

Pharmaceutical Press, London, England

Polish Scientific Publishers (PWN), Warsaw, Poland

Portland Press, London, England

Prentice-Hall of India, New Delhi, India

Royal Society of Chemistry, Cambridge, England

Sage Publications, UK & USA

Springer Science + Business Media, Berlin, Germany

Taylor & Francis, Abingdon, England

Georg Thieme Verlag, Stuttgart, Germany

William Andrew, US

Woodhead Publishing Limited, UK

World Health Organization, Department of Knowledge Management, Switzerland

World Scientific Publishers, Singapore

Permission Request Form for Book Use (Broad Request)

It is always advisable to have a standard permission request form to give to authors for use when requesting permission. Most large publishers will disregard other publisher's forms in lieu of their narrower standard forms (e.g., Forms 6.8–6.11). However, many small publishers and non-traditional publishers will sign the forms provided, and if used, they spare the requesting author/publisher the obligation of re-clearing rights for other versions, derivatives, and media.

Permission Request Form

Date _____   Permission # _____
                      Manuscript
To: Page or Figure # _____

[Author] is/are preparing a manuscript to be published by Publisher, Inc.
Author/Tentative Title _____
Estimated publication date _____ Approximate number of pages _____

    I request your permission to include the following material in this and all subsequent editions of the above-referenced book, including versions made by nonprofit organizations for use by blind or physically handicapped persons, and in all foreign language translations and other derivative works in all media of expression now known or later developed, published or prepared by Publisher, Inc. or its licensees, for distribution throughout the world.

Author(s) and/or editor(s) _____
Title of book or periodical _____
Title of selection _____ Copyright date _____
From page _____, line _____, beginning with the words _____
To page _____, line _____, ending with the words _____
Figure # _____ on page _____ Table # _____ on page _____
(If necessary attach continuation sheet)

    Please indicate agreement by signing and returning the enclosed copy of this letter. In signing, you warrant that you are the sole owner of the rights granted and that your material does not infringe upon the copyright or other rights of anyone. If you do not control these rights, I would appreciate your letting me know to whom I should apply.

Thank you,

Publisher, Inc. 15 Rue de Rivoli
Melonville, New York 12222

_____

Name

AGREED TO AND ACCEPTED:

by: _____

Signature   Title   Date

Credit and/or copyright notice: _____

_____

_____

_____

Permission Request Form for Web Site Use
(Broad Request)

See comments to Form 6.1.

Permission Request Form—Web Site

Date _____   Permission # _____

To:

I am preparing a Web site to be hosted by Publisher, Inc.
Tentative release date _____
Tentative URL: _____

　　I request your permission to include the following material in this and all subsequent versions of the Web site, published or prepared Publisher, Inc. or its licensees, including successor sites to the URL mentioned above.
Author(s) _____
Title of book, periodical or software program _____

_____
Copyright date _____ Title of selection _____

_____
Page Numbers _____

Please indicate agreement by signing and returning the enclosed copy of this letter. In signing, you warrant that you are the sole owner of the rights granted and that your material does not infringe upon the copyright or other rights of anyone. If you do not control these rights, I would appreciate your letting me know to whom I should apply.

_____
(Name of requester)

_____

_____
Return address

AGREED TO AND ACCEPTED:

by: _____
　　　　Signature　　　　　　　　Title　　　　　　　Date

Credit and/or copyright notice: _____
_____
_____
_____

FORM 6.3
Interview Permission/Release

Interview Permission/Release

May 14, 2001

Dear _____:

We appreciate your willingness to be interviewed for _____ *Magazine*. The interview is scheduled to be published by Publisher, Inc. in Volume _____, Issue _____. To help prevent any misunderstandings about the interview, please let us clarify our arrangement as follows.

You hereby confirm that you, _____, have had extensive conversations with _____, for the purpose of developing an interview for the "Features" section of _____ *Magazine*.

You understand that some or all of what you said during the interview process might appear in the interview. You understand that your statements may form the basis for conclusions and discussions regarding the subject of the interview. You realize that the interviewer may transfer or license exclusive ownership of this interview or may authorize others to publish the material, and that the material may appear in other magazines, other articles, treatises, collections, subsequent editions, and other forms any in media, and that you hereby grant us the exclusive rights to publish the interview as set forth above, and waive any claims you may have regarding publication of the interview or material from the interview, including without limitation any claims for libel, false light, or disclosure of private facts. You will not have the right to review any material prior to publication.

Please sign your acceptance of these terms on the signature line provided below, and return a copy to me.

Again, please accept our gratitude for your contribution to _____ *Magazine*.

Sincerely,

Editor

I accept the terms of this agreement:

_____
(signature)

Date: _____
Please print your name (exactly as you would like it to appear in _____ *Magazine*) and address. We will send you two complimentary copies of the issue in which your interview appears.

Permission Request Form for Use of Material in Connection with Adoption (College Publishing)—Publisher's Form (Narrow Grant)

Permission Request Form for Use of Material in Connection with Adoption

Complete the form as completely as possible and return to Permission Dept., Publisher, Inc., [address]; via facsimile to [number]; via e-mail to permreq@ publisher.com. Direct queries to [number].

YOUR MAILING ADDRESS/FAX NUMBER DATE: _____

_____

_____   _____

_____   YOUR REFERENCE NUMBER

_____

TITLE OF THE ADOPTED BOOK (AND ISBN):

_____

NAME(S) OF THE BOOK AUTHOR(S)/EDITOR(S) (do not cite chapter author(s)):

_____

EDITION NUMBER AND YEAR OF PUBLICATION: _____
MATERIAL TO BE POSTED (Solutions, Figures, Chapters, etc.):

_____

APPROX # OF STUDENTS _____ SEMESTER/QUARTER _____
PROFESSOR'S NAME _____ COURSE NAME/NUMBER _____
NAME OF YOUR UNIVERSITY/INSTITUTE/ORGANIZATION/SPONSOR:

_____

PURPOSE OF REPRODUCTION (e.g., facilitate use of adopted text):

_____

ELECTRONIC REQUESTS:
MEDIUM (e.g., intranet, Internet, CD-ROM) _____,
URL: _____,
PASSWORD PROTECTED SITE, yes ___ no ___, DURATION TO BE POSTED
ON INTERNET/INTRANET (Semester, academic year): ___
PRINT RUN OF CD-ROM: _____, FOR POWERPOINT
PRESENTATIONS: NUMBER OF HARD COPY HANDOUTS: _____.
SPECIAL CONDITIONS (e.g., customer is author of material, book is adopted
text): _____

Basic One-Time Reprint or Photocopy Permission Form

One-Time Reprint or Photocopy Permission Form

VIA Facsimile Transmission: [FAX]

[*License Date*]
[*First Name*] [*Last Name*]   **Invoice #**
[*Street Address*]
[*Company*]
[*City*], [*State*] [*Zip Code*]

Dear [*Greeting*]:

Thank you for your request of [*request date*] (ref. #___) for permission to reproduce [*number*] copies of pages [__–__] from [*author/title/ISBN*]. These copies will be used in instructor's [*name of professor*] [*name of course*] during the [*fall/spring*] [*year*] semester at [*institution*].

OR

Thank you for your request of [*request date*] (ref. #___) for permission to reproduce [*number*] copies of pages [__ through __] from [*author/title/ISBN*]. These copies will be used by employees of [*company name*] at a seminar to be held in [*location*] on [*seminar date*].

1. Permission is granted for this use, except that if the material appears in our work with credit to another source, you must also obtain permission from the original source cited in our work.

2. You must show credit to our publication on every copy that is made. Credit must include the following components: Title, author(s) and/or editor(s), Copyright © [*year and owner*]. Reprinted by permission of Publisher, Inc.

OR

Appropriate credit to our publication must appear on every copy of your work as follows: Journal Title, volume number, issue number, year (e.g., Vol. 1, No. 1, 1996), page numbers. Copyright © [*year and owner*]. Reprinted by permission of Publisher, Inc.

3. You are permitted a maximum of [*number*] copies. If you need to make a different number of copies, please let us know.

4. Our fee is $_____, payable in U.S. dollars with a check drawn against a U.S. bank within thirty days following the end of the semester. Please remit payment with a copy of this license to Permissions Department, Publisher, Inc., 10 Downing Street, New York, NY 10025, and include our invoice number on your check stub. (Our Tax ID number is:_____.)

OR

4. Our fee is $_____ payable within (120) one hundred twenty days of the date of this permission. Remittance must be made in U.S. dollars with a check drawn against a U.S. bank. Please remit payment with a copy of this license to the Cashier, Permissions Department, Publisher, Inc., 10 Downing Street, New York, NY 10025, and include our invoice number on your check stub. (Our Tax ID number is: _____.)

5. Please either sign and return one copy of this license within thirty days of the date of this license if the terms are acceptable you, or, check off the cancellation box below if you decline this license.

Sincerely,   Accepted:

                                                  _____

                                                  Cancelled:

Form 6.6
Document Delivery Agreement

Although many publishers authorize document delivery activity though collecting societies such as Copyright Clearance Center, some larger publishers will enter into separate agreements with large document supply companies. The reasons for doing so are varied, and include more direct usage data, and fewer fees deducted. In this template, the publisher specifies that articles must be downloaded individually from its Web platform whenever available. This gives the publisher the ability to count the downloads and double-check that payments are appropriate.

Document Delivery Agreement

This Agreement made and entered into as of _____, between _____, (the "Publisher"), with offices at _____, and ____, with offices at _____ ("Licensee").

WHEREAS, Publisher publishes certain journals, books, reference works, and databases (hereinafter referred to as "Publications"), which contain articles (in the event of journals) and chapters (in the event of books and reference works) written by various authors (all articles and chapters are hereinafter referred to as "Articles"); and

WHEREAS, Publisher and Licensee mutually desire to enter into an Agreement pursuant to which Licensee may reproduce and deliver copies of Articles for Licensee's customers upon order through its document delivery services and other product offering listed on Schedule 1;

NOW, THEREFORE, in consideration of the mutual agreements, covenants and obligations set forth below, the parties agree as follows:

1. GRANT OF RIGHTS. Publisher hereby grants Licensee a nonexclusive worldwide right to reproduce Articles for delivery to customers through its document delivery services, and to deliver such Articles. Articles shall include Articles from current Publications as well as former Publications in which Publisher still owns rights. Articles also include all Articles from Publications owned by Publisher's subsidiaries and affiliates. Publisher will provide a list of journals and issues, books, and reference works to which it has rights within thirty (30) days of signature of this Agreement. Publisher will provide regular updates of any changes to this list.

This license extends only to the reproduction and delivery of single Articles within a Publication as opposed to the Publication in its entirety. Articles may only be delivered to customers of Licensee by mail, courier, fax, or electronic delivery as described herein, subject to the terms hereof.

The Publisher shall retain all right, title, copyright, and other intellectual or proprietary rights in the Publications and Articles. Licensee does not acquire any intellectual property or other rights in the Publications or Articles. Neither Licensee nor its customers may modify, adapt, transform, translate or create any derivative work based on the Articles or otherwise use the same in a manner that would infringe the copyright or other proprietary rights therein. Copyright notices, other notices or disclaimers included in the Articles may not be removed, obscured or modified in any way.

Each different use of the Publisher's trademark(s) is subject to review and approval of the Publisher in the first instance.

2.   PROVISION OF PUBLICATIONS AND ARTICLES BY ELECTRONIC MEANS. Publisher and Licensee will develop a mutually agreeable method from the list of options outlined in Schedule 2 that will allow Licensee to acquire Articles from Publisher's online platform for fulfillment on an Article-by-Article basis. Licensee shall be required to fulfill any Articles available on Publisher's platform by this method. Once Licensee has acquired an Article, Licensee will send the customer an e-mail message containing a link to the Article on the Licensee server. The link is a private link unique to the customer and that particular transaction, and the number of downloads is restricted to two attempts. Both the e-mail message and the landing page with a *Download Now* button include copyright disclaimers. Once a customer has downloaded the Article they cannot reactivate the link. Articles are deleted from the Licensee server after an order has been fulfilled, or after ___ days. Licensee may only use the electronic files to fulfill customer orders on a one-time document delivery basis, in accordance with the terms of this Agreement.

For Articles that are not available on the Publisher's, or in the event of a temporary loss of access to Publisher's platform, Publisher agrees that Licensee shall have the right to scan the paper Article and deliver the scanned Article in a manner consistent with the manner of delivery described above. Licensee may retain the scanned Articles in a secure internal database in order to fulfill future orders for the same Article.

3.   ROYALTY. Publisher agrees to allow Licensee to fulfill customer orders on a one-time, pay-per-view or pay-per delivery basis. In consideration for the right of reproduction and delivery set forth herein, Licensee shall pay the Publisher a royalty for each Article as set forth on Schedule 6.

Portions of Articles are to be charged at the full Article rate. Licensee shall be responsible for bad debts from its customers and shall pay Publisher royalties on deliveries notwithstanding the bad debt. Licensee agrees to change and update Publisher royalty rates within thirty (30) days of notice.

Royalty payments will be made by Licensee to the Publisher within thirty (30) days of the last day of each Calendar Quarter as hereafter defined and will be accompanied by appropriate usage statistics consisting of the Article citation, ISSN or ISBN, imprint or geographic origin of publication, number of

copies per Title, the amount of royalty collected, type of customer (e.g., corporate, academic), and location of customer by country as outlined in a format consistent with Schedule 3. "Calendar Quarter" means three
(3) calendar months, commencing on January 1, April 1, July 1 and October 1 of each calendar year. Royalty payments and reports shall be sent to Publisher as set forth on Schedule 4.

Publisher may, no more than once per year, audit the books and records of Licensee relating to this Agreement. In the event that such an audit reveals an underpayment by Licensee in an amount greater than 5%, the costs of such audit shall be borne by Licensee.

4.   DIGITAL RIGHTS MANAGEMENT. Licensee agrees to utilize the Digital Rights Management (DRM) technology specified on Schedule 5 when the Articles are delivered electronically. Licensee reserves the right to change its DRM technologies subject to the Publisher's prior approval.

5.   NOTIFICATION TO LICENSEE'S CUSTOMERS. Licensee will retain any copyright notices that appear on Publisher's Articles when reproducing the Article and will inform its customers by a mutually agreeable legend on the cover page of any delivered documents that the Article is reproduced by Licensee under license by the Publisher and that all rights are reserved by the Publisher.

6.   REPRINTS. Bulk reprint sales in any medium are subject to separate agreements with the Publisher.

7.   QUALITY ASSURANCE. Licensee shall provide Publisher with reasonable access to its document delivery services in any form or product in which it is available pursuant to Schedule 1 for quality assurance purposes, and shall collaborate with the Publisher with respect to any quality deficiencies. Publisher's technical contact for this Agreement is identified on Schedule 4.

8.   WARRANTIES.

(a) Each party hereto mutually represents, warrants and covenants to the other, as follows:

- It has full powers to make, enter into and perform this Agreement and to take all required actions contemplated hereby to fulfill its obligations hereunder;

- It is a duly organized and validly existing corporation licensed to do business for the purposes and in the manner described herein;

- To the best of its knowledge, it is in compliance with all applicable laws and regulations and no violations of any of such applicable laws or regulations has occurred and there is no litigation or administrative proceeding pending which would affect its ability to perform its obligations hereunder; and

- No representation or warranty made and contained in this Agreement contains any untrue statement of a material fact or omits any material fact required to make any statement contained herein not misleading, and is not aware of any impending or contemplated event or occurrence that would cause any of the foregoing representations not to be true and complete on the date of such event or occurrence as if made on that date.

- Any royalty or accounting statements delivered hereunder shall be materially accurate.

(b)   Each party hereby agrees to indemnify, defend and hold harmless the other, its officers, employees and agents from any and all losses, expenses, damages and costs of suit arising from any claim, demand, action or proceeding against the indemnified party based upon any breach or alleged breach by indemnifying party of any of the representations and warranties contained herein.

9.   TERM AND TERMINATION. This Agreement will become effective as of the date and year set forth above and, unless earlier terminated in accordance with this Agreement, will continue in effect for a period of one (1) year. This Agreement shall renew automatically for successive one-year periods, unless either party provides 30-days prior written notice of its intent not to renew this Agreement. This Agreement may also be terminated upon 30-days prior written notice by either party for breach which is not cured within the notice period.

Upon termination, Licensee will delete from its databases and holdings any copies of Publications or Articles maintained or created by Licensee pursuant to this Agreement, and will pay any royalties owed as of termination.

10. NOTICES. Any notice which may be required to be given hereunder shall be in writing, and if to Licensee shall be delivered by hand, mailed by certified mail return receipt requested or sent by overnight courier to:

> [Licensee name]
> [address]

and if to Publisher, shall be delivered by hand, mailed by certified mail return receipt requested or sent by overnight courier to:

> [Publisher Name]
> [Address]

Any notice so given shall be deemed to have been given on the date of delivery, if hand delivered, on the date of mailing if sent by certified mail, and on the date of sending if sent by overnight courier. Any party hereto may change the address to which notice shall be sent by giving written notice to the other party of such address.

11. GENERAL.

(a)   The relationship between the parties is that of independent contractors and does not constitute a partnership, joint venture, or agency relationship, and neither shall have any authority to bind the other in any way.

(b)   Any information disclosed by any party (the "Disclosing Party") to any other party (the "Receiving Party") that would be understood to be confidential by a reasonable party shall be deemed Confidential and must (1) be maintained by the Receiving Party in confidence, (2) may be shown only to those employees or advisors of the Receiving Party who have a need to know the information and who are under an obligation of confidentiality, and (3) may not be disclosed by the Receiving Party to any other third parties without the consent of the Disclosing Party. Without limiting the generality of the foregoing, the terms of this Agreement are deemed Confidential.

(c)   This Agreement is personal to Licensee and may not be assigned without the prior written consent of the Publisher. Subject to the foregoing, this Agreement shall inure to the benefit of the subsidiaries, successors, and assigns of the parties.

(d)   This Agreement, including any attachments, annexes or schedules hereto and thereto, and documents explicitly referred to herein or therein (e.g., user manuals and specification documents), contain the entire understanding of the parties with respect to the subject matter contained herein and supersede all terms and conditions in any quotations, purchase orders, acknowledgements or other documents exchanged by the parties. There are no promises, covenants or undertakings other than those expressly set forth therein. No modification, amendment or waiver of any provision of this Agreement shall be valid unless in writing and signed by the parties.

(e)   Any public statements made or press releases issued in connection with this Agreement and the relationship established between the parties thereby shall be subject to the approval of both parties, which approval shall not be withheld unreasonably.

(f)   The provisions of Sections 8, 10, and 11 shall survive termination of this Agreement for any reason.

(g) This Agreement shall be governed by and construed in accordance with the laws of the State of New York. Any action, suit or proceeding arising out of or relating to this Agreement shall be commenced in a court of Competent Jurisdiction in the State of New York, County of New York, and the parties hereby consent to the jurisdiction of such courts and waive any objections to venue therein.

LICENSEE   **PUBLISHER**

By: _____   By: _____

Name: _____   Name: _____

Title: _____   Title: _____

Date: _____   Date: _____

SCHEDULE 1: LICENSEE PRODUCT OFFERINGS

SCHEDULE 2: VENDOR AUTHENTICATION

SCHEDULE 3: USAGE STATISTICS

SCHEDULE 4: PUBLISHER AND LICENSEE CONTACTS

SCHEDULE 5: LICENSEE AND DIGITAL RIGHTS MANAGEMENT

SCHEDULE 6: ROYALTIES

Permission to Use Material on Author's Own Web Site

Permission to Use Material on Author's Own Web Site

Dear:

In response to your request of _____ to post material from your book on your own Web site, permission is granted to you, on the following terms and conditions, to use selected material, not to exceed one full chapter and table of contents (the "Material") from the work named below (the "Work") for the usage (the "Usage") described below:

The Material from the Work: (specify which pages or chapter, article, figures, etc.) from (name/title/ISBN).
The Usage: post on author's Web site at URL address: _____

1. This Agreement is nonexclusive, for the English language only throughout the world, for this edition of the Work(s) and this version/ edition of the Usage for the period of time set forth in Paragraph 5 below. You may not make any other use, or authorize others to make any other use, of this Material, in any print or nonprint format, including electronic or multimedia, not explicitly stated above. You must obtain authorization from the original source to use any material that appears in the Material with credit to another source.

2. No other material from the Work(s) may be included in the Usage. It is understood and agreed that this permission does not extend to any full-text, hard-copy or online document delivery of the Material. It is understood and agreed that your Web site will provide a link to an online bookseller as well as to the publisher's Web site.

3. Credit must be given to the Work(s) and placed on every copy of the Material, and on each screen where the Material may be viewed. The credit must include the following components: Title of the Work; Name(s) of author(s) or editor(s); Copyright notice, including: the word copyright, the symbol, the copyright year, the name of the copyright owner; and the statement "This material is used by permission of Publisher, Inc."

4. This permission shall terminate automatically in the event (i) you fail to exercise the right(s) granted hereunder and make the Usage of the Material as specified within twelve months of the date of this letter; or (ii) you fail to comply with any of the terms specified herein.

5. It is understood and agreed that the Usage shall in no way render copyright in the Material in the public domain or in any way compromise the

Publisher's copyright in the Material. You agree to take reasonable steps to protect the Publisher's copyright and so to inform end-users in a manner including, but not limited to, providing full copyright credit to the Material as specified in Paragraph 3 above. You may use the material for [*time period*] only.

Please sign both copies of this Agreement and return one signed original to me.

Sincerely,   ACCEPTED:

_____

Broadcast Permission Letter with Endorsement Disclaimer

Broadcast Permission Letter with Endorsement Disclaimer

Dear:

When signed by you, this will constitute our agreement authorizing
_____ to feature in a [*description of product*] in a broadcast on [*date*] (the "Broadcast") portions of material from [*title and author*] (the "Work) on the following terms and conditions:

1.   The Broadcast may include the materials listed on Exhibit A attached hereto only in the context described by the script copy provided by you and attached hereto as Exhibit B.

2.   It is understood and agreed the Broadcast will be protected by copyright notice sufficient to meet the requirements of U.S. Copyright Law and credit will be given to the source of the materials from the Work as part of the Broadcast as follows: Copyright © [*year*] Publisher, Inc.

3.   This agreement is nonexclusive and limited to broadcast rights in the English language only. No right to use any material that appears in the Work with credit to another source is granted.

4.   You may not use the authors' names and likeness or Publisher's trademarks, service marks, name or logo in any way except as related to, and specifically authorized herein, featuring the Broadcast. No use may in any way suggest or be construed to suggest Publisher's or the authors' endorsement or support of views or statements made in the Broadcast, made by producers of or others involved in the Broadcast or made by any station which broadcasts the Broadcast.

5.   Within ten business days after the initial Broadcast, you will provide us with one complimentary copy of a DVD recording of the entire Broadcast for our review and to confirm the requirements and conditions hereunder have been met. We may retain the recording for archival purposes.

6.   It is understood and agreed that Publisher makes no representations or warranties with regard to any adaptation of the Work or any new material or other material included in the Broadcast not published verbatim by Publisher and to which Publisher holds copyright.

7. In consideration of the rights transferred herein, the fee is_____.

Please sign and return one copy of this license to me.

ACCEPTED AND AGREED:

FOR PUBLISHER, INC.   FOR BROADCASTER

_____   _____
Signature/Title   Signature/Title

_____   _____
Date   Date

De Minimis Reprint Permission—No Charge

De Minimis Reprint Permission

Dear _____ :

    RE: Your letter dated _____ requesting permission to reuse up to a maximum of 3 figures and/or 300 words in print media only from _____, a work published by Publisher, Inc.

1. Permission is granted for this use, except that you must obtain authorization from the original source to use any material that appears in our work with credit to another source.

2. Permitted use is limited to the original edition of your forthcoming work described in your letter and does not extend to future editions of your work. In addition, permission does not include the right to grant others permission to photocopy or otherwise reproduce this material except for versions made by non-profit organizations for use by blind or physically handicapped persons.

3. Appropriate credit to our publication must appear on every copy of your work, either on the first page of the quoted text or in the figure legend. The following components must be included: [*title*]. Copyright © 20__ Publisher, Inc. Reprinted by permission of Publisher, Inc.

4. This permission is for nonexclusive print world rights in the English language only. For translation rights, contact our International Rights Department. For non-print media rights, contact _____, for requests for material from our book, when you have firm plans for publishing your book in a specific non-print medium.

5. If your published work contains more than 3 figures and/or 300 words from our title, or if the material is modified in any way, this permission shall be null and void.

Sincerely,

Standard Permission Grant for Use of Material in Book (Includes E-Book Grant)

Historically, publishers only granted permission to reprint materials in the print medium and for the edition requested, while simultaneously demanding that authors clear all permissions for all editions and media. This practice has come under review, as more publishers realize that they are simultaneously publishing material in print, Web and E-book formats, and that they cannot realistically continue not to grant to others the key rights that they demand from authors. Thus some companies now routinely grant permissions for book and electronic book versions of single editions of works (*see* Clause 1), although few grant future edition rights without additional payment.

Standard Permission Grant for Use of Material in Book

Dear: _____:

> RE: Your [*date*] request for permission to republish page(s)/figure(s) _____ (the "Material") from _____ by (the "Work"). This Material will appear in your forthcoming work, _____, to be published by _____ in (the "Use").

1.   This License grants nonexclusive English language rights throughout the world for verbatim use of the Material in the above edition of your work, in print, and e-book and other electronic editions. Permission does not extend to revised editions of your work and does not include the right to grant others permission to photocopy or otherwise reproduce the Material except for versions made by non-profit organizations for use by blind or physically handicapped persons. No additions or changes may be made without our prior written consent. For translation rights, please contact the International Rights Department.

2.   Credit to our Work must appear on every copy using the Material and must include the title; the author(s) and/or editor(s); Copyright © (year and owner); and the statement "This material is used by permission of Publisher, Inc."

3.   You represent that the Use shall in no way place the Material in the public domain or in any way compromise our copyright in the Material. You agree to take reasonable steps to protect our copyright including, but not limited to, providing credit to our Work as specified in Paragraph 2 above and using appropriate digital rights management systems.

4.   Our fee is _____ payable upon signing of this License. Remit payment in U.S. Dollars with a check drawn against a U.S. bank, and a signed copy of this License to: Permissions Department, _____, and include our invoice number on your check stub. (Our Tax ID is: _____.) This License is null and void if not signed within 30 days of the date of the License or if payment is not received within 30 days of the date of the License.

5.   This License shall automatically terminate if you fail to exercise the rights granted hereunder to make the Use specified within 36 months of the date of this letter or fail to comply with the terms herein. In addition, we reserve the right to revoke this permission at any time effective upon written notice to you in the event we conclude, in our reasonable judgment, that your use of our Material in electronic format is compromising our proprietary rights in this Material.

Sincerely,
Publisher, Inc.

By _____

Accepted:

By _____

College Photocopying Permission for Unavailable Work—No Fee

College Photocopying Permission for Unavailable Work

Dear:

Thank you for your request of [*request date*] (reference number _____) for permission to photocopy _____ copies of pages _____ from [*author/title*]. These copies will be used in [*instructor's name*]'s [*course number*] course during the [*season*][*year*] semester at [*university*].

1. We license this permission with the understanding that the Work is currently unavailable for purchase and that each student who receives a set of copies will be encouraged by the instructor to purchase the Work if it becomes available during the semester.

or

We license this permission with the understanding that the Work is currently unavailable for purchase.

2. We waive all permission fees with the understanding that you are responsible for any and all expenses associated with the photocopying of this material.

3. The title of the Work, the author/editor's name, the copyright notice on the Work and the statement "Reproduced by permission of Publisher, Inc." must appear on each photocopy.

4. Permission is limited to the course and semester indicated above, and in no way extends to electronic copying.

5. Please sign and return one copy of this Agreement.

Sincerely,

ACCEPTED

_____

Permission Grant for Use of Material in Database (Broad Grant)—Database Publisher's Form

Permission Grant for Use of Material in Database

Copyright Permission

_____ grants Datapub, Inc., and persons acting with its authorization, permission to reproduce, adapt, distribute, transmit, and display the materials named below worldwide, in whole or in part and in any media, now known or later developed, but only in connection with the [title] database (the "Database") and products based thereon offered by Datapub, Inc., or any similar products or services offered by Datapub, Inc., or its successors. Datapub, Inc., agrees to provide a copyright notice, if there is one on the original, together with an acknowledgment that the materials have been reproduced with your permission.

You agree to indemnify Datapub, Inc., its distributors, and their employees, agents, and contractors against any damages or losses, including costs and fees, from any actual or alleged infringement of any copyright, trade secret, or other proprietary right arising from the materials listed below.

Citations for which copyright release is requested are attached.

_____

Name of person with authorization to grant release

_____   _____

Authorized signature   Date

PLEASE SCAN <u>BOTH</u> BOOK AND
CD-ROM BARCODES WHEN
CHECKING OUT AND IN.